The emergence of a new theory of literature in the German Romantic period constituted a decisive turning-point in the history of criticism. Prepared by new trends in critical thought during the latter half of the eighteenth century, a view of the literary work and the artistic process developed which diverged sharply from the dominant classicist understanding of aesthetics and poetics. It recognized the infinite changeability of genres, their constant mingling, and the frequent emergence of new literary forms, and asserted the rights of genius and creative imagination. It was also characterized by its intimate connection with the prevailing philosophy of its time, transcendental idealism. Professor Behler provides a new account of this crucial movement, illustrating each theoretical topic with close reference to a characteristic work by a major writer of the period.

CAMBRIDGE STUDIES IN
GERMAN ROMANTIC LITERARY
THEORY

GERMAN ROMANTIC LITERARY THEORY

ERNST BEHLER

Professor of Comparative Literature,
University of Washington, Seattle

CAMBRIDGE
UNIVERSITY PRESS

Published by the Press Syndicate of the University of Cambridge
The Pitt Building, Trumpington Street, Cambridge CB2 IRP
40 West 20th Street, New York, NY 10011-4211, USA
10 Stamford Road, Oakleigh, Victoria 3166, Australia

First published 1993

Printed in Great Britain at the University Press, Cambridge

A catalogue record for this book is available from the British Library

Library of Congress cataloguing in publication data

Behler, Ernst, 1928–
German Romantic literary theory / Ernst Behler.
p.   cm. – (Cambridge Studies in German)
Includes bibliographical references and index.
ISBN 0 521 32585 4
1. German literature – 19th century – History and criticism – Theory, etc.
2. German literature – 18th century – History and criticism – Theory, etc.
3. Criticism – Germany – History.   4. Romanticism – Germany.   I. Title.
II. Series.
PT361.B39   1993
830.9'006 – dc20 92-22039 CIP

ISBN 0 521 32585 4 hardback

Contents

Preface

Since its appearance in critical writings of the late eighteenth century, especially through the periodical *Athenaeum* (1798–1800), the early Romantic literary theory of Germany has enjoyed the reputation of having introduced a new manner of thinking about poetry and our approach to literary works in the West. This reputation has manifested itself not only in the appreciation and adoption of a new critical attitude, but also in sharp polemics against its alleged aesthetic absolutism. Such intense scrutiny has resulted in a widespread influence of early German Romantic thought on the critical scene during the nineteenth and twentieth centuries, as evidenced by its reception by Coleridge, Poe, and Baudelaire, by Scandinavian and Slavic critics, and in the literary thinking of the main Mediterranean countries of Europe. This reception has generally understood the early Romantic literary theory of Germany as a rupture with the system of mimesis and representation that had dominated European aesthetic thought during the previous centuries.

A certain disproportion can be detected between the casual origin of the theory and its actual importance and influence on successive centuries of critical thought. The formation of what we call early Romantic theory actually lasted scarcely more than six years, from about 1795 to 1801, and was the communal product of a group of about six young authors of different backgrounds and orientations who, out of mutual interests and communal literary pursuits, assembled for a few years and were ironically labelled the 'new school' or the 'Romantic school' by their contemporaries. After the turn of the century the members of the group dispersed, each taking his own path. Their manner of collaboration was by no means planned, concerted, or organized, but showed a casual and fluid type of personal interrelationship. For this reason, we should perhaps characterize their work not as a theory of literature in the sense of a doctrine, but rather as an assembly of different views about poetry from the various perspectives of these authors. Nevertheless, the initial impulse for what we consider the Romantic turning-point in the history of criticism and literary theory undoubtedly stems from the collaborative efforts of the members of this group around the end of the eighteenth century.

A phenomenon of such prominence has been the subject of many studies in Germany and other countries. The renewed interest in the origins of our modernity, stimulated by the contemporary debate about modernism and postmodernism, as well as the completion and continued work on some of the major editions of the early Romantics, permits us to take a new look at early Romantic literary theory from the perspective of the late twentieth century. This book does not aim at a systematic presentation of a doctrine containing an objective body of knowledge, but approaches the subject from its genesis, the formation of the theory in progressive stages, and from the diverse points of view of its authors. Plurality, diversity of opinion, and the developmental character of the theory, its 'eternal becoming', are the main objectives. From this perspective, early Romantic literary theory is not so much something which can be encapsulated in a chapter in the history of criticism and literary theory, but a basic reflection on poetry without limit or conclusion.

Special thanks go to Frauke Plummer, our departmental secretary, my research assistants Ann Schmiesing Linda Avraamides, and Eric Ames, but above all to my wife and colleague Diana Behler, with whom I have discussed Romanticism more than with anyone else.

Abbreviations

ALZ   *Allgemeine Literaturzeitung von Jena*, ed. Christian Gottfried Schütz and Friedrich Justin Bertuch (Jena and Leipzig, 1785–).

AWS AW   August Wilhelm Schlegel, *Sämtliche Werke*, ed. Eduard Böcking. 16 vols. (Leipzig: Weidmann, 1846).

AWS V   August Wilhelm Schlegel, *Kritische Ausgabe der Vorlesungen*, ed. Ernst Behler in collaboration with Frank Jolles. 6 vols. (Paderborn: Schöningh 1989–).

Translations
DA August Wilhelm Schlegel, *Lectures on Dramatic Art and Literature*, trans. John Black; rev. A. J. W. Morrison (London: Henry G. Bohn, 1846). Quoted from the edition of 1883 (London: George Bell, 1883).

CA   *Caroline. Briefe aus der Frühromantik*, ed. Erich Schmidt. 2 vols. (Leipzig: Insel, 1923).

CO   Antoine-Nicolas de Condorcet, *Sketch for a Historical Picture of the Progress of the Human Mind*, trans. June Barraclough (New York: Noonday, 1955).

E   *Encyclopédie ou Dictionnaire raisonné des sciences, des arts et des métiers, par une société de gens de lettres* (Denis Diderot and Jean le Rond d'Alembert), 38 vols. (Geneva: Pellet, 1777).

FDES   Friedrich Daniel Ernst Schleiermacher, *Kritische Gesamtausgabe*, ed. Hans-Joachim Birkner. 40 vols. (Berlin: de Gruyter, 1984–).

Translations and other editions
GH Friedrich D. E. Schleiermacher, *The Handwritten Manuscripts*, ed. Heinz Kimmerle, trans. James Duke and Jack Forstman (Missoula: Scholars Press, 1977).
OR Friedrich Schleiermacher, *On Religion. Speeches to its Cultured Despisers* (Cambridge University Press, 1988).
ÜR Friedrich Schleiermacher, *Über die Religion, Reden an die Gebildeten unter ihren Verächtern* (Hamburg: Meiner, 1958).

FI   Johann Gottlieb Fichte, *Gesamtausgabe der Bayerischen Akademie der Wissenschaften*, ed. Reinhard Lauth and Hans Jacob (Stuttgart: Frommann-Holzboog, 1964–).

Translations
EPW Johann Gottlieb Fichte, *Early Philosophical Writings*, trans. Daniel Breazeale (Ithaca: Cornell University Press, 1988).

FS   *Friedrich Schillers Werke und Briefe* (Weimar: Böhlau, 1953–).

FWJS   Friedrich Wilhelm Joseph Schelling, *Sämtliche Werke*, ed. Karl Friedrich August Schelling 10 vols. (Stuttgart and Augsburg: Cotta, 1861).

Translations
PA F. W. J. Schelling, *The Philosophy of Art*, trans. Douglas W. Scott. Foreword by David Simpson (Minneapolis: University of Minnesota Press, 1989).
PI *Philosophy of German Idealism: Fichte, Jacobi, and Schelling*, ed. Ernst Behler (New York: Continuum, 1987).

GOE Johann Wolfgang Goethe, *Gedenkausgabe der Werke, Briefe und Gespräche*, ed. Ernst Beutler (Zurich: Artemis, 1948–71).

HE *Johann Gottfried Herders Sämtliche Werke*, ed. Bernhard Suphan, 32 vols. (Berlin: Weidmann, 1877–1913).

Translations
OL J. G. Herder, *Essay on the Origin of Language, On the Origin of Language. Two Essays by Jean-Jacques Rousseau and Johann Gottfried Herder*, trans. John H. Moran and Alexander Gode (New York: Ungar, 1966).

HEG Georg Wilhelm Friedrich Hegel, *Werke in 20 Bänden*, ed. Eva Moldenhauer and Karl Markus Michel (Frankfurt: Suhrkamp, 1986).

Translations
EPO G. W. F. Hegel, *Encyclopedia of the Philosophical Sciences in Outline and Critical Writings*, ed. Ernst Behler (New York: Continuum, 1990).
HP G. W. F. Hegel, *The History of Philosophy*, trans. E. S. Haldane and Frances H. Simson. 3 vols. (New York: The Humanities Press, 1955).

HEI   Heinrich Heine, *Sämtliche Schriften*, ed. Klaus Briegleb. 6 vols. (Munich: Hanser, 1968).

Translations
HH Heinrich Heine, *Selected Works*, trans. Helen M. Mustard (New York: Random House, 1973).

KA   Immanuel Kant, *Werke*. 9 vols. (Berlin: de Gruyter, 1968).

Translations
CJ Immanuel Kant, *Critique of Judgment*, trans. J. H. Bernard (London: Macmillan, 1951).
CPR Immanuel Kant, *Critique of Pure Reason*, trans. Norman Kemp Smith (New York: St. Martin's Press, 1965).
PW Immanuel Kant, *Philosophical Writings*, ed. Ernst Behler with a foreword by René Wellek (New York: Continuum, 1986).

KFSA   *Kritische Friedrich Schlegel Ausgabe*, ed. Ernst Behler with the collaboration of Jean-Jacques Anstett, Hans Eichner, and other specialists. 35 vols. (Paderborn: Schöningh, 1958–).

Translations
DP Friedrich Schlegel, *Dialogue on Poetry and Literary Aphorisms*, trans. Ernst Behler and Roman Struc (University Park: The Pennsylvania State University Press, 1968).
GM Friedrich Schlegel, *On Goethe's 'Meister'*, trans. Joyce Crick, *German Aesthetic and Literary Criticism. The Romantic Ironists and Goethe*, ed. Kathleen Wheeler (Cambridge University Press, 1984).
LF Friedrich Schlegel, *Lucinde and the Frag-*

ments, trans. Peter Firchow (Minneapolis: University of Minnesota Press, 1971).

NIE   Friedrich Nietzsche, *Sämtliche Werke. Kritische Studienausgabe*, ed. Giorgio Colli and Mazzino Montinari. 15 vols. (Berlin: de Gruyter, 1980).

Translations
GT Friedrich Nietzsche, *The Birth of Tragedy and the Case of Wagner*, trans. Walter Kaufmann (New York: Random House, 1967).

NO   *Novalis Schriften. Die Werke Friedrichs von Hardenberg*, ed. by Richard Samuel in collaboration with Hans-Joachim Mähl and Gerhard Schulz. 5 vols. (Stuttgart: Kohlhammer, 1960–88).

Translations
AF Novalis, *Aphorisms and Fragments*, trans. Alexander Gelley, in *German Romantic Criticism*, ed. A. Leslie Willson with a foreword by Ernst Behler (New York: Continuum, 1982), 62–83.
HN Novalis, *Hymns to the Night and Other Selected Writings (Klingsohr's Fairy-Tale, Christendom or Europe, Selected Aphorisms)* (Indianapolis: Bobbs-Merrill, 1960).
HO Novalis, *Heinrich von Ofterdingen. A Novel*, trans. Palmer Hilty (New York: Ungar, 1964).
MW Novalis, *Miscellaneous Writings*, trans. Joyce Crick, *German Aesthetic and Literary Criticism. The Romantic Ironists and Goethe*, ed. Kathleen Wheeler (Cambridge University Press, 1984), 83–111.

TI FS   Ludwig Tieck, *Franz Sternbalds Wanderungen*, ed. Alfred Anger (Stuttgart: Reclam, 1979).

TI PH   Ludwig Tieck, *Phantasus*, ed. Manfred Frank
                (Frankfurt: Deutscher Klassiker Verlag, 1985).

TI PhK   *Phantasien über die Kunst, für Freunde der Kunst*, ed.
                Ludwig Tieck (Hamburg: Perthes, 1799). Re-
                edition by Jakob Minor (Berlin: Speemann, no
                date).

WA   Wilhelm Heinrich Wackenroder, *Herzensergie-
                ßungen eines kunstliebenden Klosterbruders*, ed.
                Ernst Benz (Stuttgart: Reclam, 1969).

                Translations
                CF Wilhelm Heinrich Wackenroder, *Confessions
                and Fantasies*, trans. Mary Hurst Schubert
                (University Park: Pennsylvania State
                University Press, 1971).
                OF Wilhelm Heinrich Wackenroder, *Outpourings
                of an Art-Loving Friar*, trans. Edward Mornin
                (New York: Ungar, 1975).

Chronology of early Romanticism

1763   Caroline Michaelis born on 2 September in Göttingen as the daughter of the Orientalist Johann David Michaelis. Educated at home.

1764   Dorothea (Brendel) Mendelssohn born on 24 October in Berlin as the daughter of Moses Mendelssohn and his wife Fromet, née Gugenheim. Educated mainly by her father.

1767   August Wilhelm Schlegel born on 8 September in Hanover as the son of General Superintendent Johann Adolf Schlegel and his wife Erdmuthe, née Hübsch. High school education in Hanover.

1768   Friedrich Schleiermacher born on 21 November in Breslau as the son of the Protestant army chaplain Gottlieb Adolph Schleiermacher. Educated in the Herrenhut schools of Silesia, at the college in Niesky, and at the seminary in Barby (all Herrenhut institutions).

1772   Friedrich Schlegel born on 10 March in Hanover. Educated at home, mainly by his brothers, especially August Wilhelm.

Novalis (Friedrich von Hardenberg) born on 2 May in Oberwiederstädt as the son of the director of the salt-mines, Heinrich Ulrich Erasmus von Hardenberg, and his wife Auguste Bernhardina, née von Bölzig. Education at home by tutors.

1773   Ludwig Tieck born on 31 May in Berlin as the son of a rope-maker.

Wilhelm Heinrich Wackenroder born in Berlin as the son of a high city official in the municipal administration.

1782   Beginning of Tieck's and Wackenroder's education at the high school Friedrichs Werd.

1783   Marriage of Dorothea Mendelssohn to the Berlin banker Simon Veit.

1784   On 15 June, marriage of Caroline Michaelis to the Clausthal physician Johann Franz Wilhelm Böhmer.

1786   A. W. Schlegel's immatriculation at the University of Göttingen for the study of ancient and modern literature; his friendship with Gottfried August Bürger starts; publications in the Göttingen *Musenalmanach* (*Almanac of the Muses*).

1787   Schleiermacher's immatriculation at the University of Halle for the study of theology and philosophy.

1788   Caroline Böhmer's return to her home in Göttingen after the early death of her husband. Acquaintance with A. W. Schlegel who courts her.

Friedrich Schlegel's apprenticeship at the Schlemm Bank in Leipzig; sudden return to his home in Hanover and preparation for university study under the tutelage of A. W. Schlegel; brief visits to his sister Charlotte in Dresden and frequenting of the gallery of antiquities.

1789   Schleiermacher in Drossen to prepare for his first examination in theology.

Publications by A. W. Schlegel in the Göttingen *Journal of Learned Subjects*.

1790   Novalis' immatriculation at the University of Jena for the study of law.

Friedrich Schlegel's immatriculation at the University of Göttingen for the study of law.

Schleiermacher as tutor in the house of Count Dohna in Schlobitten (West Prussia).

A. W. Schlegel's graduation as a *Rat* (MA).

1791   A. W. Schlegel as tutor in the house of the Amsterdam banker Henry Muilman; correspondence with Caroline Böhmer.

Friedrich Schlegel's immatriculation at the University of Leipzig for the study of law (and literature).

Novalis' immatriculation at the University of Leipzig for the study of law.

1792   Beginning of the friendship between Friedrich Schlegel and Novalis in January; expensive love affairs on the part of the two friends (August 1792 to Easter 1793).

Tieck's immatriculation at the University of Halle for the study of theology (and classical literature).

Wackenroder's preparation for the study of law in Berlin.

A. W. Schlegel collaborates with the Göttingen *Almanac of the Muses*.

Tieck's immatriculation at the University of Göttingen for the study of literature.

Caroline Böhmer settles in Mainz in the house of Georg and Therese Forster. Surrender of the fortress of Mainz to the French revolutionary army (October). Caroline's activity as a 'Clubbist' of the Republic of Mainz.

1793   Novalis' immatriculation at the University of Wittenberg (April).

Friedrich Schlegel's decision to devote himself to a theory of literature (end of May).

Tieck's and Wackenroder's immatriculation at the University of Erlangen, Tieck for the study of modern literature and Wackenroder for the study of law; communal visits to Nuremberg, Bamberg and Pommersfelden to inspect works of art.

Caroline's imprisonment at Fort Königstein following the surrender of the Republic of Mainz to the Prussian army; temporary settlement at the village of Lucka, near Leipzig, with the help of A. W. Schlegel; close contact with Friedrich Schlegel.

1794   Friedrich Schlegel assumes his private study of Greek literature in Dresden (January).

A. W. Schlegel's collaboration with Schiller's *Horae* and *Almanac of the Muses*.

Tieck and Wackenroder return to Berlin (autumn), Wackenroder as lawyer in the city administration and Tieck as a freelance writer.

Novalis obtains his law degree and assumes an administrative position in Tennstedt; acquaintance with Sophie von Kühn (15 March).

A. W. Schlegel's return to Germany (July), to Hanover and Brunswick, and assumption of a metrical translation of Shakespeare.

Meeting between Novalis, Fichte, and Hölderlin in the Jena house of the philosopher Niethammer.

Onset of Sophie von Kühn's ailment in November.

Novalis is appointed to the administration of the salt-mines in Weißenfels (30 December).

1796   Schleiermacher's appointment as preacher at the Charité in Berlin.

A. W. Schlegel's visit to his brother Friedrich in Dresden (April).

A. W. Schlegel's marriage to Caroline Böhmer (1 July); the couple settle in Jena.

Beginning of Friedrich Schlegel's collaboration with Johann Friedrich Reichardt's journal *Deutschland*; publication of his review of Schiller's *Horae* in this journal; move to Jena (beginning of August) and renewal of his friendship with Novalis; close relationship with Fichte.

Sophie von Kühn receives medical treatment in Jena and returns to Grüningen in December.

1797   Appearance of the first volume of A. W. Schlegel's Shakespeare translation (*Romeo and Juliet* and *A Midsummer Night's Dream*).

Schiller breaks with the Schlegel brothers (31 May).

Friedrich Schlegel moves to Berlin (15 July) and frequents the salon of Henriette Herz where he meets Dorothea Veit and Schleiermacher; beginning of the friendship with Schleiermacher; Dorothea assumes a love relationship with Friedrich Schlegel and leaves her family.

Sophie von Kühn's death (19 March).

Beginning of Wackenroder's illness.

1798   Wackenroder's death on 17 February.

Appearance of the first issue of the *Athenaeum* in May.

Sojourn of the early Romantics (A. W. Schlegel, Friedrich Schlegel, Caroline, Novalis, Fichte, and Schelling) in Dresden to inspect the art galleries.

Novalis' engagement to Julie von Charpentier (December).

A. W. Schlegel lectures on the philosophical doctrine of art at the University of Jena (winter semester).

1799   Dorothea's divorce from Simon Veit (January).

Publication of Friedrich Schlegel's *Lucinde*.

Appearance of Tieck's translation of *Don Quixote*.

Tieck's marriage to Amalie Alberti.

Friedrich Schlegel returns to Jena in September where the group of the early Romantics (A. W. and Friedrich Schlegel, Caroline, Dorothea, Tieck, Novalis, Schelling), with the exception of Schleiermacher, has gathered.

Acquaintance between Tieck and Novalis (17 July).

1800   Breakdown of A. W. and Caroline Schlegel's marriage and move of A. W. Schlegel to Berlin. Friedrich Schlegel obtains the doctorate and the *venia legendi* (*Habilitation*) at the University of Jena and assumes his lectures on transcendental philosophy (winter semester).

Appearance of the last issue of the *Athenaeum*.

Deterioration of Novalis' health.

1801   Novalis' death (25 March).

        Friedrich Schlegel's move to Berlin; close friendship with Rahel Levin.

        A. W. Schlegel's public Berlin lectures on literature and art.

1802   Schleiermacher as Court Preacher in Stolp (spring); beginning of his Plato translation.

        Friedrich and Dorothea Schlegel's move to Dresden (17 January); beginning of their journey to Paris (May) via Leipzig (book fair) and Weimar (première of Friedrich Schlegel's *Alarcos* at the court theatre, staged by Goethe). In Paris, Schlegel assumes lectures on German literature and philosophy.

        During the winter of 1802–3, A. W. Schlegel's public Berlin lectures on literature (mainly of Greek and Latin literature).

1803   Divorce of Caroline from A. W. Schlegel and marriage to Schelling (26 June); move of Caroline and Schelling to Würzburg.

        Appearance of the first issue of Friedrich Schlegel's Paris journal *Europa*, containing his descriptions of paintings in the Louvre; from November, private lectures for the Boisserée brothers on ancient and modern literature.

        During the winter of 1803–4, A. W. Schlegel's public Berlin lectures on Romantic literature.

1804   Schleiermacher's appointment as professor of theology at the University of Halle, including the position of University Preacher.

        Friedrich Schlegel's marriage to Dorothea on 6 April in Paris; move to Cologne in the company of the

Boisserée brothers via northern France and Belgium; beginning of the period of the Cologne lectures on philosophy.

In April, A. W. Schlegel makes the acquaintance of Madame de Staël in Berlin and moves with her to the Château Coppet on Lake Geneva.

Introduction

The emergence of the early Romantic theory of literature in Germany towards the end of the eighteenth century constitutes a decisive turning-point in the history of criticism. Incited by Lessing, Herder, and Schiller, and stimulated by Goethe's poetic creations, a new view of the literary work and the artistic process developed that differed sharply from the dominant classicist understanding of aesthetics and poetics. The European classicist tradition had stressed unchangeable norms for art, codified a hierarchical system of immutable genres, bound artistic production to an imitation of nature and an adherence to verisimilitude, and defined poetic unity according to strict rules. The early Romantic critics made decisive inroads into this classicist view of poetry by recognizing the infinite changeability of genres, their constant mixing and mingling, as well as the frequent emergence of new literary forms. They saw the poetic unity of a literary work as an inner conformity with itself, connecting a multiplicity of phenomena to a unity of its own. This task of redefinition, however, could not be accomplished by applying external rules, but was instead to be carried out by the shaping power of the imagination.

Given these features, early Romantic literary theory seems to be closely related to transcendental idealism, the prevailing philosophy of the time. In his *Critique of Judgment* of 1790 Kant laid the foundations for the autonomy of art, and for the uniqueness and distinctiveness of aesthetic, as opposed to scientific and moral judgments, thus decisively changing the ground rules in the debate about art and the beautiful that had prevailed in European criticism for centuries.[1] Other decisive

I

impulses came from Fichte and Schelling. Fichte inspired the intellectual life of his time with his reflective and self-reflective manner of thinking in terms of thought and counterthought – as evidenced by Novalis' shifts between introspection into the nature of the self on the one hand and observation of external nature on the other, as well as by Friedrich Schlegel's theory of irony, described by its author as a 'constant alternation between self-creation and self-destruction' (*KFSA* 2, 151, 172). Whereas in these early forms of transcendental idealism an antagonism between the human being and nature exists, Schelling raised this philosophy to the level of absolute idealism, achieving a complete identification of spirit and nature. This step is clearly in keeping with the new notions of symbolic and allegorical poetry in the criticism and poetic practice of the time, which led to a more profound understanding of the creative process and culminated in a striving for 'absolute poetry'.

Another important feature of early Romanticism in Germany lies in its close association with the so-called 'classicism' of Weimar, the intellectual world of Goethe and Schiller. The parallels between these two groups of authors, classicists and romanticists, seem obvious and have been the subject of many studies, which usually maintain that Romantic theory took certain positions of Goethe and Schiller to an extreme, giving a more youthful or extravagant twist to their poetic views while still basically agreeing with the classicism of Weimar.[2] One favourite formula for seeing this relationship as one of complementarity was that of 'limitation' (Weimar classicism) and 'infinity' (Jena Romanticism).[3] Outside of Germany, the antagonism between Jena, the seat of the Romantics, and Weimar, the residence of Goethe and Schiller, appears so minor as virtually to disappear, the name 'romantic' emerging as a common denominator for both groups.

These are the common views of early German Romanticism in literary history. Both of them – the assumptions of a positive relationship on the part of the Romantics to the philosophy of transcendental idealism and the poetic world of Goethe and Schiller – emphasize important features in the new theory. Upon closer consideration, however, this firm location of early

Romanticism in the intellectual landscape of the time dissolves, and a phenomenon much more complicated emerges which escapes final definition and location. This can already be seen in the attitude of the early Romantics toward the classicist and classical traditions. The prime target of the Romantic assault was not classicism as such, but the aesthetic system of the *ars poetica* and neoclassicism – in general, the view of literature as representation of reality, as imitation, as *mimesis*. In its basic attitude, early Romanticism in Germany reveals a strong affinity to classical antiquity. At best, one can speak of a shifting emphasis in the relationship to classicism, of a departure from the dominant Roman and Aristotelian influence during the classicist period in exchange for a closer bond with the Greeks, particularly the Platonic tradition. Perhaps no other literary period had a deeper impact upon early Romantic theory, at least initially, than classical antiquity, especially Greek litera-ture. In this regard, early Romanticism is an apparent expression of the 'tyranny of Greece over the German mind'.[4]

This did not interfere with the premise, however, that eventually all classicism was to be overcome, including not only the classicistic programmes of Boileau, Batteux, Dryden, and Gottsched, but also 'classical' forms of the Greek authors themselves. Classicism as such, especially in its orientation toward perfection, everlasting value, and models for imitation, did not correspond to the early Romantic understanding of human nature and the Romantic desire for free expression of the imagination. After all, Goethe had already maintained, in his essay entitled *Literary Sans-Culottism* of 1791, that no author could possibly consider himself classical, because the claim which this implied would be so elevated as to give an impression of self-acclamation.[5] Friedrich Schlegel went further still and denied the desirability of classical works in general when he said: 'Absolutely unsurpassable models constitute insurmount-able barriers to perfectibility. In this respect one might very well say: Heaven preserve us from eternal works' (*KFSA* 2, 79–80). This attitude included Greek literature and became possible because classical Greek poetry was not considered as an objective form, an 'ideal' incarnation, a prototype or model for the modern author, but rather as something one should compete and interact with, something human and natural that one should incorporate into oneself. The implications of this attitude are of special importance for the modernist character of early Romantic theory. On this premise one could indeed claim, in a paradoxical manner, that the most advanced type of modernity consists in that mentality which has the liveliest relationship with the Greeks. It also follows from this way of thinking that classicism and modernism lose their usual historical and categorical character, and become principles of a more fundamental reflection, assuming the character of ideal types in a process of intellectual interaction.

Another aspect sharply distinguishing the early Romantic mentality from every form of European classicism is its extremely favourable attitude towards revolution in general, and even to a certain degree towards the French Revolution. Contemporaries readily characterized the new critical endeavours of the early Romantics as a 'revolution', meaning of course a 'critical' or an 'aesthetic' revolution.[6] These assessments coincided with the opinions of the early Romantics about their own enterprise. The particular historical self-understanding of the Romantic critics is best illustrated, however, by the futuristic idea of infinite perfectibility.[7] Whereas during the Enlightenment the contemporary age was taken as a standard for previous epochs, the Romantics regarded their own time as part of an all-pervasive moment of becoming, and saw themselves moving towards ever new possibilities in the future. They viewed poetry as an absolutely 'progressive' realm involved in a process of endless development. The idea of infinite perfectibility also applies to their own criticism and theory of literature, and corresponds to the inexhaustibility of interpretation, to the infinite potentialities in the understanding of literary works that yield new meanings from ever new modes of historical consciousness.

Similar observations can be made about early Romantic theory from the point of view of idealistic, transcendental philosophy. Here the Romantic theory is usually regarded as an application of doctrines developed by Kant, Fichte, and

Schelling to the realm of poetry. Hegel attempted to impress this interpretation upon our understanding of Romanticism, insisting that the early Romantic form of subjectivity, with its 'non-philosophically executed turn', was nothing but an extravagant offshoot of Fichtean philosophy (*HEG* 20, 415). In a less polemical fashion, this view of early Romantic theory can be described as an extension of a larger philosophical process of that time, namely, the aesthetic formulation of subjective idealism, the elaboration of the poetic side of transcendental idealism. Yet, in the end, early Romanticism is just as little an extension of the idealism of Kant, Fichte, and Schelling as it is a mere offshoot of classicism and the classicist theory. Here again, the early Romantic mentality adopted an attitude that showed little interest in historical frameworks of philosophy, the content of philosophical knowledge, the results of philosophizing, or systems of thought. Instead, it departed from these reference points and arrived at its own medium of reflection, that is, at art, poetry, and literature, independent of historical relationships. This invasion of reflection, theory, and philosophy into the territory of art, poetry, and literature can be interpreted as another feature of the modern aspect of Romantic theory, the consciousness of literary modernism, as a process best described as a 'poetry of poetry' that blends critical, reflective discourse with its own creative invention. One could also describe the intrusion of reflection into the realm of the aesthetic and the imaginative as a combination or junction of poetry and philosophy. This is a model of interplay which regards the two poles, poetry and philosophy, spontaneity and reflection – like the former model of classicism and modernism – as interdependent and complementary, as ideal types of intellectual interaction. If we adopt this model, we transcend the dominance of one single principle (reason or imagination, theory or creation, classicism or romanticism) in favour of a pluralistic movement of counteractive and interactive principles that seem to oppose, but in their interaction actually generate and maintain each other.

One can also view the self-reflective style of early Romantic theory in terms of its historical consciousness and thereby return to the topic of classicism. From this point of view, the absolute has vanished and the classical structures of complete identity and full self-possession are no longer regarded as valid. Here, too, there is no utopian promise, and the absolute expectations of the future are no longer valid. What we have instead is a universally progressive poetry, the 'real essence' of which is 'that it should forever be becoming and never be perfected' (*KFSA* 2, 183; *LF*, 175). This is not to be interpreted as a loss, however, but rather as the actual human condition and as an enormous source of creativity. If total communication is impossible, if language provides no direct path to reality, then we are left with indirect communication, figurative language, metaphor, allegory. What matters even more is not to spoil this delicate position of the in-between that typifies the truly modern attitude by coarsely constructing an absolute past, a golden age, as the classicists have done, or, conversely, by upholding an absolute future, a utopia, as certain philosophers of the time attempted to do. Similar observations could be made in the field of hermeneutics. The early Romantic theory of understanding should not be regarded as a historical phase or a step into a generally developing history of hermeneutics, as has often been maintained,[8] but as a much more radical reflection upon the possibility of understanding which takes into account the amount of incomprehensibility, indeed, of not-understanding, constituted in every act of understanding.

If one pursues this line of thought, one soon realizes that early German Romanticism also has few links with the classicism of Schiller and Goethe. From the beginning, the early Romantic reflection upon poetry transcends the scope of any national literature and extends to the broad field of world literature or, more precisely, to Western literature as demarcated by names such as Pindar, Sophocles, Dante, Calderón, and Shakespeare. Conversely, the category of modern or Romantic literature as established in the new theory is one that a whole generation of European authors in the Mediterranean, northern, and Slavic countries of Europe adopted for their own endeavours, and in which they recognized themselves.[9] As far as the direct relationship of the early Romantic theory to Goethe and Schiller is concerned, one soon realizes that a reflective critique was at work here that did not cease to 'annihilate' certain authors of the Enlightenment (Nicolai, Kotzebue, Merkel) or representatives of the classicist and sentimental tradition (Jacobi, Wieland, Herder). Indeed, this critique soon extended to Schiller, and then to Goethe himself, and finally established a notion of absolute poetry that no Romantic work could possibly equal. At this point, we again notice a movement away from any historical relationship and reference, towards a transcendental or anthropological realm of more general significance, although the discourse continues to be organized in terms of historical names and historical references. In other words, we encounter in these instances the absolutely progressive and exponential character of early Romantic theory.

A further attempt to classify early Romantic theory has occasionally been made from the point of view of the encyclopaedia,[10] a predominant theme of the time which is usually combined with the function of education, as in the old notion of cyclical education, *enkyklios paideia*. Yet here again, we encounter the typical attitude of early Romanticism in the sense of suspending firm reference points and regarding the principles of such an encyclopedia as in a peculiar state of oscillation, of hovering. The most impressive development of this theme in terms of a literary encyclopaedia is certainly the famous discussion of Shakespeare in Goethe's novel *Wilhelm Meister's Apprenticeship*, where it is argued that Shakespeare, in whom nature and art are one, seems to have a special connection to the creative world spirit.[11] Consequently, the modern human being can find no better path to an encyclopaedic education than through this poet, who, having special access to the structure of the world, functions as its interpreter. Hegel, in contrast, promulgated the idea of a philosophical encyclopaedia. Inasmuch as philosophy, as a fundamental science, contains the principles of all other sciences within itself, he argues that philosophy is the true encyclopaedia and doctrine of education, and he consequently regards the literary encyclopaedia as empty and useless for the young mind.[12] In contrast to these poetic or philosophical encyclopaedias, the early Romantic theory can be described as an interaction of the literary and the philosophical encyclopaedias – not as their synthesis, to be sure, but as an attempt to think philosophy from the point of view of poetry and poetry from the point of view of philosophy. Similar interactive relationships exist in this theory between poetry and prose, genial inspiration and criticism, understanding and incomprehensibility, truth and error, the inner and the outer world, this life and the beyond. By operating in this manner, early Romantic theory manifests itself as a basic reflection upon poetry and literature that eludes any final formulation and does not result in an ultimate doctrine.

Outlining early Romantic theory in these terms, we realize that we are dealing with a phenomenon that is hard to locate in a particular historical environment and has a future-oriented thrust in which features of our own modernity become obvious. As the examples of interpretation mentioned above have shown, there have always been attempts to limit early Romantic theory to some historical context and thereby enclose it in the past. But these attempts have always had a counterpart in so-called 'actualizations' of early Romantic theory in more recent and contemporary trends of criticism, such as new criticism, philosophical hermeneutics, the critical theory of the Frankfurt School (especially that of Adorno), the critique of subject philosophy (Heidegger), and deconstruction in the writings of Derrida, Lacoue-Labarthe, Nancy, and Paul de Man.[13] In view of its actuality and modernistic character, early Romantic theory has also become, next to Nietzsche, the main target of any fundamentalist critique of modernity and postmodernity. In Germany the contemporary critique of ideology identifies early Romanticism as the first step into 'aesthetic modernism', an attitude marked by a loss of all bonds with communal rationality, communicative reasoning, consensus, and so forth.[14]

Another important aspect of the theory of literature in early German Romanticism is that it is not the completed product of one single mind, but an open, fragmentary, ever-changing thought process to which authors of the most diverse backgrounds made their contributions – authors who, in spite of their intellectual diversity, considered themselves at least for some period of time the originators of a 'new school' of literature and criticism. This 'school' comprised a variety of talents – from learned and scholarly critics like the Schlegel brothers to a mining engineer like Novalis, from a freelance writer like Tieck and a legal administrator like Wackenroder to a trained Protestant theologian like Schleiermacher. All were in their twenties when their theory of literature originated through mutual discussion and interaction. Depicting such a complex phenomenon poses a real challenge, one which is attempted in this text through a sequential examination of the main developments in the early Romantic theory of poetry. Hence the following chapters are arranged in accordance with the predominant themes of early Romantic reflection. We are dealing with a brief period of about six to seven years, from 1794 to around 1800. During these years, such vast domains as the literature of the Greeks and the Romans (Ch. 2, pp. 72–130, below), the period of the 'Romantic authors' (Dante, Boccaccio, Calderón, Shakespeare: Ch. 3, pp. 131–80, below), the new philosophy of transcendental idealism (Ch. 4, pp. 181–221, below), modern painting and music (Ch. 5, pp. 222–59 below), the theory of language and understanding (Ch. 6, pp. 260–305, below), and new possibilities for 'pure' and 'absolute' poetry were explored (Ch. 3, pp. 154–64, below and Ch. 4, pp. 201–11, below). Although these periods of literature and modern art formed the basis for reflection and research on the part of the Romantics, the chapters are not arranged solely in terms of these historical studies, but rather according to the themes which arise from them. As will be seen in the following discussion, history and theory are indeed inseparable in early Romantic discourse, since theory evolves directly from the study of historical phenomena and manifests itself in historical references and images.

The first chapter gives a brief portrayal of the intellectual environment in which early Romantic theory originated, focusing on the city of Jena and its university. This seat of philosophers of transcendental idealism lies only a few miles from Goethe's Weimar, which was also the residence of Wieland and Herder. Schiller, a professor of history at the university,

lived in Jena until 1799 and then moved to Weimar to become
more actively involved in Goethe's reforms of the court theatre.
The formation of the Romantic school in Jena is the occasion for
brief biographical introductions of its main representatives,
including Caroline and Dorothea Schlegel, as well as for a
discussion of the terms 'romantic' and 'romanticism'. The
second chapter, based on the specific investigation of Greek
literature by Friedrich and August Wilhelm Schlegel, particularly of lyric poetry, the epic, and drama, considers the
theme of poetic unity as an important means of defining what is
poetic. Such a study of Greek and Roman literature, however,
inevitably raises questions about our own relationship to the
Greeks and thereby approaches the theme of literary modernity
in a way reminiscent of the famous debate between the ancients
and the moderns during the seventeenth and eighteenth
centuries. The third chapter finds its historical bearings in the
equally intense study of modern literature by the Schlegel
brothers, which included writers neglected or even rejected by
the classicist theory. In a decisive revision of the literary canon
of the time, authors such as Dante, Boccaccio, Cervantes,
Shakespeare, and Calderón became the leading figures for the
Romantic view of literature, while among contemporary
authors only Goethe was considered worthy of inclusion. Yet
this chapter primarily examines the type of literature and the
mode of organization and construction that the Romantic
critics found in these authors. Irony, in Friedrich Schlegel's
Romantic understanding of the term, is one of the main themes
of this chapter, which also covers the topic of 'transcendental
poetry' and the theme of mythology in its relationship to
literature. The fourth chapter expands upon these ideas and
introduces Novalis, a writer through whom early Romantic
theory gained a new and important dimension. Up to then, this
theory had been one of the subject, of subjective idealism, and
the potentialities of the human mind. But Novalis began to
include not only the natural world surrounding us within his
thought, but also the world beyond. By reflecting upon
relationships between the inner and the outer world, the realms
of this life and the hereafter, Romantic theory came to embrace

new territories and assumed a mysterious, mystical, even religious, character that was, nevertheless, originally free from dogma or religious orthodoxy. The fifth chapter introduces aesthetic considerations that had previously remained outside the scope of early Romantic theory. Wackenroder and Tieck began to concentrate on painting and music in their early study of Italian Renaissance painting and the old German art of Dürer, in addition to their preoccupation with music. In his sketches of these areas, Wackenroder formulated insights into the nature of art which, although more spontaneous and less learned, were in some ways parallel to those articulated by the Schlegel brothers. The link between the Jena group (the Schlegel brothers and Novalis) and the Berlin circle (Wackenroder, Tieck) not only expanded Romantic theory by adding significant new themes, but also led to a larger representation of the new school, especially when Tieck found a natural ally in Novalis. With Friedrich Schlegel's move to Berlin in 1797 and his close intellectual alliance with Schleiermacher, the Romantic school continued to expand. The sixth chapter attempts to show how the themes of the encyclopaedia, hermeneutics, and language theory gained prominence in early Romantic theory.

Each of the following six chapters on the evolution of early Romantic theory also features, by way of example, a certain theme, event, or book in which the individual chapter finds its most concrete expression. Always engaged in an active relationship with historical events, early Romantic theory also remained in lively contact with the literary life of its own time. Thus, the additional examples in each individual chapter illustrate the original historical context of early Romantic theory, but are also meant to depict particular aspects and implications of this theory more vividly than a purely theoretical discussion would allow. The first chapter examines the relationship of the early German Romantics to the French Revolution. August Wilhelm Schlegel's condemnation of Euripides then accentuates the discussion of poetic unity and modernity (Ch. 2), whereas Friedrich Schlegel's essay on Goethe's novel *Wilhelm Meister* exemplifies the potentialities of

Romantic literature in the novel (Ch. 3). The mythological tendencies of Romantic theory and its integration of manifold realms are illustrated by Novalis' fragmentary novel *Heinrich von Ofterdingen* (Ch. 4), and the chapter on the theory of painting and music (Ch. 5) is augmented by a discussion of Tieck's novel *Franz Sternbald's Journeys* with its many interwoven dialogues on art. Friedrich Schlegel's novel *Lucinde* (Ch. 6), known primarily for its advocacy of greater autonomy for women, is discussed in terms of its reception by the reading public and its thematization in Romantic writings. The entire process begins with Friedrich Schlegel's intensive study of Greek poetry in 1794, while its conclusion is marked by Novalis' death in 1801. This is accompanied by a number of ruptures and disagreements among the participants in the new school that eventually brought an end to early Romantic literary theory in Germany, followed by its transformation into many forms of Romanticism and its lasting importance for critical theory ever since.

CHAPTER I

Formation and main representatives of early Romanticism in Germany

During the last decade of the eighteenth century, Jena was a lovely residential area in Thuringia mostly known for its excellent and progressive university. The city, situated in close proximity to the Wartburg, had been a traditional stronghold of Protestantism. This spirit animated the university, which since its founding in 1558 had maintained its reputation as an intellectually independent, self-governed institution. Its founder was the Saxon Elector, Johann Friedrich, called the 'magnanimous'. Among the German universities of the time, Göttingen and Leipzig certainly predominated, but Jena, although relatively small, was attractive to students and scholars because of the spirit of innovation and open-mindedness which contrasted favourably with the stale atmosphere of the Enlightenment still dominant at these other institutions.

All of the representatives of early Romanticism were university students, and most of them had followed curricula in the humanities, primarily in literature (both ancient and modern) and philosophy. August Wilhelm Schlegel had pursued all his studies in classical and modern literature at Göttingen University, where he obtained a degree granting him the title of 'counsel', perhaps comparable to the present MA degree. Friedrich Schlegel studied law at Göttingen and Leipzig without obtaining a degree, but later, in 1800, became a Doctor of Philosophy of the University of Jena. Tieck and Wackenroder studied at the universities of Erlangen and Göttingen. Wackenroder obtained a law degree from Göttingen, but was also drawn into literary courses by Tieck, who made the study of literature his main object. Schleiermacher's field of study was theology, first pursued at private pietist institutions. But he completed his education at Halle University, where he also studied Kantian philosophy and classical philology with the great Hellenist Friedrich August Wolf. Only Novalis began his studies at the University of Jena, where eventually most of the Romantics would gather, but his choice was simply based on the university's close proximity to his home. He studied law in Jena, continued these studies at Leipzig University together with Friedrich Schlegel, and eventually moved to Wittenberg, where he obtained his degree.

JENA AND EARLY ROMANTICISM

Novalis' studies at Jena University provide us with some information about this institution at the time of the Romantics. He entered the university in 1790 at the age of eighteen, and although his field of study was law, he took courses on Kantian philosophy with Karl Leonhard Reinhold and in modern history with Schiller. Three letters of this time, two of them to Schiller (*NO* 4, 89, 98) and one to Reinhold (*NO* 4, 91), show his boundless veneration for Schiller and his desire to follow in the latter's footsteps. Schiller, however, at the request of Novalis' father, explained the advantages which a law degree held over poetry and metaphysics to the young student and persuaded him to continue this course at Leipzig University. Because of the proximity of his paternal home in Weissenfels to Jena, however, Novalis frequently returned to the city. One such visit has special importance, perhaps simply because it has been registered. It took place in May 1795 shortly after the formation of early Romantic theory had begun in the house of the Jena philosopher Friedrich Immanuel Niethammer. Fichte, who had recently been appointed to the university, was also present at this meeting, as was a young poet from Swabia, one of Schiller's friends who had been on a brief visit to Jena. His name was Friedrich Hölderlin. We know very little about the meeting, and although there has been much speculation about the content of the conversation,[1] Niethammer simply wrote in his diaries: 'Talked much about religion and revelation and in this regard many questions remain open for philosophy' (*NO* 4, 588).

Schiller was certainly one of the luminaries at the university. As the author of *History of the Defection of the Netherlands* (1788) and *History of the Thirty Years War* (1791–3), he had been appointed as a professor of history in 1788. His inaugural lecture of May 1789 on 'What Is and to What End Does One Study Universal History?' was a memorable event at the university. Schiller was of Swabian origin and had connections with the most important publisher of the time, Johann Friedrich Cotta of Tübingen. Through Cotta, he published two prominent journals in which the most respected minds of the time participated. Both were edited in Jena and were directly related to the Romantic school, first in a cooperative and later in a polemical sense. These were the *Horae* (1795–7), adopting the Greek mythological name for the hours, and the *Almanac of the Muses* (1795–1800), an annual which contained the usual popular information included in traditional yearbooks about astronomical configurations, weather forecasts, and the yearly calendar, but also supplemented such data with poetry by various authors. Some of the poems were set to music by famous composers with scores accompanying the poems in the almanac. The most popular and traditional yearbook at that time was the one known as the *Göttingen Almanac*, which was edited by Johann Heinrich Voß, the translator of Homer. By founding a new, substantially revised almanac, Schiller implied that the *Göttingen Almanac* was no longer up to date and had ceased to represent the best type of poetry produced in Germany, which was now, he made clear, to be published in his own almanac. His *Horae*, however, was less progressive in content. Containing mostly prose fiction and theoretical essays, the first issues of the periodical appeared in 1795, after the Reign of Terror in France (1793–4) had ended and a new constitutional government had been formed. Yet the effects of the Reign of Terror were still noticeable among some intellectuals in Germany, and Schiller himself reacted to the 'torturers' in Paris, as he called Robespierre and his Jacobins, with special horror. A direct result of this reaction, the *Horae* were meant to be a periodical absolutely silent about the tumultuous events of the day, an organ in which a spirit of order and humanity was to guide humankind toward its truly important tasks.[2] This is worth mentioning because of specific clashes which the Romantics had with the *Horae* after an initially harmonious period of collaboration. Indeed, the founding of the *Horae* can be viewed as the ultimate reason for Jena's becoming the centre of early Romantic literary theory. After Schiller had enlisted A. W. Schlegel as one of his most prolific contributors, he persuaded him to come to Jena in 1796 for closer collaboration, and this eventually made Jena the site for the formation of the Romantic school. Another important journal published in Jena was the *Allgemeine Literaturzeitung (ALZ)*, a paper for the critical review of the most important publications in the humanities. Founded in 1785, the *ALZ* was edited by Christian Gottfried Schütz and Friedrich Justin Bertuch and recruited the most illustrious literary authors of the time as its reviewers. A. W. Schlegel became perhaps the most prominent contributor to this journal, the author of about 300 of its reviews; and many of the events connected with the Romantic group in Jena are reflected in the *ALZ*.

The host at the meeting of Novalis with Fichte and Hölderlin, Friedrich Immanuel Niethammer, was an influential teacher of philosophy, but his chief service to the new spirit at the university was his founding of the *Philosophical Journal of a Society of German Scholars* in 1795, the leading philosophical journal of the time. To understand its importance, one must consider that Niethammer's undertaking almost coincided with Fichte's move to Jena in 1794. The journal became the main organ for formulating the principles of transcendental idealism, and many of Fichte's and Schelling's early writings first appeared in it. Fichte later joined Niethammer as its editor. The other philosopher at Jena mentioned in the context of Novalis' early studies at the university, Karl Leonhard Reinhold, was a Kantian and author of the *Letters on Kantian Philosophy* (1786), first delivered as a university lecture course. At the time at which our investigation begins, Reinhold had already left for a position at Kiel University, and his departure in 1794 became the immediate occasion for Fichte's appointment. Reinhold remained attached to the intellectual world of Jena, however, and even transferred the basis of his 'elementary philosophy' from Kant to Fichte – a major success for the acceptance of Fichte's doctrine. Yet Reinhold later abandoned the Fichtean position, becoming an ardent opponent of what he called the 'mischief of speculation'.

Friedrich Hölderlin does not play a major role here because his visit to Jena was accidental and did not lead to any contact with the Jena Romantics, except for the brief encounter with Novalis. But the philosopher Fichte did have a great impact on the development of the university as well as on the early Romantic school. He had joined the university at the beginning of the summer semester of 1794, and his appointment contributed considerably to the reputation of the university as an innovative, progressive, future-oriented place of study. Until then, Fichte had spent most of his time as a private tutor in Zurich. After a brief visit to Kant in Königsberg in 1792, Fichte anonymously published his *Critique of all Revelation*, perhaps an outcome of his conversations with Kant and generally regarded as a text by Kant. When Kant revealed the work's true authorship, Fichte's fortune was made. Two further publications by Fichte attracted widespread attention and were directly related to the French Revolution. Living in Zurich, Fichte was deeply familiar with the events in neighbouring France, but unlike Schiller, and despite a strong conservative reaction in Switzerland to the terror and persecution of the royal family, he remained a proponent of the revolution. Edmund Burke's constitutionalist *Reflections on the Revolution in France* of 1790 had been translated by Friedrich Gentz into German in 1791 and formed the starting-point for a number of anti-revolutionary treatises. Responding to them, Fichte singled out August Wilhelm Rehberg's *Investigations into the French Revolution* (1792) and wrote his *Contribution to Correcting the Public's Judgments about the French Revolution* (1793), soon followed by his *Reclamation of Freedom of Thought, To The Princes of Europe* (1794) – publications which had wide repercussions in Germany. In the first, to the horror of many of his contemporaries, Fichte deduced the people's right to a revolution from the principles of reason. On 17 August 1795, Friedrich Schlegel wrote to his brother:

The greatest metaphysical thinker *now* living is a most popular author. You can see this in his famous *Contribution* in which Rehberg is pierced. Compare the ravishing rhetoric of this man in the *Lectures on the Vocation of the Scholar* to Schiller's stylized exercises in declamation. He is one for whom Hamlet sighed in vain. Every trait of his public life seems to say: this is a *man*. (*KFSA* 23, 248)

The *Lectures on the Vocation of the Scholar* of 1794 were among Fichte's first publications after his move to Jena. They were not delivered at the university, however, but counted among his 'popular' writings first presented to the public on Sundays. Fichte attempted to communicate with the public in non-technical language in order to promote the ultimate goal of his 'doctrine of knowledge', the infinite perfectibility of the human being. Like no philosopher before him, he placed all value on the future and told his audience, in a language clearly anticipating early Romantic discourse on poetry, that the final end of our history 'is completely unachievable and must always remain so – so long, that is, as man is to remain man and is not supposed to become God' (*EPW*, 152). In an interesting twist of wording, Fichte considered it the goal of man never to achieve his goal and declared it to be the 'vocation of man' to be in an 'endless approximation toward this goal' (*EPW*, 152, 160).

Fichte's university lectures, however, were devoted to an endlessly repeated attempt to introduce his audience to the true standpoint of transcendental idealism, which encountered enormous, and for Fichte, desperate, difficulties. Hegel later reported sarcastically that students not capable of moving their minds over to that standpoint had become mad (*HEG* 2, 398). If we attempted to render Fichte's standpoint in ordinary language, we could say that we have contact with being only in the medium of consciousness and that both being and consciousness cannot be separated from each other in our experience of the world. Even an expression like 'the world' would not be precise enough in this context, since there is no 'world' outside of my consciousness, but only my experience of it through my consciousness. In this sense, Kant had already introduced this type of knowledge as 'transcendental knowledge' and stated in the *Critique of Pure Reason*: 'I call transcendental all knowledge which is not so much occupied with objects as with the mode of our cognition of objects' (*KA* 3, 43). Traditional philosophy, one could say, assumes a pregiven reality of objects, whereas transcendental philosophizing views them in their interrelationship with the knowing subject. Fichte said this much better himself when in a letter of 23 June 1804 to P. J. Appia he argued:

All philosophy up to Kant had being as its object. Because of a lack of attention, all [philosophers preceding Kant] overlooked the fact that there is no being except in a consciousness and, conversely, no consciousness except in relation to being; that therefore the proper *As Such*, as the object of philosophy, can be neither being, as in all pre-Kantian philosophy, nor consciousness – which, however, has not even been attempted – but only the absolute unity of the two beyond their separateness.

This is still very much the Kantian position according to which a realm of reality, although unknowable, is postulated as an enigmatic 'thing in itself'. The real difficulty of transcendental speculation sets in, however, when Fichte attempts to absorb this 'remnant' of reality, the thing in itself, by declaring it nothing 'in itself' but only something for the ego and therefore created by the ego. Thus, he says, there is really no being without consciousness and no consciousness without being. We come to an absolute principle prior to its division into being and consciousness, the Archimedean point on which Fichte's philosophy actually turns. In his early period he called this principle 'the ego' in the sense of a general, absolute spiritual principle in which subjectivity and objectivity, ideality and reality coincide. This is one point in which Fichte went resolutely beyond Kantian philosophy and what was then somewhat disdainfully called the 'Kantian dualism'. He further deduced all specific forms of consciousness, and also practical philosophy, from this highest point of identity (or the absolute) through mere thinking, through pure reflection. This procedure bestows a degree of abstraction upon Fichte's philosophy which is hard to match and eventually led to its failure, its ill-famed 'incomprehensibility'.

On the whole, one can characterize Fichte's early philosophical attempts at Jena University as a foundational drive comparable to that of Descartes. While able to impart decisive impulses to his fellow philosophers, such as Schelling and Hegel, Fichte was not capable of moving the larger academic or intellectual community to his position and engaged in one frustrating attempt after the other to 'introduce' his 'doctrine of knowledge'. This title of his new philosophy has also been the subject of ridicule and misunderstanding, but it is actually very simple and clearly says what it means, namely, a doctrine, a theory of knowledge, an analysis of how we know things. It was certainly an important success for Fichte when Karl Leonhard Reinhold embraced Fichte's position as relevant, even basic, to his 'elementary philosophy'. But a devastating blow came when Kant, repeatedly asked for his opinion about the doctrine of knowledge, finally stated in the Jena *ALZ* of 28 August 1799 that he considered Fichte's philosophy 'a completely untenable system' and reduced it to 'mere logic', characterizing its metaphysical results as 'useless hair-splittings'. With their own modes of speculation, both Schelling and Hegel soon left Fichte behind. The early Romantics, Friedrich Schlegel and Novalis in particular, were perhaps the most responsive recipients of Fichte's philosophy, although they, too, became less interested in the 'doctrinaire of knowledge', as Friedrich Schlegel put it (*KFSA* 23, 343), than in the general thrust of this philosophy independent of any contents of knowledge and solely focused on its free manner of reflection.

In addition to its 'incomprehensibility', the Fichtean philosophy suffered from its outspoken 'atheism' in its reception at Jena. The use of this term was initiated from outside by citizens of Jena, by administrators, perhaps also by the duke of Saxony-Weimar and his minister of education, Goethe, but did not really coincide with Fichte's own working. Yet the negation of an extra-worldly principle followed necessarily from the monism of this philosophy and its integration of ideality and reality, subjectivity and objectivity. When a disciple of Fichte's, Friedrich Karl Forberg, published an article on religion in Niethammer's *Philosophical Journal* (1798) and reduced religion in Fichtean terms to a belief in a moral world order, an anonymous text appeared in Jena with the title 'Writing of a Father to His Son on Fichte's and Forberg's Atheism'. As a result, the *Philosophical Journal* was banned in the duchy and the university threatened with closure. Fichte, in his frank manner, wrote *Appellation to the Public. A Writing Begged to be Read Before being Confiscated* (1799). Not realizing the danger of the situation and not in the least concerned with rhetorical compromises, he outlined his philosophical position with all possible clarity. The duke attempted to settle the issue by having the academic senate give Fichte a reprimand, but Fichte retorted officially in a letter to the senate that he would not accept a reprimand. Not expecting them to accept it, Fichte submitted his resignation to the senators, and this indeed marked the end of his academic career at Jena. He was dismissed from the university and in the summer of 1799 went to Berlin, where the Prussian king granted him residence. There he maintained his contacts with Friedrich Schlegel, who also lived in the Prussian metropolis at the time and who brought Fichte in touch with Schleiermacher and Tieck.

Fichte's true successor at Jena University was Schelling, who had, however, already been appointed professor of philosophy upon Fichte's recommendation in 1798, and therefore did not actually take over Fichte's chair. Before that, Schelling had become one of the most active and dynamic contributors to the *Philosophical Journal*. It was in this periodical that he published the series of his 'Philosophical Letters on Dogmatism and Criticism', exhibiting for the first time his particular 'standpoint' in philosophy, namely, that there are actually two equally valid 'systems' or points of view, that of the *subject* and that of the *object*, which cannot be subsumed or absorbed by the one or the other but constitute a relationship of mutual support or mutual veneration. Schelling first made this decisive point in a letter to Hegel on 5 February 1794, which reads:

Meanwhile, I have become a Spinocist! Do not be surprised. You will soon hear how. Spinoza was the world (the object as such in opposition to the subject) – everything. For me this is the *ego*. The proper distinction between critical and dogmatic philosophy appears to me to be that the one proceeds from the absolute ego (still undetermined by any object) and the other from the absolute object or non-ego. The latter in its utmost consequence leads to Spinoza's system, the former to the Kantian.

Schelling's statement: 'Meanwhile, I have become a Spinocist', is therefore not to be interpreted as an uncritical acceptance of the 'dogmatic' philosophy of Spinoza, but rather as a maintenance of the absolute object (nature, the world) against the absolute ego (consciousness in the manner of Kant and Fichte). Schelling's version of transcendental idealism cannot be limited to the rational, conscious, and free dimensions of the ego, but requires complementation from the side of nature, the unconscious, and the irrational. Nature and spirit appear as two corresponding spheres of a universal process in which the absolute manifests itself. They correspond to each other most intimately and constantly reveal analogies. According to a famous dictum, nature is visible spirit and spirit is invisible nature. Schelling thereby proceeds to an absolute idealism of the perfected unity of the real and the ideal, to an ideal-realism, or a philosophy of identity.

Schelling was also one of the most successful academic teachers, who at the age of twenty-three actually dominated the scene at Jena University. We have a later report about Schelling's activity as a teacher from Henry Crabb Robinson dating from the winter semester of 1802–3, when Schelling had begun his first lecture course on aesthetics.[3] The report relates Robinson's activities on 14 November 1802 and is still of relevance as an account of Jena University during the Romantic age. Robinson lived in the house of the philosopher Jakob Friedrich Fries and began his day by comparing Schelling's *Journal on Speculative Physics* with his lecture notes from the day before 'to squeeze out a little sense or meaning'. At ten o'clock he had a lecture by the president of the university, Voigt, on experimental physics, but lamented that Voigt 'with utter want of taste and propriety will incessantly digress from his object and convert his physical lectures to moral and edifying sermons'. After lunch, he went to the two o'clock lecture on 'anthropology' by 'Mr Privy Councillor' Justus Christian von Loder – 'unquestionably the best delivered and most useful of all I hear'. Soon afterwards he rid his imagination of 'rotten carcasses and smoked skeletons' by attending Schelling's lectures on aesthetics, 'hearing the modern Plato read for a whole hour his new metaphysical Theory of Aesthetic or the Philosophy of the Arts'. In spite of the 'obscurity of a philosophy compounded of the most comprised abstraction, and enthusiastic mysticism', this lecture offered Robinson 'particular ingenious remarks' and 'extravagant novelties'. This impression was not diminished by Schelling's 'contemptuous treatment of our English critics'. Among other things, Schelling attempted to show 'to what *bestialities* (the very words) the empirical philosophy of Locke leads and how the mind of man is *brutalised* unenlightened by science'. In similar manner, Schelling polished off Burke, Horne, 'the "thick-skinned" Johnson', and the "shallow" Priestley', and declared 'that it is absurd to expect the science of beauty in a country that values mathematics only as it helps to make spinning jennies and stocking-weaving machines and beauty only as it recommends their manufactories abroad'. At such remarks, Robinson sighed and thought to himself: 'too true'. After this lecture, he took a walk with friends on the 'Philosopher's Path' above the city and then went to Schelling's 'grand lecture on Speculative Philosophy' at four o'clock. Here he found about 130 inquisitive young men 'listening with attentive ears to the exposition of a philosophy in its pretentions more glorious than any publicly maintained since the days of Plato and his commentators, a philosophy equally inimical to Locke's empiricism, Hume's scepticism, and Kant's criticism, which has been but the ladder of the new and rising sect'. Robinson watched with a detached smile as the large audience patiently listened to the presentation 'which filled their heads only with dry formularies and mystical rhapsodical phraseology'. Evenings were devoted to translating Goethe and to books on 'natural or speculative philosophy'.

THE WORDS 'ROMANTIC' AND 'ROMANTICISM'

Jena soon became the centre for a group of young critics who promoted a new style of thinking and judging in matters of literature and taste, and created an attitude that, for lack of a better name, received the designation 'romantic'. The history of this word has received extraordinary attention in modern scholarship and will concern us here primarily as it relates to the theory of literature.[4] In the vocabulary of the major European nations towards the end of the eighteenth century, the word could be used in a variety of contexts. It referred to particular phenomena of literature ('wild romantic tales'), features of the informal, irregular English garden ('in shapes romantic'), modes of feeling (*amour romanesque*), or to eccentric forms of behaviour (*romantischer Charakter*). The basic meaning of all of these usages, however, was 'associated with the expansive effect that romances exerted upon the imagination of their readers'.[5] Hence the understanding of the word 'romantic' 'in the sense of "romance-like", "pertaining to romances", "as in a romance rather than in real life"', and consequently, 'as "fictitious", "untrue", "extravagant", "improbable", or "absurd"'.[6] The romances one thought of in this context were, of course, primarily the legends surrounding Roland and the Arthurian Knights, but the term also included the many 'purely fictitious imitations' of these legends which the printing press had transformed into a '"mass medium" available to anyone who had learned to read and could pay a modest price'.[7]

If, among these broad usages, one concentrates on the sense of the unreal or fictitious, the critical meaning of the word 'romantic' refers to a type of literature which had not found recognition among the critics and theoreticians as part of the established canon. There was always both a broader and narrower meaning of the word, the broader referring to any 'romance-like' literature, including Dante, Tasso, Cervantes, and Shakespeare, and the narrower relating more directly to literature springing from the romance, such as the novel. In the broader sense, Boileau spoke quite disdainfully in his *Art of Poetry* of 1674 about literatures from 'beyond the Pyrenees' indulging in the exotic marvellous, expressing the 'glittering folly' of the Italians, or the 'insignificance' of the 'heroes of the novel'.[8] In a more precise manner, the great *Encyclopaedia* of 1751–72 relates 'romanesque', the prevailing synonym for romantic, to 'everything that belongs to the novel', things or persons, such as: 'Une passion *romanesque*; un ouvrage *romanesque*'.[9] Significantly, the word 'romantic' is, in the French language, directly related to the word for novel (*roman*), whereas in the English language this relationship is established via the romance and has therefore a more indirect, mediated character. This semantic linkage between romantic and roman or romance is lacking in German, where there are 'well-established adjectives referring to the three classical genres – *episch*, *lyrisch*, and *dramatisch*', but 'no such word referring to the novel (*Roman*)'. As Hans Eichner has pointed out, it is likely, and in some texts of the Schlegels even obvious, that 'around 1800, *romantisch* could be used to fill the gap, and – given a suitable context – was readily understood to have the same semantic relationship to *Roman* that *dramatisch* has to *Drama*'.[10] This usage did not become established, however, and remained essentially a terminological extravagance of the early Romantic critics. Because of the broad meaning of their term for the novel (*Roman*), which practically comprised the entirety of modern literature, it was also of little generic significance for their own theory.

Generally speaking, there are two basic meanings of the term in the literary criticism of the late eighteenth century, a chronological and a typological one. The chronological referred to a tradition of literature originating in the Middle Ages and pervading literary writing in modern Europe, but which was held in low esteem by neoclassicists and even excluded from the literary canon. The typological referred to certain exotic traits in literature, including compositional and structural ones, which were originally expressed in Romanesque literature, but which were now found everywhere. Friedrich Schlegel still used the word in these two ways, although the valorization associated with them changed profoundly in his texts. The typological dimension of the term, which derived from a mixing or crossing of styles, is obvious in his statement: 'According to my point of view and my usage, that which is romantic presents a sentimental theme in a fantastic form' (*KFSA* 2, 233; *DP*, 99). The chronological character of the term is noticeable when Schlegel says with regard to post-medieval literature: 'This is where I look for and find the Romantic – in the older moderns, in Shakespeare, Cervantes, in Italian poetry, in that age of knights, love, and fairy-tales in which the thing itself and the word for it originated' (*KFSA* 2, 325; *DP* 101).

To throw into relief these different nuances in the term, one has to turn to the great shift in the meaning of 'romantic' brought about by the Schlegels towards the end of the eighteenth century. A. W. Schlegel talks about this process in retrospect at the beginning of his third Berlin lecture in the series on Romantic literature of 1803–4, distinguishing between 'distinctively modern poetry' and that derived from classical antiquity. He considers it one of both his own and his brother's main achievements in criticism to have exposed the different spirit of the two types of literature, even the 'opposition prevailing between the two', as well as the fact that in speaking critically about them, one must proceed from 'differently modified principles in order to recognize each without pre-judicing one by the other' (*AWS V* 2, 3). In similar terms, he outlines this distinction at the beginning of the first of the three sets of lectures (1801–2), considering it essential for the history of art to 'recognize the opposition between modern and ancient taste'. During the age of Louis XIV, this difference was debated in terms of preferences ('la querelle des anciens et des modernes'), but only as a difference in degree, not in essence. These critics usually compared only those authors with the ancients who had modelled themselves on them (Corneille, Racine, Molière), and not those who were essentially different (Dante, Boccaccio, Calderón, Shakespeare). Only recently,

Schlegel maintained, had literary critics come to realize that those truly epoch-making works 'stood in their entire direction, in their most essential effort in contrast with the works of antiquity, and still had to be recognized as excellent' (*AWS V* 1, 195). Schlegel considers it splendid that the character of ancient poetry has been called 'classical' and the modern 'romantic', because this implies that what had earlier been considered the entire sphere of art is really only half of it, and can therefore now be better comprehended. He condenses this consideration into the formula of an 'antithesis of ancient and modern taste' and considers it the task of theory to show that 'opposite things are of the same dignity and should enjoy equal rights' just as 'our own entire existence rests on the alternation of opposites constantly resolving and renewing each other' (*AWS V* 1, 196).

Most prominent critical minds ignored this *sui generis* character of the moderns and did not realize that 'romantic, that is, genuinely modern works, not organized according to the models of antiquity and still to be considered as valid according to the highest principles', were not simply 'wild effusions of nature', not merely 'nationally or temporarily interesting' works, but true, universal, and everlasting poetry. Schlegel is thinking not only of the various classicist schools of modern times, but also of a mind like that of Winckelmann, who completely misjudged the most genuine creations of modern painting (e.g. Raphael) 'by misunderstanding the best in them as approximations to antiquity' and decidedly rejecting 'every way in the fine arts except the one taken by the ancients' (*AWS V* 3, 4). This position ultimately implies 'that there *should* be no romantic poetry, even if something like that had existed'. Those more sympathetic to the moderns but lacking a sense for these structural differences, like Lessing, had to 'withdraw behind the indistinct concept of genius and its privileges' to support their favourite authors against the 'authority of presumed rules' (*AWS V* 1, 5). As far as the word 'romantic' is concerned, Schlegel offers an etymology similar to the one indicated above: 'I should like to remark here that the same *romantic* poetry is well chosen also in this historical consideration. For romances are what one called those new dialects that originated from a mingling of Latin with the language of the conqueror; hence romances (novels) are the poems written in these dialects from which romantic is derived' (*AWS V* 3, 12).

Schlegel admits that Romantic poetry is undoubtedly much closer to our mind and feeling than the classical and seems to have had 'authority' weighing against its general recognition (*AWS V* 3, 8–9). In another instance, where he talks about the two halves of poetry, Schlegel indicates that Romantic poetry might so far have been only 'a transition, a becoming', to the extent that 'only the future will deliver the part corresponding to classical poetry and the opposite whole' (*AWS V* 1, 196). In these instances he seems to include his own time and efforts in a Romantic period roughly corresponding to the modern age. There are many other early Romantic writings in which this assumption is corroborated. When Novalis, for example, reproaches Goethe for not being romantic enough and proposes to restore the romantic style with his own novel, *Heinrich von Ofterdingen*, he seems to favour the romantic. But in general, the meaning of 'romantic' did not coincide with 'modern', but rather comprised only highlights of the modern period, phases of reappearance followed by decline. Independently of the romantic, the modern had its own particular qualities, too. Lessing is a case in point, especially if one compares him to Shakespeare. One conversation partner in Friedrich Schlegel's *Dialogue on Poetry* attempts to make this point and tells his interlocutor: 'If you really want to see a clear difference, just read *Emilia Galotti*, which is extremely modern and yet not in the least romantic, and then think of Shakespeare, in whom I would like to fix the actual centre, the core of the romantic imagination' (*KFSA* 2, 335; *DP*, 100–1).

There are many instances in which the romantic comes as close as possible to the early Romantics' own position and where it even loses its chronological, historical character of designation and enters an anthropological, transcendental, absolute realm and becomes synonymous with the poetic. These occur when the romantic is designated as an essential element of poetry as, for instance, in another section of the *Dialogue on Poetry* in which the interlocutor says that 'the romantic is not so much a literary genre as an element of poetry which may be more or less dominant or recessive, but never entirely absent'. He then continues to tell his interlocutor that 'according to my views, I postulate that all poetry should be romantic' (ib.). The most famous text for this transition of the romantic into the transcendentally and absolutely poetic is the famous Fragment 116 of the *Athenaeum*. From the beginning, Friedrich Schlegel seems to ignore chronological considerations of poetry according to epochs and phases, and declares: 'Romantic poetry is a progressive, universal poetry' (*KFSA* 2, 182; *LF*, 175). We have only the single universal process of Romantic poetry, which, during the course of its development, comes to a synthesis or a saturation of the most enormous antitheses – those of poetry and philosophy, poetry and prose, poetry and rhetoric, and poetry and life – and furthermore reconciles the strokes of genius with the labour of criticism, artistic poetry and natural, spontaneous poetry. This process of universal integration moves on to ever higher levels which seem to open the way 'to an infinitely increasing classicism'. Romantic poetry is something, in other words, that entirely absorbs us into its course and makes us a part of it. This is all the more so since the movement is not toward some ultimate goal where Romantic poetry could realize its true nature, be objectified, and find rest. Such perfection and cessation apply only to 'other types of poetry', like the classical or the classicistic which 'are finished and now capable of being fully analysed', whereas Romantic poetry, precisely because of its incompletion, is infinite: 'The romantic kind of poetry is still in the state of becoming, and that is, in fact, its real essence: that it should forever be becoming and never be perfected. It can be exhausted by no theory and only a divinatory criticism would dare try to characterize its ideal.' At this point Schlegel comes closest to an identification of Romantic poetry with poetry itself, concluding that 'the romantic kind of poetry is the only one which is more than a kind, that is, as it were, poetry itself: for in a certain sense all poetry is or should be romantic' (*KFSA* 2, 183; *LF*, 175–6).

In general, however, there remained a slight distance between the Romantic and the theoretical position of this group of critics, soon given various labels, but not that of 'Romantic' or the 'Romantics'. The most frequent designation was 'school', as in the 'new school' or the 'Schlegelian school of poetry'. In this sense, Friedrich Schlegel says retrospectively in the preface to the second edition of his *Dialogue on Poetry* of 1823 that his efforts and those of his friends were frequently characterized as 'the new school' and that his *Dialogue* would preserve the memory of that 'collaboration of talents' (*KFSA* 1, 573). The name 'school' still appears in the title of Heinrich Heine's book of 1836, *The Romantic School*, but by that time the meaning of 'romantic' had changed profoundly. When in 1805 the Homer translator Johann Friedrich Voß moved to Heidelberg and came into head-on conflict with Clemens Brentano, Achim von Arnim, Josef Görres, and Friedrich Creuzer – that is, with the Heidelberg Romantics – a change took place in meaning, making 'Romantic' a polemical, caricaturing designation.[11] Voß and his followers, in other words, applied the term originally used for an older style of European literature to the proponents of this style themselves and gave it a satirical twist with reference to 'our romantics'. The designation was also used to ridicule the Christian, particularly Catholic, tendencies among the Romantics. A new journal founded by Cotta in Heidelberg, the *Morning Paper for Educated Classes*, served as the springboard for these satirical attacks, but by the end of the second decade of the nineteenth century, the word 'romantic' had clearly assumed a contemporary meaning, not necessarily satirical and polemical. When Friedrich Bouterwek, a learned scholar, although no friend of the Romantics, came to the eleventh volume of his *History of Modern Poetry and Eloquence*, for instance, he mentioned 'the new school which, lacking another name, may be called the romantic'. Eichendorff, in his *On the Ethical and Religious Significance of the More Recent Romantic Poetry in Germany* of 1847, attempted to be more precise and spoke about a 'modern', 'contemporary', or 'second' Romanticism.

By that time, however, the term 'romantic' had assumed an entirely negative connotation as something reactionary in nature. At precisely mid-century, in 1850, Hermann Hettner complained in his book, *The Romantic School in its Inner Relationship with Goethe and Schiller*, that the 'concept of romanticism had become a mere party slogan with us' and described its meaning simply as 'reactionary, but not simply as reactionary as such, but reactionary out of doctrine and education'. Such a reactionary person, according to Hettner, preferred the old not on the basis of accidental, exterior preferences, but 'because the ready-made, sealed off, and sensually perceivable forms of the dead past appear to him infinitely more agreeable and poetic than the new, which still has to become and can never offer concrete shapes and firm reference points' to the confused imagination.[12] Hettner was by no means a spokesman for Romanticism, rather an enemy, but declared it a great injustice that people had come to consider 'romantic and reactionary as identical without further ado'. Rudolf Haym, in his book of 1870 entitled *The Romantic School*, displayed a similar attitude.[13] He declared in his introduction that Romanticism enjoyed no favour at that time in Germany, stating, however, that the mood of 1870 was no longer as hostile as that of 'the battle of the forties', when people 'waged war against the romantic with passion and hatred and believed they had to fight it with fire and sword' and when 'the sciences, the state, and the church' saw themselves invaded by Romantic ideas that seemed to endanger their freedom. The main reason for such an attitude was that the 'founder and disciples of the romantic spirit of literature obviously had sympathies with the Middle Ages, with its presumption of faith, its loose governmental structures, its wild but poetically proliferating individualism'. Indeed, though the Romantic became identified with the reactionary, Haym also noticed in the radicalism of its opponents an ingredient of intolerance similar to what they intended to fight in the Romantics.

Among these ardent opponents of Romanticism during the thirties and forties, we find the representatives of the 'New Germany' (*das Junge Deutschland*), authors like Heinrich Heine, Arnold Ruge, Theodor Echtermeyer, even the early Kierkegaard of *On the Concept of Irony* (1841). Heine was the most successful satirist in pointing out the 'reactionary' tendencies of Romanticism. 'What then was the Romantic school in Germany?' Heine asked rhetorically, answering: 'Nothing but the resuscitation of the poetry of the Middle Ages in its songs, paintings and architecture, in art and life. This poetry, however, had found its origin in Christianity and was a passion-flower rising from the blood of Christ.'[14] Heine, of course, knew better, but his formulations proved particularly suited to making the epithet of reactionary stick. Another slogan on Romanticism that became prominent during this campaign derived from Goethe, who had once said: 'The classical I call the healthy, and the romantic the sick' (*GOE* 24, 332). Goethe had not intended to launch a polemic against his contemporaries, but used the terms 'classical' and 'romantic' in broader typological connotations. Nevertheless, his comment was soon turned against the Romantics of his time, especially Novalis, whose biography seemed to corroborate Goethe's statement, and Romantic art was declared decadent and degenerate. Another important reference point in the campaign of the forties against Romanticism was Hegel, who in prominent contexts within his philosophy had turned against the Romantic kind of subjectivity and declared it an irreverent, insubordinate, irresponsible type of subjectivity without any commitment, indeed, the 'apex of subjectivity separating itself from the unifying substance' (*HEG* 20, 415–18).

In his book of 1870 Haym concluded that 'this time, as was said earlier, is behind us', and he viewed it as a nightmare.[15] His task was now to investigate the past historically and ascertain the 'contribution to the history of the German spirit' made by the early Romantics. This is the subtitle of Haym's book, which was published around the time of the founding of the Second Empire and coincided with the elaboration of a history of German national literature. Haym's investigation of the early Romantics employed the older title of the 'Romantic school', which proved, however, too severely burdened by negative associations acquired during the forties to be used as a suitable critical term. Haym's book itself is the best evidence for this. He constantly evaluates the early Romantics according to standards which are by no means their own, comparing them to Goethe, Schiller, Hegel, and Schelling, and depicting them as searching for an ideal of organic unity which is actually denied by their own theory. This inappropriateness seems to be the reason why both the opponents (Ricarda Huch, Carl Schmitt, Georg Lukács) as well as the proponents (Oskar Walzel, Josef Körner, Paul Kluckhohn) and the lively debate on German Romanticism in the first half of our century used the more neutral, single designations 'Romantic' and 'Romanticism'. The terms 'early Romantic' and 'early Romanticism' seem to have emerged from these debates for the purpose of distinguishing the Jena group from the later forms of Romanticism and of emphasizing the strongly theoretical and revolutionary character of their literary work as well as their broad historical and international orientation towards world literature instead of a national German literature. These terms became more established following the Second World War and are now the common designations for this special and early form of German Romanticism.

THE MEMBERS OF THE EARLY ROMANTIC SCHOOL

An introduction of the main representatives of early German Romanticism can best begin with AUGUST WILHELM SCHLEGEL, who was not only the oldest and most established author of the group but also the one who chose Jena as the centre for its union. Born on 8 September 1767, he was the son of an old family of Protestant pastors that traced its origins back to the days of the Reformation. His father, Johann Adolf Schlegel, and uncle, Johann Elias Schlegel, had been prominent critics and literary figures of the eighteenth century, and his mother, Johanna Christiane Erdmuthe, née Hübsch, was the daughter of a mathematics professor. A. W. Schlegel received an excellent education, especially in Classics, and from 1786 to 1791 studied at the University of Göttingen with the famous Hellenist Christian Gottlob Heyne, with whom he also published his early scholarly research. During these years he entertained a cordial relationship with the aging poet Gottfried August Bürger, author of the ballad 'Lenore' and editor of the

Göttingen *Almanac of the Muses*, in which A. W. Schlegel's first poetry appeared. When Schiller published a devastating review of Bürger in the *ALZ* reproaching him for 'sins against good taste' and substantiating these reproaches with references to unfortunate biographical details of Bürger's life, A. W. Schlegel not only lent Bürger his literary support, but also developed a life-long aversion to Schiller. After a short period of collaboration with Schiller's *Horae* and *Almanac of the Muses*, a complete break between the Schlegel brothers and Schiller finally ensued in 1797. In one of his later writings, A. W. Schlegel mentions with satisfaction that Schiller's feud against Bürger had carried its own nemesis with it in that Bürger's 'Lenore' and other ballads now compared most favourably with Schiller's own poetic achievements in the ballad (*AWS* 8, 71–2). During his years at Göttingen University, A. W. Schlegel fell in love with Caroline Michaelis, the daughter of a professor of Oriental literature, and devoted his early love poetry to her, but Caroline was not inclined then to respond to his courtship.

By the time A. W. Schlegel completed his studies of literature in May 1791, he had established himself as a promising young scholar and poet, but for lack of a better opportunity he accepted the position of tutor in the house of the Amsterdam banker Henry Muilman. For several years he lived in a French- and Dutch-speaking community, and a generous salary secured him economic independence early in life. When Schiller planned the *New Thalia* in August 1791, he invited A. W. Schlegel to collaborate with him, but still feeling hurt about Bürger, A. W. Schlegel refused to join the contributors. The situation had changed by 1794, when Schiller projected the *Horae* and the *Almanac of the Muses* and again invited A. W. Schlegel to participate. Bürger had died on 8 June 1794, and now various friends, including his brother Friedrich, urged Schlegel to accept. For A. W. Schlegel, participation in such important journals implied the possibility of a return to Germany. He contributed some of the more interesting pieces to the *Horae*, among them some sensational annotated metrical translations of Dante's *Inferno*, a work then little known in Germany. His interest in Dante had been sparked in Göttingen, where he had published a longer essay on the Italian poet for Bürger. Initially, A. W. Schlegel was on his way to becoming the translator of the *Divine Comedy*. In Amsterdam, however, he changed direction and turned to Shakespeare. Some of the earlier pieces he sent in for the *Horae* were indeed his first translations of scenes from *Romeo and Juliet* and *The Tempest*, and his literary theory was clearly decisively influenced from Shakespeare. Among the theoretical writings published in the *Horae* were two substantial critical pieces, one entitled 'Something about William Shakespeare on the Occasion of *Wilhelm Meister*' (*AWS SW* 7, 324) and the other consisting of 'Letters on Poetry, Metrics, and Language' (*AWS SW* 7, 98), which revealed A. W. Schlegel's characteristic approach to poetry via language.

Summoned by his brother, friends, and especially Schiller, A. W. Schlegel returned to Germany in July 1795. He first lived in his parental home in Hanover but soon moved to Brunswick, apparently to look for a position as instructor at the Carolinum, a prominent educational institution there. Johann Joachim Eschenburg, who had produced a prose translation of Shakespeare's complete works, was a professor of modern literature at the Carolinum, and Schlegel was eager to have an opportunity to discuss with him his new project, a metrical translation of Shakespeare. But a major attraction was undoubtedly Caroline, who now lived with her mother in Brunswick and appeared more receptive to his courtship. Schiller, however, obviously seeking A. W. Schlegel's participation in the editorship of the *Horae*, urged him to move to Jena and promised to help him obtain a professorship at the university. On 1 July 1796, the 'Ducal Saxon Counsellor in Jena, August Wilhelm Schlegel' was married to Caroline Böhmer, born Michaelis, in St Catherine's church in Brunswick, and the young couple immediately moved to Jena. They soon acquired the big house on Löbdergraben which was to form the centre for the 'new school' and was later known as the 'house of the Romantics'.

Collaborating with his wife on some of his projects, A. W. Schlegel embarked upon an influential and productive career in Jena. It was here that his Shakespeare translation originated and his first lecture course on aesthetics was delivered. In 1798 he founded the *Athenaeum* with his brother Friedrich, a periodical which became the leading publication of the early Romantics. Most of these events will be discussed in later chapters in more detail. In 1801, however, Schlegel moved to Berlin. His marriage with Caroline had come to an end and both agreed to a divorce. Caroline became Schelling's wife and left Jena for Würzburg. In the autumn of 1801, A. W. Schlegel began his Berlin lectures on literature and art, which he continued each autumn and winter in three series until the spring of 1804. When Madame de Staël visited Berlin during that spring, A. W. Schlegel accepted her offer to become her advisor and the educator of her children. From then on, he lived at Coppet on Lake Geneva in the French part of Switzerland. A mutual pact bound him to Madame de Staël until either party should die, and following Madame de Staël's death on 14 July 1817, A. W. Schlegel received flattering offers from the newly founded Prussian universities of Berlin and Bonn. As he preferred an institute at which he might further his recently begun Sanskrit studies, A. W. Schlegel chose Bonn in 1818. He bought the now famous house on the Rhine and, according to Heine, went to his university lectures in a carriage drawn by several horses. He died on 12 May 1845, at the age of seventy-eight, active as a critic until the end of his life, in spite of the raging campaign against Romanticism already long underway.

His younger brother FRIEDRICH SCHLEGEL, was in appearance a much less pretentious character, but in terms of critical demands, he was more dynamic and less inclined to compromise than his brother. Born on 10 March 1772, he was from early on a withdrawn and reflective person. As an adolescent he locked himself up in the evening in the collection of antiquities in Dresden, then housed in Brühl Terrace on the River Elbe. There he sought privacy and leisure among the statues of the Greek gods, solitude which he needed to let his imagination flow. Extremely gifted in ancient languages, especially Greek, he acquired an excellent knowledge of the ancient world, taking Winckelmann as his intellectual guide. Friedrich Schlegel described this early state of mind as one of 'total absolute scepticism, theoretical and moral' (*KFSA* 1, xci) and considered that the only firm points in his life were the ideal of classical beauty and something he vaguely described as a 'longing for the infinite' (*KFSA* 23, 24). The first ideal describes his aesthetic inclination, and the second his philosophical interest, which focused on Plato, but soon extended to Kant and Fichte.

The younger Schlegel began his studies as a law student in Göttingen and, following his brother's departure, continued at the University of Leipzig. There he met Novalis, a fellow student, and the two became close friends. In reality, however, Schlegel felt more inclined towards the study of literature, having chosen law not only upon parental insistence, but also in order to secure a firm and stable position in life for himself, for he was plagued by melancholy and had a suicidal tendency. He discussed at length the pros and cons of law versus literature in his correspondence with his brother, who encouraged him to choose literature. At the end of May 1793, almost in a single day, he decided to make the study of the nature of literature his life's work (*KFSA* 23, 96). His original publication was to be an exchange of letters with his brother on this subject, taking Shakespeare, Goethe, and also Schiller as media for their reflection. There is sufficient material in their correspondence to indicate how this critical, fictional correspondence would have looked: it was like an exchange of opinions of two very different minds, one oriented towards philosophy, theory, and the most recent Kantian aesthetic doctrines, and the other more empirically inclined, discussing poetry on the basis of metre, language, rhythm, and so forth, and having little use for abstract theories. But upon a sudden impulse, Friedrich Schlegel decided to begin his study of literature and poetry in classical Greece, where he thought poetry to be 'native' (*KFSA* 23, 180), and to articulate his theory through the medium of Greek literature. For this purpose, he withdrew entirely from the world in which he had lived so far and moved to Dresden in January 1794. Here he spent the next two-and-a-half years as a virtual recluse, reading and rereading his classical authors and trying to build, as he put it, a history of Greek literature (*KFSA* 23, 179). When his brother or Novalis mistook his work for historical studies, he protested and explained that it was of much greater importance, that it actually implied an aesthetics, 'a natural history of the beautiful and of art' (*KFSA* 23, 188, 204). It was during this time in Dresden that Friedrich Schlegel wrote those critical essays through which, as Dilthey put it, 'he gained a position in the literary world overnight'.[16]

Friedrich Schlegel had sent his manuscripts at random to various publishers. One of them, Salomon Michaelis, showed the proofs of the 'Essay on the Study of Greek Poetry' to friends whom he met in Leipzig, the Hellenist Friedrich August Wolf from Halle University and Johann Friedrich Reichardt, a composer, writer, and influential editor of literary journals. Michaelis wanted to demonstrate what kind of author he had just acquired, and Reichardt tore the text, so to speak, right out of his hands and published preliminary extracts in his periodical *Deutschland*, for which Friedrich Schlegel then became the 'star author'. When *Deutschland* could not be continued because of difficulties with the censorship, Reichardt founded a new periodical in 1797, the *Lyceum of Beautiful Arts*, in which Schlegel was even more prominent. Reichardt, however, was known as a strong adherent of the French Revolution and his journals manifested a glowing republicanism – a bias with which many of his contemporaries took issue. In fact, he had founded *Deutschland* to create a contrast to Schiller's *Horae*. Reichardt's revolutionary penchant matched Friedrich Schlegel's own opinions quite well, yet Reichardt's strong bias against Schiller and Goethe was an ill omen for a young author who wanted to establish his critical career in Germany (*KFSA* 23, 324).

Through a particular series of events, Schlegel was drawn ever more deeply into a position that almost necessarily resulted in open hostility towards Schiller. When he reviewed Schiller's *Almanac of the Muses* of 1796 for Reichardt, his brother visited him in Dresden, and the two decided to insert a few satirical comments on Schiller's poem *Dignity of Women*, which had appeared in that periodical and viewed women in the tra-ditional manner as subservient to men. Schlegel wrote in his review that the poem was not poetic enough but could be improved if one casually confused the stanzas and read them backwards, an idea clearly stemming from his brother, A. W. Schlegel. Continuing, he said that Schiller's presentation was again 'idealized', but in a reverse way, in a downward direction, beneath the truth, and he demanded that men like those depicted in the poem be bound by hand and foot and the women tethered (*KFS* 2, 6). Schiller responded with a number of satirical epigrams on Friedrich Schlegel in the *Xenia*, which he and Goethe published in the 1797 edition of Schiller's *Almanac of the Muses*. These are distichs, a poetic form that applies to a couple of verses, usually rhymed and expressing a friendly thought, as by Martial in his thirteenth book of epigrams, but which here in the *Xenia* took on a biting, polemical note. Schiller's epigrams on Friedrich Schlegel took issue with his seemingly absolute veneration of the Greeks, with what Schiller called 'Graecomania'. Schlegel seemed amused by the attack and enjoyed it out of an urbane liking for public literary polemics. By that time, he had already followed his brother to Jena and also prepared his countermove, which appeared in his review of the latest issues of Schiller's *Horae*. The monthly periodical was having obvious difficulties in maintaining its originally high level of criticism, and many contributions were simply translations, some even of ancient texts. Friedrich Schlegel concluded his review with the laconic observation that the periodical had now entered the 'epoch of translations' and that one had translated 'excellent, medium, and poor originals in an excellent medium, and poor manner' (*KFSA* 2, 47). Infuriated, Schiller now cancelled all further collaboration with Friedrich Schlegel's brother, and both brothers, in turn, responded by no longer mentioning Schiller.

When Friedrich Schlegel moved to Jena in the summer of 1796, he renewed his friendship with Novalis (who lived near the city), and immediately established contact, which was to turn into a close friendship, with the philosopher Fichte. Schlegel spent some time with the Hellenist F. A. Wolf in Halle reviewing the individual chapters of his *History of Poetry of the Greeks and the Romans* with him before publishing the first volume in 1798. Primarily, however, the 'critical air in Jena' motivated him to curtail his classical studies in favour of modern and contemporary literature. As he wrote to a friend shortly after his arrival in Jena, he realized that he had been on his way to 'petrifying' himself in the study of the ancients (*KFSA* 23, 332). Unfortunately, the dispute with Schiller cast its shadow over Schlegel's first sojourn in Jena from August 1796 to July 1797. Goethe, who did not like disruptions, convinced him during a walk on the Philosopher's Path that it would be better for him to spend some time elsewhere, and Schlegel decided to move to Berlin. There he met Wackenroder, Tieck, and Schleiermacher, whom he incorporated into the group of the early Romantics. When the *Athenaeum* began appearing with a Berlin publisher, Friedrich Schlegel assumed the main editorship of the periodical. Above all, while in Berlin, he met Dorothea Veit, with whom he lived for the rest of his life and who became his wife in 1804. When he returned to Jena in the autumn of 1799, Schlegel's Berlin friends, except for Schleiermacher, followed him and the school was almost fully united in Jena. After the dissolution of the group, Schlegel and Dorothea lived in Paris and Cologne, both converting to Catholicism, before finally settling down in Vienna in 1808. Schlegel became a Counsellor in Metternich's government and gave a good number of lecture courses to the public, the Vienna lectures of 1812 on ancient and modern literature among them, before he died on a lecture tour to his favourite city, Dresden, on 12 January 1829, at the age of fifty-six.

CAROLINE SCHLEGEL did not really emerge on her own as an author, but had a decisive influence upon the formulation of early Romantic theory. She collaborated with A. W. Schlegel on some of his articles, probably also on his Shakespeare translation, and in his later writings A. W. Schlegel acknowledged 'the help of a witty woman who had all the talents to shine as a writer but whose ambition was not focused on that' (*AWS SW* 7, xxxiv). The daughter of Johann David M. Michaelis, a professor of Oriental languages and literatures who taught at Göttingen University for forty-six years, Caroline was first married to Dr Johann Franz Wilhelm Böhmer, a physician who died shortly after the birth of their daughter Auguste. Caroline returned to her parental home in Göttingen, where she became a kind of muse among students and scholars. Showing little interest in A. W. Schlegel's courtship, she nevertheless maintained a correspondence with him while he lived in Amsterdam. Caroline was a close friend of Therese Heyne, the daughter of the famous Hellenist at Göttingen and wife of Georg Forster, a well-known author of the time who had accompanied Cook on his second voyage. Forster had a position as a librarian in Mainz, where the Elector attempted to attract German intellectuals and scientists. Not knowing what to do with her life, Caroline settled in Mainz in 1792 to be close to her friend Therese, whose marriage with Forster had become difficult. Caroline attempted to help Therese, but during the course of events was actually drawn closer to Forster.

In the autumn of 1792 Mainz was occupied by the French revolutionary army under General Custine. The Elector and his staff left town in a hurry, and the German intellectuals, led by Forster, proclaimed the existence of the Republic of Mainz and announced their desire for its integration with the Republic of France. They founded the Mainz Republican Club, known as the 'Clubbists', and Caroline, Therese, and their friend Meta Forkel, the wife of a Göttingen historian of music, became prominent members of this club and wore the revolutionary cockade and other insignia of the revolution. Taking her children, Therese left her husband in December 1792 for Switzerland, later to become the wife of the author and diplomat Ludwig Ferdinand Huber. On 30 March 1793, Forster went to Paris and put forward a motion in the French National Assembly to integrate the Republic of Mainz into the Republic of France. Left by his wife and children, denounced by his country, and disillusioned by the terror in Paris, he died the following year. Caroline had personal connections with the French headquarters in Mainz that continued when General Custine was replaced by General d'Oyré. This general's adjutant was his nephew, the nineteen-year-old officer of the 91st Regiment, Jean-Baptiste Dubois-Crancé. Meta Forkel remembers an evening in February 1793 when they danced the 'Carmagnole' with the French, one of the most popular songs of the French Revolution, which has as its refrain: 'Dansons la

Carmagnole! Vive le son du canon!' As she later recollected, Caroline had begun an affair with Jean-Baptiste Dubois-Crancé on that evening.[17]

By the end of March 1793 Mainz was encircled by the coalition army, and the French army began to withdraw. Caroline then left Mainz with her daughter to move to friends in Gotha, where, as a proscribed person, she could stay only temporarily and incognito. When she ran into the Prussian army in the vicinity of Frankfurt, she was held in close custody in the fortress Königstein, and at the beginning of June, she was under simple arrest in Kronenburg. In Königstein she discovered that she was pregnant, something which a prolonged imprisonment would have revealed. Writing to all of her friends for help, Caroline informed only A. W. Schlegel about her true situation. She had set for herself a certain time-limit of around the middle of July, by which date she wanted to die if she were not released. Schlegel procured poison for her and arrived from Amsterdam on 10 June to be with her 'in life or death' (*CA* 1, 303). Three days later she was freed by an order from the Prussian King Friedrich Wilhelm that had been obtained by her younger brother. Schlegel first brought her incognito to the house of the Leipzig publisher Göschen, but then to Lucka, a little village in the vicinity, where she lived in the house of farmers as a woman from Hamburg whose husband was not yet in a position to support her. Schlegel had to hurry back to Amsterdam, and the only one to take care of Caroline during the following months was the young law student Friedrich Schlegel, who came almost daily on horseback from Leipzig. On 3 November 1793, Caroline gave birth to her son Julius, described in the church register of Lucka as the son of 'Madame Krantz, married to Julius Kratz, a travelling shipping agent from Hamburg, who has lived here for some time', and Friedrich Schlegel was listed among the child's sponsors (*CA* 1, 204).

During these few months, Caroline exerted a deep influence upon Schlegel, who depicted her in his *Lucinde* as the female figure who becomes 'a firm centre and the basis for a new world' for the protagonist of the novel, Julius. Julius indeed recognized in himself the 'vocation for divine art' through her influence (*KFSA* 5, 49). Three years later, Friedrich Schlegel wrote to Caroline on 2 August 1796: 'Today it is three years since I saw you for the first time. Think only that I stood before you and silently thanked you for everything you have done for me' (*KFSA* 23, 326). Soon after the birth of Caroline's son Julius, the paths of Caroline and Friedrich Schlegel separated, and they began a correspondence. Schlegel undertook his work on the Greeks in January 1794 in Dresden, and Caroline went to her mother in Brunswick, where she learned of the death of her son, whom she had left in the temporary care of the farmer's family. A. W. Schlegel returned to Germany in July 1795 and married Caroline in the following year. From then on she was a particularly stimulating and attractive member of the Romantic circle. As mentioned earlier, her marriage to A. W. Schlegel lasted until 1801, after which Caroline married the philosopher Schelling. In September 1803, shortly before this marriage, she was reunited with her friends Therese Forster and Meta Forkel, this time in the house of Schelling's father in Murhard, in Swabia. Therese Forster was now Ferdinand Huber's wife, and Meta Forkel was the wife of Johann Heinrich Liebeskind. When someone asked about the 'Carmagnole' during the course of the conversation, Therese Huber simply took his arm and that of someone else, singing and dancing the revolutionary song 'avec toute la folie nationale'. The attempts of her friends to detect a trace of recollection on Caroline's face were in vain, however, and they found 'rien, rien du tout'.[18] The after-effects of this period are not be found in Caroline, but rather in Friedrich Schlegel. They are manifest in his emancipatory essay on Greek women preceding his *Lucinde* (*KFSA* 1, 45–115), his review of Condorcet directly motivated by Caroline (*KFSA* 7, 3–10), the essay on republicanism of 1796 (*KFSA* 7, 11–25), the article on Georg Forster of 1797 (*KFSA* 2, 78–99), and especially in his general attitude toward the French Revolution, which had changed remarkably since 1794.

NOVALIS is the pen name of Friedrich von Hardenberg and a Latin rendering of his family name ('fallow land'), meaning something that has to be cleared, ploughed, and cultivated.

Using this name for the first time when he published his fragments *Pollen* in the *Athenaeum*, he added the motto at the beginning of the text: 'Friends, the soil is poor, and we have to spread seed abundantly in order to enjoy even a merely modest harvest' (*NO* 2, 413). Novalis came from an aristocratic family of Lower Saxony that traced its origins back to the twelfth and thirteenth centuries. His father had a salt-mine business, and Novalis followed him in this profession. A devout pietist, his father was deeply convinced of the human being's general sinfulness, which had to be mastered with ascetic rigour. His father's first wife had died early, but his second wife, Auguste Bernhardine Bölzig, bore him eleven children, the last at the age of forty-five. Most of the children, however, died between the ages of twenty and thirty, and Novalis, always rather frail, also died when he was only twenty-nine years old. In an early letter to Schiller of 7 October 1791, he described his experience of the world in striking fashion:

I live and move in the fresh autumn air, and new streams of vivacity flow into me with every breath of air. The beautiful scenery and a good-natured innocuousness into which I feel dissolved, charm me into the blossoming realms of fantasy surrounded by the same magic and thin mist as the distant landscape beneath my feet. I enjoy myself with the last smile of life departing from nature and the mild sunny glance of a chilling heaven. Fertile ripeness begins to turn into decomposition, and for me the view of a slowly waning nature is almost richer and greater than its unfolding and enlivening in the spring. I now feel more disposed toward noble and sublime sentiments than in the spring, when the soul floats in idle, voluptuous receptiveness and enjoyment instead of withdrawing into itself and becoming attracted to and dissipated by every inviting object. The disappearance of so many beautiful, lovely objects makes the feelings so much more compounded and interesting. I therefore never feel so purely disposed and receptive to all impressions from the higher, more sacred muse than in the autumn. (*NO* 4, 98–9)

Novalis was born on 2 May 1772, in Oberwiederstedt, Thuringia, in his family's country house. He began his study of law at Jena University, continuing at Leipzig University, where his close friendship with Friedrich Schlegel began. Hearing of their frivolous mode of life – the two young men had love affairs with two sisters of the high society in Leipzig – Novalis' father came to Leipzig in person to separate the two and had his son continue his studies at the more rigorous Lutheran University of Wittenberg. The correspondence between the two friends, Novalis with his capricious nature and both uncommonly passionate and easily inflamed, counts among the finest pieces of early German Romantic literature.

Novalis moved to Wittenberg in May 1793, passed his examinations a year later, and in the autumn of 1794 began his administrative career at the salt-mines in Tennstedt in the northern part of Thuringia. Not far from Tennstedt lies Grüningen, a little place where Captain Johann Rudolf von Rockenthien had married the widow Sophia Wilhelmine von Kühn, whose thirteen-year-old daughter Sophia became the great love of Novalis' life. In spite of her youth, the two became engaged in March of the following year. Sophia's special attraction undoubtedly derived from her candid, spontaneous nature, combined with considerable precocity, but increased by a disease that manifested itself in November 1795. Suffering from an infection or abscess of the liver, Sophia had to undergo three operations, real tortures at that time, and showed admirable equanimity in her agony. The operations, necessitating painful repeated cleansings of the wound, were carried out in Jena. During these operations Novalis composed a literary character sketch of Sophia entitled 'Klarisse' (*NO* 4, 24), an amazing piece because of the most heterogeneous aspects Novalis had noticed in her young life. The wound became severely infected and had to be cleansed again, but around Christmas things seemed to look better, and Sophia received permission to go home to Grüningen.

In the meantime, Novalis' reunion with Friedrich Schlegel had taken place. On the way to Jena, Schlegel visited his friend in Weissenfels and found him preoccupied with the reading of Fichte, whom Schlegel had already begun to study. In his letter of invitation, Novalis had mentioned: 'My study has the same name as my fiancée, Sophia is her name and philosophy the soul of my life' (*NO* 4, 188). Schlegel visited Sophia several times in the Jena hospital where she underwent her operations. In

January Novalis wrote to him: 'If I were to lose Söffchen
[Sophia], God only knows what would become of me' (*NO* 4,
195), indicating that her state of health had deteriorated. His
next letter of 14 March 1797, begins with the statement: 'Your
letter has reached me in a desperate situation. I have returned
from Thuringia with the firm conviction that Sophie has only a
few more days to live' (*NO* 4, 204). She died shortly thereafter,
at which time a deep transformation took place in Novalis.
Instead of coming to Jena to take up the study of Fichte with
Schlegel, he turned to Grüningen to be in the vicinity of the
grave of his beloved and carry out the project of following her in
death. Only through a cautious correspondence and the
tentative mailing of interesting materials was Schlegel able to
lead his friend back to his philosophical interests. On 7 May
1797, he sent him a copy of his brother's German translation of
Romeo and Juliet, which had just appeared. The volume also
contained the translation of *A Midsummer Night's Dream*, and
Novalis took special note of the famous lines:

> The poet's eye, in a fine frenzy rolling,
> Doth glance from heaven to earth, from earth to heaven;
> And as imagination bodies forth
> The forms of things unknown, the poet's pen
> Turns them to shapes, and gives to airy nothing
> A local habitation and a name.   (v, 1)

At that time Novalis began to conceive of his particular form
of transcendental idealism as a fusion of idealism and realism in
which subject and object became idential. Intending to leave
Schelling 'far behind' (*NO* 4, 255), he conceived of the world as
a 'universal trope' or a 'symbolic image' of the human spirit
blending this world and the beyond, the interior and the
exterior worlds, the human being and nature (all of which is
discussed in greater detail in Ch. 4 below). Novalis continued to
be a contributing member of the Romantic group, although he
published very little, out of consideration for his family, and
only under his pen-name. Most of his writings were published
after his death, first in the two-volume edition brought out by
Friedrich Schlegel and Tieck in 1802. Yet he exchanged some of

his manuscripts with Schlegel, who sent him his notebooks. Novalis died of pulmonary disease, having been miserably ill during the last months of his life. Schlegel was at his death-bed and wrote to his brother on 27 March 1801:

Yesterday I returned from Weissenfels, where the day before I saw Hardenberg die. It is certain that he had no idea of his death, and in general one would not believe it possible for someone to die so gently and beautifully. He was, as long as I saw him, of an indescribable cheerfulness, and although the great weakness hindered him in talking during the last days, he took part in everything most amiably, and I prize it above all to have seen him. Please communicate this to Tieck and Schleiermacher. All details will be reserved for conversation.

When Friedrich Schlegel moved to Berlin in July 1797, Reichardt introduced him to the literary circles of this city. In one of them, the salon of the elegant Henriette Herz, wife of Marcus Herz, a well-known physician and head of the Jewish community in Berlin, he made the two most important acquaintances of his sojourn, those of Schleiermacher and Dorothea Veit. FRIEDRICH SCHLEIERMACHER impressed him with his training in philosophy, especially that of Kant, and his pronounced interest in questions of morality and general conduct of life, the art of living. This interest can be partly explained by Schleiermacher's profession as a Protestant pastor and his appointment at the Charité, a public hospital. But Schleiermacher developed the theme of morality far beyond theological or religious aspects to include topics such as the social position of women, problems of economy and society, themes of communication and mutual understanding. Friedrich Schlegel soon moved into Schleiermacher's Charité apartment, and the friendship that ensued remained dominated by these themes of common interest. Schleiermacher never went to Jena, but established a close personal contact with A. W. Schlegel during the latter's visits to Berlin in connection with Shakespeare performances on the Berlin stage. When Friedrich Schlegel returned to Jena in the autumn of 1799, Schleiermacher edited the *Athenaeum* in his stead, and together they planned the new German translation of Plato, which was carried out, however, by Schleiermacher alone.

Schleiermacher was born into a Protestant family of pietistic orientation, his father and mother both coming from families of pastors. Born on 21 November 1768, he was given the full name of 'Friedrich Ernst Daniel', but was simply called 'Friedrich'. Receiving a religious education which emphasized the ancient languages but also had a strong pietistic flavour, Schleiermacher originally attended a seminary of the Moravian Brethren, which usually trained theologians in the Moravian manner. After serious discussions with his father, however, he managed to continue his studies at the University of Halle, where he also found an opportunity to study Kantian philosophy and to work with F. A. Wolf on classical subjects. After finishing his theological examinations in May 1790, he initially held positions as a tutor and teacher, and finally gained an appointment as a preacher to the Charité.

Schleiermacher's connection with the early Romantics was a problematical matter for his superiors, and he repeatedly received admonitions from August Friedrich Wilhelm Sack, an influential person in the Protestant hierarchy of Berlin, especially when he began to review Schlegel's *Lucinde* in his *Intimate Letters* on that book. Yet, with his great sense of personal independence, Schleiermacher wrote back to Sack and justified what he was doing in intellectual and rational terms. After the dissolution of the Romantic circle, he began a most illustrious theological career, first teaching at Halle University, where he pursued the themes of morality and hermeneutics, progressively in a wider theological context. When the University of Berlin was founded in 1810, Schleiermacher became its leading theologian. His best known accomplishment during that period is his *Doctrine of Faith* (2 vols., Berlin, 1821–2), which became the standard work of Protestant theology almost into the twentieth century, until the time of Karl Barth's 'theology of crisis' and *On the Letter to the Romans* (1918). Schleiermacher saw religion as dominated by a 'feeling of absolute dependency upon God'. In its attempt to demarcate religion as a distinct and legitimate realm of human experience, however, his work still shows a strong relationship to early Romantic theory. This link is visible even in the title and in a self-assertive manner, if one compares

Schleiermacher's 'doctrine of faith' with Fichte's 'doctrine of knowledge'. In spite of his many academic and administrative obligations, Schleiermacher continued to preach publicly until the end of his life. He died on 12 February 1834, at the age of sixty-six.

DOROTHEA SCHLEGEL was the eldest daughter of the influential philosopher Moses Mendelssohn, one of the main representatives of the Enlightenment in Germany and in his attitudes of tolerance, especially in religious and philosophical matters, the model for Lessing's *Nathan the Wise*. She came to the Romantic group with a broadly educated and sharp intellect, but also a personality of unusual warmth and passion. In contrast to that of the Schlegels, Novalis, and Schleiermacher, her education embraced the arts, music, and painting. Her two sons, Philipp and Johannes Veit, became famous painters of the Nazarene school in Rome, and Philipp later moved to Frankfurt to be the director of the Staedel Museum; her brother, Abraham, was the father of the famous composer Felix Mendelssohn-Bartholdy. The first letters we have from Dorothea are a very critical description of a Gluck opera performance to Rahel Levin (*KFSA* 23, 62) and a discussion of how her father's works should be edited with Friedrich von Blankenburg, a Leipzig critic she had just visited (*KFSA* 23, 4). The last of these letters also reveals Dorothea's sharp disagreements with her mother on the editorial project.

Dorothea Mendelssohn was born on 24 October 1764 in Berlin, and her mother, Fromet, was the daughter of Abraham Gugenheim of Hamburg. Her first name was Brendel, which she changed to Dorothea after her acquaintance with Friedrich Schlegel. According to the customs of Jewish families of that time, her father had given her in marriage at the age of eighteen to the banker Simon Veit in Berlin, who was not only considerably older, but had no interest whatsoever in the subjects Dorothea loved. She bore him four children, two of whom died in infancy, and spent her time in the intellectual circles of her friends, especially Henriette Herz and Rahel Levin, where artists, writers, and aristocrats met, and no distinctions were made in terms of social difference. Here she met Schleiermacher, Reichardt, Tieck, the brothers von Humboldt, and others, and a wide gap between her home life and her real interests ensued. Friends noticed how unhappy Dorothea was in her marriage, and Henriette Herz proposed on several occasions to negotiate a divorce from Veit. But because of her children, Dorothea felt obliged to stay where life had placed her. But when, in the late summer of 1797, she met the young author Friedrich Schlegel, this attitude changed. Henriette Herz reports that an almost visible spontaneous attraction between the two took place during their first encounter, and they fell in love at first sight.[19] Now Dorothea asked for a divorce, which after a period of separation from her family was granted at the beginning of 1799. Philipp, the younger son, who was only three years old, stayed with his mother, whereas Johannes remained with Veit.

Three weeks after the divorce, Dorothea wrote to her friend Karl Gustav von Brinkmann, a Swedish diplomat in Berlin:

Think of how I feel, since for the first time, I have experienced that I am free from fearing to have to tolerate an unpleasant conversation, an uncomfortable presence, or even a humiliating coarseness. I can hardly feel it myself – even now I am like someone who has carried a heavy weight for a long time and still believes she feels it after she has long been rid of it. Now I am what I should have been for a long time, dear friend! Now I am happy and *good* – no longer any horrors, no humiliation, perhaps you would no longer find me as hard. I live in peace with everything that surrounds me. (*KFSA* 23, 224)

A marriage had originally not been intended because of the seemingly insurmountable difficulties, but eventually it took place in 1804 in Paris. When Schlegel returned to Jena in September 1799, he introduced Dorothea to the group. Dorothea published a romantic novel, *Florentin*, in 1801 under Schlegel's name and assisted her husband in most of his projects. After his death she received a pension from the Austrian emperor, but in September 1830 she moved to Frankfurt to live with her son Philipp and his family, where she died in 1838.

LUDWIG TIECK was the most versatile poet and narrative writer of the Romantic group. Already in 1797, before knowing him personally, A. W. Schlegel reviewed his *Knight Bluebeard* and *Puss in Boots*, which had appeared under the pseudonym Peter Leberecht ('live well') and which had been highly praised in the *ALZ*. In the very first lines, Schlegel called him a true poet who was able to unfold seemingly insignificant material into a comprehensive dramatic action and to give the 'airy nothing-ness a local habitat' (*AWS SW* 11, 136). Tieck was born on 31 May 1773 in Berlin as the son of a rope-maker. His mother was of a pious and his father of a practical nature, but Tieck left all of this behind when he entered the high school Friedrichs Werd in Berlin at the age of nine, where he displayed his talents for writing, drama, and recitation. His school was an excellent institution for someone of his talents and had instructors who knew how to stimulate their pupils in such activities. Already in these early years, Tieck acquainted himself with a great variety of literature: the works of Goethe, Schiller, Shakespeare in the translation of Eschenburg, *Don Quixote* in the translation of Bertuch, and the comedies of the Danish author Holberg. In Reichardt's house, Tieck met various musicians and actors who came to Berlin, and he used his own pronounced histrionic talent, supported by his sonorous voice, in many amateur performances. In this society, Tieck met the younger sister of Reichardt's wife, Amalie Alberti, who first became his sweet-heart, and then, in 1799, his wife. At the age of sixteen, he had already composed dramatic scenes entitled 'Summernight', reminiscent of Shakespeare, and a great number of melo-dramatic tales and thrillers, sometimes simply as continuations of stories that his teachers at the gymnasium had begun in instalments to earn extra money and then hired him to complete for them. Through these early exercises – although they were chiefly aimed at a reading public which asked for little more than excitement – Tieck learned how to write at a relatively young age. In 1792, after finishing his school education, he became a student at the University of Halle where he studied classical literature with F. A. Wolf. Halle, however, was too pedantic and scholastic for Tieck's taste, and so he moved to Göttingen, which was certainly the best university for the study of literature to be found at the time. He concentrated on English literature, particularly Shakespeare and Ben Jonson, but also attended courses on Spanish authors; he became a great translator, collaborating in A. W. Schlegel's Shakespeare translation and producing his own new translation of Cervantes' *Don Quixote*.

When his friend Wackenroder began his studies at the University of Erlangen in 1793, Tieck joined him to be in his company. The summer semester at Erlangen was of great importance for the two in their studies of modern European painting, especially of the Italian Renaissance and Dürer's old-German style. But in the winter, Tieck returned to Göttingen with Wackenroder, remaining there until the autumn of 1794, when Wackenroder started his career as a legal administrator in Berlin and Tieck began his life as a freelance author. He had published his novel *William Lovell* in three volumes (1795–6) and his *Popular Fairy-Tales by Peter Leberecht* (1797), and was on the way to his novel *Franz Sternbald's Wanderings* (1798), to *Prince Zerbino, or the Journey to Good Taste* (1799), and his two-volume *Romantic Poetry* (1799–1800), which contained the tragedy *Life and Death of St Genevieve*, when he personally met the Schlegels. Tieck was well-read, and he had a keen intelligence and a quick power of comprehension, but he was not at all theoretically oriented. His contributions to the theory of early German Romanticism will mainly be discussed from the perspective of fiction, especially his novel *Franz Sternbald*. When he joined the Romantic group in Jena in the summer of 1799, Tieck had the closest contact with Novalis. Throughout his life, he worked on a comprehensive study of Shakespeare, which he never completed. Later, he moved to Dresden, where he became the director of the court theatre and continued his highly influential role as a writer of narratives, especially in the genre of the novella. With the help of his daughter Dorothea and her husband Wolf Graf von Baudissin, he completed A. W. Schlegel's Shakespeare translation – but not without altering his friend's versions. He died in April 1853 at the age of seventy-nine.

WILHELM HEINRICH WACKENRODER was born in 1773, the same year as Tieck, in Berlin, where his father held a high position in the city's Prussian government. His father had distinguished himself during the Seven Years War, when Berlin was occupied by the Russians, and he had been an admirer of King Frederick II of Prussia, as he had the same sense of duty and devotion to the state. Paying great attention to the education of his son, Wackenroder's father wanted his son to follow in his footsteps as a Prussian administrator. Wackenroder himself, however, displayed an early talent for music and musical composition, and his close friendship with Tieck drove him even further in the direction of the arts. In a schematized manner, critics have often emphasized the antagonism of art and practical life in Wackenroder, even to the point of attributing his early death to his inability to resolve this conflict. This is, of course, exaggerated and can only be maintained if one overlooks a good number of biographical facts in Wacken-roder's life. Yet in his writings, he anticipated this antagonism, which was to become a favourite theme of the late nineteenth century, especially in the early works of Thomas Mann. It should be noted that this antagonism places both life and art in a precarious position, in that art is viewed from the perspective of life and life from that of art, each having to maintain or justify itself from the opposite point of view.

In the spring of 1793, Wackenroder took up his study of law at Erlangen University in the company of Tieck. They attended lectures on classical poetry together, but more important than these academic experiences was their contact with the southern German and Bavarian landscape full of Baroque art and remnants of the Middle Ages. For the young men from Berlin this was an entirely new world, which they absorbed with astonishment and admiration. They took trips to the cathedral of Bamberg, the art galleries in the château of Pommersfelden, to Nuremberg, the former centre of old-German art and Dürer's city, as well as to the areas of Bayreuth, Bohemia, and the Fichtel Mountains. In the autumn, they continued their studies at Göttingen University where Wackenroder, in addition to law, studied older German literature, the history of art with Johann Dominique Fiorillo, and the history of music with Johann Nikolaus Forkel, whom we had met earlier as Meta Forkel's husband. These studies were all of great importance for his *Outpourings of an Art-Loving Friar*. Here in Göttingen he also studied Giorgio Vasari's *Lives of the Most Excellent Painters, Sculptors, and Architects*, another important source for his own book.

He began working on the manuscript shortly after his return to Berlin, when he found employment in the judicial administration of the city. Nobody knew about the manuscript, and he showed it only to Tieck while they were on a trip to Dresden, but it was not published until after his death. In short, we know very little about the events in Wackenroder's life. When Friedrich Schlegel moved to Berlin, he wrote to his brother in Jena that of this 'entire art school' in Berlin, Wackenroder was his favourite intellect, and added: 'He has perhaps more genius than Tieck, but the latter certainly more understanding' (*KFSA* 24, 4). This obviously refers to Wackenroder's lack of worldly experience and Tieck's abundance of it. On 18 December 1797, Schlegel wrote: 'Wackenroder has been very ill, but now is out of danger' (*KFSA* 24, 66). Then, quite abruptly, we read on 17 February 1798: 'Wackenroder has died. He had a putrid fever and afterwards was melancholy for several months or, as others say, mad' (*KFSA* 24, 89). In spite of his early death and lack of contact with the members of the Romantic group (except for Tieck and Schlegel) Wackenroder was one of its most influential figures. His impact continued through Tieck and gave Romantic theory an important and lasting new dimension in the realms of painting and music.

EXAMPLE: EARLY ROMANTICISM AND THE FRENCH REVOLUTION

The strong affinity of early German Romanticism to the French Revolution is in many ways obvious and has been emphasized repeatedly in the critical literature. The common denominator lies in the overcoming of the old European order, the ancient regime, here in literature and poetic theory, there in society and politics. Other features of Romantic theory, such as the abolition of a hierarchical system of genres, the removal of the difference between poetry and prose, and the end of demarcation lines between poetry and philosophy, for example, follow quite naturally from this basic premise, as well as from the new esteem for popular literature and the acknowledgement of the entire Romantic tradition of Europe in general. The opposition of classicistic and Romantic orientations in theory and criticism thereby assumes an obviously revolutionary character. This became especially manifest in later phases of European Romanticism, during the first decades of the nineteenth century, particularly in the Mediterranean countries of Europe where there had been a strong classicist tradition, such as France, Italy, and Spain. In these countries, Romanticism came to mean a revolutionary uprising against traditional forms of the past, and it was equated with being modern, belonging to the future, and having irrevocably broken with the tradition.

This affinity of early Romantic theory to revolution was noticed by contemporaries like Adam Müller, who referred in his critical writings to the 'literary revolution, occasioned by the critical philosophy, inspired by Goethe's, Winckelmann's, and Wolf's views of classical antiquity, and executed by Friedrich Schlegel, who was assisted by his brother's attractive mode of expression'.[20] Foreign visitors like Madame de Staël and Henry Crabb Robinson shared this impression. When Robinson came to Germany in 1800, he referred to Friedrich Schlegel as a leader of a literary school that had brought about an aesthetic revolution.[21] Schlegel himself, in one of his earliest writings, had stated that the task was nothing less than to produce an 'aesthetic revolution' (*KFSA* 1, 269, 272, 359). His famous *Athenaeum* Fragment 216: 'The French Revolution, Fichte's doctrine of knowledge, and Goethe's *Wilhelm Meister* are the greatest events of the age' (*KFSA* 2, 198), expresses this connection directly and comprehensively, although no text of early Romanticism is mentioned in it. The fragment attempts to associate the three most innovative events of the concluding eighteenth century, and besides the French Revolution, it refers to Fichte's new philosophy and Goethe's latest novel as a work that takes a new step in narration and poetic structuring.[22] These last two events, however, correspond most intimately to tendencies in early Romantic theory itself. Later historians have been quite affirmative in relating early German Romanticism to the French Revolution. One even spoke of the three *R*s (Reformation – Revolution – Romanticism) in the sense of a progressive line of emancipation,[23] although this was by no means a dominant attitude in German historiography (as we saw earlier in the equation of 'Romantic' with reactionary).

The conditions for a positive attitude toward the revolution had been quite favourable in Germany. There was, first of all, no dominant native theory of classicism to combat in this country, and all the signs seemed to indicate a great reversal in the order of things which would give this hitherto neglected country its appropriate place in the European intellectual community. In paragraph 85 of his *Education of the Human Race*, Lessing had proclaimed: 'It will come, it will certainly come, the time of perfection.'[24] Herder had interpreted the course of history as a wandering of the divine spirit through the nations, drawing one country after the other to the dawning light and thereby also giving the disadvantaged German nation its opportunity. Such sudden alternations in history had been described as revolutions by Herder (*HE* 4, 565), and the revolutionary consciousness among German philosophers was just as strongly developed. In the preface to the second edition of his *Critique of Pure Reason* of 1781, Kant illustrated his philosophical achievement, his 'reversal of the common manner of thinking', with the image of revolution, characterizing his critical philosophy as a revolution in thought and relating it to the Copernican revolution in the sciences (*KA* 3, 12). Fichte's thought is also of a profoundly revolutionary character. In its desire to be entirely by itself and with itself – that is, to be completely free – his Ego constantly encounters barriers and finds itself in otherness and alienation. After overcoming one barrier, the Ego is confronted with yet another, and so the transcendental thought process moves on for Fichte towards ever higher determinations. Hegel later described this mode of philosophizing through revolutionary dialectics as 'a continuous alternation of negation and affirmation, an identity with itself that immediately succumbs to the negative, but is then immediately reconstituted' (*HEG* 20, 403). With regard to the impact of the revolution upon his generation, Hegel said in retrospect: 'All thinking beings shared in the jubilation of this epoch. Emotions of a lofty character stirred men's minds at that time; a spiritual enthusiasm vibrated through the world, as if the reconciliation between the divine and the secular was now first accomplished' (*HEG* 12, 529; *HP*, 447). Goethe expressed this enthusiasm in *Hermann and Dorothea*, Novalis in his early poetry, and Hölderlin in hymnic poems which evoked the hour of freedom in the image of the coming century.

This attitude changed profoundly by 1794, the time of the beginning of early Romanticism in Germany. The September massacres, the execution of the French royal family, and the bloody Reign of Terror that saw the daily execution of sixty to eighty people in public had turned the original enthusiasm for the revolution into profound aversion, even on the part of those who had been most strongly in favour of it. By 1795, most of the early Romantics considered the French Revolution a failure, a morally and politically shipwrecked adventure in history. Henriette Herz speaks in her memoirs of a 'bloody, world historical tragedy' converting 'enthusiastic adherents' to 'embittered enemies of the revolution'.[25] Schiller wrote on 8 February 1793 to Christian Gottfried Körner: 'For a fortnight now, I have not been able to read French newspapers any more because I am so disgusted by these miserable torturers' (*FS* 26, 326). Caroline Böhmer felt disinclined to open French newspapers out of a fear of seeing well-known heads rolling towards her (*CA* 1, 338). Jean Paul described this sudden change in his essay on Charlotte Corday of 1800:

The tornado of the century, the ice-cold storm of terrorism, finally descended from the hot cloud and struck down life. Not those tortured or whose lives were sacrificed suffered most bitterly, but those for whom each day murdered one great hope of freedom after the other, who died anew with every victim and for whom the weeping image of a dying empire wrapped up by chains and vampires gradually appeared as the result of all these sacrifices.[26]

Authors like Wieland, Wilhelm von Humboldt, and Goethe did not need the signs of terror to fill them with deep doubts, even dread, over the French Revolution. According to his *Diaries and Annals* of 1789, Goethe behaved so strangely after the outbreak of the revolution that he appeared to some of his friends to be mad.

Authors like Friedrich Schlegel who would have been inclined to condone these events from a broader world-historical perspective considered the sudden disapproval of the French Revolution as a sign of the 'delicate morality of a century' that had become 'too tender and soft-hearted to be able to see tragedies' (*KFSA* 2, 207). Yet Schlegel, too, came to despise the French Revolution, precisely because of its failure in terms of world history. The French Revolution was for him only 'the highest thing the French have' (*KFSA* 18, 77), namely an expression of their 'antireligious religion' (*KFSA* 18, 227). To consider the merits of the revolution politically and constitutionally would necessarily lead to a 'perspective of pettiness' (*KFSA* 18, 237) because the constitution was the 'ridiculous aspect of the French Revolution' (*KFSA* 18, 243). Here the French had 'constituted many things, but no constitution' (*KFSA* 18, 243). In a fragment from the *Athenaeum*, Schlegel summarized what he called the 'usual points of view' of his time concerning the French Revolution. One was to regard the event 'as the greatest and most remarkable phenomenon in the history of nations, as an almost universal earthquake, an immeasurable flood in the political world'. Another was to see it 'as a prototype of revolutions, as the absolute revolution per se'. These were not Schlegel's own perspectives. He saw the revolution simply 'as the centre and apex of the French national character, where all its paradoxes are thrust together; as the most frightful grotesque of the age, where the most profound prejudices and their most brutal punishments are mixed up in a fearful chaos and woven as bizarrely as possible into a monstrous human tragicomedy' (*KFSA* 2, 247–8).

Novalis offered a similar critique. What is important for both Schlegel and Novalis, however, is their vision of a much greater revolution than the French one, a revolution that permeated the age in all spheres of life, including poetry and philosophy. They saw behind the French Revolution a revolution of truly world-historical dimensions, an event which encompassed their own theory. Novalis regarded the French Revolution as only a partial aspect of an impending general upheaval of much vaster magnitude leading to a new age. He also thought that this partial attempt had failed. Whoever was mesmerized by this event would necessarily misinterpret the fundamental course of history. Such a shortsighted spectator, Novalis thought, recognized only the 'symptoms' of the great turnabout and did not realize that the French Revolution was 'nothing but the crisis of beginning puberty' (*NO* 2, 459). A true 'intellectual astronomer' of history, however, had long since recognized that 'powerful inundations', 'changes in climate', and 'intense incitations' had manifested themselves and that the results would constitute the 'content of a new age of history' (*NO* 2, 489–90). Novalis was so convinced of the historical relativity of the French Revolution that he said: 'If the revolution is truly historical, every contemporary must be able to find in himself its causes and its real essence' (*NO* 3, 490). In this sense, Schlegel and Novalis were profoundly revolutionary thinkers who developed their thoughts on the French Revolution and its significance to a new level of historical reflection. As Richard Brinkmann puts it, they treated the French Revolution in a manner 'of high originality and importance that simultaneously had the quality of the typical, the historically representative'.[27]

Novalis was seventeen years old when the French Revolution began. Of all of the early Romantics, he was most strongly disposed to the magic words of a revolutionary philosophy of history: the golden age in the past and the corresponding future realm of perfection. Yet, through a constant oscillation between these two poles, by seeing the state of perfection now as something lost in the past, and then as an achievement still in the future, he secured himself against either a one-sidedly utopian or a pessimistic philosophy of history and saw the true historical status of the human being as something between the two extremes. In this way, he used the idea of a golden age in the past simultaneously with and alongside the notion of a revolution which abruptly changes and constantly upsets our present state of experience. In this spirit, he wrote: 'Adam and

Eve. What was effected by a revolution has to be suspended by a revolution. Bite of the apple' (*NO* 2, 275). And he said even more paradoxically: 'Many anti-revolutionary books have been written for the revolution. Burke has written a revolutionary book against the revolution' (*NO* 2, 459).

In this oscillating manner of thinking, operating between opposites without overcoming them, accepting the antinomies as natural, Novalis reflected upon the two forms of government of democracy and monarchy. On the surface, the two seem to constitute 'an insoluble antinomy – the advantages of the one to be terminated by the opposed advantage of the other' (*NO* 2, 503). It is usual that 'young people' are on the side of democracy and elder representatives of the family on that of monarchy and that 'an absolute difference in inclinations' is responsible for this opposition: 'The one likes changes – the other does not.' At this point, Novalis seems to propose a scheme of individual psychological development as an explanation for the different points of view, and thereby to hierarchize them. He apparently continues in this direction when he adds: 'Perhaps in certain years we all like revolutions, free competition, contests and similar democratic phenomena. But for the greatest majority these years pass – and we feel attracted by a more peaceful world in which a central sun dominates the dance and one would rather become a fixed planet than enter a destructive battle for the leadership of the dance' (ib.). This, however, is not Novalis' own position, as is obvious from the conclusion of the fragment, in which he proposes to become 'at least politically as well as religiously tolerant' and to concede the possibility that 'a human being could be inclined differently from us'. Such a tolerance would eventually lead to the 'sublime conviction of a relativity of each positive form' and thereby to the 'true independence of a mature spirit with regard to every form that is nothing but a tool for it' (ib.).

Novalis adds to this observation: 'The time must come when political entheism and pantheism are most intimately connected as interactive members.' 'Entheism' in this fragment is the designation for monotheism, and in political terms, it stands for the monarchic sysem, while pantheism is the doctrine according to which God is everywhere and which therefore corresponds to democracy in the political realm. Monarchy and democracy, in other words, are the poles between which our thinking oscillates, the phenomena of an interactive quality that determine each other. If we try to apply these thoughts to the political reality of Novalis' time, he would argue that we are not talking about a true monarchy when we turn to pre-revolutionary France or to most of the reigning houses in Europe. They have long since ceased to be monarchies (*NO* 2, 472), and people have taken them much too seriously in considering their abolition as a 'life-endangering and contaminating sickness' (*NO* 2, 465–6). Such interpreters do not go beyond the symptoms and do not notice that this so-called sickness is nothing other than the 'incipient puberty' of humanity (ib.). As the comets are the 'revolutionary torches of the entire world system', namely signs of a change of a profounder nature, the French Revolution is an analogous type of torch which indicates an impending change in our history (*NO* 2, 489–90).

We have discussed this aspect earlier. What is important in this context is Novalis' emphasis on interaction, on mutual determination, on a reciprocal saturation of two utterly opposed political systems, democracy and monarchy. He expresses these views mainly in his unpublished fragments, but also in a collection of fragments with the title 'Faith and Love. The King and the Queen', which he published in the *Yearbooks of the Prussian Monarchy*. This publication aroused some indignation but it was perhaps not sufficiently read or understood to constitute a major provocation. A colleague and friend, the District Magistrate Just, wrote to Novalis after reading the text that he would do well to hold on to his head if the French came, but that any monarch would feel cheated if he hired him as an inveterate monarchist (*NO* 4, 505). In one of these fragments we read: 'There will be a time, and this soon, when people will generally be convinced that no king can subsist without a republic and no republic without a king, that both are like body and soul, and that a king without a republic and a republic without a king are words without significance. The king always arose together with the true republic, and the republic together with the true king. The true king will be a republic, and the true republic king' (*NO* 2, 490).

This is a typical example of early Romantic reflection. To appreciate it fully, we must realize that Novalis is using his terms in the classical sense of a single person's rule as monarchy and the people's rule as a republic. In this sense, the two are irreconcilable. Yet Novalis maintains that a 'true republic' is king just as a 'true king' is a republic. We could describe this position by saying that it is equally impossible to think of the absolute king and the absolute republic in isolation and that our task is rather to think of the king from the perspective of the republic and the republic from the perspective of the king. But such terminological clarifications were not the business of Novalis, who preferred to think in an oscillating manner in terms of transitions and wished to be a 'true observer' operating with the 'magic wand' of analogy (*NO* 3, 517–18). The most important document for this interpretation of the French Revolution which sees it as part of a larger process is his little essay *Christendom or Europe* of 1799. No one will read this text today as a document of the 'romantic reaction', as Georg Lukács proposed toward the end of the 1940s, or as a 'revocation of realism, Enlightenment, Reformation, modern science, and bourgeois emancipation', as Hans Meyer tried to do as late as 1959.[28] In its formal aspects, the text is a speech with a rhetorical structure. With regard to its content, we could call it an address to the age on the most important tasks of the epoch – tasks which arose after the revolution, after the failure of the revolution, especially in Germany.[29] Novalis concentrates on the great change which became evident in his time and expresses the conviction 'that the time of resurrection' has come and that the history of modern unbelief which culminated in the French Revolution is the 'key to all the colossal phenomena of modern times' (*NO* 3, 516).

How are we to interpret this? After describing in images of an idealized period of the Middle Ages a harmonious political community resting on hierarchy and subjugation, Novalis describes modern discontinuity as beginning with the Reformation. He presents a process which is characterized in most later histories of philosophy as one of progressive emancipation and self-liberation. He sees one line of development as proceeding from the Reformation to the Enlightenment and Revolution, and defines a historical tradition which was later made famous by Hegel and Marx. Yet, Novalis gives a negative note to these events by presenting them not as sign posts of emancipation, but as manifestations of modern unbelief. 'Knowledge and possession' replaced faith and love, modern politics dissolved the old universalism, and everything contributed to the dominance of calculating rationalism. 'The result of the modern manner of thinking was philosophy, and this was taken to include everything opposed to the old, hence in particular every attack on religion' (*NO* 3, 515). With these observations, Novalis describes the Enlightenment – an Enlightenment, however, devoid of its usual splendour. Philosophy transformed the 'infinitely creative music of the cosmos' into a 'monotonous rattling of an infinite mill driven by the stream of accident'. No other enthusiasm was left but the enthusiasm for philosophy. France was the 'seat of this new faith' where poetry was decried, the holy offended by sarcasms, and the light adored 'because of its mathematical obedience and insubordination' (*NO* 3, 516). Everywhere in Europe there arose the 'new European guild: the philanthropists and enlighteners' (ib.), marking the climax of modern unbelief. The 'great iron mask' walking around in the French Revolution bearing the name Robespierre sought 'religion as the centre and the force of the republic'. From an original negation of religion he rose to its recognition and became its high priest. Novalis is referring to the monstrous 'Gospel of Liberty' addressed to the supreme being by the French Republic and issued by Robespierre in May 1794; he perceives the cold madness of this gesture but takes it as a sign of the great reversal which he expected not from France, though, but from Germany.

This leads to Novalis' own conception of revolution. Whereas in other European countries we can expect a 'new and higher religious life' only in the time after the 'peace' – that is, after the disturbances stemming from France have been quelled – in Germany we already realize 'with full certainty the traces of a new world' (*NO* 3, 519). These are obvious in the progress towards a 'higher epoch of culture', in a 'tremendous fermentation in the sciences and the arts', and in a 'versatility without comparison'. All these signs are still 'incoherent and crude', but they indicate to anyone with a 'historical eye' a 'universal individuality, a new history, a new humanity'. Novalis is obviously referring to the developments in poetry and philosophy of which early German Romanticism forms a part. If we ask more precisely about the nature of this epoch-making, however, he retreats into mythical, poetic language and says with a surrealistic touch:

The newborn will be an image of its father, a new golden age with dark, infinite eyes, a prophetic, miraculous and healing time, a consoling and life-engendering time – a great time of reconciliation, a Savior native to humankind like a true genius, not visible but believed in, and adored by his believers in manifold forms, consumed as bread and wine, embraced as the beloved, breathed as air, heard as word and son, and absorbed with heavenly pleasure as death, with the most intense pain of love, into the inner part of the dissolving body. (*NO* 3, 519–20)

As to the time at which this transition will occur, Novalis is somewhat vague. In the rhetorical fervour of his speech, he assures his audience: 'When and how soon? You should not ask that. Have patience, and it will come, it must come, the holy time of eternal peace when the new Jerusalem will be the capital of the world. And until then, be cheerful and courageous in the dangers of the time, companions of my belief, proclaim with word and deed the divine gospel, and remain faithful to the true and infinite faith unto death' (*NO* 3, 524).

In similar manner, Friedrich Schlegel saw his time as a period of great upheaval and the French Revolution as only a partial expression of this change. The general tendency of the epoch was that of humanity struggling to enter a new phase of development, a new history. Schlegel wished to be able 'to draw a profile of the giant' but was aware of the great difficulties in correctly understanding and punctuating the contemporary period, and he readily admitted that the citizens of a later period 'will probably think much less of us than we do now, and consider a great deal of what we now simply marvel at as only the necessary preliminary exercises of humanity' (*KFSA* 2, 249; *LF*, 234). The intellectual side of this revolution consisted for him mainly in the 'history of philosophy from Kant to Fichte', which appeared as comprehensive to him as the 'history of philosophy from Descartes and Bacon to the latest English and French philosophers' (*KFSA* 18, 67). The most important impulse in this 'transcendental view' came from Fichte, who had 'shaken consciousness in its innermost creative depths' and had organized 'free self-reflection' as an art. This had caused far-reaching 'revolutions in other realms of human thinking and creation', especially in poetry, which in its higher forms is 'only another expression of the same transcendental view of things' (*KFSA* 3, 5). As in the well-known Fragment 116 on the three 'greatest tendencies of the age', Schlegel juxtaposes philosophical, poetic, and aesthetic revolutions to the French Revolution and says: 'Whoever is offended by this juxtaposition, whoever cannot take any revolution seriously that is not noisy and materialistic, has not yet achieved a lofty, broad perspective on the history of mankind' (*KFSA* 2, 198; *LF*, 190). All these movements derive from the 'centre', that is, from 'humanity' itself. They manifest the 'fomenting gigantic power of the age' (*KFSA* 2, 261; *LF*, 246), which for Schlegel is the 'first true age' (*KFSA* 2, 262; *LF*, 256) in which the 'sun really begins to rise' (*KFSA* 2, 265; *LF*, 249). Their common tendency is a great religion of humanity, a dynamic pantheism animated by the 'revolutionary desire to realize God's realm on earth' (*KFSA* 2, 201; *LF*, 222). According to the 'Speech on Mythology', humanity is struggling 'with all its power to find its own centre' (*KFSA* 2, 314; *DP*, 83). This religion will 'swallow the French Revolution', and the 'highest destination and dignity' of the latter will perhaps appear to 'future history' as having been 'the most vigorous incitement of this slumbering religion' (*KFSA* 18, 94).

In June 1795, deeply engrossed in his studies of ancient Greek literature and its relationship to the modern age, Friedrich Schlegel received a letter from Caroline who addressed him by his nickname and said:

Fritz, there are two books which you must read, and one of them deals with the problem of knowledge. This is *Condorcet*. He belongs to your field – since you want to determine the level of culture of a people and the value of this culture according to the notion that we can form of the earliest human perfection. Condorcet does not know anything about your great turning-point in history, but more about the turns into infinity than you and I have ever dreamed about. (*KFSA* 23, 235)

The other book mentioned by Caroline is that by S. C. F. Fulda on German history and is of little importance in the context of revolution. Condorcet's text, however, was of prime significance not only for a world-historical understanding of the French Revolution, but also for Schlegel's and his friends' own undertakings in the field of theory.[30]

Caroline referred to Condorcet's latest work, his *Sketch for a Historical Picture of the Progress of the Human Mind* of 1794, a text sketched out in great haste in hiding from his Jacobin persecutors during the short time left to him before his death. This work, although highly eclectic and sketchy, is the classic exposition of the doctrine of the infinite perfectibility of the human race. In a positivistic manner and in the style of a 'mathématique sociale', Condorcet concentrated on the dependence of each instance on the preceding ones and its own impact on the following ones and thereby attempted to demonstrate the unlimited progress of humanity as a natural law (*CO*, 2) – provided, of course, that 'the earth occupies its present place in the system of the universe, and as long as the general laws of this system produce neither a general cataclysm nor such changes as will deprive the human race of its present resources' (*CO*, 3). Condorcet's model of science is definitely a mathematical one. Hence his insistence on the truly indefinite and infinite process of perfectibility, which by its very character does not permit a limit, a term, or a goal of its development. He expressly says:

Such is the aim of the work that I have undertaken, and its result will be to show by appeal to reason and fact that nature has set no term to the perfection of the human faculties: that the perfectibility of man is truly indefinite: and that the progress of this perfectibility, from now onwards independent of any power that might wish to halt it, has no other limit than the duration of the globe upon which nature has cast us. (*CO*, 3)

Condorcet's starting-point for his calculation was the human ability, in contrast to that of the animals, to form simple and compound concepts as well as simple and compound ideas from individual sense-impressions and to generate moral principles from the feeling of pleasure and displeasure (*CO*, 1). The sensualist philosophy of Locke and Condillac formed the nucleus of perfectibility for him, and the origin of language and the creation of new sign systems were essential to his notion of perfectibility. This is perhaps the most important line of development in this thought, leading to ever new combinations and pointing to the creation of a mathematical language and an entirely artificial system of signs. The decisive turning-point in this history of humanity is consequently not the advent of Christianity nor the change from a local to a universal development, but the 'invention of alphabetical writing' followed by the art of printing and a computerized means of transmitting knowledge. Another path runs from tribal society to pastoral, agricultural, and industrialized forms of society, and other approaches pursue models of differentiation in additional spheres of life. Condorcet divides history into ten epochs, the ninth of which forms the period of the Enlightenment from Descartes to the foundation of the French Republic and is marked by three great accomplishments: the philosophy of Locke and Condillac, which permitted an entirely natural explanation of our ideas and moral concepts; the political principles of Rousseau; and the doctrine of the infinite perfectibility of the human species as formulated by Turgot, Price, and Priestley (*CO*, 166). The tenth depicts 'future progress of the human mind' in the sense of general education, universal suffrage, freedom before the law, freedom of thought and freedom of speech, the right of self-determination for colonized peoples, the fair distribution of wealth, insurance and pension-rights, social medicine, equal rights for women, and so on (*CO*, 203–35). A special point in Condorcet's philosophy of perfectibility concerns the effects of a 'conserving medicine' and is directly related to his mathematical concept of indefinite progress and limitless perfectibility, of a movement without a final goal. Such speculation finds its greatest obstacle in the invariable nature of the human being, the most conspicuous expression of which is death. Progress in 'médecine préservatrice' is expected to diminish the 'organic degeneration' of the human being, to permit the decisive step beyond the permanence of an invariable human nature, and actually to raise the process of perfectibility to new levels (*CO*, 236–7).

Friedrich Schlegel adopted the theory of infinite perfectibility from Condorcet in the summer of 1795. One can find similar conceptions of history in Kant's and Fichte's notions of an infinite progress of history approaching its goal only in stages through an infinite approximation. The use of the term 'perfectibility', however, with the addition of the word 'infinite', precludes any final perfection as an ultimate stage and is indeed most unusual in the German thought of the time, especially in the mathematical expression of these concepts. Schlegel first applied the term in his writings on Greek literature, and no other theory refuted the notion of an absolute classicism more thoroughly for him than Condorcet's idea of infinite perfectibility.[31] In this conception, the goal of the historical movement was also detached from any form of arrival, and a final perfection was precluded in the past as well as in the future. In German philosophy, especially in Kant and Fichte, the historical movement did have such a point of arrival, if not in reality, then in thought. This was the full deployment of all human faculties in the perfected society of a fulfilled republicanism, and this, despite its humanism, was a metaphysical idea. Such a human state appeared so far removed from the present German misery, however, that Kant could visualize it only as a peripheral concept in history, and Fichte actually described it as unrealizable, as a regulative ideal. But for both Kant and Fichte, human nature, the subject, determines the course of history as the final goal, as a structural axiom, as the totality of meaning. In contrast to this, the system of infinite perfectibility has no such principle, either as an origin or as a goal. The movement described in the process of infinite perfectibility is a decentred movement, yet the lack of centre is not experienced as a loss of centre but as the normal state of affairs. In German philosophy, the movement of history remained determined by a firm principle of arrival, if only in the sense of approximation. Friedrich Schlegel referred to Herder and Kant, and saw Herder as taking 'tradition and education' as the principles underlying the coherence of history (*KFSA* 1, 629), while Kant projected everything into the future and adopted a 'teleological point of view', taking the harmonious formation of all human faculties in a free republican society as his reference point for history (ib.). Indeed, the common denominator of German thought during the eighteenth century seems to have been the idea of an education of the human race, a progressive perfection of humanity, a rounding off of human nature – in short, a thinking in terms of the transcendental subject.

In a fragment of 1796, Friedrich Schlegel emphasizes 'absolute infinity' by underlining 'absolute' twice and marking the remaining stages as never ending, as truly infinite. The fragment reads: 'Analysis of ABSOLUTE infinity, of the progress still remaining. Not only matter is inexhaustible, but also form; each concept, each proof, each sentence is *infinitely perfectible*. Mathematics is not excluded from this. Enormously important is the *perfectibility of mathematics* for philosophy, the doctrine of science, and logic' (*KFSA* 18, 506). Basic concepts of early Romantic theory have a revolutionary character and are expressed in revolutionary vocabulary. On the level of transcendental reflection, the revolution as political insurrection finds its counterpart in the logical insurrection of scepticism. The insurrection of scepticism forms an essential element of Romantic irony, and constitutes a countermovement of enthusiasm and scepticism described by Schlegel in many instances as a 'constant alternation of self-creation and self-destruction' (e.g., *KFSA* 2, 127, 149, 151, 172). However, just as permanent insurrection in political life would result in anarchy, permanent scepticism would lack any forward-moving power of thought. Schlegel observes in *Athenaeum* Fragment 97: 'As a temporary condition scepticism is logical insurrection; as a system it is anarchy. Sceptical method would therefore more or less resemble insurgent government' (*KFSA* 2, 179; *LF*, 173). He also viewed Romantic poetry as an 'absolutely progressive poetry' involved in a process of constant becoming and an endlessly developing march. Romantic poetry, he declares in Fragment 116 of the *Athenaeum*, 'alone is infinite, just as it alone is free; and it recognizes as its first commandment that the will of the poet can tolerate no law above itself' (*KFSA* 2, 183; *LF*, 175). Schlegel was obviously convinced that opposition, contradiction, antinomy, and antithesis are essential to our existence. As he puts it, 'for someone who has attained a certain level and universality of education, the inner self is a continuous chain of the most colossal revolutions' (*KFSA* 18, 82; 2, 255).

It was of great importance for the formation of Friedrich Schlegel's thought that at an early stage of his critical work he became familiar with Condorcet's doctrine of the infinite perfectibility of the human race. Traces of Condorcet are numerous in his writings. Yet, he did not by any means simply take over Condorcet's theory of infinite perfectibility, but eventually recast it in his own terms. When he formulated his own theory of history in the medium of romantic poetry, there is no longer any trace of the French model. However, the thought of a decentred movement irreducible to a foreknown goal remained the same. He writes in *Athenaeum* Fragment 116: 'Other kinds of poetry are finished and are now capable of being fully analysed. The romantic kind of poetry is still in the state of becoming: that, in fact, is its real essence: that it should forever be becoming and never be perfected. It can be exhausted by no theory and only a divinatory criticism would dare try to characterize its ideal' (*KFSA* 2, 183; *LF*, 175).

This infinite becoming, irreducible to a knowable principle with regard to beginning or end, seems to express the new Romantic philosophy of history most concisely and to demarcate its difference from the Enlightenment and the idealistic view of history. The revision embodied in this new formulation of infinite perfectibility seems to have been directly provoked by the course the French Revolution had taken. In a subtle double gesture, the new Romantic conception of perfectibility maintains both scepticism towards any achievable final goal and belief in the pursuit of such a goal. One way of describing this position is through Schlegel's frequent use of formulas such as 'as long as' or 'not yet'. In this sense, Schlegel justifies fragmentary writing 'as long as' we have not yet established the completed system of knowledge, and he demands irony 'wherever philosophy appears in oral or written dialogues – and is not simply confined to rigid systems' (*KFSA* 2, 152; *LF*, 148). In a similar sense, philosophy is in need of 'genial inspirations' and 'products of wit' as long as it is not yet entirely systematic. This will change, Schlegel assures us, once we move on to a secure methodology. Yet, as we realize at this point, the words 'as long as' and 'not yet' do not designate a temporary deficiency or a transitoriness to be overcome by fulfilled knowledge, but are ironic expressions of the actual state of our knowledge, its permanent form. Schlegel said: 'One can only become a philosopher, not be one. As soon as one thinks one is a philosopher, one stops becoming one' (*KFSA* 2, 173; *LF*, 167).

CHAPTER 2

Poetry in the early Romantic theory of the Schlegel brothers

The Schlegel brothers did not originally conceive of poetry in the larger context of a comprehensive aesthetics or an encyclopaedia of the sciences and the arts, but as a topic that directly formed the centre of their interest and spontaneously occupied their investigations. We could also say that their entire thinking about art had a character determined by poetry and that their later aesthetic works and encyclopaedic projects took their starting-point from there.[1] Poetry was the primary subject of reflection for these critics, at least during the early Romantic period. Indeed, the Schlegels were unique in making the investigation of the nature of poetry the vocation of their lives and in seeing the clarification of this question as the particular contribution they wanted to make.

The intention can be seen in Friedrich Schlegel's decision, datable almost in terms of a particular day, to choose the investigation of the 'art of poetry' or the 'poetic work of art' as the 'destiny' of his life (*KFSA* 23, 96), while A. W. Schlegel had already made this decision during his studies at Göttingen University (1786–91). This highly conscious and persistently pursued objective is easily overlooked in the intellectual panorama of that time because one usually associates the Schlegels with more general trends such as the new stimulus in poetry or the lively development of philosophy and aesthetics. Indeed, they took part in these endeavours by contributing, as A. W. Schlegel did, to Schiller's *Horae* and the *Almanac of the Muses*, or in Friedrich Schlegel's case, by immersion in the philosophical life of Jena. For the intellectual orientation of the Schlegels, however, and their historical position, these were in fact only marginal efforts, because their main activity was the consistent pursuit of a theory of poetry.

According to an early project of January 1793, this theme was to be explored in a communal correspondence 'on poetry' (*KFSA* 23, 81). Although the project never materialized, various attempts are sufficiently recognizable in the letters exchanged about it. Friedrich Schlegel appears as a critic who, in his brother's opinion, was dangerously close 'to construing a poet according to concepts 'a priori' (*KFSA* 23, 129). Indeed, he frequently felt induced to defend the 'system' against his brother, or at least the 'spirit of the system, which is something entirely different from the system' (*KFSA* 23, 130). A. W. Schlegel always appears in this debate as someone who insists on concrete and observable data such as metre, rhythm, rhyme, and language. These differing views reveal the separate speculative and empirical starting-points of the Schlegels, their individual profiles. A. W. Schlegel pursued the project of a correspondence on poetry much more seriously than his brother. In November 1793, he wrote his 'Considerations on Metrics' for him in a sequence of letters (*AWS SW* 7, 98–194) that formed the origin of his 'Letters on Poetry, Metre, and Language' published in Schiller's *Horae* (*AWS SW* 7, 98–194). Friedrich Schlegel's early projects, as for instance his manuscripts 'On Beauty in Poetry' of 1794–5, emphasize the question of unity in literary works (*KFSA* 16, 5–31). One of his first remarks on this subject stems from the end of May 1793 and reads: 'Manifoldness must necessarily be tied together to an inner *unity*. Everything must operate towards one, and the existence, position, and significance of everything else must necessarily result from this one. That which unites all parts, which animates the whole and keeps it together, the heart of the poem, is often deeply concealed' (*KFSA* 23, 97).

This attempt to create a new foundation for poetics evolved from the Schlegels' conviction that the question of what poetry actually is had hitherto been wrongly addressed by focusing exclusively on formal requirements that could never manifest anything truly poetic. They found this erroneous approach in Aristotle, who had determined the requirements for poetry too

one-sidedly in terms of the epic, in the Roman representatives of
an *ars poetica*, or the theoreticians of classicism who searched for
normative principles but could only formulate rules. Lessing,
too, had searched for a 'poetic Euclid', as if such a manual
could be established for poetry (*AWS V* 1, 211). Their general
rejection of the tradition of poetics did not, however, prevent
the Schlegels from finding decisive inspiration for their own
thinking in rhetoricians of late antiquity, such as Dionysius of
Halicarnassus, or in Plato, or even in Aristotle, as well as in
Dante, Boccaccio, Shakespeare, Goethe, and Schiller. In their
opinion, the fundamental question about what poetry is had to
be raised completely anew. Before examining the best-known
contribution by the Schlegels to this topic – namely – their
distinction between ancient and modern, classical and romantic
poetry, the discussion will focus on their structural analysis of
poetry, which has hitherto received less critical attention. These
two approaches, however, the historical and the structural, will
never be easily disentangled in the case of authors whose
aesthetic motto was: 'The best theory of art is its own history.'[2]
One important aspect of their new investigation into the nature
of poetry concerned the function of the imagination. As far as
German philosophy is concerned, Kant had already taken up
this issue in his critical philosophy as well as in the aesthetic
dimension of his thought. One way of approaching the
Schlegels' notion of poetry and the poetic is via their understanding of the imagination as a creative principle, especially in
its distinction from the Kantian analysis of this faculty.

THE THEORY OF THE IMAGINATION

The main difference between Kant's aesthetics and the early
Romantic theory of poetry concerns the understanding of the
imagination. Kant obviously does not grant the imagination the
high status bestowed on it by the early Romantics, for whom it
is capable of creating consummate works. The imagination, for
him, is rather a sensuous faculty capable of apprehending a
multitude of appearances and representing this multiplicity in
the scheme of 'manifoldness'. It is understanding that unifies

this manifoldness, according to Kant, and thereby engenders concepts. Discussing this function of the imagination in the *Critique of Pure Reason*, he does not yet touch upon the 'aesthetical', preferring to focus primarily on the 'logical' aspect of our intellectual operations. More precisely, Kant says that although the imagination is a faculty of 'sensuality', its manner of activity already has the effect of a 'synthesis of spontaneity' by determining sensuality, or a given manifoldness of sensuality, a priori. This manner of activity, or this ability to synthesize, is to apprehend a manifoldness in the scheme of manifoldness. Looked at more closely, however, such spontaneous activity is not one of the imagination alone, but reveals an interaction with the faculty of understanding, and is indeed an 'effect of understanding upon sensuality' (*KA* 3, 119–20).[3] Kant obviously does not see the imagination as independent, but bound to the understanding and even subordinate to it. This aspect of the *Critique of Pure Reason* directly exhibits the low degree of auto-activity which Kant accords to the imagination. The first visible sign of spontaneity and creative activity discernible on this level is actually that of the understanding, which is located in the realm of the logical and not attributable to the aesthetic powers of the mind.

To be sure, in his *Critique of Judgment*, Kant granted the imagination a larger scope of activity. This is obvious first of all in his analysis of our aesthetic judgment of taste, in his looking at the aesthetic experience from the perspective of the spectator, the recipient. According to a famous new formula, these aesthetic judgments of taste result from a 'free play of imagination and understanding' (*KA* 5, 217–18; *CJ*, 52). Here, too, we find an interference of the understanding with the imagination, because Kant obviously cannot conceive of a free spontaneous activity of the imagination on its own. In contrast to the cooperation between imagination and understanding in the realm of the logical, however, the dominance of the understanding is now much reduced, even suspended. This manifests itself in a 'free play' between the two faculties, but also in the fact that the aesthetic experience does not result in a concept for which the guiding power of the understanding would be needed. Yet the aesthetic experience is not merely subjective for Kant like the 'taste of the tongue, the palate, and the throat' (*KA* 5, 212; *CJ*, 46), but something 'capable of being universally communicated' (*KA* 5, 217; *CJ*, 51), of being 'deemed valid for everyone', of finding the 'concurrence of others' (*KA*5, 216; *CJ*, 50). The beautiful is, in short, something 'which pleases universally without requiring a concept' (*KA* 5, 219; *CJ*, 54). It is in these formulations that the Kantian notion of the imagination finds a more distinct delineation within the aesthetic realm, although we realize that it always remains bound to the understanding and never emerges in its distinct autonomy.

In a similar manner, Kant describes the activity of the imagination from the point of view of the creator – the artist, or genius. Genius is essentially the 'faculty of presenting *aesthetic ideas*'. Kant understands by this a 'representation of the imagination which occasions much thought, without, however, any definite thought, i.e., any *concept* adequate to it; it consequently cannot be completely compassed and made intelligible by language' (*KA*, 5, 314; *CJ*, 157). At this point, Kant perhaps comes closest to the conception of the imagination as a productive faculty, and it is also in this section that most of his examples derive from poetry. He mentions that the poet creates intuitions that transcend all forms of experience, sensualizes ideas 'of invisible beings, the kingdom of the blessed, hell, eternity, creation, etc.', and with the aid of the imagination, presents human experiences such as death, envy, and all the vices, as well as love, fame, and the like, even beyond all limits of our experience. Kant says that the imagination gives these ideas and concepts a motion, a movement occasioning 'more thought than can ever be comprehended in a definite concept and which consequently aesthetically enlarges the concept in an unbounded fashion' (*KA* 5, 315; *CJ*, 158). This is for Kant the creative aspect of the imagination. Here again, imagination and understanding are the constituent principles, and it is only in their cooperation of free play that the creative activity of genius finds expression (*KA* 5, 316). Genius is for Kant the 'happy relation' between these faculties that 'no science can teach and no industry can learn' and that enables the artist to find an expression for his ideas in language, painting, or statuary, which makes them universally communicable (*Ka* 5, 317; *CJ*, 160).

The Schlegels had the impression that Kant, in spite of his powerful advocacy of the autonomy of art in his *Critique of Judgment*, had not accorded sufficient autonomous activity to its central source, the imagination, in that he had either linked or subordinated it to understanding and reason. In this manner, a false note entered his doctrine of the beautiful, which had to be retuned by presenting the imagination in its full potentiality and specific manner of activity. According to their different personal tempers, the Schlegels settled their differences with Kant in their individual ways: Friedrich Schlegel by ignoring Kant and developing his own view of the imagination, and A. W. Schlegel by conducting a detailed argument with Kant. To assume, however, that the Schlegels opposed Kant's theory of the imagination with one of their own, or that their poetic theory proceeded from the imagination as its ground and first principle, would be an incorrect reading of their texts. This would bring into their argument a systematic tendency that simply does not exist. We should rather take their often fragmentary and mostly casual observations on the imagination as individual views and insights that attempt to point to the particular mode of operation of this often neglected faculty, its energy-specific activity. A. W. Schlegel accomplishes this by contrasting his understanding of the imagination with that of Kant. Friedrich Schlegel often confronts the unifying power of the imagination with that of reason and discovers a greater suppleness in the former, a sharper rigidity in the latter. One can call this procedure a 'theory of the imagination' only by insisting on the particular Schlegelian meaning of the word 'theory', which, in accordance with its classical Greek origin, is a mental view, a visual perception, and not at all a systematization or construction of the results and contents of knowledge (*KFSA* 2, 337).

If one wishes to characterize the imagination as a particular human faculty, Friedrich Schlegel seems to argue, it distinguishes itself from reason[4] by its intensely individual, subjective, and personal manner of operation. By using in this instance the word 'poetry' for imagination, he says at the beginning of his *Dialogue on Poetry*: 'There is only one reason, and for everyone it remains the same; but just as every human being has his own nature and his own love, so does he bear within him his own poetry' (*KFSA* 2, 284; *DP*, 53). This does not imply a poetic solipsism which encloses us in the world of the imagination, because it is our task 'to grasp every other independent form of poetry in its classical power and abundance' (ib.), a feat which is possible because this power is operative in all of us in a more or less intense form. In addition, the imagination is an immensely social faculty which is capable of furthering sociability. According to Friedrich Schlegel's *Athenaeum* Fragment 116, we should 'make poetry lively and sociable, and life and society poetical' (*KFSA* 2, 182; *LF*, 175).

From this point of view, one could consider the imagination as a form of knowledge, an epistemological faculty that recognizes its objects in a much more individual and intimate manner than reason and understanding, which operate according to transcendental concepts and laws. Friedrich Schlegel even seems to assume that the imagination is the primary faculty in our encounter with the world, and that reason begins to operate only after we have established a poetic relationship with our environment. The world, in this conception, appears like a work of art, as a poem, as the 'riches of animating nature with her plants, animals, and formations of every type, shape, and colour', as an 'unconscious poetry which stirs in the plant and shines in the light' (*KFSA* 2, 285; *DP*, 53–4). We are able to comprehend this original poetry directly and transform it into language, a 'poetry of words', because 'a part of the poet, a spark of his creative spirit, lives in us and never ceases to glow with secret force deep under the ashes of our self-induced unreason' (ib.). Indeed, from the point of view of knowledge, the imagination seems to have supremacy over reason if we compare the two in epistemological terms. Whereas reason tends to unify its elements of knowledge as concepts, the imagination not only tends to embrace the greatest abundance and manifoldness, but also includes the comical, droll, and quaint features of life that reason is inclined to eliminate. For this view of the world, Schlegel uses words like 'chime of life' or 'music of life', and in his review of Tieck's translation of *Don Quijote*, he speaks directly of the ability of poetry 'to fantasize the music of life' (*KFSA* 2, 282–3). In a fragment of 1798 he says of this fantastic view: 'The world considered as music is an eternal dance of all beings, a universal song of all living creatures, and a rhythmical stream of spirits' (*KFSA* 18, 202). In the 'Speech on Mythology', the task of poetry is to cancel 'the laws of rationally thinking reason, and to transplant us once again into the beautiful confusion of imagination, into the original chaos of human nature' (*KFSA* 2, 319; *DP*, 86).

These remarks should not be understood as if Friedrich Schlegel wished to set up a new universal realm of the imagination, of poetry and mythology, that would end the dominance of reason and now, conversely, subject reason to the imagination. Yet, this is how he is often interpreted in the contemporary critique of ideology.[5] In reality, his aim was to establish the imagination in its own right alongside reason and to determine it on the basis of its natural function, which was not sufficiently recognized in idealistic philosophy and determined too exclusively from a rational perspective to allow for the development of the new theory of poetry which the Schlegels hoped to achieve. This aim already anticipates Friedrich Schlegel's later critique of idealism, reason, and pure thought, on the grounds that reason, because of its specific mode of activity, is not capable of producing anything but structures of mere thought and thereby moves along the thread of thought, describing a circle around itself which is void of any positive content.[6] At the time of early Romanticism, however, he developed a programme for the 'union of poetry and philosophy', and the 'new mythology' was conceived as 'the most artful of all works of art' (*KFSA* 2, 312; *DP*, 82).[7]

A. W. Schlegel developed this point more precisely in his critique of Kant's notion of the imagination. His argument can be found in his Berlin lectures of 1801–2 on literature and art, which seek to present early Romantic theory in a coherent and generally understandable manner. His main objection against Kant is that he has not grasped the activity of the imagination in the realm of artistic beauty, but has borrowed it from his conception of the understanding.[8] Beauty, in Kant's *Critique of Judgment*, is not something genuine which can be explained by itself, but only 'the form of objects as they correspond to the demands of understanding' (*AWS V* 1, 231). Similarly, Kant did not consider the imagination 'independently as poetic imagination, but only in its relationship to the understanding' (ib.). According to A. W. Schlegel, such divisions into faculties result from Kant's poor and narrow conception of the beautiful, most obvious in the fact that he separates the beautiful from the sublime (*AWS V* 1, 234–6). In relating the perception of the beautiful to the understanding, Kant had to deny any relationship between the beautiful and the infinite because the understanding is a faculty 'occupied with pure finitude' (*AWS V* 1, 231). Separating the 'height of understanding from artistic genius', he therefore needed something in addition to genius 'for the production of the highest in art'. All these distinctions follow for A. W. Schlegel from Kant's much too narrow concept of the beautiful (*AWS V* 1, 239).

Kant lacked, in short, any understanding of the 'symbolic nature of the beautiful' and simply could not rise to that 'absolute and indivisible act through which genius produces its artistic creation' (*AWS V* 1, 240). He wished to segregate the animalistic, sensuous side of our nature from its reasonable, spiritual counterpart. As A. W. Schlegel put it:

What we have praised about art in general, namely, that it accomplishes for perception what the highest philosophy achieves through speculation, can be made clear here by means of an example. Transcendental intuition teaches us that body and soul are not originally opposed but one; from this point of view, we consider bodily organization as a radiation of the spirit. When in an artistic work body and spirit merge in perfect harmony, the merely animalistic disappears as well as the merely rational, and the ideal, the truly human, the divine, or whatever expression one wishes to use emerges.

A. W. Schlegel refers to the figures of gods and heroes in classical plastic art or the tragic personae in classical drama who are 'truly ideal' in so far as this interpenetration of animality and humanity has taken place in them. In a similar manner, a poem or any other work of art can be called ideal 'when matter and form, letter and spirit have penetrated each other to the point of complete indistinguishableness' (ib.). The same is true for the reverse manner of integration 'when the spirit is drawn down into a complete harmony with animality' and does not reveal the least sign of conflict. In the realm of plastic art, he refers to satyrs and sileni, or in poetry to the masks of Aristophanes. These figures are permitted to be 'immoral', because in reality they do not exist. Morality is suspended in their case, just as in that of the divine figures. (*AWS V* 1, 240–1).

Such artistic creations, however, cannot be the work of genius as Kant understood the term, that is, as a 'blind tool of nature' (*AWS V* 1, 241). His definition of genius could be applied virtually unchanged to the artistic drives of animals, to the production of beehives, beavers' lodges, and silk worm cocoons, for example – works that are not freely produced by these animals themselves, but rather by nature working through them (*AWS V* 1, 242). Schlegel quotes with amusement Kant's statement according to which neither Homer nor Wieland would be able to indicate how their 'imaginative and at the same time thoughtful ideas' originated in their minds. As far as Wieland is concerned, he adds sarcastically that this was an 'unfortunate choice', 'because Wieland knows very well, and if he should have forgotten, others do and can very well indicate, from which French and other authors he has collected his ideas' (*AWS V* 1, 242). In another instance, A. W. Schlegel describes Kant as first scratching out the eyes of genius and later, to remedy the damage, putting on the spectacles of taste to produce an aesthetic judgment (*AWS V* 1, 243). He also says: 'According to Kant, genius, like the mother bear, gives birth only to raw offspring which have to be formed through taste, but this can hardly be reconciled with the assumption that genius is supposed to provide the rule for art' (ib.).

It appears sufficiently clear at this point that, together with his polemic against the imagination 'as an entirely blind and passive natural drive', A. W. Schlegel rejects the organic, natural, unconscious origin of art implied in Kant's aesthetics and in strong opposition insists on the highly conscious, intentional, and reflective character of artistic creation. This is completely in line with his other statements on poetry. In his 'Letters on Poetry, Metre, and Language' of 1795, he makes a special issue of the question of whether the poet is a 'favourite of nature' who, without knowing how, transforms words of ordinary language, a language of need and restriction, into heavenly song. His answer is that there is no such 'natural' origin of poetry and that poetic creation is an intentional work, a craft, working in the material of language (*AWS SW* 7, 98–9). Also in other instances, in his Jena and Berlin lectures on aesthetics, Schlegel rejects the notion of an original, natural, pregiven poetry from which artistic, 'artificial' poetry is allegedly derived. To put his view of this relationship in extreme terms, in terms of earlier and later, he claims that artistic poetry came first and a natural poetry became conceivable only after the former had come into existence (*AWS V* 1, 256–7). In other words, there was no original state of poetry from which our poetry has fallen, but poetry, like all of our activities, takes place on this side of the fall (*AWS V* 1, 254). In another instance, he takes up Schiller's distinction of a 'naive' and a 'sentimental' poetry, also conceived in terms of an origin and a fall from this origin or a separation from nature. Schlegel thinks that this distinction cannot lead very far because the entire dichotomy is construed from the perspective of the sentimental. In a rhetorical manner he asks: 'For whom could the naive be naive but for the sentimental?' (*AWS V* 1, 222).

A. W. Schlegel's main point is that 'true poetry is seldom correctly understood and that the specific action of the imagination appears unnatural to those who themselves have no spark of it' (*AWS SW* 7, 93). If we perceive an object in the medium of the imagination, each part of it 'must be coloured by this medium'. In drama, for instance, the poetic appears as 'historical', as a real human occurrence, although 'its untruth is not at all concealed' and we know from the beginning that it is fiction. Yet the poetic presentation of the event is able to bring the essentials of the matter before us in a much clearer and more lively manner than the 'most scrupulous protocol'. The dramatist accomplishes this effect by lending his personages 'a more perfect organ of communication' than human beings possess. Whereas in real life the force of passion and other occurrences often inhibit their expression and stifle the faculty of communication, the poet can remove such hindrances. When in Shakespeare's *Romeo and Juliet* Juliet learns of Romeo's death after her awakening and is summoned by the friar to flee, she simply says: 'Go, get thee hence, for I will not away' (v, 3, 165).

A. W. Schlegel thus wants to say that with poetry we enter a world with its own laws, proportions, relations, and measurements that stand out from those of the real world in a most meaningful manner. He refers to Circe in Calderón's *El mayor encanto, amor*, who says that, for her, the stars are letters on the blue page of the sky (*AWS V* 1, 719). A particularly prominent example of poetic diction is the discourse of love in poetry. Such speech cannot function without images, but they rise above 'the entire other world' as if they 'had lost the measurement of the real' and strayed to the limit of things 'as far as the wings of the imagination will carry them and without any feeling of an aberration' (*AWS SW* 7, 94). In order to illustrate the language of love, Schlegel refers again to *Romeo and Juliet*, which he regards as a lyrical type of drama, and says: 'The more remote and dissimilar the images are, the more meaningful their similes must appear' (*AWS SW* 7, 95). Love is in its essence an experience of 'uncomprehended contradictions', something that transcends reason and cannot at all be grasped by reason. Even if responded to by the 'most beautiful reply', love cannot 'dissolve into complete harmony' and therefore has a tendency 'to manifest itself antithetically' (ib.). Considering the autonomous life and legislation of poetry in the realm of language, Schlegel also emphasized the 'wordplay' in poetry, especially that of lyric poetry, as particularly significant.[9] His argumentation for the appropriateness of wordplays results from the auto-legislation of the imagination, its energy-specific mode of operation also manifest in the ability 'to play significantly with similarities of tones'. A wordplay is for A. W. Schlegel 'a comparison between the meaning of words and their sound'. He refers to his favourite lyric poet, Petrarch, whose 'marvellous images and metaphors, constantly returning opposites and gentle mystical suggestions', cannot be translated into any language of reason or understanding. Another illustration of the language of the imagination would be the 'daring metaphors and antithetical richness of words' expressed in grief over the 'loss or the death of the beloved' (*AWS SW* 7, 96).

We will come back to these linguistic aspects of A. W. Schlegel's theory of poetry after first investigating the particular notion of mimesis which results from his concept of the imagination. He dealt with the relationship between reason and imagination in an image-laden critique of the Enlightenment in his Berlin lectures on literature of 1803. He offered the comparison that the human mind was divided like the outer world 'between light and dark' and that 'the alternation of day and night' would be a 'fitting image for our spiritual existence' (*AWS V* 1, 524). Whereas in the 'sunshine of reason' we are bound to the 'conditions of reality', these are suspended during the night and enveloped in a 'benevolent veil'. A 'view into the realms of possibility' opens up. In this sense, reason and imagination form the 'common basic force of our being', reason insisting absolutely on 'unity', imagination playing its game in the realm of 'infinite manifoldness'. This 'darkness' in which the root of our existence disappears is for Schlegel the 'charm of life', the 'soul of all poetry'. In order to emphasize its mode of existence entirely independent from reason, he refers to dreams in which the imagination 'plays free from all coercion' (*AWS V* 1, 527). Of course, people know how to interpret dreams in a rationalistic manner, Schlegel continues sarcastically. Yet the Homeric Greeks were already clever enough to distinguish between 'meaningful and merely accidental' dreams. Whoever has not had dreams in his life, Schlegel concludes, that at least testify to a highly marvellous, even bizarre freedom of the imagination, is not overly burdened with poetry (ib.).

The specific question to which all this leads concerns, of course, the relationship between poetry and reality – in other words, the mimetic character of poetry. In tackling this problem, A. W. Schlegel takes the Aristotelian dictum from the

Poetics, 'the beautiful arts are mimetic', as his starting-point and reinforces it with the classicistic mandate: 'Art should imitate nature' (*AWS V* 1, 252). Whether his interpretation of Aristotle or Boileau is correct is not at issue here. We are interested only in his notion of imitation. If one takes nature not in a restricted or subjective sense but rather as the 'quintessence of all things', Schlegel maintains, then it is evident 'that art has to take its subjects from nature, because there is nothing else' (*AWS V* 1, 257). 'The elements of artistic creation, however transformed they become through its marvellous activity, must always be borrowed from a given reality.' From this point of view, one does not have to prescribe that art should imitate nature, since this occurs by itself, and the Aristotelian sentence need only be modified to read: 'Art should form nature' (ib.).

However, if one concentrates on the process of forming and creating as it is executed by the imagination, Schlegel continues, one soon discovers that this is not a copying of something already existing that would give art short shrift. It is rather an original type of creating, organizing, forming of living work comparable to Prometheus 'when he formed the human being from earthly clay and animated him through a spark taken from the sun' (*AWS V* 1, 258). According to Schlegel, however, only one of all the theoreticians of art at that time understood the artistic act of creation in this manner. This was Karl Philipp Moritz, who in 1788 wrote *On the Formative Imitation of the Beautiful*.[10] At the time, Moritz had no philosophy at his disposal which would have been adequate for his 'speculative spirit'. This is the reason why he easily 'lost himself in solitary mystical aberrations' (*AWS V* 1, 259). But the beautiful was for Moritz the 'perfected which in itself can be embraced by our imagination as an autonomous whole'. The only truly autonomous whole, in fact, is the 'great coherence of the whole of nature', which transcends the measurement of our perception. Because of the 'insoluble enchainment of things' every 'individual whole' is necessarily 'only imagined'. Yet just like the 'great whole', it must be formed according to the same rules and, supported by its centre, rest in its own existence. Each artistic work is, therefore, a formation in the sense of this 'highest beauty in the great whole of nature'. A. W. Schlegel adds to Moritz's theory: 'Superb! Both the relationship to the infinite inherent in beauty and the striving of art for inner perfection have found here the most fortunate expression' (ib.).

Schlegel complements this theory simply by locating the principle of creative nature in the human being, in his 'interior', at the 'centre of his being', and in 'intellectual intuition' – terms which seem to imply the imagination. The particular manner in which nature appears in the human being determines his artistic activity. In Schlegel's own words: 'The clarity, the emphasis, the abundance, and manifoldness in which the universe mirrors itself in a human mind, and in which this mirroring mirrors itself in him, determines the degree of his artistic genius and enables him to form a world within the world' (*AWS V* I, 259). With these observations, however, the principle of an imitation of nature turns into its contrary, since it now reads: 'In art, the human being is the norm of nature' (ib.).

In order to distinguish art from nature even more clearly, Schlegel discusses toward the end of this lecture the notions of manner (*Manier*) and style (*Stil*) which were prominent in the literary debate of the time.[11] He shows his preference for style and illustrates this by turning to Shakespeare, whose style functions as 'a system of his particular art, an amazingly thorough and deeply thoughtful one which changes in accordance with the different subjects of his dramas in the most manifold fashion' (*AWS V* I, 264). Manner, in contrast, is a much too personal and intimate operation that unexpectedly reintroduces nature. Schlegel explains this by deriving manner, *maniera*, from *manus*, 'the conducting of the hands', that is, from personal properties permitting the 'intrusion of bodily habits'. *Stylus*, however, 'is the stylus used by the ancients to write on wax tablets'. Schlegel says: 'This one does not belong to us, it is a tool for our free activity. The quality of the stylus certainly determines that of our written character, but we have chosen it ourselves and can exchange it for another' (ib.).

A. W. Schlegel's observations lead back to that self-consciousness and reflexivity in the early Romantic conception of poetry which were mentioned at the beginning of this chapter. Self-consciousness and reflexivity are two features nowhere more noticeable than toward the end of A. W. Schlegel's lectures on the Enlightenment, where he attempts to describe, convinced as he is of having taken a momentous step, the 'beginning of a new time' that he and his friends had tried to propagate in manifold ways (*AWS V* 1, 538). He sees the 'seeds of becoming', the origin of a 'new time' especially in the fact that a 'heightened consciousness', a new 'level of self-under-standing' has become manifest 'as never before in philosophical enterprises'. Clearly, Schlegel's sentimentality towards the 'new' and 'revolutionary' is obvious in his opinion that 'the contemporary poet has to be better aware of the nature of his art' than previous great poets and this 'higher reflection' now has to be submerged again into the 'unconsciousness' (*AWS V* 1, 540–1). The above statements give rise to important reflections on Schlegel's preferred type of artistic poetics in contrast to a theory of unconscious creation – reflections that will be pursued at a later opportunity.

THE POETIC UNITY OF THE LITERARY WORK

As far as imitation of nature and the mimetic character of poetry are concerned, Friedrich Schlegel took a position similar to that of his brother, although his paradigms derive from classical poetry and sometimes use a different language and induce a different line of thought. He illustrates his theory mainly with three authors of Greek literature – Homer, Aristophanes, and Sophocles. 'Freedom of the poet' in the face of the pre-existent world of nature, society, and tradition (myth and history) was a decisive principle for him (*KFSA* 1, 502), although he was aware of the fact that, in relationship to these pre-existent entities, the poet is 'not entirely free', or free only in a particular way relative to his individual work of poetry. Yet, in spite of all these considerations according to which the poet must, for instance, pay heed to the 'requirements of the place', it remains for him a prime task to demonstrate his 'superior power' (*KFSA* 1, 52).

Homer is for Schlegel the example of a poetry that is 'less an ideal beauty than a faithful copy of nature' and in which the poet acts as a 'true reflection of his own world and surroundings' (*KFSA* 1, 49). Schlegel reduces the basis of Homer's doctrine of art to a laconic dictum deriving from a classical saying: 'To know much, especially of previous times, and to be able to say it effectively and structuredly' (*KFSA* 1, 450). Indeed, saying something 'effectively and structuredly' becomes the essential point in Schlegel's own theory and relates to free creation on the part of the poet. This can also be expressed by another judgment of one of the ancient critics to whom Schlegel often refers at this time: 'Homer, favoured by an enthusiastic nature, had formed in an artful manner manifold narrative songs to a charming order' (*KFSA* 1, 564). This emphasizes the freedom of the poet in a striking manner, because it is manifest in a genre that tends towards the imitation of nature. This freedom is also evident in the many 'deceptions' of Homer that are reminiscent of what he himself said about those of Odysseus, i.e., that he invented many deceptions that seemed like truths (*KFSA* 1, 455). Pindar said directly of Homer that his lies, through their winged art, obtained a certain dignity (*KFSA* 1, 454). These two directions of poetry, the mimetic and the freely creative, appear in the two epics of Homer with a respective preponderance, in that the *Iliad*, with its tendency toward 'passionate vigour and heroic greatness', refers to the ideal world of tragedy and even represents a 'youthful announcement' of it, while those 'who seek only nature in art' will prefer the *Odyssey*, because it offers 'a beautiful mirror of human life' (*KFSA* 1, 482). As far as the preponderance of poetic freedom and imitation in Homer was concerned, Schlegel followed the opinion expressed by Polybius, who said that Homeric poetry was composed of 'history, diathesis, and myth; of tradition, arrangement, and invention; the purpose of history was truth, that of arrangement perspicuity, and that of invention pleasure and amazement' (*KFSA* 1, 455).

With Aristophanes, a poet appears instead in whom 'poetic playfulness' assumes the 'freest scope'. Schlegel says: 'The degree of female licentiousness and depravity represented by

Aristophanes is surprising and exceeds all belief.' At first glance, nature appears altered in his plays 'according to the requirements of comedy and idealized into the comical (the worse)' (*KFSA* 1, 64). Anyone who considered women's scenes like those in his *Lysistrata* or *Ecclesiazusi* a 'literally true painting of real events' could be regarded as being incapable of sound judgments (*KFSA* 1, 111). And yet, Schlegel thinks, these comic representations were not without all connections to reality; rather, comedy borrowed its subject from reality by 'further developing it according to the requirements of the comical ideal' (ib.). On this basis, Schlegel can see in the Aristophanean comedy 'a copy of nature, sometimes even a portrayal of an individual character' and say that this comedy 'contains innumerable traits that are borrowed from reality and is an irrefutable document for the history of morals' (*KFSA* 1, 64). Yet as in the case of Homer, it will not be easy 'to distinguish with certainty and reliability the delicate borderline between the real and the ideal in Aristophanes' (*KFSA* 1, 111).

Like his brother, however, Friedrich Schlegel clearly distinguished the true imitation, i.e., an artistic formation, from the mere 'copy of nature' (*KFSA* 1, 59). 'The privilege of nature is fullness and life; the privilege of art is unity', he declared categorically. 'Whoever denies the latter, whoever conceives of art only as a remembrance of the most beautiful nature, denies it all autonomous existence' (*KFSA* 1, 38). In this way, Schlegel's reflections on the specific functioning of the imagination and its relationship to a pre-existent nature come to a focus in the notion of poetic unity, the particular organization or structure of a literary work. The task of poetry is: ' *To weave together a multitude to one, and to perfect this weaving as an absolutely accomplished whole*' (*KFSA* 1, 295). It is obvious that this whole is not that organic, naturally grown unity that was the model in the aesthetic theory of German idealism. The artistic, artful character of Schlegel's notion of unity is also evident in his carefully chosen terminology. He uses words like 'structure' (*Gliederbau*), 'weaving' (*Verknüpfung*), 'organization' (*Organisation*), 'formation' (*Gebilde*), and 'the form of the poem' (the Greek *morphe epeon*) (*KFSA* 1, 451). The most perfect work of art appears, in his opinion, in the domain of poetry, because poetry permits the best solution of the task of integrating the most comprehensive manifoldness with the highest possible unity. Poetry has no limits, no restrictions in this regard, because it is 'not limited by any material, neither in circumference nor in vigour', because its medium, 'arbitrary sign language', is 'human work and therefore infinitely perfectible and corruptible' (*KFSA* 1, 294). Again, we recognize language as the most important basis for the poetic theory of the Schlegel brothers.

At this point in his discourse, Schlegel constructs a hierarchy of the arts, which is otherwise alien to his aesthetic considerations – a hierarchy based on their material, their medium of expression – and he gives the lowest rank to plastic art. He must have felt the inappropriateness of such a scheme himself, and he is eager to add that, if one compares the arts, there can be no question of 'a greater or minor value of purpose' because that would sound like the question 'of whether Socrates or Timoleon was more virtuous' (*KFSA* 1, 294). Yet he maintains that, in the accomplishment of 'weaving', there can be gradations of 'more or less', and that poetry in this regard occupies the absolutely highest position (*KFSA* 1, 294–5). He substantiates his opinion with the thought that a singular artistic phenomenon becomes complete only 'through the *context of the entire world* to which it belongs'. The plastic artist who does not have such a context makes up for this lack by presupposing the world in which he and his work are at home, by creating an '*analogue of unity*' (*KFSA* 1, 295). The lyric poet and the musician create their unity through the 'homogeneity of some situations that are isolated from a whole series of connected situations' (ib.). '*Completeness of connection*', from this point of view, is achievable only by the tragic poet. Schlegel says: 'Only the tragic poet whose goal is to connect the widest circumference with the strongest rigour and the highest unity is able to give his work a complete organization whose beautiful structure is not disturbed by the smallest want and the slightest superfluity' (*KFSA* 1, 296). This consideration necessarily leads Schlegel to consider Greek tragedy, especially that of Sophocles, as the absolute artistic expression. This is the point of view of his 'On the Study of Greek Poetry' (which he had already repudiated, however, at the time of its publication in January of 1797) (*KFSA* 2, 146–7).

From this perspective, Greek drama permitted the 'freedom of the poet' to a degree hitherto unknown. Whereas 'even the most artful epic and lyric poems of the older Hellenes still had a footing and a fundament' either in mythology or reality, poetry appears in Greek drama 'as absolutely divorced from the real world' (*KFSA* 1, 502). This is obvious not only in the changes to established mythological events, which now became 'more noticeable and sudden', but also even in the fundamental aim of dramatic presentation 'to make the most remote appear immediately present' (ib.). Schlegel says: 'Because of the inner wholeness (totality) of its autonomous creations from mere and pure semblance, the dramatic genre deserves in the fullest sense to be called poetic art which, according to the ancients, consisted in the production of lasting works' (*KFSA* 1, 502).[12] Action, for instance, now assumes a meaning of its own, so autonomous that Schlegel would like to eliminate the word entirely from the interpretation of the epic (*KFSA* 1, 473). Similar observations could be made about the character of poetic unity, which appears only in drama as an 'absolutely complete and entirely perfected poetic whole in itself', whereas in the epic, 'this derivation of all threads of a work from one initial point and the relation to one final point is lacking' (*KFSA* 1, 472).

Friedrich Schlegel illustrates this character of Greek tragedy above all with reference to Sophocles, who, in his opinion, modified certain 'hard' features in the works of Aeschylus and was not yet familiar with the unrestrained luxury present in the dramas of Euripides. Sophocles' particular excellence consisted in his own manner of 'weaving' together, of organization, of structuring. His manner of composition has become 'canonical' for Schlegel, 'similar to the proportions of the famous Doryphorus by Polycleitus' (*KFSA* 1, 297). Schlegel says: 'The mature and developed organization of each whole is perfected to such a *completeness* that it is not disturbed by the smallest gap or superfluous touch. *With necessity* everything develops from one, and even the smallest part obeys absolutely the *grand law of the whole*' (ib.). The following sections in this characterization of Sophocles are simply variations of this fundamental quality of unity on the basis of manifoldness and difference. The central notion is structure, and the lawfulness in the interconnection is freedom or play. Another important feature is described by means of words like 'positioning' and 'grouping': 'The larger whole as well as the smaller parts are distinctly divided into the richest and simplest compounds and pleasantly grouped' (*KFSA* 1, 298). Schlegel repeatedly emphasizes a particular aesthetic rhythm animating the work, describing it as an alternation of 'struggle and peace, action and contemplation, humanity and fate' (ib.). This alternation is of great importance for the frightening, upsetting events in tragedy that are balanced by moments of 'emotion'. Mere terror would freeze us to unconsciousness. Sophocles knew how to blend terror and sympathy to create a most perfect balance, and the total impression of his tragedy is one of reconciliation (*KFSA* 1, 298–9). In a more formal type of analysis, Schlegel presents Sophocles' language as the height of 'Attic charm' and the '*perfection* of Greek language' in general (*KFSA* 1, 299). He does not name any titles, but the work he has in mind is doubtless the Oedipus trilogy, particularly the conciliatory ending in *Oedipus at Colonus*.

Already in his essay 'On the Study of Greek Poetry', Schlegel identified Shakespeare's *Hamlet* as the example of an utterly organized, formed, and 'woven' work of modern poetry, 'which so far is the most exquisite of its kind as far as the perfect connection of the whole is concerned' (*KFSA* 1, 246–9). In considering this early text, we must, of course, bear in mind that Sophocles represents the 'maximum' of poetry in the reality of ancient, 'objective', and natural poetry (*KFSA* 1, 218), whereas Shakespeare is the culmination or 'summit' of modern, subjective, and artful poetry (*KFSA* 1, 249), so that the qualities of Sophocles and Shakespeare show a symmetrical correspondence. Whereas the main impression gained from Sophoclean tragedy is harmony and reconciliation, *Hamlet* is the most accomplished presentation of 'indissoluble disharmony', of a disproportion in the 'thinking and acting power'. The mind splits and is 'torn apart, as on the rack, in opposite directions'. The 'total impression' is a 'maximum of despair', and the 'last and single result of all being and thinking' appears here as the 'eternal, *colossal dissonance* infinitely separating humanity and fate' (*KFSA* 1, 247–8). In spite of this fundamental difference, however, the principle of poetic unity is precisely the same in Sophocles and Shakespeare. The 'individual parts' in *Hamlet* develop with the same necessity as in the works of Sophocles 'from one common centre and are retroactive to it': 'Nothing is alien, superfluous, or accidental in this masterpiece of artistic wisdom' (*KFSA* 1, 247).

A. W. Schlegel chose mostly works of modern, Romantic literature to exemplify the notion of differentiated poetic unity. The most famous example is his essay 'On Shakespeare's *Romeo and Juliet*' of 1797 (*AWS SW* 7, 71–97), in which he attempts to demonstrate how the interaction of different parts, elements, characters, and traditions operates in a highly complex work of modern drama and to show that these components belong so necessarily to one another that it would be impossible to change even one without altering the structure of the whole. This essay is of special importance, because it forms the nucleus of A. W. Schlegel's entire Shakespeare criticism, which, for a certain period of the nineteenth century, made him the most prominent and influential Shakespeare critic.[13] We would certainly not be mistaken in assuming that the aesthetic notion of structure which became dominant in the new criticism of our century has one of its roots in this brief essay which appeared in Schiller's *Horae* in 1797.

In order to show the conscious, intentional shaping of poetic unity in the most effective manner, Schlegel insists that Shakespeare based his *Romeo and Juliet* not on his own invention, but on the narration of Luigi da Porta, and devoted his entire geniality to its shaping, its dramatic organization, its structuring as a drama. Shakespeare was not interested in the 'what' but in the 'how' (*AWS SW* 7, 71). Everything that charms, touches, and captures us in the drama is merely a blank page in the prose text, so that we must insist on the notion of 'creation out of nothingness' to do justice to Shakespeare's work of art. Another way of describing the completely different level of Shakespeare's art in comparison to the material he utilized is for A. W. Schlegel to say that, by accepting the story described in the text, the poet, with bound hands, transfigured letters into spirit and a mechanical elaboration into a poetic masterpiece (*AWS SW* 7, 75).

Only through this dramatic shaping and connecting can the drama attain that kind of coherence and unity which is its particular beauty. In order to describe the poetic unity of *Romeo and Juliet*, Schlegel quotes Lessing, who declared that this drama was the only one to his knowledge that depicted love but was also composed with the help of love (*AWS SW* 7, 97). He further develops this thought by showing the lyrical character of the drama, its atmosphere of youth, of spring, of freedom, of remoteness from the artificial relationships of society, and of proximity to nature. This becomes obvious when Romeo compares Juliet's eyes to the stars of the sky, when the two lovers are surrounded by trees the tops of which are bordered by the silver of the moon, or when their parting hour is not announced by a stroke of the bell but by the nightingale. Yet this centre of love has a dual structure, in that the drama is marked by a 'great antithesis, in which love and hatred, the sweetest and the most acerbic, festivities and dark misgivings, caressing embraces and sepulchres, budding youthfulness and self-destruction stand close to each other' (*AWS SW* 7, 87).

A. W. Schlegel engages in detailed arguments with all those critics who, for dramaturgical or literary reasons, attempted to eliminate or reduce certain scenes and even suggested that, for a more pathetic effect, Juliet should wake up shortly before Romeo's death, after he has taken the poison. Against these critics, especially Samuel Johnson and David Garrick, he insists on the 'completeness of the tragic action' in this drama, its fitting character in the sense of a true identity with itself. To be sure, Shakespeare is a most generous poet, Schlegel admits, and his art does not know that 'rigorous separation of the accidental and the necessary which is the distinguishing feature of tragic art among the Greeks'. His manner is generosity, 'generosity in everything, except in that which can have an effect only when used sparingly' (*AWS SW* 7, 89). In this way, some of the minor characters are drawn 'according to the law of suitability, with few yet distinct traits' (ib.). With regard to the more pathetic ending, he says: 'There is a degree of shock above which everything that is added either turns into torture or slides off the mind without any effect' (*AWS SW* 7, 91).

Obviously, all of these considerations of dramatic structure, characters, scenes, poetic diction, wordplay, and so on, serve the purpose of arguing for a coherent unity of the play in which nothing can possibly be altered, as well as refuting all those who take offence or displeasure at certain features and want to change them. Schlegel's translation of *Romeo and Juliet* shows that he was familiar with every word of it. He mentions the lines he could not translate because of the idiomatic difficulties of the puns. He does not limit the antithetical abundance of expression to the joyful side of passion, but sees it as equally powerful in the pain over the loss or death of the beloved, and concludes: 'Indeed, one can call this poem a harmonious miracle whose elements could be welded together only by that heavenly force. It is at the same time charmingly sweet and painful, pure and passionate, tender and violent, full of elegiac softness and tragic shock' (*AWS SW* 7, 97).

ANCIENT AND MODERN, CLASSICAL AND ROMANTIC POETRY

The Schlegelian distinction between ancient and modern, classical and Romantic poetry follows from a broad comparative view of European literature in its ancient and modern phases, and can be seen as an investigation into the origins of our own modernity. Looked at from this perspective, the distinction is a late echo in German criticism of the struggle between the ancients and the moderns (*la querelle des anciens et des modernes*) – a literary debate between the proponents of an ancient or a modern orientation in literature and criticism. This is a famous literary controversy, basic to the notion of literary modernity, which during the seventeenth and early eighteenth centuries was mostly conducted in France and England, and in which Germany, because of the relatively undeveloped state of its literature and lack of a classicism of its own, did not yet participate. Inspired by the importance of the age of Louis the Great and the excellence of its poets Corneille, Racine, and Molière, or convinced of the unique dramatic genius of Shakespeare, critics like Fontenelle, Saint-Evremond, and Perrault in France, and Swift and Dryden in England, attempted to shake off the classicist requirements for literature and to grant the modern age its right to independence and self-confidence. We notice that the ideas of progress and perfectibility in literature lurk behind their efforts and that their attempts show that their age had not only outgrown Aristotle's *Physics*, but also created artistic beauties unknown to that philosopher's *Poetics*.

However, whereas the idea of a continuous progression was recognized without hesitation in philosophy and the sciences, and constituted a well-developed doctrine at that time, the notion of infinite perfectibility in poetry and the arts did not find recognition until the end of the eighteenth century, until the beginning of early Romanticism.[14] With regard to the historical status of the sciences and the arts, the realms of reason and imagination, European classicism and the Enlightenment show a characteristic antagonism. The sciences appeared to be involved in an interminable progression, whereas the arts were thought of as always returning in cyclical motion to that position of good taste and correct norms from which they had departed in periods of decay and barbarism. The obvious guiding principle in this antagonism of progress in the sciences and cyclical motion in the arts was obviously the assumption that philosophy and science are as infinite as nature, whereas poetry and the arts have a certain point, determined by man's invariable nature, beyond which they cannot go. The most concise formulation of this principle concerning the invariability of taste and human nature can be found in the great *Encyclopaedia*: 'The fundamental rules of taste are the same in all ages because they derive from invariable attributes of the human mind.'[15] Even a future-oriented author like Diderot shared this opinion. His conception of genius and the work of art produced by genius seems to require an infinite perfectibility as its basis. But Diderot maintained the theory of cyclical motion for the arts when he mentioned, in a famous pronouncement, a 'decree pronounced for all things in this world', namely, 'the decree which has condemned them to have their birth, their time of vigour, their decrepitude, and their end'.[16] The most authoritative and classical formulation of this principle can be found in the introduction to Voltaire's *Age of Louis XIV* of 1751 where Voltaire asserts that, as far as the history of art is concerned, we have already repeated this cycle four times and that only four ages count within the history of the arts: the age of Philip and Alexander in classical Greece; the age of Caesar and Augustus in classical Rome; that of the Medici in the Renaissance; and finally, that age which Voltaire presents as the age of Louis XIV.[17] Yet, Voltaire no longer considered himself part of that period and viewed himself only as its historiographer, that is, as being already outside of it and on the side of a new decline.

Friedrich Schlegel deals most comprehensively with the problem of modern art and poetry in relation to the ancients in his essay 'On the Study of Greek Poetry' of 1795.[18] The text shows a direct reference to the classicist struggle between the ancients and the moderns, and proposes on several occasions to resolve this old controversy. Schlegel is convinced that his view of the problem will eliminate 'the quarrel about classical and modern aesthetic culture', that the 'entirety of ancient and modern art history will surprise through its inner coherence and completely satisfy through its absolute purposefulness' (*KFSA* 1, 354). The notion of an infinite perfectibility is essential to this solution of the problem, and it makes his text one of the first in European critical theory that deals with the struggle of the ancients and the moderns in terms of a fully developed philosophy of history.

Schlegel's view of the relationship of the moderns to the Greeks, as expounded in his 'On the Study of Greek Poetry', gains profile if we project it against Schiller's and Goethe's positions in this controversy. Schiller apparently took his stand on the side of the moderns. Goethe confirmed Schiller's modern posture, referring to the time of his first conversations with him when Schiller, as Goethe put it, preached the 'gospel of freedom', whereas Goethe did not want to see 'the rights of nature' diminished and, out of his great predilection for ancient poetry, was often unjust toward the moderns (*GOE* 16, 876–7). These discussions of their predilections led to Schiller's essay *On Naive and Sentimental Poetry* of 1794–6, which is his most important contribution to this controversy and through which he sought to settle the argument. At first, Schiller appears to share the cult of Greece of his time, when he characterizes the inception of modernity as the 'beginning of moral and aesthetic decay' (*FS* 20, 432). Yet, Schiller certainly does not summon the modern author to return to the unity with nature which, in his view, characterized the classical age, and says of this unity: 'It lies behind you, must eternally be behind you' (*FS* 20, 428). The ideal of the modern author is an infinite one that can never be fully accomplished. Yet, it is obvious to Schiller 'that the goal toward which man is striving through culture is infinitely preferable to the goal he is reaching through nature' and that there is no question 'which of the two with regard to the ultimate goal deserves preference' (*FS* 20, 438).

Comparing the type of the naive poet to that of the sentimental with reference to these concepts of nature and culture, Schiller assumes that the former merely follows 'simple nature and feeling', whereas the latter reflects upon his impressions, relates his subject to an idea, and always has to struggle with antagonistic concepts. Schiller thereby comes to the result that the naive poet 'is powerful through his art of limitation', whereas the sentimental is powerful through 'his art of infinity' (*FS* 20, 440). 'The former certainly fulfils his task', he says, 'but the task itself is a limited one; the latter does not entirely fulfil his, but the task is an infinite one' (*FS* 20, 474). Although the essay *On Naive and Sentimental Poetry* clearly reveals a preference for the modern author, we should be careful not to identify the naive poet fully with the ancient and the sentimental with the modern. To be sure, these concepts have a certain historical tinge, but Schiller introduced them as typological categories. He saw sentimental poets in the ancient world and depicted Goethe as a Greek in the sentimental age.

Goethe seems to have been unreservedly on the side of the ancients in this controversy. He never left a doubt about his great predilection for classical poetry and said in his *Maxims and Reflections*: 'When we confront ourselves with antiquity and look at it seriously with the intention of educating ourselves, we gain the impression of becoming real human beings' (*GOE* 9, 587). Yet under the influence of Schiller, Goethe also recognized the merits of the moderns and maintained that the two manners of poetizing, the naive and the sentimental, should agree to recognize each other on equal terms (*GOE* 16, 876–7). Ultimately, however, Goethe did not use the designations 'classical' and 'Romantic', 'ancient' and 'modern', as categories to distinguish historical ages, but as supratemporal characteristics to describe artistic styles, attitudes, and approaches to life and art. This is obvious in his descriptions of so-called 'fortunate talents' like Raphael, Shakespeare, or Rubens. If such an attitude receives the designation 'Greek', Goethe connects with it the aclassical and ultimately 'sentimental' demand that one should become a Greek, as in the postulate: 'Everybody should be in his way a Greek! But he should be it' (*GOE* 13, 846).

In his essay *Winckelmann and His Age*, Goethe sees the moderns as throwing themselves in every respect 'into the infinite', whereas the ancients 'felt a characteristic need to remain firmly within the pleasant confines of the beautiful world'. Most of these comparisons and confrontations seem to underscore Goethe's preference for the ancients. Ancient education resulted in a harmonious formation of all human faculties, whereas modern education emphasizes specialised talents. The moderns may be able to realize the 'extraordinary', but the ancients put the human being in the centre. Modern education has splintered the human being and accomplished a 'scarcely remediable division within the healthy human powers' (*GOE* 13, 416–19). Yet, when these comparisons extend to himself, it becomes obvious that Goethe did not see himself as a happy Greek, but put himself into the camp of the moderns. Karl Ernst Schubarth, an enthusiastic Goethe critic of that time, had compared Goethe with Shakespeare and come to the conclusion that Shakespeare was always able to hit the right point 'with supreme self-assurance, without any reasoning, reflecting, subtilization, classifying, and exponentiating', whereas Goethe, when pursuing the same goal, always had to struggle with adversities to overcome them. 'Here our friend hits the nail on the head', Goethe agreed and added: 'It is precisely where he finds me at a disadvantage compared to Shakespeare, that we are at a disadvantage compared with the ancients' (*GOE* 13, 842).

Yet the most complex philosophical position in this quarrel between the ancients and the moderns comes to light if we turn to Friedrich Schlegel's attitude as he formulated it in his essay 'On the Study of Greek Poetry'. His apparently uncompromising veneration of Greek culture has already been mentioned. In different contexts he maintains that Greek poetry was 'a general natural history of the beautiful and of art' (*KFSA* 23, 188, 204), that it provided for all ages 'valid and critical perceptions' (*KFSA* 1, 318), and that its peculiar feature was 'the most vigorous, pure, distinct, simple, and complete reproduction of general human nature' (*KFSA* 1, 276). With regard to the theory of poetry, he claimed that Greek poetry offered 'for all original concepts of taste and art a complete collection of examples so surprisingly suitable for the theoretical system as though formative nature had, so to speak, condescended herself to anticipate the desires of reason striving for knowledge' (*KFSA* 1, 370). The 'forms' of this world 'do not appear as being made or having come into existence, but as eternally present or originated by themselves' because they do not reveal 'the slightest reminiscence of labour, art, and need' (*KFSA* 1, 298). Schiller used terms like 'fever' and 'Graeco-mania' to characterize Schlegel's attitude toward the Greeks, and Rudolf Haym comments: 'Never, not even in related remarks by Wilhelm von Humboldt, Schiller, and F. A. Wolf, were the Greeks, their culture and poetry, more thoroughly elevated to the infinite'.[19]

Correspondingly, Friedrich Schlegel speaks of the works of

Greek poetry in superlatives like 'purest beauty', 'unpretentious perfection', and 'proper dignity'. These works seem to exist 'only for themselves' (*KFSA* 1, 298). In a more theoretical formulation, he designates the character of these works as a self-identity in the sense of a complete conformity with themselves (*KFSA* 1, 296). Schlegel was convinced that Greek poetry had actually reached this 'ultimate limit of natural form', this 'highest peak of free beauty'. The 'golden age' is the name for this state, he observes, and adds: 'The pleasure afforded by the works of the golden age of Greek art admits, to be sure, of an addition, but is still without any disturbance and need – *entirely self-sufficient*. I know no more appropriate name for this peak than the *highest beauty*' (*KFSA* 1, 287). In a final rounding off of this image, Schlegel adds of Greek poetry: '*Prototype of art and taste*' (*KFSA* 1, 288).

The only disturbing element in this characterization of the 'highest beauty' consists in the words 'admits, to be sure, of an addition'. With these words, Schlegel's attempt at a construction of an absolute classicism inevitably takes a turn towards a theory of modernity.[20] For if one examines the meaning of these words more closely, one soon comes to features of Greek beauty, of all beauty, which in the last analysis make any notion of classicism and every idea of a golden age impossible or allow them to be used only as marginal concepts, as ironical metaphors. In this manner, Schlegel immediately adds to his notion of the 'highest beauty': 'By no means a beauty above which a more beautiful could not be thought; but only the most comprehensive example of the unattainable idea, which here, so to speak, becomes fully visible' (*KFSA* 1, 287–8). The unattainability of the idea and the 'limits of art' are explained in terms suggesting the principle of perfectibility: 'Art is infinitely perfectible, and an absolute maximum is not possible in its continuous development, but a conditioned, relative maximum, an insurmountable fixed approximation' (*KFSA* 1, 288) – that is, a maximum for a particular period or epoch in this continuous development, an age. Works of art, in other words, can only be an example 'in which the comprehensive task of art becomes as visible as it can in a real work

of art' (*KFSA* 1, 293). Among these examples, the works of art
of the golden age of classical Greece certainly occupy a high
rank. They are '*the peak in the natural culture of beautiful art*' and
therefore for all times the '*high prototype of artistic progression*'
(ib.). Yet, this does not alter the fact that they represent not an
absolute accomplishment that could not occur in any period but
only a maximum of classical, natural culture, in other words, a
'relative maximum' (*KFSA* 1, 634), a maximum for that
period.

As becomes obvious, Schlegel makes a sharp distinction
between a natural and an artificial, artistic period in the
development of European art and attributes the natural element
entirely to the classical period, whereas the modern has become
separated from nature and is engaged in an infinite progression
of artificial, artistic development. He insisted on a clear
'opposition', an 'antithesis', or an 'antinomy' between the
classical and the modern worlds (*KFSA* 2, 188–9). In classical
antiquity, the entire cycle of art and literature had been
completed in an organic and natural development. With the
dawn of modernity, however, art had entered into an endlessly
developing process. The moderns are capable of ever new and
unimaginable achievements, but total perfection is unattainable
to them and is at best a regulative ideal. Yet these two worlds of
classicism and modernity, antithetically opposed to each other,
are nonetheless related to each other, and through their
mediation an entirely new stage in the formative process of
literature can be expected. By establishing the intrinsic difference between the historical moment of Greek antiquity and
the historical moment of modern Europe, Schlegel attempted to
prepare the way for this turning-point. This is especially obvious
in the last sections of his essay. He attempts to mediate between
the two worlds by bringing modernism into a competitive
relationship with classicism. Modern poetry is thereby placed
on a course that makes it strive towards ever higher accomplishments.

To characterize this dual tendency of the essay, one can also
say that it reveals an inner tension, a constant rhetorical
overstating, even a sense of being torn between two absolute

values, between ancient and modern poetry. Tension within the text can easily be illustrated by two sentences which seem to express absolutely opposed value judgments concerning these two worlds: 'Only in one people [the classical Greeks] did beautiful art correspond to the high dignity of its destination' (*KFSA* 1, 275) – 'The sublime destination of modern poetry is therefore nothing less than the highest goal of all poetry, the greatest that can be demanded from art and after which it can strive' (*KG5FSA* 1, 255). According to whether one puts the emphasis on the first or on the second aspect, the text can read as a plea for the ancients or the moderns. The categories designating these two opposed aspects of ancient and modern poetry are the 'objective' and the 'interesting'. This is indeed the first pair of concepts in which Schlegel delineates the difference between the ancients and the moderns. The characteristics of objective poetry are that no interest, no claims to reality are involved in it but that it represents a mere 'play' or an 'appearance (*Schein*) as universal and lawful as the most absolute truth' (*KFSA* 1, 211). The core of this appearance is the 'purely human', the 'truly divine: purest humanity' (*KFSA* 1, 279, 277). It manifests itself clearly in Homer's epics, in the lyrical poetry of the Greeks, which also has this 'tendency toward the objective' by always approaching the 'purely human' (*KFSA* 1, 363), as well as in classical tragedy, the most comprehensive expression of this human and thereby 'objective' orientation. Modern, interesting poetry, in contrast, shows a complete lack of any orientation. As a whole it appears like a huge chaos, 'an ocean of conflicting forces in which the particles of dissolved beauty, the fragments of smashed art, stir in a confused manner and in a muddy mixture' (*KFSA* 1, 223). Shortly before, Schlegel had said: 'Lack of character appears to be the only character of modern poetry, confusion the common feature of its mass, anarchy the essence of its history, and scepticism the result of its theory' (*KFSA* 1, 222). These are only first impressions, however, which Schlegel attempts to integrate with other values, such as the 'ingenious originality', the 'interesting individuality', and the 'isolated egoism' of the modern artist (*KFSA* 1, 223, 239). He thus aims at a new vision of unity for the modern age that permits it to view its poetry as a coherent whole, as the opposite pole to that of classical antiquity. He elaborates progressively the 'peculiar traits of modern poetry', distinguishing it 'from all other poetries of history in the most distinct manner' and considers it of great importance that the origin and purpose of modern poetry 'can be deduced only from a common inner principle', doubtless that of a free progression (*KFSA* 1, 225–7).

If one asks in approximately what period of time Schlegel locates this transition from a natural to an artistic type of formation, the answer must be that this was the time at which a more universal principle of culture (reason, humanity as such, freedom) replaced the former national and more particularistic interests. In one instance we read: 'The old and the new system diverge most obviously where a national religion is replaced by a universal one' (*KFSA* 1, 635). This would make Christianity the distinctive point of separation between the ancient and the modern worlds and push the beginning of modernity back to an amazingly early date. Yet, Schlegel obviously thought less about the religious and more directly about the generally human aspects of this change and considered it essential for the transition to the 'system of perfectibility' to coordinate 'morals and the state to ideas of pure reason'. He sees the beginning of the 'history of free people' at that point 'where freedom in mass has the preponderance' and 'where the entire culture of a whole mass has torn away from the tutelage of nature and risen to autonomy' (*KFSA* 1, 635). In his review of Herder's 'Letters on the Furtherance of Humanity', he assumed that this striving, manifest with the beginning of Christianity, 'to realize the absolutely perfect and infinite, was a lasting quality among the incessant change of the times and the greatest difference among peoples, of that which with the best justification can be called modern' (*KFSA* 2, 49). Later he wrote in the *Athenaeum*: 'The revolutionary desire to realize the kingdom of God on earth is the elastic point of progressive civilization and the beginning of modern history. Whatever has no relation to the kingdom of God is of strictly secondary importance' (*KFSA* 2, 201; *LF*, 193). When Schlegel actually analyzes modern poetry and speaks about its earliest representatives, the 'older moderns', in a concrete manner, however, we are in the period of Dante and Boccaccio, in the late Middle Ages. This places an enormous interval or 'intermezzo' between the earliest manifestations of modernity and the actual appearance of the modern age. Yet, Schlegel is of the opinion that a basic reformation of the human being first had to be completed before the character of modern culture could manifest itself. The new manner of feeling 'needed time' to 'become, grow, and develop, before art could direct it arbitrarily' (*KFSA* 1, 235).

Classicism, in Schlegel's notion of historical development, always remains present, however, at least in the sense of an ideal, an 'eternally present beauty'. Classicism and modernity enter into a relationship of close interaction, a rapport lacking in French, English, and all other treatments of the quarrel between the ancients and the moderns. In contrast to Schiller's concept of a constant progression in history, modernity does not separate itself from classicism, but maintains a lively relationship with the ancient world. The poorer version of modernity, one could say, is a mere separation from classicism, a mere progression. Genuine modernity has an equal relationship with classicism and is in a dynamic position to that world. This is obvious in the fact that we can relate to the models of the ancient world in a most lively 'interaction', provided that in imitating them we never pay attention to the 'letter', that is, the outer form, the historical garment, but only to their 'spirit' (*KFSA* 1, 346–7). One cannot restore the classical age by returning to a past historical time, however perfect such an age may have been. One must produce instead a timely effort. What the moderns should seek is not the restitution of classical mythology, but the creation of an up-to-date 'new mythology', not the rejuvenation of the Homeric epic as desired by Schelling and Hegel, but rather the creation of the modern novel as an expression of subjective transcendental poetry. In this sense, Greek classicism reaches up to our own age across the millenia, and Goethe in poetry (*KFSA* 1, 261) or Johannes von Müller in history (*KFSA* 1, 343) appear as the true imitators of the Greeks, as their equal partners. To take the reverse view, modernism reaches back into classical antiquity and, confronted with Euripides, looks into its own face. Schlegel says: 'In this manner, Socrates, and even further back, Pythagoras, are at the beginning of modern history, that is, the system of infinite perfectibility by daring for the first time to establish morals and the state according to ideas of pure reason' (*KFSA* 1, 636). Plato's 'poetical philosophemata' and 'philosophical poemata' appear as works of art in the modern sense (*KFSA* 1, 332). In a similar manner, the 'sublime urbanity of the Socratic muse', i.e., Socratic irony (*KFSA*, 152; *LF*, 283), can be understood as the language of the modern human being.

In these instances, Friedrich Schlegel's notion of infinite perfectibility, as he had adopted it from Condorcet's philosophy, becomes obvious. He uses this notion in his characterization of ancient poetry, where he designates the accomplishments of the Greeks as a 'relative maximum' (*KFSA* 1, 288), and in his depiction of modern poetry, when he summarizes it as 'interesting poetry'. The 'interesting' is for him a 'necessary precondition of infinite perfectibility' (*KFSA* 1, 214) simply because a highest form of the interesting or a most modern form of the modern cannot be conceived of. In a later instance, we read of the artistic, artificial character of modern culture: 'Nothing in general is as evident as the theory of perfectibility. The pure principle of reason concerning the necessary infinite perfectibility of the human race is without any difficulty' (*KFSA* 1, 263). The 'highest ugliness' is 'in the strictest sense of the word' just as impossible for Schlegel as the 'highest beauty', and the argument is in both cases the same: 'An absolute maximum of negation, or accomplished nothingness, can be given in our representation just as little as an absolute maximum of the positive; on the highest level of ugliness there is still something beautiful' (*KFSA* 1, 313). In another instance, Schlegel relates infinite perfectibility to poetry in general, deriving it from the medium of poetry, the arbitrary language of signs. He says: 'It would be most daring to posit for painting and music an ultimate limit of perfection. How much less can such a limit be determined for poetry that is not limited, either in circumference or in vigour, by any particular material?

Whose tool, the arbitrary language of signs, is human work and therefore infinitely perfectible and corruptible?' (*KFSA* 1, 294).

This theory, like no other, ruled out any attempt in Schlegel's thought to envisage an absolute classicism or an absolute work of art. His preference for Condorcet's theory of infinite perfectibility as against any idealistic notion of an infinite progress of perfection seems to be based on the fact that the goal which Condorcet envisages is independent of any preconceived notion such as the complete development of all human faculties or the perfected social and political life of human beings in a fully developed republicanism. Such a movement was truly infinite and not determined by the desires of the human subject. We have shown earlier how this notion of infinite perfectibility was transformed into Schlegel's idea of an infinitely progressive poetry.[21] Not only the unattainability but also the inconceivability of a final goal was indelibly linked for him with the dissolution of absolute classicism. In his approach to European literature, too, he departed from any excessive veneration of the ancients at the expense of the moderns. He wrote of his essay 'On the Study of Greek Poetry' at the time of its publication: 'My essay on the study of Greek poetry is a mannered prose hymn to the objective quality in poetry. The worst thing about it, it seems to me, is the complete lack of a necessary irony; and the best, the confident assumption that poetry is infinitely valuable – as if that were a settled thing' (*KFSA* 2, 147; *LF*, 143–4). He saw himself now in a 'liberal relationship to antiquity' because he was 'no longer passively and by nature' classical but could 'deliberately attune himself classically' (*KFSA* 1, xc), 'quite arbitrarily, just as one tunes an instrument, at any time and to any degree' (*KFSA* 2, 154; *LF*, 149). As he later said in the *Athenaeum*, he was able to transport himself arbitrarily 'now into this and now into that sphere, as if into another world, not merely with one's reason and imagination, but with one's whole soul; to relinquish freely first one and then another part of one's being, and confine oneself entirely to a third; to seek and find now in this, now in that individual the be-all and end-all of existence, and intentionally forget everything else' (*KFSA* 2, 185; *LF*, 177). Schlegel adds that only a mind 'which simultaneously contains within itself a plurality of minds and a whole system of persons, and in whose inner being the universe which, as they say, should germinate in every monad, has grown to fullness and maturity' is capable of this attitude (ib.). At this point, it becomes obvious that Schlegel is no longer using the classical and the modern as historical designations for epochs in European history, but essentially as categorical, transcendental, typological terms, as names for intellectual attitudes of an atemporal and ahistorical character that relate to each other in a manner of oscillation or alternation.

In A. W. Schlegel's writings, as earlier noticed,[22] the difference between ancient and modern literature appears as that of classical and romantic poetry, the old structure of two completely different worlds between which the critic attempts to mediate. This subject of A. W. Schlegel's Berlin lectures (1803–4) re-emerges in the famous and neat distinctions of his Vienna lectures of 1808 on dramatic art and literature, which, according to Goethe (*GOE*, 24, 405–6), soon travelled round the globe and mirrored the aspects and ambitions of generations of 'romantic' authors at that time. According to the first of these lectures, Greek culture and art was 'a perfect, natural education', Greek religion the 'worship of natural forces and of earthly life', and the Greek form of beauty that of a 'purified, ennobled sensuality'. The Greeks had achieved everything that could be accomplished within the structures of finiteness, and their entire art and poetry was the 'expression of the consciousness of this harmony of all forces', the 'poetics of joy' (*AWS SW* 5, 12–13). In the Greek world, the human being felt 'self-sufficient', had 'no sense of defect' and strove 'for no other perfection than what he really could attain through his own powers' (*AWS SW* 5, 15). This state of affairs changed dramatically with the introduction of Christianity, the 'guiding principle in the history of the modern peoples'. Next to Christianity, 'the Germanic line of the Nordic conquerors' brought new life into the degenerating old world and instilled a new sense of 'chivalry' as well as a 'more decorous spirit of love as an enthusiastic dedication to genuine womanliness' (*AWS*

SW 5, 14). A. W. Schlegel concludes: 'Chivalry, love, and honour are, next to religion itself, the objects of the natural poetry that poured out in the Middle Ages in incredible abundance and preceded a more artistic culture of the romantic spirit' (*AWS SW* 5, 15).

In order to capture the spirit of this modern or Romantic poetry, A. W. Schlegel proceeds to contrast it with ancient, classical poetry, saying: 'The poetry of the ancients was the poetry of possession, our poetry is that of yearning; the former stands firmly on the ground of the present, the latter sways between memory and presentiment.' He adds that in Romantic poetry not everything 'dissolves in monotonous lament nor does melancholy always have to express itself obtrusively', but admits that the mood in Romantic poetry 'will always bear traces of its origin in a nameless something' and that feeling in general has become 'more fervent, fantasy less corporeal, thought more contemplative'. Whereas the Greek ideal of humanity was 'perfect concord and symmetry of all powers, natural harmony', the moderns show an 'awareness of inner dissension, which makes such an ideal impossible'. Their poetry therefore attempts to mediate between these two worlds: 'Sensual impressions must be hallowed, as it were, through their mysterious alliance with more noble feelings; the mind, in contrast, wishes to record its presentiments and ineffable contemplation of the infinite metaphorically.' Whereas in Greek poetry and art we find an 'unconscious unity of form and content', the modern seeks a 'more intimate penetration of both' by being content with an 'aspiration toward the infinite only by approximation' (*AWS SW* 5, 17).

A. W. Schlegel's position in the face of these differences is that of a mediating critic who wants to reconcile conflicting and oppositional tendencies of taste and give all true poetry and art its due recognition (*AWS SW* 6, 159). In a practical 'application' of this principle, he refers to a wide array of works of art and says:

The Pantheon is no more different from Westminster Abbey or Saint Stephen's in Vienna than the structure of a tragedy by Sophocles from a drama by Shakespeare. The comparison of these marvels of poetry and architecture could probably be extended even further. But does our admiration of the one really compel us to disparage the other? Can we not admit that each in its own way is great and marvellous, even though the one is and should be quite different from the other? Let the example stand. We do not want to dispute anyone's preference for the one or the other. The world is vast, and many things can exist in it side by side'. (*AWS SW* 5, 11–12)

In this advocacy of mutual tolerance, the earlier notion of an interaction between the ancient and the modern, the classical and Romantic styles of literature found a less demanding, yet more conceivable and acceptable expression. It was indeed mainly in A. W. Schlegel's sense that this fundamental distinction of ancient and modern, classical and Romantic poetry found its reception in other European countries.

EXAMPLE: A. W. SCHLEGEL AND THE EARLY ROMANTIC *DAMNATIO* OF EURIPIDES

In his Berlin lectures of 1802–4 on aesthetics, A. W. Schlegel claimed that his younger brother had been the first in the modern age to discern the 'immeasurable gulf' separating Euripides from Aeschylus and Sophocles, thereby reviving after more than two thousand years the ancient assessment of the Greeks themselves (*AWS V* 1, 753). The elder Schlegel noted that certain contemporaries of Euripides felt the 'deep decline' – both in his tragic art and in the music of the time and that Aristophanes, with his unrelenting satire – had been designated by God as Euripides' 'eternal scourge'. Plato, in reproaching the poets for fostering the passionate state of mind through excessive emotionalism, also pointed to Euripides. A. W. Schlegel believed that his younger brother's observation of the profound difference between Euripides and the two other Greek tragedians was an important intuition which required detailed critical and comparative analysis for its sufficient development. By appropriating this task to himself, A. W. Schlegel inaugurated a phenomenon which we may describe as the nineteenth-century *damnatio* of Euripides. The repercussions of A. W.

Schlegel's judgment on the tragic poet are evident throughout the nineteenth century, and the early Romantic critique of Euripides came to its climax in the early writings of Nietzsche, especially in *The Birth of Tragedy from the Spirit of Music*.[23]

The condemnation of Euripides by the early German Romantics was not an extravagant and isolated moment in their critical activity, but a central event in the progressive formation of a new literary theory. Greek literature, especially classical tragedy, formed a corner-stone of this literary theory, and the evaluation of Euripides was an essential part of it.

One decisive reason for the prominence of Greek tragedy in the aesthetics of the Schlegels is their attempt to substitute a genuine form of drama for one they considered distorted. Lessing and others had sufficiently proven for Friedrich Schlegel 'that the principles of French tragedy were absolutely false, its presuppositions and conditions completely arbitrary and wrong, the apparent attempt to restore the old tragedy an entire failure, and the whole out of line and void' (*KFSA* 3, 38). Yet, the Schlegels approached tragedy not predominantly from the point of view of poetics, *ars poetica*, and rules, but from that of philosophy. They saw in Aristotle the beginning of a trend that, over the centuries, had resulted in a complete misunderstanding of tragedy. They attempted, as would be said later of Nietzsche, to restore to Greek tragedy the element of religion, which Aristotle had eliminated from it.[24] They saw tragedies as symbolic representations of the most central aspect of humanity: the struggle between man and fate, the conflict of freedom and necessity. Schiller had introduced this new view of tragedy and interpreted the message of tragedy as the victory of the moral law in spite of the protagonist's physical defeat. Similarly, for Schelling and Hegel tragedies became paradigms of an unfolding dialectic re-establishing law and order after an unintended catastrophe. Marx interpreted tragedy according to his own understanding of the dialectics of world history and saw in it the emergence of deeds and events the moment for which had not yet arrived, which had come 'too early'. It is obvious that Nietzsche's Dionysian interpretation of the message of tragedy – that 'beneath the whirl of phenomena' and the

constant destruction of phenomena, 'eternal life flows inde-
structibly' (*NIE* 1, 115; *BT*, 109–10) – is inseparable from this
sequence of philosophical interpretations of tragedy in nineteenth-century Germany. For the Schlegels, tragedy illustrates
man's conflict with fate, and the dominant aspect of tragedy is
an aesthetic one deriving its beauty from that harmony between
man and fate, drama and mythology, action and chorus which
was noted earlier. But in emphasizing this harmony as the
highest accomplishment of tragedy, the Schlegels inevitably
came to reject that poet who appeared to have lost all these
qualities, Euripides.

In his Vienna lectures on the history of ancient and modern
literature (1812), Friedrich Schlegel insisted that the chorus was
inseparable from the structure of ancient tragedy in its lyrical
thrust and nature – a feature that modern poets had come to
recognize through their imitative efforts to assimilate the
genre. Perfect harmony and an appropriate relationship between chorus and dramatic action were, therefore, the most
essential requirements for ancient tragedy. While in Sophocles
both elements were in complete harmony, Schlegel continued,
the chorus in Euripides appeared 'as if it occupied its position
only because of old right and habit, and otherwise rambled
about through the entire realm of mythology' (*KFSA* 6, 58).
Earlier in these lectures, Schlegel had defined the notions of
'clarity of reason in the arts and sciences' and a 'striving for
harmony in the order of life and the cultivation of the mind' as
the predominant features of Greek life during the second, most
brilliant period of its intellectual and aesthetic history (*KFSA*
6, 35–6).

The transgression of the basic requirements of harmony is a
recurrent theme in Friedrich Schlegel's critique of Euripides
and is by no means limited to the relationship between action
and chorus. In one of his earliest sketches on aesthetics (1795),
he claims that 'many-sidedness and facile grace in the arrangement and alternation of the means of poetry – language,
metre, style' must serve an expressive necessity; otherwise, they
testify to a 'decayed art'. In this instance, he considers Euripides
conspicuous for this type of seductive, yet false appeal (*KFSA*

16, 7). In a letter to his brother written towards the end of 1795, Schlegel observes that Euripides' 'rhythmic beauty', so praised by the ancients, was actually inferior to that of Sophocles and had gained pre-eminence only because Euripides strove for it 'in isolation' at the expense of the 'whole, which from now on was destroyed, and whose harmony was forever ruined' (*KFSA* 23, 268). Regarding their creation of characters, for example, Schlegel believes that Sophocles bestowed upon his characters as much beauty as the requirements of the whole and the conditions of art permitted, while Euripides allowed in his characters as much 'passion (*Leidenschaft*) as possible, whether noble or ignoble, without regard for the whole and the requirements of art' (*KFSA* 1, 62).

This theme of passion is as central to Friedrich Schlegel's arguments against Euripides as that of harmony. 'In his ideal, his genius, and his art, everything is present in the greatest abundance', he had said in 1794 (*KFSA* 1, 61), 'only harmony and conformity are lacking. With vigour and ease he knows how to touch and excite us, how to penetrate to the very marrow, and how to attract through an abundance of alternations. Passion, its rise and fall, especially in its impetuous eruptions, he depicts in an unrivalled fashion.' As in the case of Medea or Phaedra, 'even high-mindedness and greatness are not of an enduring nature for him, as for Sophocles, but violent manifestations of a passion, a sudden enthusiasm'. Not infrequently Euripides spoils the nobility expressed in even these impulsive outbursts because 'just as in his artistic ideals, so in his personal genius there is a lack of harmony and restraint. He does not know how to curb and control himself as an artist and is often carried away during the execution of an individual part, a favourite theme, so much so that he completely loses sight of the whole.'

One characteristic feature of Euripides' subjective and individualistic manner is strikingly obvious in his attitude as a misognynist. 'Euripides is a woman-hater', Friedrich Schlegel declared, 'and takes occasion, whenever he can, to declaim in the harshest manner against the female sex' (*KFSA* 1, 63–4). Schlegel had expressed an emancipatory point of view in some of his early essays on Greek literature.[25] But while he saw in Euripides' 'foolish and silly hatred of women' the 'animosity of the offended party' rather than the 'arrogance of an unjust oppressor' (*KFSA* 1, 115), he seems more concerned with the artistic implications of this attitude than with its social impact. He finds it amazing and unique in the history of a literature in which nothing was merely accidental and personal that Euripides gives such prominence to so individual an attitude. 'The reason for this fault lies in the character and the ideal of this poet', Schlegel claims, 'because his general anarchy quite naturally made him more lenient toward his personal peculiarities' (*KFSA* 1, 64).

Friedrich Schlegel interpreted these qualities as characteristic of Euripides' era itself: a period of transition, a descent from the Sophoclean heights of Greek poetry to an unheard-of 'aesthetic luxury' (*KFSA* 1, 60). Although their works vary in genre, modes of expression, moral and philosophical level, and the like, the main representatives of this period – Plato and Xenophon, Aristophanes and Euripides – were thought by Schlegel to possess many traits in common. He considered it unfair that the Athenians should both sense their own decline and at the same time blame and even detest poets who, like Euripides, represented and expressed this decline through tragedy (*KFSA* 1, 323). But above all, Schlegel saw the particular nature of the new style in Euripides' tragedy not as an expression of weakness and decadence, but of fullness and abundance. There are passages, he would argue, that exhaust all aesthetic patience, but even these are part of the particular beauty that Euripides has created: 'He has never elevated himself to beauty of character, but in passion he is unsurpassed' (*KFSA* 1, 63). In describing this new style – as represented in the panegyrical speeches of Lysias, in the works of Aristophanes, Euripides, and Isocrates – as one of 'luxuriant exuberance', Schlegel reminded his readers that a work of art could be 'empty' and still 'luxuriant' (*KFSA* 1, 160). 'There are many faults among the Greek poets, before which the modern ones can feel safe', he said, illustrating his point by referring to the richness of Aristophanes. 'The man in whom Aristophanes' impetuous sacrilege inspires only anger betrays not only the limitations of his reason, but also a shortcoming in his moral nature. For this poet's lawless excesses are not only seductively attractive because of their luxurious abundance of the most sumptuous life, but also captivatingly beautiful and sublime through a profusion of sparkling wit, exuberant spirit, and moral power' (*KFSA* 1, 323).

Contrary to his brother's assertion, Friedrich Schlegel did not first present this image of Euripides in his essay 'On the Study of Greek Poetry' of 1795–7, but in several earlier articles on Greek literature. In fact, the essay 'On the Study of Greek Poetry' culminates in a section that praises Sophocles' tragedy as the unsurpassed climax of its genre (*KFSA* 1, 296–301) and mentions Euripides only once, in a relatively positive manner (*KFSA* 1, 323). Schlegel's earliest published essay, 'On the Schools of Greek Poetry' (1794), presents Euripides as a decisive figure in a fourfold cyclical development of Greek poetry from

(1) 'harsh greatness' (Aeschylus), to (2) the 'highest beauty' (Sophocles), to (3) 'vigorous, yet anarchical debauchery' (Euripides), and, finally, to (4) 'exhaustion' (*KFSA* 1, 14–15).

His most vivid and sympathetic characterization of Euripides is to be found in the essay 'On Female Characters in the Greek Poets', which appeared in 1794 in the *Leipzig Monthly for Ladies* and emphasizes the 'passionate' features of Euripides' characters. Schlegel felt that Euripides excelled when his subject-matter forced him to combine passion with beauty, as in Iphigenia, and when he had to present a beautiful scene in order to touch the audience all the more profoundly, as in Agamemnon's sacrifice of his beloved daughter (*KFSA* 1, 62). Yet 'beauty of character' counts among the exceptions in this poet; 'his proper terrain was passion, whose depths he knew fully', and there is 'no richer or more moving picture of female pain than in the *Troades*' (*KFSA* 1, 63). In his *Dialogue on Poetry* (1800), Schlegel mainly reiterates his earlier ranking of the three Greek tragedians, but alters an important facet of his image of Euripides by reducing 'vigour' and 'abundance' to 'weakness' (*KFSA* 2, 293). In his Paris lectures on European literature (1803), he considers Euripides' chief merit his 'single lyrical-musical passages' and finds in this 'snatching and aiming at single beauties' an analogy to modern opera (*KFSA* 11, 81–2). His notebooks occasionally reveal quite modernistic features of Euripides. A note from 1797, for example, observes that 'Euripides is to be considered as an attempt at a synthesis of poetry and philosophy' (*KFSA* 16, 314); another, from 1803, assigns Sophocles to 'pure drama' and Euripides to the 'musical play', that is, to the 'Romantic' drama (*KFSA* 16, 516).

In his basic view of ancient tragedy, A. W. Schlegel followed his brother's opinions in declaring that Aeschylus represents 'the great and austere', Sophocles the 'harmoniously perfect', and Euripides the 'luxuriant yet disintegrated' tragic style (*AWS V* 2, 334). In his detailed treatment of Greek tragedy, he places greater emphasis on such particulars as metre, poetic diction, and theatrical practicalities than his brother had done. But above all, from the beginning of his involvement with the ancient tragedians, A. W. Schlegel makes Euripides an issue of public debate, first in Germany, especially in the literary circles of Berlin and Weimar; then, following the publication of his *Comparison between the 'Phaedra' of Racine and that of Euripides* (1808), in France; and finally, in the wake of his lectures on dramatic art and literature (1808), among literary circles across Europe.

A. W. Schlegel simplified his brother's complex and ambiguous image of Euripides to an almost entirely negative one. He actually maintained that, to acquaint oneself with the 'genuinely great style' of ancient tragedy, one can limit oneself to Aeschylus and Sophocles and simply ignore Euripides (*AWS V* 2, 351), as he himself had done in 'The Art of the Greeks', an elegy of 1799 dedicated to Goethe (*AWS SW* 2, 5–11). In the *Poetic Almanac*, which he edited with Tieck, he published an epigram entitled 'The Tragedians' (*AWS SW* 2, 35):

> Aeschylus conjures up Titans and calls down Gods;
> Sophocles graciously leads the row of heroines and heroes;
> Euripides finally, as a sophistic rhetorician, gossips at the
> market-place.

Reaction came in Karl August Böttiger's *Prolusio de Medea Euripidis*, wherein Böttiger, referring to a pathetic speech by Medea, stated that Euripides' insolent censors would not, despite all their efforts, be able to produce anything comparable. Schlegel retorted to Böttiger that this had not been the issue in his epigram and continued with a sarcastic lesson on the task of the critic (*AWS V* 2, 360). In this debate, the discussion of Euripides in Romantic Germany after the turn of the century assumed a style typical of the elder Schlegel.

In October 1801, A. W. Schlegel completed his drama *Jon*. The work was staged by Goethe in the Weimar court theatre on 2 January 1802 and by Iffland in the Berlin Theatre in May of the same year. Although it was not published until May 1803, the play was already the source of intensive debate in 1802, one of the main issues being its relationship to Euripides' *Ion*. It had by no means been A. W. Schlegel's intention simply to adapt Euripides to the modern stage. As with Goethe's approach to his subject-matter in *Iphigenia*, Schlegel wanted instead to create his own tragedy on the basis of an ancient drama. He insisted that the originality and individual poetic unity of his work arose from one central dominating idea, in spite of similarities in plot and action to the Euripidean *Ion* (*AWS SW* 9, 201). Böttiger had written a biting critique of Schlegel's *Jon* for the *Journal of Luxury and Fashion*, but Goethe intervened to prevent its appearance.[26] On 19 January 1802 the poet Christoph Martin Wieland wrote to Böttiger: 'I, for my part, keep silence about all this nuisance and am translating Euripides' *Ion* for the *Attic Museum*, and for this very year.'[27] He obviously wanted to enable readers to compare the two authors' treatment of the same subject-matter. When during the summer of 1802 similar articles appeared, A. W. Schlegel published an essay 'On the German *Jon*' in which he explained that he had 'developed the historical aspect of the fable into one of a more general interest' and created a 'heroic family portrait' (*AWS SW* 9, 207).

Since there had been so much talk about the relationship of his work to that of Euripides, A. W. Schlegel did not miss the opportunity to point out to his readers that Euripides' tragedy was unsatisfactory in the 'poetic and moral (these two coincide

here), as well as the historical realm' (*AWS SW* 9, 205). For
him, Euripides' *Ion* was based on the 'violation of moral
relationships between persons because of the sanctioning of a
continuing lie on the part of the adopted son towards his father,
and the wife towards the husband, who thereby and without
any guilt is, so to speak, expelled from the union of a confiding
love' (*AWS SW* 9, 203–4). He also emphasized the weak role of
the chorus, Mercury's awkward exposition at the beginning,
and the lame appearance of Minerva toward the end, characterizing the entire work as containing, like most of Euripides'
plays, 'beautiful parts' but 'on the whole...loosely and
miserably composed' (*AWS SW* 9, 206). His intention had been
'to do better than Euripides' (*AWS SW* 9, 200), and if his *Jon*
had accomplished its goal, then it would itself provide a critique
of the Euripidean *Ion* (*AWS V* 2, 377). Aristophanes had given
us all that could be said about the 'deep corruption and inner
wretchedness of that poet', Schlegel thought, but had been
misunderstood because his comedies had been taken as 'mere
farces and pasquilian mischief' (*AWS SW* 9, 203).

The opportunity for a comprehensive evaluation of Euripides
did not arise until 1801, when A. W. Schlegel began his lectures
on aesthetics in Berlin. The second cycle of these lectures,
presented in the winter of 1802–3, contained a comprehensive
section on Greek tragedy. Although these lectures were widely
attended by the public and parts of them were circulated in
manuscript form,[28] they remained unpublished until 1884,[29]
when they had already become a historical document. But A.
W. Schlegel fully integrated the section on the Greek tragedians
into his lectures on dramatic art and literature delivered in
Vienna in 1808, which subsequently appeared in four German
editions (1809, 1816, 1845, 1846), and numerous translations
appeared into almost every European language, including an
English version by John Black that was distributed in the
United States.[30] To understand Schlegel's image of Euripides
fully, one should begin with his initial conception of the
tragedian, as manifest in the Berlin lectures of 1802–3.

After a positive characterization of Aeschylus and Sophocles,
in which Sophocles' *Oedipus at Colonus* appears as the *non plus ultra*

of Greek tragedy, A. W. Schlegel declares that Euripides had 'not only destroyed the exterior order of tragedy, but also missed its entire meaning' (*AWS V* 1, 762). Anticipating Nietzsche's definition of literary *décadence* as an insurrection of the parts against the whole (*NIE* 6, 27; *BT*, 170), he sees in Euripides 'the magnificent formation of tragedy hurrying towards its dissolution' and declares:

If works of art are to be considered as organized wholes, then this insurrection of the individual parts against the whole is precisely what in the organic world is decomposition. It is all the more hideous and disgusting, the nobler the structure that is now being destroyed by it, and in the case of this most excellent of all poetic genres, must inspire the greatest repugnance. Yet most human beings are not as susceptible to this spiritual decomposition as to the physical one. (*AWS V* 1, 752)

In the first place, Euripides abandoned the idea of fate. To be sure, fate appears frequently in his works, but in a superficial, merely conventional manner and does not create a sense of a genuine conflict between human freedom and fateful necessity (*AWS V* 1, 747). Euripides' chorus no longer has any structural interrelationship with the action and has become instead an non-essential, episodic ornament. The great freedom in the treatment of myth, which was one of the privileges of tragic art, has in Euripides become 'capricious arbitrariness' (*AWS V* 1, 750); because he overthrew everything familiar and habitual, he was compelled to introduce prologues reporting the circumstances and foretelling the development to come. These prologues make the beginnings of Euripidean tragedies 'very monotonous' and aesthetically awkward (ib.). The trochaic tetrameter, used by Sophocles whenever he wanted to express a 'sudden passionate motion', appears in Euripides much more frequently. This 'luxuriant versification' transformed 'ancient severity into irregularity' (*AWS V* 1, 752).

Another basic alteration A. W. Schlegel sees in Euripides is that he no longer believed in the gods in the simple manner of the people and, as an artist, took every opportunity to introduce allegorical interpretations that revealed how ambiguous his piety actually was. He had passed through the school of the philosophers – not through the Socratic one, as many believed, but through that of Anaxagoras – and enjoyed the friendship of Socrates (*AWS V* I, 748). This philosophical background manifests itself in the 'vanity' of Euripides' constant allusions to philosophical and moral pronouncements (*AWS V* I, 749). These occasionally exhibit a dubious morality, as in Hippolytus' apology for perjury (*Hipp.* 612), or Eteocles' defence of injustice committed in the pursuit of power (*Phoen.* 524–5), frequently quoted by Caesar as a pragmatic basis for getting things done in government (ib.). Indeed, immoral ideas not infrequently gain the upper hand in Euripides' plays, and lies and other mischief are occasionally excused because of underlying noble motivations. Moreover, like his brother, A. W. Schlegel observes that Euripides was a woman-hater, and considers his many references to the inferiority and unreliability of the female sex to be a further aesthetic failure (*AWS V* I, 750).

A. W. Schlegel shared his brother's view that passion and passionate exchange were the main characteristics of Euripidean tragedy, but gave it a much less favourable interpretation than Friedrich Schlegel had done. He felt that many critics had misunderstood Aristotle's reason for calling Euripides the most tragic of all ancient poets.[31] Aristotle was, in fact, simply referring to Euripides' mastery of the art of exciting the passions (*AWS V* I, 747). If the purpose of tragedy was indeed to purge the passions through the arousal of terror and pity, some pieces of Euripides certainly offer this potential. But we should also remember Plato's complaint that the mimetic poets exposed their audience to the power of the passions and made them emotionally self-indulgent by constant use of exaggerated and melting lamentations.[32] A. W. Schlegel was convinced, as we noted earlier, that Euripides, the most popular tragedian of the time, was the immediate target of Plato's attack (*AWS V* I, 747). He declares: 'With luxuriant softness he lavished "material" attractions which captivate only the exterior sense' (*AWS V* I, 748). Euripides never missed an opportunity to allow his characters to indulge in animated but useless fervour. His old people forever lament the inconvenience of age, and by exposing his characters' weaknesses and debilities, expressed in naïve, involuntary declarations, he appealed to the low and common in human nature. In using the term 'material', Schlegel adopts an expression employed by Winckelmann with the meaning 'sensual' and 'low' (ib.). Euripides, for the first time, had made love the main subject of his dramas – the wild passion of a Medea or the unnatural desire of a Phaedra (*AWS V* 1, 750). Whenever he had an opportunity, Euripides pursued whatever was touching, and for that reason not only sacrificed decency, but also abandoned coherence and harmony, so that some of his dramas seem to have been tossed together by the wind. A. W. Schlegel's characterization of Euripides does not, however, conclude on this entirely negative note. The unevenness of the poet also has some virtue. Euripides is especially good in depicting sick, lost, and passionate souls, and is truly excellent with subjects requiring emotion along with moral beauty, as with, for example, Alcestis and Iphigenia. Only a few of his dramas are wholly without truly beautiful parts (*AWS V* 1, 753). Yet it is clear that A. W. Schlegel did not see the excellence of Euripides, as his brother did, from the point of view of a modern, progressive philosophy of history, but from a conservative perspective in which literature is judged according to pre-existent models.

A. W. Schlegel's Berlin lectures on tragedy included a comparison of Aeschylus' *Choephoroe*, Sophocles' *Electra*, and Euripides' *Electra* (*AWS V* 1, 754–67) that was later incorporated as a separate chapter into his Vienna lectures on dramatic art and literature (*AWS SW* 5, 147–62). The purpose of this section was to 'bring into the clearest light', by way of a 'parallel between three plays on the same subject', the relationship of Euripides to his 'great predecessors'. The result is predictably unfavourable to Euripides. Aeschylus approached the 'terrifying aspect' of his subject and transposed it into the 'realm of the dark gods'. Sophocles lent it a 'marvellous organization' and concentrated the main interest on Electra, thus giving the entire subject a new twist. In spite of the horrible deed, we sense a 'heavenly serenity' and the 'fresh air of life and youth' in Sophocles' version. Euripides, however, presents us with a 'rare example of poetic senselessness'. Why, for instance, does Orestes tease his sister so long without making himself known to her? In his treatment, the event is no longer a tragedy, but merely a 'family portrait in the modern sense of the word' (*AWS V* 1, 761–2).

The 'parallel', as a literary genre, was favoured by the Schlegel brothers because it permitted them to point out excellence or faults in concrete fashion. This form of critical approach owes much to the *Bioi paralleloi* of Plutarch and had become popular in the *querelle des anciens et des modernes* (with Perrault, for example) because it could be used to defend the modern position. The most famous of such 'parallels' by the Schlegels is surely A. W. Schlegel's comparison of the *Phaedra*s of Racine and Euripides, published in French in 1807.[33] As he wrote to the Countess Luise von Voss on 20 June 1807, he had just finished 'something anti-French on Racine's *Phaedra*', which was being printed in Paris and would certainly bring down upon himself all the *beaux esprits* of that city.[34] Indeed, by devaluating through this 'parallel' one of the *chefs-d'œuvre* of the French classicistic theatre, A. W. Schlegel soon became the target of the leading newspapers in France.[35] One critic called him the 'Domitian of French literature, who desired to knock it down with one single stroke' (*AWS SW* 7, 26). But Goethe greatly appreciated the *Comparaison*,[36] and Madame de Staël was also an admirer.

Without going into every detail of a rich book – one that secured for him a pre-eminence in European literary criticism – we can say briefly that A. W. Schlegel carried out his comparison in three main steps. He first showed that, contrary to the assumptions of the classicistic theory, Greek and French tragedy are diametrically opposed (*AWS SW* 14, 336). He then proceeded to prove in a detailed analysis that, in order to write a tragedy according to the prerequisites of French *goût*, Racine had to make a considerable shift in the focus of the drama so as to minimize tragic necessity and fatality; he had, furthermore, to strip from the main characters that 'ideal beauty' which constitutes the charm of the masterpieces of classical antiquity and seems to introduce us to a race of nobler mortals who are almost divine (*AWS SW* 14, 378). Finally, A. W. Schlegel inquired into the nature and goal of tragedy in general, and into the difference between ancient and modern tragedy; on this basis he arrived at the goal of the entire undertaking, a conclusive depreciation of Racine in favour of Euripides.

Arguing from the viewpoint of the poetic and aesthetic principles of early German Romanticism, Schlegel asserted – not without some arrogance – that knowledge of Greek tragedy had progressed since the days of the classicistic critics (*AWS SW* 14, 335) and could no longer be based on Aristotle, who had shown little understanding of it. With some irony, he admits that Racine was certainly the most able representative of the French theatre, uniting in the cultivation of his mind the most salient and refined traits of the age of Louis XIV, whereas Euripides, despite his capacity for 'ravishing beauty', was most uneven in his art and already manifested the 'degeneration' of Greek tragedy (*AWS SW* 14, 337–8). Moreover, A. W. Schlegel did not question the 'inimitable beauties of poetic and harmonious diction' in Racine (*AWS SW* 14, 334) – indeed, he repeatedly mentioned his liking for them. But in fact, a quite negative evaluation of Racine's poetic language emerges from his comparison of Racine's 'pompous, overcharged, and exaggerated declamations' with the 'exact, circumstantial, and thereby picturesque narration in a noble but simple style that is supposed to be the natural language of tragic characters'. In Euripides 'there is nothing too much. Everything seems to indicate how this inevitable misfortune has occurred' (*AWS SW* 14, 370–1).

The assumption of the French classicists that their theatre (and their tragedy especially) rested on the same principles as that of the Greeks, and that it reflected a continuation – although at an infinitely higher level of perfection – of ancient drama, A. W. Schlegel dismissed as mere illusion (*AWS SW* 14, 335). In a later section, he attempted a definition that ironically summarized the main prerequisites of tragedy according to the classicistic theory: 'serious representation, in dialogue form and elevated style, of one action, completed, and capable of inspiring terror and pity' (*AWS SW* 14, 385–6). We have seen that the Schlegels no longer judged tragedy according to the rules of a 'poetics', but from a philosophical perspective that allowed them to inquire into the innermost metaphysical principle underlying the tragic fiction. This principle was for them 'fatality' in Greek tragedy, and 'providence' in modern tragedy (*AWS SW* 14, 388). Since modern authors perceive the moral relationships and destinies of man in a fashion opposite to that of the ancients, A. W. Schlegel argued, it is not astonishing that, in imitating classical tragedy, they attached themselves 'more to the form than to the base on which this superb edifice rests'. Most frequently, however, when they crafted their fiction, they simply 'arranged it in the common frame of five acts, and while observing the unities of time, space, and the other theatrical conventions, they believed they had fulfilled their task without troubling themselves with any ulterior goal' (*AWS SW* 14, 392). Another feature sharply distinguishing ancient from modern tragedy was for Schlegel the preponderance of love as the dominant passion on the modern stage. Aeschylus and Sophocles excluded love almost entirely from their drama because it was tragedy's task to allow the dignity of human nature to appear, while love was considered a passion man shared with animals (*AWS SW* 14, 339). A. W. Schlegel was, of course, aware of the refinement of the concept of love during the development of Western literature, and was himself a pioneer in the discovery of the Provençal literature of the Middle Ages.[37] Yet he insisted that, in order to elevate the particular drama of Euripides to its tragic heights, the poet needed an 'irresistible fatality' – in this case, the incestuous love of Phaedra for her stepson Hippolytus, with its catastrophic result. It was therefore imperative for the dignity and effect of tragedy to keep the horror of incest ever-present in the imagination of the spectator: 'in this regard, moral and aesthetic needs coincided' (*AWS SW* 14, 339–40).

The shift of focus in Racine's tragedy, and his consequent neglect of the element of necessity, manifests itself for A. W. Schlegel first in the title and the role accorded to the main characters. Euripides focused his whole composition on the virtue of the young hero, while Phaedra was merely the instrument of the action: thus the title, *Hippolytus*. Racine, on the contrary, presented Hippolytus as 'effaced and pale', and

lent his heroine considerable graces and seductive qualities in
spite of her 'monstrous aberration'. Although his drama was
entitled *Phaedra and Hippolytus* in the first production, the second
name was later dropped, with good reason (*AWS SW* 14,
340–1). Euripides' Phaedra possesses the greatest simplicity and
is a completely consistent character, mourning the evils of
human life and revealing strains of lyrical beauty when she
abandons herself to the wanderings of her imagination (*AWS
SW* 14, 341–2). Racine's Phèdre, in spite of her rhetorical *élan*,
appears to Schlegel 'arid and meagre'. Yet the major fault of
the French version lies in Racine's attempt to avoid as much as
possible the idea that Phaedra's passion is an incestuous one
(*AWS SW* 14, 344). 'The frenzy of passion', he says, 'resembles
the exaltation of virtue, in that it cancels out calculations of
personal interest and makes one defy all dangers and sacrifice all
advantages. One therefore forgives a human being misled by a
passion that causes misfortune to others' (*AWS SW* 14, 347).
Towards the end of her tragedy, the French Phèdre shows fear,
whereas the Greek Phaedra has nothing to lose: 'She draws
Hippolytus along into the abyss into which she has first thrown
herself' (*AWS SW* 14, 355).

A. W. Schlegel is especially startled by Racine's alleged
inability to recognize Hippolytus' true character. The French
author's muse was 'la galantérie', and he therefore invested all
his poetic energy in depicting an 'affectionate woman', leaving
Hippolytus rather 'insignificant', in effect highlighting one
character at the expense of another (*AWS SW* 14, 358–9). The
Hippolytus of Euripides possesses the 'austere purity of a
virginal soul', comparable to a figure like the Belvedere Apollo.
Only such a figure, with his 'imperturbable calm' and devotion
to the goddess Diana, could provide an appropriate contrast to
the aberrations of Phaedra's voluptuous passion (*AWS SW* 14,
364–5). Similarly, according to A. W. Schlegel, Racine mis-
rendered the character of Theseus by presenting the first
lawgiver of Athens as a philandering vagabond, whereas in
Euripides the venerable hero maintains his dignity as husband
and father even in the most extreme moments (*AWS SW* 14,
371–8). 'In poetry as well as in the sculpture of the ancients,

there reigns, even in the most violent situations, a certain moderation derived from magnanimity. These energetic souls, a great expert in antiquity [Winckelmann] once said, resembled the sea, the bottom of which always remains calm, although the surface is agitated by tempests' (*AWS SW* 14, 366).

In short, A. W. Schlegel wanted to demonstrate through this comparison the complete disparity of ancient tragedy and French *tragédie classique*, with its demands of verisimilitude and 'poetic justice' based on the standards of the seventeenth century during the age of Louis XIV. He considered the restriction of the action to one single day an actual violence of probability: 'I am therefore asking whether it is not offensive to all verisimilitude if one represents to us human actions of the highest importance punished and recompensed, in such a short space of time?' (*AWS SW* 14, 380). If one inquires into the basis for our satisfaction and our sympathy with the violent and painful actions represented in tragedy, he argued, one discovers that it is 'the feeling of the dignity of human nature awakened in us by grand models, or the trace of a supernatural order imprinted and somehow mysteriously revealed in the apparently irregular course of events, or the reunion of these two causes' (*AWS SW* 14, 384). Seneca had said that a great man fighting against adversity was a spectacle worthy of gods (*AWS SW* 14, 385). If one questions further the role of destiny and adversity in the fiction of the tragic poets, one must conclude that in Greek tragedy it has a deeply religious cause, in 'fatality' – not in the sense of arbitrary decisions by the gods, but that fatality which reigns even over the gods (*AWS SW* 14, 387).

At the time of the appearance of his *Comparaison*, A. W. Schlegel had entered a religious phase. He had become acutely aware that such fatality stood in flagrant opposition to the Christian belief in a providence that seemed to cancel the possibility of genuine tragedy (*AWS SW* 14, 388). But his sense of the impenetrability of providence had exposed a new basis for tragedy in the apparently checkered order of things in this world. His recent discovery of Calderón as the foremost Christian tragedian had prompted his translations of selections from this Christian style of tragedy in his volumes of 1803 entitled, *Spanish Theatre*,[38] and he discussed its character in an essay of the same year.[39] A third tragic system appeared to be represented by Shakespeare, most remarkably in his *Hamlet*. Schlegel called this 'philosophical tragedy', or the tragedy of speculation, of 'perpetual, unending reflection on the purpose of human existence – a reflection whose Gordian knot is finally cut by death' (*AWS SW* 14, 393–4).

Although Greek tragedy was for A. W. Schlegel based on an irreconcilable and unyielding conflict between 'moral liberty' and 'fatal necessity', he saw the idea of a reconciling providence foreshadowed in at least some of the ancient works. To be sure, terror dominates in the tragedy of Aeschylus; his *Agamemnon*, *Choephoroe*, and *Eumenides* constitute a single chain of vengeance. Yet, this sequence of revenge comes to an end under the influence of divine wisdom, represented by Minerva (*AWS SW* 14, 389–90). The rigorous power of fatality is even more remarkable in Sophocles, whose Oedipus is cast from the height of a glorious life into disgrace and frightful desperation; but at the end of his life, embraced by the tenderness of his daughters, he finds a haven of peace. The tomb of a man from whom one would have turned away during his life becomes a blessing to the land that preserves it (*AWS SW* 14, 391). Euripides, from this religious point of view, offers a double face. On the one hand, he respects the religion that protects him; but on the other, he exhibits the philosophical pretensions of a sophist. He gives preference to tenderness and sensibility, searches for brilliant effects and sacrifices the unity of the whole for the sake of the fascinating parts. And yet, Schlegel admits, 'beyond all these faults, he is gifted with an admirable facility and an eminently amiable and seductive genius' (*AWS SW* 14, 391).

In addition to this remarkable appreciation of Euripides' poetic qualities, A. W. Schlegel even came to recognize the 'religious' and metaphysical aspect of *Hippolytus*. For here, no human foresight can avert the fatality of the drama. Phaedra is the victim of a fatal hatred on the part of Aphrodite, and Hippolytus dies as the result of her eternal rivalry with Artemis, the object of Hippolytus' devotion (*AWS SW* 14, 395–6). The scene in which Artemis approaches the dying Hippolytus represents the highest manifestation of human dignity in the reconciliation between father and son, a scene which 'alleviates hard fatality as much as was possible'. Here Artemis reveals to Hippolytus and to Theseus the true cause of the misfortune that has destroyed Phaedra and Hippolytus, as well as Theseus. Of the dialogue of these three characters Schlegel says: 'I know of nothing at all, either in ancient or in modern tragedy, that is more touching' (*AWS SW* 14, 402–3). To pay tribute to the poetic genius of Euripides and to give his French readers some flavour of its beauty, he translated the entire scene into French (*AWS SW* 14, 398–402).

It should be clear that A. W. Schlegel's image of Euripides was by no means as one-sidedly negative as is often claimed, but showed a remarkable understanding of his poetic qualities. But unlike his brother, who had also perceived Euripides' departure from the classical standard while viewing him from the perspective of a progressive conception of literary history, A. W. Schlegel had the habit, as Heine put it, of 'always whipping the back of a younger poet with the laurel-branch of the older one' (*HEI* 3, 415). He was not able to integrate the two aspects of Euripides into one unified image; his evaluation remained ambivalent and unreconciled. When he integrated the predominantly negative sections on Euripides from his earlier Berlin lectures into his lectures on dramatic art and literature, however, he realized that they would appear to conflict with the favourable judgments of the *Comparaison* and felt that he could not 'arbitrarily change measure and weight' (*AWS SW* 5, 132). He tried to solve the problem by stating that, viewed independently 'without consideration of his predecessors', Euripides deserved the highest praise, but serious blame when seen in the context of poetic development: 'Of few authors can one truthfully say so much good and bad.' Similarly, his *œuvre* contained, for Schlegel, this double aspect: 'sometimes he has enchantingly beautiful passages; in other places he sinks into real vulgarity' (*AWS SW* 5, 131–2). With this brief qualification, Schlegel proceeded once more to demonstrate how Euripides brought about the collapse of Greek tragedy. He did not go beyond the essence of his Berlin lectures but simply rounded out his presentation, raising it to that level of style for which the lectures on dramatic art and literature have become famous.

It was in the four editions of this work and its many translations that Schlegel's image of Euripides travelled around the world, exerting considerable influence on classical scholarship in Germany and beyond. Most importantly, Schlegel's image of Euripides had a decisive influence on the philosophy of tragedy that forms the intellectual background for Nietzsche's first major work, *The Birth of Tragedy*. Schelling's lectures on the philosophy of art (1803–4) follow Schlegel's Berlin lectures in their discussion of tragedy, presenting Euripides as 'separated' from his two predecessors because of the 'material' motivations in his arousal of our sympathies, his manipulation of myth, and his introduction of prologues. He is great in depicting passion, not in presenting beauty (*FWJS* 5, 708–11; *PA*, 261–3). Schelling's discussion is little more than a condensed and superficial version of A. W. Schlegel's ideas, which are themselves a summary of what Friedrich Schlegel had written. In Hegel's lectures on aesthetics it is again Euripides who first attempted to make his appeal through 'subjective compassion' and departed from the 'rounded plasticity' of the earlier characters in Greek tragedy (*HEG* 15, 546, 562). In his *Lectures on the History of Philosophy*, Hegel sees in this trend the first symptoms of the 'principle of decay' (*HEG* 12, 318).

Even Friedrich Schlegel, when he delivered the lecture courses of his own later period, came quite close to his brother's views on Euripides. In his lectures on the history of ancient and modern literature (1812), he maintained a high opinion of Aristophanes, for whom, as for the tragic poets, he had been a pioneering champion in European literary criticism. Yet, he now felt that the 'abundance of ingenious invention and comic wit' in the work of Aristophanes was closer to the 'grand style of the serious poets' than to the 'rhetorical softness and sentimental property' of a Euripides (*KFSA* 6, 42), and he noted with pleasure that when Aristophanes, as a comic poet, lashed out against the tragic poets, he attacked Euripides relentlessly but treated Sophocles with 'noticeable consideration, even with a deeply felt respect' (*KFSA* 6, 43). In his lectures on the philosophy of history, delivered in 1828 shortly before his death, Friedrich Schlegel spoke with emotion about the high rank of the 'ideal of beauty, in character and noble disposition' that marked the golden age of Greek poetry, with which his own studies in the humanities began:

No nation has been able to attain the charm and grace of Homer, the sublimity of Aeschylus, and the beautiful nobility of Sophocles. Yet perhaps it is wrong even to strive for this, because the truly beautiful and grand can never be attained by way of imitation. Euripides, however, who fully belongs to a period dominated by rhetoric, will only be included with his predecessors by those who are incapable of comprehending and appreciating the grand spirit in all its majesty. (*KFSA* 9, 187)

Nietzsche was probably ignorant of the opinions of these critics when he first took up the theme of Euripides and Greek tragedy and gave it a new impulse. But in time, A. W. Schlegel's work became known to Nietzsche not only through his teacher Friedrich Wilhelm Ritschl, A. W. Schlegel's colleague at Bonn, but also through his own studies when he began preparations for *The Birth of Tragedy*.[40]

CHAPTER 3

The theory of Romantic poetry

With his move to Jena in August 1796, Friedrich Schlegel's interests came to focus more and more on modern and contemporary literature, as well as on the philosophy of his time. He was still working on his *History of the Poetry of the Greeks and the Romans* and spent part of the winter with F. A. Wolf in Halle to bring the initial sections of this work into their final shape. Yet, after the first volume appeared in 1798, he actually abandoned this project, which had served as the starting-point for his search into the nature of poetry. Instead he composed the grand essays of these years (1796–8), intense studies of Jacobi, Forster, Lessing, and Goethe (*KFSA* 2, 57–146). Their common theme can be described as a particular type of writing that has left behind the habitual distinctions between poetry and prose, science and art, literature and philosophy. The writers discussed, all great literary authors themselves, were equally prominent in philosophy and the theoretical discussion of issues of the modern world. Although strongly bound in their mode of expression to drama, lyric poetry, the novel, or the philosophical treatise, they represent in large sections of their literary production what Schlegel at that time considered the modern bourgeois prose writer. Since their mode of viewing the world was no longer the absolute understanding of the traditional philosopher nor the holistic manner of the older poets, nothing appeared to be more appropriate than to expound their ideas and their art of writing in the form of the essay, and thereby initiating a genre projected in Friedrich Schlegel's notebooks as the new 'German essay' (*KFSA* 18, 219). He also included Kant in this type of writing by dealing with the philosopher's 'popular' texts, such as *On Eternal Peace*, and discussing themes like universal republicanism and the world republic within and beyond the Kantian models of thought (*KFSA* 7, 11–25). Above all, Schlegel began a new style of fragmentary writing when he published a collection of 127 'Critical Fragments' after his first sojourn in Jena in the late summer of 1797. Considering the great variety of topics raised in them, it would be difficult to single out one overriding theme. One question, however, was asked with a particular persistency in these fragments, and it concerns what is most meritorious in contemporary poetry and criticism (e.g., *KFSA* 2, 162).

The framework for this shift to modern and contemporary issues is still the former interrelationship of the classical and Romantic styles, of ancient and modern literature. In his fragment from the *Athenaeum* on Romantic poetry as a 'progressive universal poetry', Friedrich Schlegel describes the progressive course of modern literature as one of an 'infinitely increasing classicism' (*KFSA* 2, 183; *LF*, 175). In the 'Essay on the Different Styles in Goethe's Early and Later Works' from his *Dialogue on Poetry*, he presents the ultimate goal of all literature as 'the harmony of the classical with the Romantic' (*KFSA* 2, 346; *DP*, 112). During the ensuing discussion of the course of literature in the modern world of infinite perfectibility, one of the conversation partners reminds the others of the importance of the ancient prototype, that is, of classical literature, saying: 'Do not forget the model (*Vorbild*) which is so essential for orienting ourselves in the present and at the same time constantly reminds us to rise up to the past in order to work toward a better future' (*KFSA* 2, 350; *DP*, 116). In other instances, however, the emphasis on modernism and Romanticism is so strong that the impact of classical antiquity is no longer felt. The fragment on Romantic poetry as a progressive universal poetry, for instance, concludes with the statement: 'The Romantic kind of poetry is the only one that is more than a kind, that is, as it were, poetry itself; for in a certain sense all poetry is or should be Romantic' (*KFSA* 2, 183; *LF*, 175–6). On other occasions, the former oscillation between Romanticism and classicism, modernity and antiquity, transforms itself into different modes of intellectual inter- and counteractions, such as infinity and limitation, exuberance and restraint, self-creation and self-annihilation. After the union of the early Romantics in Jena had begun in 1796, the main accomplishment in theory formation clearly manifests itself in the realm of modern or Romantic literature and also includes an intensive historical exploration of the neglected Romantic tradition of European literature.

A. W. Schlegel's critical interests had consistently taken modern, Romantic literature as their starting-point, especially Dante and Shakespeare. His move to Jena coincided with the inception of his new metrical translation of Shakespeare. In the spring of 1797, his German versions of *Romeo and Juliet* and the *Midsummer Night's Dream* appeared, followed by seven more volumes and sixteen additional dramas by 1801. Soon after settling in Jena, he became one of the most influential and prolific contributors to the *ALZ*, writing about 300 reviews of the most prominent literary publications by 1800. 'What an army!' Dorothea exclaimed to Schleiermacher when A. W. Schlegel published the list of these anonymous contributions in order most effectively to stifle certain rumours spread by the editors of this journal about the alleged lack of significance of his reviews. The list contained comprehensive critical essays on Goethe's *Hermann and Dorothea*, on J. H. Voß's German translation of Homer, on Schiller's *Horae*, and on Herder's *Terpsichore*. Another recurrent topic in these reviews is the practice and theory of literary translation. Shortly after his arrival in Jena, A. W. Schlegel was appointed professor of philosophy at the university, and he offered a number of courses on literary and critical subjects. The most prominent among them was a course throughout the academic year of 1798–9 entitled on 'The Philosophical Doctrine of Art', one of the first comprehensive treatments of aesthetics in Germany, in which Schlegel further explored his particular approach to poetry with reference to phenomena such as language, rhythm, and mythology, earlier developed in his 'Letters on Poetry, Metre, and Language' in Schiller's *Horae* (1797).

The main literary event after Friedrich Schlegel's move to

Berlin was the foundation of the periodical *Athenaeum* in 1798, which was coedited by August Wilhelm and Friedrich Schlegel and became the most conspicuous publication of the early Romantics in the field of theory and criticism.[1] The periodical existed for three years, until 1800, and its three volumes contain essays, fragments, fictitious dialogues, advertisements, letters, announcements, and reviews – examples of the most imaginative and versatile ways of communication, of 'configurated thought'. Among these various contributions, the collection of 451 fragments, known as *Athenaeum* fragments, and Friedrich Schlegel's *Dialogue on Poetry* are perhaps the most important for the formation of early Romantic theory. The bulk of the fragments derives from Friedrich Schlegel, but other members of the group, like his brother and Schleiermacher, also contributed a smaller number to them. Novalis published his own collection of fragments in the *Athenaeum*, which bears the poetic title of *Pollen* (*Blütenstaub*), and Friedrich Schlegel added a further series in the third volume with the title *Ideas*. His *Dialogue on Poetry* has four sections around which the conversations are grouped: 'Epochs of Poetry', a brief survey of the history of poetry in the West; 'Speech on Mythology', an animated summons to create a new mythology; 'Letter on the Novel', a discussion of the Romantic style in the context of the novel; and 'Essay on the Different Styles in Goethe's Early and Later Works'. These texts are often considered independently, but they actually form part of the context of the entire *Dialogue*. One can also see in this *Dialogue* a re-enactment of conversations among the early Romantic group at Jena.

TRANSCENDENTAL POETRY AND DOUBLE REFLECTION

Even Friedrich Schlegl's classical studies of this period assumed a tendency toward the modern era, or at least contributed considerably to the emerging theory of modern or Romantic poetry. While still in Dresden, he had agreed to contribute pieces on rhetoricians of the late antiquity to Wieland's *Attic Museum*. This periodical pursued the purpose of acquainting its readers with masterpieces of Greek poetry, philosophy, and rhetoric, and can be seen as an expression of the manifold humanistic tendencies of that time. Wieland obviously wanted to take advantage of Friedrich Schlegel's growing reputation as a classical scholar, whereas the young critic seems to have accepted the rather tedious task of translating and commenting on old rhetoricians in order to acquaint himself with unusual pieces of intellectual and critical history. Wieland had first asked him for a translation of a funeral oration, an *epitaphios*, by Lysias, the third of the Attic orators. Schlegel completed this task by supplying an introduction to the oration as well as a translation of it, followed by a critical judgment, a translation of an additional speech by Lysias (this time a fiery polemic delivered at an Olympic festival against the tyrant Dionysius of Sicily), and then a final commentary (*KFSA* 1, 133–68).

Wieland and his coeditor Karl August Böttiger were delighted by such a meticulous display of classical scholarship, and this gave Schlegel the opportunity to propose as his next venture into the field something more to his own taste, that is, the translation of a literary evaluation, a piece of criticism, an 'artistic judgment'. The subject of this evaluation was Isocrates, who, as the fourth of the ten Attic orators, was a contemporary of Sophists like Gorgias and Prodicus, an acquaintance of Socrates, and is known to us from the ending of Plato's *Phaedrus*. The author of the judgment, however, was one of Schlegel's favourite rhetoricians, Dionysius of Halicarnassus (30–8 B.C.), author of a treatise on the composition of words (*De compositione verborum, Peri syntheseos onomaton*), on the art of how to produce beautiful prose. Whereas the Lysias text dealt with a goal-oriented speech, a funeral oration, that is, a lower type of functional rhetoric, the one by Dionysius expounded an aesthetic judgment on Isocrates, one of the finest rhetoricians of classical antiquity. It was itself written in the high style of rhetoric and non-functional speech, and treated a subject which, although written in prose, nevertheless had all the qualities of a poem, a *poema*.

Dionysius had an eye for such qualities and sharpened Schlegel's sense for the art of beautiful prose as written by modern prose writers such as Jacobi, Forster, Lessing, Kant, and

Goethe. A. W. Schlegel showed a similar interest in Dionysius of
Halicarnassus and dealt with him in his lectures on literature
and art (*AWS V* i, 214–15). Guided by this rhetorician of the
late antiquity, the Schlegels undermined one of the main
principles of the classicistic *ars poetica*; this is difficult for us to
notice because their position has since become common opinion.
Unlike the classicists, they came to recognize works of prose, like
the novel, or rhetorical products, like the epigram, the essay, the
speech, and even certain writings in philosophy and history, as
poetry in the genuine sense of the word. In his *Epistola ad
Pompeium*, Dionysius had designated works by Herodotus and
Thucydides as *poemata*, as poems. In his book entitled *The
Composition of Words*, he had pointed out the deep kinship
between prose rhythm and poetic metre, and observed that
certain figures in the Hellenic art of prose related to rhyme in a
manner similar to the relationship between the prosaic numerus
(rhythmic euphony of free speech) and poetic metre (*KFSA* i,
185, 197). Dionysius was also the originator of comparisons
between works of rhetoric and the plastic art of Polycleitus and
Phidias (*KFSA* i, 172). He thought that Plato's dialogues and
the writings of Isocrates 'were not like written ones but
resembled the hollowed out and profiled work of a sculptor'.
Friedrich Schlegel wanted to improve on Dionysius' statement
by maintaining that it was as if Isocrates' writings were 'carved
and rounded out with chisel and file' (*KFSA* i, 196).[2]

These views were of great importance for the early Romantic
conception of literature, and contributed directly to the
abolition of the basic difference between poetry and prose. In
the introduction to a collection of essays on classical antiquity
entitled *The Greeks and the Romans*, for instance, Friedrich
Schlegel had characterized the history of Greek poetry 'in its
whole circumference' as comprising quite naturally certain
works of rhetoric, history, and philosophy. He justified this
concept with reference to a remark by Dionysius of Halicarnassus according to which the history of Thucydides is 'at the
same time a beautiful poem' and continued that 'although in
the speeches by Demosthenes and the Socratic dialogues,
poetizing imagination is restricted by a distinct purpose of

reason, it is nevertheless not deprived of all freedom and thereby not released from the duty to play beautifully: for the beautiful ought to exist, and every speech, the main purpose or secondary purpose of which is the beautiful, is totally or partially poetry' (*KFSA* 1, 205–6). As far as modern poetry was concerned, this notion of literature determined the Schlegels' turning towards authors of prose, the so-called 'symbolic form' in modern works of prose and rhetoric, the 'characterization of German classics' in the genre of the prose essay, but above all toward the novel as the most prominent literary art form of modernity. This new trend becomes obvious in A. W. Schlegel's insistence on the poetic qualities of Goethe's novel *Wilhelm Meister*, however superfluous and stilted such an approach might appear today. Towards the end of his essay 'On Goethe's *Hermann and Dorothea*', which is, of course, an epic text, and having discussed in great detail the nature of the epic metre in the sense of 'perseverance in change' and 'identity of self-consciousness', A. W. Schlegel continues:

This theory of epic rhythm deserves a detailed explanation. It is also important because it permits an application to the novel. A rhythm of narration relating to the epic one, approximately as the rhetorical numerus relates to poetic metre, would perhaps be the only means of making a novel poetic not only in its general structure but also in its detailed execution, although the manner of writing must remain of course purely prosaic. And this seems to be actually accomplished in *Wilhelm Meister*. (*AWS SW* 11, 220)

Yet, the modern, artistic concept of literature did not come into its own until the activity of reflection and auto-reflection entered this domain and became its animating force. This component in the Schlegel brothers' view of modern literature has a strong relationship to the transcendental philosophy of the time, especially to Fichte, with whom, according to many critics, the modern age of reflection had begun.[3] Fichte's concept of the pure Ego or the 'Ego as such' that determines itself through reasoning made philosophy a pure thinking of itself. As Hegel puts it, Fichte brought the 'knowledge of knowledge to consciousness' and conceived of philosophy as an 'artistic consciousness, a consciousness of consciousness, so that I have a consciousness of what my consciousnes is doing' (*HEG* 20, 393). The intelligence, as Fichte conceives of it, 'looks at itself' and in this looking penetrates 'immediately all that it is'. This 'immediate union of being and looking' was for Fichte the true nature of the intelligence, which consisted in metaphorical language 'in a double series', that of 'being and looking, of the real and the ideal' (*FI* 4, 196–7).

The most salient step in Friedrich Schlegel's critique of Fichte occurred, however, when he began a fragment of the *Athenaeum* with the statement: 'There is a kind of poetry whose essence lies in the relation between the ideal and real, and which therefore, by analogy to philosophical jargon, should be called transcendental poetry' (*KFSA* 2, 204; *LF*, 195). At this point, Schlegel had entered the Fichtean terrain of transcendental philosophy and recognized that artificial, reflective thinking is an essential element of poetry. He saw the essence of this poetry as including 'the producer along with the product', i.e., the poet together with his poem, thereby effecting an 'artistic reflection and beautiful self-mirroring' for which he found the best examples 'in Pindar, in the lyric fragments of the Greeks, in the classical elegy, and, among the moderns, in Goethe'. Such a poetry should represent itself in all its representations and 'always be simultaneously poetry and the poetry of poetry' (ib.). In his fragment on Romantic poetry as a universal progressive poetry, Schlegel described the 'poetic reflection' of transcendental poetry in the image of an endless series of mirrors, saying that this poetry is able to 'hover at the midpoint between the portrayed and the portrayer, free of all real and ideal self-interest, on the wings of poetic reflection, and can raise that reflection again and again to a higher power, can multiply it in an endless succession of mirrors' (*KFSA* 2, 182–3; *LF*, 175).

As is obvious from these statements, Schlegel understood the meaning of 'transcendental' in its original sense. Kant had defined this term when, in the introduction to the second edition of his *Critique of Pure Reason*, he called 'transcendental' that mode of cognition which is not so much interested in the mere cognition of objects, but in our manner of recognizing objects

(*KA* 3, 43), and thereby joined the subject of knowledge and its object in an inseparable way. Fichte's usage of the term 'transcendental' emphasized the reflective action on the part of the subject in this relationship. Friedrich Schlegel's new version of the term, however, abolished the distinction between philosophy and poetry by referring the reflective part of this interaction also to poetry and by rephrasing the notion of reflection as a 'poetic reflection' that includes 'the producer along with the product' (*KFSA*, 204; *LF*, 195), 'the portrayed and the portrayer' (*KFSA* 2, 182; *LF*, 175). Whereas the rhetoricians of the late antiquity had encouraged him to cross the borderline between poetry and prose, the impact of transcendental philosophy abolished the distinction between poetry and philosophy for him, and gave the Schlegelian notion of literature its decisive and modern character. Friedrich Schlegel described this notion of literature on many occasions as going beyond the distinctions of poetry and prose, poetry and philosophy, and the term 'transcendental poetry' is indeed only one among many designations for this phenomenon. He presents the aim of 'Romantic poetry' as not 'merely to reunite all the separate species of poetry and put poetry in touch with philosophy and rhetoric', but also to 'fuse poetry and prose, inspiration and criticism, the poetry of art and the poetry of nature; and make poetry lively and sociable, and life and society poetic; poeticize wit and fill and saturate the forms of art with every kind of good, solid matters for instruction, and animate them with the pulsations of humour' (*KFSA*, 182; *LF*, 175).

Another concept for the poetic prose of transcendental literature is that of 'symbolic form'.[4] Lessing was a master of it, and even more so Plato, but Fichte, too, can be counted among its representatives. In his writings around the turn of the century – especially the conclusion of the essay on Lessing and the introduction to the anthology of Lessing (1804)[5] – Friedrich Schlegel developed this notion of symbolic form mainly on the basis of philosophical writings. He could have expounded this concept just as easily with reference to poetic texts, since the aim was precisely that synthesis of philosophy and poetry or that overcoming of the difference between philosophy and poetry which is characteristic of 'transcendental poetry'. Two features are essential for the type of text that lends itself to a symbolic form: the movement or pathway of thought, that is, its anti-systematic tendency, and the resulting desire to shape this thought-process artistically, as an art form. At the time in question, Friedrich Schlegel liked to describe the pathway of thought in terms of mathematical symbols and cited some philosophers for whom everything is circular, others who think in the form of triplicity, and yet another group for whom the ellipse is characteristic. The group of authors he had in mind were writers in the form of 'crooked lines, who, although progressing with noticeable steadiness and regularity, can manifest themselves only in fragments because one of their centres lies in the infinite' (*KFSA* 2, 415). Schlegel found this form in Plato and Lessing, and attempted to design a model of prose writing which excelled in 'higher art and form' (*KFSA* 2, 413–14). The pathway of thought was to find expression in 'peculiar combinations of thought', in 'surprising turns and configurations that reach out ever further beyond themselves' (*KFSA* 3, 51). Such a text would constitute the intended union of philosophy and poetry, and simultaneously be truly 'universal'. 'Universality is the successive satiation of all forms and substances', Schlegel said in Fragment 451 of the *Athenaeum*. 'Universality can attain harmony only through the conjunction of poetry and philosophy; and even the greatest, most universal works of isolated poetry and philosophy seem to lack this final synthesis. They come to a stop, still imperfect but close to the goal of harmony' (*KFSA* 2, 255; *LF*, 240).

One model for the symbolic form of prose writing was the Socratic dialogue as Plato had created it. But this form was by no means bound to the imitation of a conversation and could manifest itself whenever 'an oscillating change of thought in continuous interconnection' took place (*KFSA* 3, 99–100). Another favourite medium for the symbolic form was the essay, especially with regard to an 'interactive development of thought' (*Wechsel-Gedankenentwicklung*: *KFSA* 18, 173), 'dialectics with the public' (*KFSA* 18, 364). The most developed description of this type of text can be found in the dedication *For Fichte* of Schlegel's edition of *Lessing's Thoughts and Opinions* of 1804. The following quotation refers to Plato, Lessing, Fichte, and to any other of the prose writers considered in Schlegel's theory of poetic prose, and is in all likelihood a hidden quotation from Plato. It should be kept in mind, however, that the description offered here is equally valid for predominantly poetic texts, as will become more evident in the example of Goethe's *Wilhelm Meister* in the appendix to this chapter. Schlegel refers directly to Plato's writings when he says:

A denial of some current prejudice or whatever else can effectively surmount innate lethargy constitutes the beginning; thereupon the thread of thought moves imperceptibly forward in constant inter-connection until the surprised spectator, after the thread abruptly breaks off or dissolves in itself, suddenly finds himself confronted with a goal he had not at all expected: before him an unlimited, wide view, but upon looking back at the path he has traversed and the spiral of conversation distinctly before him, he realizes that this was only a fragment of an infinite cycle. (*KFSA* 3, 50)

IRONY AND FRAGMENT

Nothing comes closer to this reflective type of literature than irony, and irony is virtually identical with that self-reflective style of poetry that became accentuated during early German Romanticism and constitutes a decisive mark of literary modernism. Irony is also the most famous part of early Romantic theory and became so closely associated with it that the two are often regarded as identical. If we consider the history of irony in the European tradition as a rhetorical figure and a literary device, the early Romantic period marks a turning-point, and, like the theory of literature in general, shows the beginning of a modern trend that is still our own. This theory of irony, however, is almost exclusively Friedrich Schlegel's work. Novalis had his doubts whether 'what Friedrich Schlegel characterizes so precisely as irony' was not 'the result and character of circumspection, of a true presence of the mind' that would better be designated as 'genuine humour'

(*NO* 2, 428–9). A. W. Schlegel relegated irony to the 'ante-chamber of poetry' (*AWS SW* 6, 200) and declared with regard to tragedy: 'where the genuinely tragic begins, all irony certainly ceases' (*AWS SW* 6, 198–9). Friedrich Schlegel's treatment of irony cannot be reduced to a ready-made theory, but consists of a great number of statements that certainly show a coherence but also exhibit constant changes in emphasis and approach. The most productive way of dealing with this enormously complex topic is the genetic way, the discussion in successive fashion of his three collections of fragments relevant to the notion of irony. These are the 'Critical Fragments' (1797), the '*Athenaeum* Fragments' (1798), and the 'Ideas' (1800). Before that, however, a brief look at the history of irony and at Schlegel's innovative approach to the subject is appropriate.[6]

Modern critics credit Friedrich Schlegel with innovation in the field of irony and refer to his new usage of the word irony as the 'coinage of a concept' (*Begriffsschöpfung*).[7] Hegel called Schlegel the 'father of irony' and the 'most excellent ironical personality' (*HEG* 11, 233) – epithets which were not, however, intended as compliments. Adam Müller characterized Schlegel's new understanding of irony as the re-establishment of an originally Greek concept.[8] Norman Knox, who has studied the history of irony, detects a decisive change in the usage of the term toward the end of the eighteenth century but believes that the new concept did not arise from the head of a new Aristotle and find expression in a critical scheme, but rather evolved from the everyday criticism prevalent during the latter decades of the eighteenth century.[9] Whatever the origin of the new concept may be, until far into the eighteenth century, irony had the consistent and coherent connotation of an established form of speech or communication that could be reduced to the simple formula, 'a figure of speech by which one wants to convey the opposite of what one says' (*E* 19, 86). This is a quotation from the French *Encyclopédie* of 1765 and contains the essence of the definitions of irony found in numerous handbooks of various European literatures as they had developed from older manuals of rhetoric concerning the art of public speaking and persuasion.

If we were to define the place of irony in the schematized structure of classical rhetoric, we would first find it in the column of the tropes, that is, among indirect modes of speech, or particular verbal constructions (including question, antici-pation, hesitation, consultation, apostrophe, illustration, feigned regret, and intimation). The most basic characteristic of all forms of classical irony is always that the intention of the speaker is opposed to what he actually says, that we understand the contrary of what he expresses in his speech. We should perhaps add to this description that, according to ancient opinion, in order to distinguish irony from mere lying, the entire tenor of speaking, including intonation, emphasis, and gesture, was supposed to help reveal the real or intended meaning.

Irony is mostly discussed by the classical rhetoricians in the context of peculiar idiosyncracies of style. Aristotle mentions irony in the third book of his *Rhetoric*, which is devoted to style, and presents it as a 'mockery of oneself': 'Some of the forms befit a gentleman, and some do not; irony befits him more than does buffoonery. The jests of the ironical man are at his own expense; the buffoon excites laughter at others.'[10] From other passages of his works, especially his *Ethics*, we know that Aristotle conceived of irony as a noble self-deprecation. 'Irony is the contrary to boastful exaggeration', he says, 'it is a self-deprecating concealment of one's powers and possessions – it shows better taste to deprecate than to exaggerage one's virtues.'[11] Cicero, who introduced the term into the Latin world and rendered it as 'dissimulation' ('ea dissmulatio, quam Graeci eironeia vocant'),[12] discusses irony in his work *On the Orator* in connection with figures of speech. He defines irony as saying one thing and meaning another, explaining that it has a very great influence on the minds of the audience and is extremely entertaining if presented in a conversational rather than declamatory tone.[13] Finally, Quintilian assigned irony its position among the tropes and figures discussed in the eighth and ninth books of his *Oratorical Education*, where its basic characteristic is that the intention of the speaker differs from what he actually says, that we understand the contrary of what he expresses in speech ('in utroque enim contrarium ei quod dicitur intelligendum est').[14] In addition to these two modes of irony, however, Quintilian mentions a third which transcends the scope of mere rhetoric, or what Friedrich Schlegel would call single ironic instances, and relates to the whole manner of existence of a person. Quintilian refers directly to Socrates, whose entire life had an ironic colouring because he assumed the role of an ignorant human being lost in wonder at the wisdom of others.[15]

As this observation indicates, Quintilian, as well as Cicero and other rhetoricians, regarded Socrates as the master of irony, the *eiron*. Originally, however, the words *eironeia* and *eiron* had a low and vulgar connotation, even to the extent of invective. We come across these terms in Aristophanes' comedies, in which the ironist is placed among liars, shysters, pettifoggers, hyprocrites, and charlatans – in other words, with deceivers.[16] Plato was the first to present Socrates as an ironic interlocutor who, by understating his talents in his famous pose of ignorance, embarrassed his partner and simultaneously led him into the proper terrain of thought. With the Platonic Socrates, the attitude of the ironist was freed from the burlesque coarseness of classical comedy and appeared as that refined, human, and humorous self-deprecation that made Socrates the paragon of a teacher.

Yet, even in Plato's dialogues, where the attitude of Socratic irony is so obviously present, the term 'irony' itself still retains its derogatory cast in the sense of hoax and hypocrisy and, as such, evinces the Sophist attitude of intellectual deception and false pretension. In his *Republic*, for example, Plato depicts the scene in which Socrates deliberates in characteristic fashion on the concept of *dikaiosyne*, justice. At a crucial point in the discussion, his conversation partner Thrasymachus explodes, requesting Socrates to desist from his eternal questioning and refuting, and finally to come out with a direct statement and reveal his own opinion. Again assuming his stance of ignorance, Socrates replies that it is utterly difficult to discover justice and that they should have pity rather than scorn for him. At this point, Thrasymachus bursts out: 'By Heracles! Here again is the well-known dissimulation of Socrates! I have told these others beforehand that you would never answer, but take refuge in dissimulation.' The Greek term rendered here as 'dissimulation' is, of course, *eironeia*, irony.[17]

From many other instances in Plato's dialogues we know that the pretended ignorance of Socrates was considered by many of his contemporaries as chicanery, scorn, or deceptive escapism, all of which made him deserve the epithet *eiron* (ironist). Only with Aristotle did the word 'irony' assume that refined and urbane significance which marks the character of 'Socratic irony'. This important change in meaning can be detected in Aristotle's *Nichomachaean Ethics*, where *eironeia* and *alazoneia*, understatement and boastfulness, are discussed as modes of deviation from truth. Aristotle, however, held the opinion that irony deviates from truth not for the sake of one's own advantage, but out of a dislike of bombast and to spare others from feelings of inferiority. Irony was, therefore, a fine and noble form. The prototype of this genuine irony was to be found in Socrates, and with this reference, irony received its classical definition.[18] Some of the other instances in which Aristotle mentions irony also reveal a Socratic image. In his *Physiognomy*, Aristotle describes the ironist as possessing greater age and having wrinkles around his eyes, thus reflecting a critical power of judgment.[19] In his *History of Animals*, Aristotle considers eyebrows rising up toward the temples as marks of the mocker and ironist.[20]

These physiognomical features which predestined Socrates as the master of irony are also referred to in Plato's writings about the philosopher. They are obvious in the speech in the *Symposium* delivered by Alcibiades in Socrates' honour, wherein Alcibiades compares Socrates with the sileni, those carved figurines with satyr-like and grotesque images on the exterior, but which are pure gold inside. This is obviously a reference to the contrast between the philosopher's outer appearance, his protruding lips, paunch, and snub nose, and his personal rank and intellectual quality. This contrast can also be seen as a form of ironic dissimulation, as a 'mask', and was to become a famous and continuous theme in European literature. Toward his fellow citizens, Socrates assumes the mask of one who tends to appreciate handsome young men and convivial symposia, who is to all appearances universally ignorant and unfit for any practical activity. But beneath the surface, we discover that he is independent of the attractions of physical beauty as well as those of wealth and popular esteem, and that he possesses self-control to an unparalleled degree. Using the Greek term *eironeia* for this type of dissimulation, Alcibiades explains to his drinking companions: 'He spends his whole life pretending and playing with people, and I doubt whether anyone has ever seen the treasures that are revealed when he grows serious and exposes what he keeps inside.'[21]

When Friedrich Schlegel decided to extend the restricted use of irony, as encountered in the rhetorical tradition of Europe, to works of Boccaccio, Cervantes, Sterne, and Goethe, and wrote in 1797 that 'there are ancient and modern poems which breathe throughout, in their entirety and in every detail, the divine breath of irony' (*KFSA* 2, 152; *LF*, 148), he gave irony a completely new scope and effected a fundamental change in the concept in Western literary theory. The authors he mentioned certainly would have been astonished to hear him interpret their literary creations as displaying irony – to say nothing of Shakespeare and other older models of so-called ironic style. Schlegel himself described his novel treatment of literary works as a move away from the search for 'beautiful instances and single images' which was so dominant in eighteenth-century criticism to the comprehension of the entirety of works of the imagination and the expression of this insight in words (*KFSA* 3, 296). Indeed, in this reference to the entirety of literary works, Schlegel's new understanding of irony bears a strong resemblance to his other innovations in literary criticism.

This change of meaning in the notion of irony can be dated in a precise manner and actually occurs in Fragment 42 of the 'Critical Fragments,' beginning with the blunt statement: 'Philosophy is the real homeland of irony, which one would like to define as logical beauty' (*KFSA* 2, 152; *LF*, 143). This statement implies that, contrary to the entire rhetorical tradition of Europe according to which irony is a distinct figure of speech, the real origin of irony is to be found in philosophy, more precisely in a particular philosophical type of argumentation practised by Socrates and developed as a form of art by Plato. Schlegel calls this technique 'logical beauty', but the technical term for it is Socratic or Platonic 'dialectics', thought and counterthought as a progressive movement of thinking. In fact, Schlegel's statement continues directly with the argument that 'wherever philosophy appears in oral or written dialogues – and is not simply confined to rigid systems – there irony should be asked for and provided' (ib.). This is entirely in line with his general image of Plato, as present in the previous section on transcendental poetry. In his Paris lectures on European literature of 1804, he formulated this image of Plato more pointedly, saying: 'Plato had no system, but only a philosophy. The philosophy of a human being is the history, the becoming, the progression of his mind, the gradual formation and development of his thoughts' (*KFSA* 11, 118). A little later in these lectures he says:

We have mentioned already that Plato only had a philosophy, but no system; just as philosophy in general is more a seeking, a striving for science than science itself, this is especially the case with that of Plato. He is never finished with his thought, and this constant further striving of his thought for completed knowledge and the highest cognition, this eternal becoming, forming, and developing of his ideas, he has tried to shape artistically in dialogues. (*KFSA* 11, 120)[22]

Friedrich Schlegel was, of course, aware of the rhetorical tradition in which irony was transmitted and had found its habitual place in Europe. But this rhetorical irony, bound to individual instances, to particular figures, appeared to him minor and insignificant compared to the philosophical homeland of irony where it could manifest itself 'throughout'. He said: 'Of course, there is also a rhetorical species of irony which, sparingly used, has an excellent effect, especially in polemics; but compared to the sublime urbanity of the Socratic muse, it is like the pomp of the most splendid oration set against the noble style of an ancient tragedy.' The most important sentence occurs in the middle of the fragment and states that it is not rhetoric but poetry that can equal philosophy in the use of irony 'throughout', in the entirety of a work, and not simply in single and isolated instances. In order to appreciate this fully, one has to take into consideration that Schlegel had abolished the line of demarcation between philosophical and poetic discourse, as was explained in the previous section of this chapter. The sentence reads: 'Only poetry can also reach the heights of philosophy in this way, and only poetry does not restrict itself to isolated ironical passages, as rhetoric does.' After this equation of Socratic philosophy and modern poetry in the works of Boccaccio, Cervantes, Shakespeare, and Goethe is established, Schlegel concludes with the statement that actually constitutes the turning-point in the history of the concept of irony and has been quoted above: 'There are ancient and modern poems that are pervaded by the divine breath of irony throughout and informed by a truly transcendental buffoonery.' What he understands by the 'divine breath of irony' is described with reference to the internal mood of these works of literature. It is a 'mood that surveys everything and rises infinitely above all limitations, even above its own art, virtue, or genius' (ib.). The fragment, however, like all complex and condensed statements, has also an afterthought, which consists in the words 'transcendental buffoonery'. A buffoon is a clown, and after irony has been introduced in elevated fashion as Platonic discourse and Socratic incompletion, it appears appropriate to remind the reader of the human character of limitation and confinement, a feature which is also apparent in the outer appearance of Socrates and is expressed by Schlegel in the final words of the fragment, 'the mimic style of an averagely gifted Italian *buffo*' (ib.).

Fragment 108 of the 'Critical Fragments' focuses more directly on Socratic irony, but it does not convey anything not already mentioned in Fragment 42 of the same collection, except for the paramount topic of communication, for Schlegel now refers to the 'impossibility and necessity of complete communication', which is mediated by irony. Instead of paraphrasing this fragment, it is perhaps best to reproduce some of its statements in their entirety:

In this sort of irony, everything should be playful and serious, guilelessly open and deeply hidden. It originates in the union of *savoir vivre* and scientific spirit, in the conjunction of a perfectly instinctive and a perfectly conscious philosophy. It contains and arouses a feeling of indissoluble antagonism between the absolute and the relative, between the impossibility and the necessity of complete communication. It is the freest of all licenses, for by its means one transcends oneself; and yet it is also the most lawful, for it is absolutely necessary. (*KFSA* 2, 160; *LF*, 156)

There are some other passages in the 'Critical Fragments' that illustrate this change in the meaning of irony from the classical, rhetorical concept to its modern connotation as being coextensive with speech, writing, and communication. These fragments add little to what has already been discussed. One of them, however, introduces a new note on the concept of irony, although the term itself does not occur in it. The reference is to a rhythm of 'constant alternation of self-creation and self-annihilation' (*KFSA* 2, 151; *LF*, 146–7) that becomes the dominant theme in the exposition of irony in the *Athenaeum* (e.g., *KFSA* 2, 172, 217). In its dual movement of affirmation and negation, of enthusiasm and scepticism, this ironic alternation between self-creation and self-annihilation is simply another formulation for what had previously been presented as poetic reflection, as transcendental poetry, and it shows that Schlegel's notion of poetry and literature actually coincides with this dual movement in the creative mind. To underline this fact, one could add that practically all polarities which have occurred so far in the description of Schlegel's theory of literature can be related to this alternating rhythm of self-creation and self-annihilation, that is, the antitheses of classical and Romantic, poetry and philosophy, the Ego and the world. The speaker of Schlegel's 'Speech on Mythology' refers to the 'structure of the whole' in the works of Shakespeare and Cervantes and describes it as 'this artfully ordered confusion, this charming symmetry of contradictions, this wonderfully perennial alternation of enthusiasm and irony which lives even in the smallest parts of the whole' (*KFSA* 2, 318–19; *DP*, 86). A similar and recurrent formulation of the same phenomenon is the phrase 'to the point of irony' or 'to the point of continuously fluctuating between self-creation and self-annihilation' (*KFSA* 2, 172, 217; *LF*, 167, 205). In a certain respect, this is the point of highest perfection – a perfection, however, that is conscious of its own imperfection and inscribes this feature into its own text. Another and perhaps better way of characterizing the dual movement of self-creation and self-destruction inherent in reference 'to the point of irony' would be to say that this is by no means a deficiency, but rather the highest level we can reach, and in aesthetic terms, also one of charm and grace.

In his early writings on Greek poetry, Friedrich Schlegel represented the dual movement of self-creation and self-destruction as a self-destructive reaction to a primordial Dionysian ecstasy and said: 'The most intense passion is eager to wound itself, if only to act and to discharge its excessive power' (*FSA* 1, 403). One of his favourite examples of such an action was the *parabasis* of classical comedy, that is, the sometimes capricious, frivolous addresses of the poet through the chorus and the coryphaeus to the audience that constitute a total disruption of the play. In a fragment of 1791, Schlegel says summarily: 'Irony is a permanent *parabasis*' (*KFSA* 18, 85), interpreting the emergence of the author from his work in the broadest sense and relating it to ancient and modern literature in all its genres. With specific reference to the comic exuberance exhibited through *parabasis* in the comedies by Aristophanes, Schlegel said:

This self-infliction is not ineptitude, but deliberate impetuousness, overflowing vitality, and often has not a bad effect, indeed stimulates the effect, since it cannot totally destroy the illusion. The most intense agility of life must act, even destroy; if it does not find an external object, it reacts against a beloved one, against itself, against its own creation. This agility then injures in order to excite, not to destroy. (*KFSA* 1, 30)

In the medium of modern literature, Schlegel described the ironic mood in Goethe's *Wilhelm Meister* by referring to the author's 'illusion of dignity and importance, mocking itself gently', and to the occurrence of a 'delicate breath of poetic pedantry on the most prosaic occasions' (*KFSA* 2, 138; *GM*, 66).

The collection of fragments with the title 'Ideas', which appeared in 1800 in the last volume of the *Athenaeum*, does not contain many entries on irony. There is one fragment, however, hardly more than one line long, that introduces a larger, almost cosmic view of irony. It reads: 'Irony is the clear consciousness of an eternal agility, of an infinitely abundant chaos' (*KFSA* 2, 263; *LF*, 251). If one stresses the feeling of one's own insignificance, transitoriness, and fragmentation implied in this fragment, one comes close to the notion of melancholic irony, which became a famous topic in Romantic theory after the turn of the century, although the fragment can, of course, also be read in a more confident vein. That Friedrich Schlegel's thought was inclined in that direction, or at least not closed off from it, becomes obvious in some of his later pronouncements on irony. In his Cologne lectures of 1804–6 he says in a philosophical context that irony brings to our attention the 'inexhaustible plenitude and manifoldness of the highest subjects of knowledge' (*KFSA* 13, 207). In his Dresden lectures of 1829, delivered shortly before his death, he claims: 'True irony... is the irony of love. It arises from the feeling of finitude and one's own limitation and the apparent contradiction of these feelings with the concept of infinity inherent in all true love' (*KFSA* 10, 357).

Against this larger background of European literature and Friedrich Schlegel's own varied use of irony, the relationship between irony and the fragment as a literary means of communication becomes apparent. The notions of the fragment and the fragmentary are indeed central to early Romantic theory but often lead simply to an abbreviated, pointed type of writing whose antecedents are to be found in the epigram in classical literature and in the maxim, the 'pensée', in modern European writing. In the spring of 1791, Chamfort's *Maxims and Thoughts, Characters and Anecdotes* had appeared in German translation, and A. W. Schlegel had already reviewed Chamfort's *Oeuvres* in 1795, praising the *Maxims* of Volume 4 as the most valuable part of the edition (*AWS SW* 11, 297–304). It is certainly no coincidence that Friedrich Schlegel published his collection of 'Critical Fragments' soon afterwards and frequently insisted thereafter that he had found his natural form of literary communication in this genre. He also indicated that this kind of fragment had antecedents in the Roman epigram ('I, the restorer of the epigrammatic genre', *KFSA* 18, 130) and the French maxim ('I have just sent a *critical Chamfortade* of several sheets into the world, that is, to the printing-press', *KFSA* 24, 21).[23] In one of his fragments, he defined the nature of this genre, saying: 'A fragment, like a miniature work of art, has to be entirely isolated from the surrounding world and be complete in itself like a porcupine' (*KFSA* 2, 197; *LF*, 189).

If we look at Friedrich Schlegel's fragments and some of his own statements on them more closely, however, we soon realize that what he has in mind is not a classical or classicistic form of brief, isolated statements like the epigram and the maxim, but a type of fragmentary writing that does not necessarily have to break apart into splinters of thought, but can also manifest itself in more coherent texts like the essay, the dialogue, the lecture, and still reveal a fragmentary, incomplete, perspectivistic, or asystematic outlook. Prototypes for this much more basic fragmentary kind of writing can be found in Hamann (*Diary of a Christian*: 'Crumbs') and Herder (*On Recent German Literature. First Collection of Fragments*). Schlegel's favourite 'fragmentary' author of the eighteenth century was Lessing, whom he characterized as 'absolutely fragmentary' (*KFSA* 3, 79). If this was not always apparent from Lessing's own writings, Schlegel broke them up even further, as in his anthology of Lessing, to show how basically fragmentary Lessing really was.[24] Lessing lived, according to Schlegel, in a time of 'not yet', a period of fermentation and preparation, that is, of the new German literature. In such periods, 'particular literary devices or writings become necessary which have only the firm aim of inciting, examining, and nourishing the productive power' (*KFSA* 3, 83). Yet we know from earlier occasions that Schlegel did not use the metaphor of 'not yet' to denote a transitory stage to be overcome by a completed form of knowledge and literary writing, but saw in it the appropriate form of human comprehension and communication. In this respect, Plato was also for him a prefiguration of fragmentary thinking. The devices employed, if not to transcend this state of affairs then at least to keep us aware of it, were for Schlegel a certain type of writing, and in this sense the fragment reveals its close relationship to irony.

Whereas authors such as Hamann, Herder, and Lessing can be seen as 'fragmentary' writers, we can speak of a consciously established genre of the fragment only at that moment when, in 1797, Friedrich Schlegel entitled a collection of 127 individual thoughts 'Critical Fragments' (*KFSA* 2, 147–63; *LF*, 143–59). This was followed in 1798 by a more comprehensive collection of 451 entries to which other members of the early Romantic group (August Wilhelm and Caroline Schlegel, and Schleiermacher) contributed and which bore the simple title *Fragments* (*KFSA* 2, 165–255; *LF*, 161–240). Shortly before, in 1798, Novalis had published a collection of 114 fragments with the title *Pollen* (*NO* 2, 412–63). In that same year, Novalis made public his fragments 'Faith and Love, or the King and the Queen', dealing with his ideal of the state (*NO* 2, 485–98). In 1800 Friedrich Schlegel's series of prophetic and solemn fragments appeared bearing the title *Ideas* (*KFSA* 2, 256–72; *LF*, 241–56). These published series of fragments had parallels in thousands and thousands of unpublished fragments, especially in the notebooks of Friedrich Schlegel and Novalis. These various collections and compilations of fragments constitute a particular genre of thinking in fragments or writing in fragments that became typical of early German Romanticism and lasted for the short period from 1797 to 1800.[25] To be sure, Friedrich Schlegel continued to jot down masses of fragments in his notebooks until his death, but he never published a fragment again after 1800. What is denied in these collections of fragments is systematic coherence, or Hegel's doctrine: 'The truth is the whole.' Completion and totality in any realizable fashion are questioned by a type of writing that, from the outset, rejects any type of closure and postpones it to an unrealizable future.

ROMANTIC POETRY AND THE NEW MYTHOLOGY

As far as the image of literary history is concerned, the Schlegels still saw themselves, at the turn of the century, within the framework of a large historical development extending from the Greeks into their own time. Yet, their work had increasingly focused on that Romantic tradition of European literature after which their own endeavour was later named. The exploration of Dante and Shakespeare had been followed by an equally intense study of Cervantes, Boccaccio, and Petrarch. In the summer of 1802, A. W. Schlegel began his translations of Calderón,[26] whereas Friedrich Schlegel explored Provençal literature and Portuguese poets, like Camoes (*KFSA* 3, 17–37). Two meanings of the term 'romantic' became more and more prominent in their work: the historical, relating to that tradition of European literature unjustly suppressed by classicistic taste and of which the Schlegels became the pioneers; and the normative, according to which the romantic is an 'element of poetry, that may predominate or recede to a greater or lesser extent, but must never be wholly absent' (*KFSA* 2, 335; *DP*, 101). It is this second notion that needs a more thorough analysis.

Because of the predominance of the novel in the Romantic tradtion and the semantic affinity of the term 'romantic' to the German word for the novel (*Roman*),[27] critics have often been inclined to reduce the Romantic theory of the Schlegels to a theory of the novel. There is no question that Friedrich Schlegel at least had a particular predilection for the novel and made several statements on the pre-eminence of the novel in modern, Romantic literature that have since become famous.[28] But he also expanded the notion of the novel so far beyond generic limitations that it almost coincided with his notion of Romantic poetry, and is therefore of little help for a clarification of these matters. A much better approach to the notion of Romantic poetry is to look at it rather from the point of view of its task, its object, its rendering of the infinity of life and nature, as well as its artful manner of creation. In his review of Tieck's translation of *Don Quixote*, Friedrich Schlegel expressed his satisfaction at the fact that the German public no longer mistook Shakespeare for a 'raving mad Storm and Stress poet', but had begun to appreciate him as 'one of the most purposeful artists'. This gave hope that, one day, Cervantes would no longer be seen as a mere joker, because 'as far as concealed purposefulness was concerned, he might be just as wily and cunning' as his fellow English poet (*KFSA* 2, 283). Schlegel also found this highly artistic quality in the prose of Cervantes and claimed that it was 'the only *modern* prose we could juxtapose to the prose of a Tacitus, Demosthenes, or Plato, just because it is so thoroughly modern as the other is classical and still in its manner just as artfully formed' (ib.). He adds: 'In no other prose is the position of words so entirely symmetry and music; no other uses the differences of styles so entirely as floods of colour and light; no other is in the general expressions of social life so refreshing, lively, and picturesque' (ib.).

An even better example of this appreciation of the Romantic style of literature is his characterization of Boccaccio. He considers his essay on this author as dealing with the most interesting thing there is in the world, namely, with 'truth which is one with beauty' (*KFSA* 2, 373), and thereby assigns to Romantic poetry the highest possible task, the creation of a symbolic image of life and existence. Whereas Cervantes, Shakespeare, and other Romantic poets approached this task by focusing on its objective side, or the side of the object (that is, the infinity of life and nature), Boccaccio, especially in the novellas of his *Decamerone*, took the opposite path in shaping 'a subjective mood and point of view' and attempting to render this attitude 'indirectly and, so to speak, allegorically' (*KFSA* 2, 393). This 'indirect representation of the subjective' seems to be the particular charm of his novellas. Their 'indirect and veiled' character occasionally gives them an even greater attraction than the direct and immediate lyrical mode of communication (*KFSA* 2, 394). The 'indirect and hidden subjectivity' of these novellas, however, does not preclude a marked tendency towards the objective side. This is manifest not only in their painstaking adherence to peculiarities of the locality and society to which the narration relates, but especially in the view of life which is invisibly shaped by the poet through his varying moods.

Friedrich Schlegel finds this particular feature of the novella already preformed in its original character. Basically, the novella is an anecdote, an unknown story, told in society, and exciting a certain interest among its members. This interest, however, has nothing to do with issues like 'the coherence of nations, or of times, or the progressions of humanity and the relationship of education to them', or with any other such topics of a larger significance (*KFSA* 2, 394). The novella is a story that does not belong to that type of history, but rather shows a predisposition towards irony which is already present at the moment of its birth. Its main effect is to interest, and the best way for the narrator to show his 'art of narration' is to start with an 'anecdote that, strictly speaking, is not even an anecdote', in other words, with an 'agreeable nothingness', and deceivingly entertain us with it by adorning it so copiously with his art that we will be pleased to let ourselves be deceived and even become earnestly interested in it (ib.). Another possibility for this 'artful narrator' would be to renarrate familiar stories in such a way that they appear as new ones and to convey his personal view of life through these different arrangements. In any case, we would not listen to such stories with rising interest if we did not become interested in the author himself, and receive through his subjective, indirect communication an image of life in its infinitely unpredictable course, an image which other Romantic authors convey more from the objective side (*KFSA* 2, 395).

Through these and other investigations, the notion of the Romantic became more and more synonymous with the truly poetic, and progressively split off from the earlier designation of modern poetry that had constituted the counterpart to the truly classical in the sense of antique poetry. The 'modern' came to denote a certain type of literature which might indeed be artistic and artful in its composition, but lacked a genuinely Romantic character. The Schlegels had originally relegated the entire tradition of classicistic poetry, especially French classicism and *tragédie classique*, to this category of literature. Yet, the more their exploration of the Romantic tradition, and especially of authors like Dante, Boccaccio, Petrarch, Cervantes, Shakespeare, and Calderón, progressed, the more restricted their recognition of the truly poetic became – although, as was pointed out earlier, the notion of the poetic also applied to prose writers in the field of the rhetorical essay or history, and to philosophers like Plato. We now find on the list of 'modern' authors not only names like Pope and Voltaire, but also Lessing, at least as far as his dramatic *œuvre* is concerned, and even Goethe.

If one asked what constituted the truly Romantic for the Schlegels in contrast to the merely modern, no quality would perhaps be more important than a certain radiance, or fluorescence, of the literary work which makes it transcend the necessarily limited scope of human language and open a vista into the infinite. Indeed, this relationship to the infinite seems to mark the difference between Romantic and modern literature, in that modern literature is thoroughly confined, although in a highly artistic fashion, to the human sphere of the subject, whereas the Romantic style attempts to transcend the merely human world and to create an image of the 'infinite play of the world' (*KFSA* 2, 324; *DP*, 89), a view of the universe created by the imagination, yet broken and reflected by the indirect communication of irony (*KFSA* 2, 324; *DP*, 100). This does not imply that the rigorous structural principles developed earlier in the context of Greek literature are relinquished, but simply adds another dimension to them. 'A work is shaped', Friedrich Schlegel says in the *Athenaeum*, 'when it is everywhere sharply delimited, but within those limits limitless and inexhaustible; when it is completely faithful to itself, homogeneous, and nonetheless exalted above itself' (*KFSA* 2, 215; *LF*, 297). His characterizations of Cervantes and Boccaccio made this absolutely clear with reference both to the objective and the subjective side of artistic creation. This relationship to the infinite is not to be interpreted in a religious sense either, and lies completely within the 'aesthetic horizon', which Friedrich Schlegel had earlier claimed is the only horizon for the poet (*KFSA* 1, 328–9). Yet one senses in these views of an 'absolute' and 'pure' poetry an attitude which more than anything else in the early Romantic theory breaks through the confines of the traditional world of the subject and introduces features of modernity of a yet unheard-of power and Dionysian resonance. This is the 'mystical' aspect of early Romanticism which is strictly abhorred and avoided by A. W. Schlegel. Friedrich Schlegel and Novalis liked to indulge in it, referring to it ironically as their attempt at founding a new religion.[29] The best-known designation for this new tendency, however, is that of a 'new mythology'.

Certainly, the mythological aspect of literature is also strongly emphasized by A. W. Schlegel. It is an essential point of his literary theory, emphasized in the first sentence of the section on myth in his Jena lectures entitled 'The Philosophical Doctrine of Art' (1798): 'Myth, like language, is a general, a necessary product of the human poetic power, an arche-poetry of humanity', so to speak (*AWS V* 1, 49). He considers mythology a 'metaphorical language' of the human mind created according to the needs of the human being in which 'everything corporeal is animated' and 'the invisible is made to appear' (ib.). As these formulations indicate, mythology does not belong to some early and bygone phase of humanity for A. W. Schlegel, but like language, forms an essential accompaniment of the human being, a structural principle of his mind. Like language, mythology might lose some of its strength and colours through the process of rationalization, but even in its state of reason, the human mind mythologizes.

Particular mythologies, like that of the Greeks, show stages of development and may eventually die out as the creed of a particular people. Even if they are dead as far as general belief is concerned, they can be recreated, if only fragmentarily and in particular images, through intentional usage by modern artists. A great deal of modern painting and poetry is based on such arbitrary recreations of ancient, especially Greek and Roman, mythologies. But independently of these artistic tendencies, our basic manner of experiencing the world will always have a mythologizing trend which expresses itself in a metaphorical transformation of everything with which we have contact. This tendency should not be misunderstood and minimized as a mere allegorical rewording of complicated concepts, which would be a deliberate method of illustration, but seen as a much more fundamental, involuntary action of forming images with the imagination (*AWS V* 1, 50). In this sense, the mythological or mythologizing tendency of the human mind is a basic aspect of our nature without which human experience would not be possible. Once formed and shaped to a coherent whole, a particular mythology, while never true poetry itself, can become a 'means for attaining poetry' (*AWS V* 1, 49).

In his Berlin lectures of 1801, A. W. Schlegel amplified these views considerably in both their general epistemological and historical aspects. The more important feature of his notion of poetry is, of course, the philosophical, theoretical aspect of the human mind's fundamental tendency to mythologize, to find metaphorical expressions for its experience. Imagination is the basic power of the human mind, A. W. Schlegel argues in these lectures, and he concludes: 'The original action of the imagination is the one through which our own existence and the entire outer world gains reality for us' (*AWS V* 1, 440). The basic activity of the imagination must, however, be carefully distinguished from its artistic and intentional use. Whereas the spontaneous imaginative experience can be illustrated by the phenomenon of dreaming, poetry in the specific artistic sense can be characterized as an artificial recreation of that mythical state, a 'deliberate and waking dreaming' (*AWS V* 1, 441). This wide range of mythology is already indicated by the Greeks, who considered it the common ground of poetry, history, and philosophy. As far as poetry is concerned, mythology provides it with a much more elaborate material than mere nature. 'Mythology is nature in a poetic garment, it is itself already in a certain sense poetry' (*AWS V* 1, 451). But upon closer scrutiny, mythology embraces everything that can become an object for the human mind. Mythology provides a complete view of the world and is therefore also the basis of philosophy (*AWS V* 1, 452). A. W. Schlegel believes that the most recent doctrines of modern physics could easily be transformed into mythical images (453).

Against this background of a universally metaphorical and

mythological organization of the human mind, A. W. Schlegel's conception of poetry – in the narrower sense of an artistic activity – gains its characteristic shape. Whereas the other arts have a certain range of representation which is determined by their media of expression, the medium of poetry is the one in which the human mind gains consciousness of itself and is able to connect its representations in an intentional mode of expression. This medium is language. 'Language', A. W. Schlegel says, 'is not a product of nature, but a reproduction of the human mind that deposits in language the origin and relationship of all its representations, the entire mechanism of its operations. It is therefore so that, in poetry, something already shaped is reshaped, and the formative capacity of its organ is just as limitless as the ability of the human mind to return into itself through ever more highly developed reflections' (*AWS V* 1, 387–8). In the early stages of its formation, language produces, just as necessarily and unintentionally as its own body, a poetic view of the world dominated by the imagination, which is mythology. This is, so to speak, the higher form of the first poetic representation of nature through language. Self-conscious poetry goes one step further by treating mythology poetically and by poeticizing it. In this way, the process continues, since according to Schlegel poetry 'will never leave the human being in any stage of his further development': 'Just as poetry is the most original, the arche- and mother-art of all the others, poetry will also be the ultimate perfection of humanity, the ocean into which everything will return, however far it may have moved away from it in various forms' (*AWS V* 1, 388).

All these careful considerations of the relationship between mythology and poetry are left far behind, however, when Friedrich Schlegel, in his 'Speech on Mythology' of 1800, at once declares in impetuous language: 'I will come straight to the point. Our poetry, I maintain, lacks a focal point, such as mythology was for the ancients. One could summarize all the essentials in which modern poetry is inferior to the ancient in these words: We have no mythology' (*KFSA* 2, 312; *DP*, 81). Here, mythology obviously is no longer understood as a primordial metaphorical functioning of the human mind, but as a coherent view of the world as it supposedly existed in classical India, in Greece, Rome, and among the modern Christian nations of Europe in a communal medium of universal understanding operating through images, metaphors, and allegories. Schlegel deplores the lack of such a communal basis particularly with regard to literature and poetry, but one senses that he actually misses in his age a general foundation for all types of intellectual discourse including philosophy, the interpretation of history, and the moral, social, and political tasks of the time. Addressing himself only to the poets of his period, he says: 'You above all others must know what I mean. You yourselves have written poetry, and while doing so much often have felt the absence of a firm basis for your activity, a matrix, a sky, a living atmosphere' (ib.).

This is the negative aspect of the diagnosis. Yet Schlegel hastens to add with no less categorical assurance: 'But, I add, we are close to obtaining one [a mythology] or, rather, it is time that we earnestly work together to create one' (ib.). It is in this context that he introduces the notions of an 'old' and a 'new' mythology and projects the new mythology as the great task to which he is summoning his age. What he understands by this new mythology, however, is more hinted at than actually described or defined. In one of these instances within his speech he mentions the 'revolution' of his age, its 'great maxims', and the 'phenomenon of all phenomena', namely, 'that mankind struggles with all its power to find its own center', and that it must 'either perish or be rejuvenated'. He has, of course, high hopes and opts for an 'age of rejuvenation' in his time (*KFSA* 2, 314; *DP*, 83). The same thought occurs towards the end of the speech where he says that what matters now is to promote 'those great principles of general rejuvenation and of eternal revolution' (*KFSA* 2, 322; *DP*, 88). In his 'Ideas', written at about the same time, he refers to the 'fermenting gigantic power' of his age and sees 'violent convulsions', all stemming from the centre, from mankind, and leading to a 'great rebirth of religion, a universal metamorphosis' (*KFSA* 2, 261; *DP*, 246). These statements already reveal vital aspects of the new mythology. The most important one is perhaps that the new mythology is not a gift of nature, not a product originating by itself, but the result of our own efforts and simultaneously not only a creation of the imagination, but also one of thought, of the deepest reflection. Schlegel says:

For it [the new mythology] will come to us by an entirely opposite way from that of previous ages, which was everywhere the first flower of youthful imagination, directly joining and imitating what was most immediate and vital in the sensuous world. The new mythology, in contrast, must be forged from the deepest depths of the spirit; it must be the most artful of all works of art, for it must encompass all others; a new bed and vessel for the ancient, eternal fountainhead of poetry, and even the infinite poem concealing the seeds of all other poems. (*KFSA* 2, 312; *DP*, 81–2)

What connects the new with the old mythology is, of course, the overall unity in its view of the world, the character of bed and vessel for the fountainhead of poetry, its function as a universal horizon of meaning, as it supposedly existed in the old mythologies and religions. How such a decisive concentration or self-reflection of the human mind can be accomplished is indicated, for Friedrich Schlegel, by a 'significant hint' of his time, by the 'great phenomenon of our age', by idealist philosophy, in the course of its development from Kant to Fichte. This idealism established in the intellectual world a 'firm point from which the creative energy of humanity can safely expand, developing in all directions, without losing itself or the possibility of return' (*KFSA* 2, 313; *DP*, 82–3). In a remark which is usually taken to refer to the effects of Fichte's philosophy, Schlegel adds: 'All disciplines and all arts will be seized by the great revolution' (*KFSA* 2, 314; *DP*, 83). Idealism, the true 'spirit of that revolution', is, however, not yet the full manifestation of the new mythology, but 'only a part, a branch, a mode of expression of the phenomenon of all phenomena' of the age. Just as the inner life of the mind consists in a 'perennial alternation of expanding from and returning to itself', idealism has to immerse itself in the same movement and 'transcend itself in one way or another, in order to return to itself and remain what it is'. In this manner, there will arise from the matrix of idealism 'a new and equally infinite realism', and through this decisive process, idealism will simultaneously be the example and source of the new mythology (*KFSA* 2, 315; *DP*, 84).

How is this to be understood? Like Novalis, Friedrich Schlegel points to a 'new life' manifesting itself 'in the most splendid manner through the infinite abundance of new ideas, general comprehensibility, and a lively efficacy' (*KFSA* 2, 314–15; *DP*, 83). This is obviously a reference to the rejuvenation of intellectual and literary life in Germany at that time, of which early Romanticism formed a part. In other instances he mentions 'physics' as a sign of this trend (*KFSA* 2, 314, 321–2; *DP*, 83, 88) and obviously means the new philosophy of nature arising out of Schelling's ideal realism as a complete philosophy of subject and object. Yet, above all, Schlegel refers to a transcendence of philosophy through poetry, to the fusion of philosophy and poetry, reflection and creation, the ideal and the real, as it had been proclaimed in early Romantic theory. The early Romantic project thereby becomes one with the new mythology, and this name can be interpreted as just another designation for poetry in this endless chain of new reflections. As a matter of fact, Schlegel actually says:

I, too, have long borne in me the ideal of such a realism, and if it has not yet found expression, it was merely because I am still searching for an organ for communicating it. And yet I know that I can find it only in poetry, for in the form of philosophy, and especially of systematic philosophy, realism can never again appear. But even considering a general tradition, it is to be expected that this new realism, since it must be of idealistic origin and must hover, as it were, over an idealistic ground, will emerge as poetry which indeed is to be based on the harmony of the ideal and real. (*KFSA* 2, 315; *DP*, 84)

The new mythology provides the ground for this new poetic view of the world. In two instances, Schlegel illustrates his point with reference to Spinoza, the philosopher of realism and nature pantheism. As if to prevent us from equating realism totally with philosophy, however, he entirely disregards the systematic philosopher, the author of demonstrations in the mathematical manner, and concentrates solely on Spinoza's imagination, his view of the whole of the world, of the all-in-one and the one-in-all (*KFSA* 2, 316–17, 321; *DP*, 84–5, 87). Spinoza's particular manner of considering things in terms of the world is obviously introduced as a paradigm for the poetic view of the new mythology and its 'hieroglyphic expression of surrounding nature' (*KFSA* 2, 318; *DP*, 85), its ability to let us perceive what usually escapes consciousness (ib.), and to let everything appear 'in relation and metamorphosis' (*KFSA* 2, 318; *DP*, 86). Another example of the mythological view of the world is the 'marvellous wit of Romantic poetry', which does not manifest itself so much 'in individual conceptions but in the structure of the whole' and is exemplified by Cervantes and Shakespeare (*KFSA* 2, 318–19; *DP*, 86). In this context, we could also list the suspension of the 'laws of rationally thinking reason' and the combined effort to transplant us 'into the beautiful confusion of the imagination' (*KFSA* 2, 317; *DP*, 86), as well as many other characteristics of Romantic poetry which were mentioned earlier. Friedrich Schlegel's presentation makes it sufficiently clear, however, that the new mythology is not a research project to be carried out in the near future, but one of those more fundamental tasks that, upon reflection, manifest both the impossibility and the necessity of their realization. Schlegel distances himself from this project by letting it be introduced overzealously by his speaker. 'I will come right to the point', he says. 'Our poetry, I maintain, lacks a focal point, such as mythology was for the ancients' (*KFSA* 2, 312; *DP*, 81). Towards the end, he says: 'And thus let us, by light and life, hesitate no longer, but accelerate, each according to his own mind, that great development to which we are called' (*KFSA* 2, 322; *DP*, 88). One could, therefore, very well apply to the new mythology what Schlegel had earlier said about systems: 'It is equally fatal for the mind to have a system and not have a system. One will simply have to decide to combine the two' (*KFSA* 2, 173; *LF*, 167).

EXAMPLE: GOETHE'S *WILHELM MEISTER* AND THE EARLY
ROMANTIC THEORY OF THE NOVEL

The completion of the novel *Wilhelm Meister's Apprenticeship* exemplified not only the high poetic standing Goethe had acquired since his Italian journey, but also a new step in the history of the modern novel. Through a manner of composition of unprecedented compactness and complexity, Goethe's novel diverged radically from the novels of the eighteenth century. The manner in which narration and action are represented, the integration of the protagonist Wilhelm into the world and society, and the shaping of the events which lead him to this result correspond in such a balanced manner that the novel conveys an impression of absolutely organized coherence. This, at least, is the way in which Goethe's novel was received by his contemporaries, with the effect that expectations of the whole genre of the novel were raised to a higher level. Schiller, Wilhelm von Humboldt, Jean Paul, and Hegel attempted to comprehend the innovative features of Goethe's art of the novel. Yet, nowhere were the particular characteristics of *Wilhelm Meister* more enthusiastically perceived and articulated than among the early Romantics, especially the Schlegels, Novalis, and Tieck.

The spontaneous affinity of the early Romantics to Goethe's novel has often been analysed.[30] The most extravagant statement certainly derives from Friedrich Schlegel, who wrote without further ado: 'The French Revolution, Fichte's philosophy, and Goethe's *Meister* are the greatest tendencies of the age' (*KFSA* 2, 198; *LF*, 190). One way for the early Romantics to illustrate the novelty of Goethe's *Wilhelm Meister* was the approach in terms of genre, from the aspect of the novel. One can observe a tendency in German criticism at that time to derive the classical epic and the modern novel from the same source, namely epic narration, and to consider the epic and the novel as different manifestations of one and the same type of narration. Schelling, Hegel, and even Goethe shared this opinion, which still dominates Georg Lukács's theory of the novel. For the Schlegels, however, this was much too global a view of the modern novel that could not do justice to its particular historical character nor to its peculiar manner of narration. For these critics, the neatly delineated system of genres of the classical world was completely different from the poetry of modern Europe, which did not permit clear-cut generic distinctions but showed a process of constant trans-formation and new combinations of existing genres. The novel was for the Schlegels the most conspicuous expression of this fluid, indeterminable spirit of modernity. To derive this genre from the classical epic meant to overlook its peculiar nature.

Attempts at imitating the classical epic in the Romantic age, like those of Ariosto, demonstrate clearly enough that, com-pared to that of Homer, the art of narration had entered a new phase in which the unity of the classical epic could no longer be achieved. This becomes obvious when, in these modern epic creations, a slight persiflage or irony alien to the classical style of uninterrupted narration becomes noticeable (*KFSA* 1, 334). In contrast to Schelling and Hegel, who regretted the inability of their age to produce a true epic (*FWJS* 5, 328; *PA*, 212–21; and *HEG* 15, 338–9), Friedrich Schlegel said with a more distinct awareness of modernity: 'In vain do we hope for a Homer' (*KFSA* 1, 334), and he made this statement with obvious satisfaction. In his 'Letter on the Novel' of 1800, he rejected the prevailing opinion of his time that the novel had the closest relationship to the narrative or epic genre and insisted that it was a modern art form *sui generis* that could not be reduced to or derived from any classical genre (*KFSA* 2, 335–6; *DP*, 101). He substantiated his argument with the observation that narration is only one of the elements of the novel, saying that he could not imagine a novel that was not composed of narration, song, and a number of other forms, and thereby maintaining that the novel had a completely different structural principle than the epic (*KFSA* 2, 336). His central argument, however, concerns the narrative attitude of the author of the novel, which for him is fundamentally different from that of the epic narrator. He declares: 'Nothing is more contrary to the epic style than when the influences of the subjective mood become in the least visible, not to speak of the author's inclination to abandon himself to his humour and play with it, as often happens in the most excellent novels' (*KFSA* 2, 336; *DP*, 102). A. W. Schlegel used similar arguments to support the contention that the novel's poetic unity was entirely different from that of the epic. He stressed that Homer is completely without passion in his work and, as Aristotle had already remarked, says as little as possible on his own initiative (*AWS SW* 11, 190–1). Homer's epic is a 'calm represenation of progression', and the hexameter is only the 'expression and audible image' of this quiet rhythm (*AWS SW* 11, 192). The novel represents the spirit of modernity in such characteristic fashion for Friedrich Schlegel that it is actually the only modern genre that can be put on a par with the achievement of classical antiquity, that is, tragedy (*KFSA* 2, 335; 16, 88).

This prominent position of the novel in the history of modern literature reveals itself for the Schlegels in a remarkable way. At the beginning of this history, Cervantes undoubtedly reached the summit of the art of the novel and accomplished in it what Dante and Shakespeare had achieved in different genres. European literature, however, had since fallen into a decline of almost two hundred years, until the first signs of a reawakening of poetry became noticeable towards the end of the eighteenth century (*KFSA* 1, 335–6; 16, 158). This development also determined the art of the novel. During the seventeenth and eighteenth centuries, the novel was represented by authors who were not equal to Cervantes, but merited interest because of the 'originality of imagination' displayed in their works and features like irony, humour, and 'witty form'. After all, the power of imagination cannot be equally abundant at all times and in all countries (*KFSA* 2, 331). Such authors included Swift, Sterne, Fielding, Diderot, and Jean Paul. Not gifted by nature as great poets and 'quite remote from real art', in fact, more at home among 'so-called scholars and learned people' than in true poetry, these intellectuals had to make efforts and develop idiosyncratic techniques in order to work themselves into the art of writing novels (*KFSA* 2, 331–2) – just as Friedrich Schlegel himself had to do when writing *Lucinde*. Then, towards the end of the eighteenth century, Goethe appeared and marked a turning-point with his *Wilhelm Meister*, producing, after a long pause, a new and genuine poetry as a genuine poet. In his essay 'On the Study of Greek Poetry', Friedrich Schlegel had indeed hailed Goethe as the 'dawn of true art and pure beauty' (*KFSA* 1, 260). Together with Dante and Shakespeare, Goethe formed the 'great triple chord of modern poetry' (*KFSA* 2, 206; *LF*, 197). Novalis said that Goethe was '*now* the true vicar of the poetic spirit on earth' (*NO* 2, 495), and A. W. Schlegel called him the 'restorer of poetry in Germany' (*AWS V* 2, 252).

The point about the restoration of poetry deserves some attention, because it concerns the revival of poetry in the genre of the novel, that is, in a prosaic form, a form of poetry in prose. The result was that a genre which had not previously been recognized as a medium of poetry came to the fore. From the point of view of the classicistic theory of literature which was still valid at the time of the early Romantic critique of *Wilhelm Meister*, a prose work like the novel had to be considered unpoetic. Indeed, the novel was not included among the poetic genres of classicism. This exclusion of the novel as a work of poetry is hard for us to imagine today, but it is visible, for instance, in the correspondence between Schiller and Goethe, when Schiller writes to Goethe on 20 October 1797: 'The form of *Meister*, like every form of the novel in general, is absolutely not poetic, it is and lies solely and totally in the realm of reason, is subject to all of its demands, and shares all of its limits' (*FS* 29, 149). Of course, Schiller had also detected a true poetic spirit in *Wilhelm Meister*, but he could not go so far as to recognize the novel as true poetry and continued his letter to Goethe by observing: 'Since it is a true poetic spirit utilizing this form and expressing in it the most poetic situations, a peculiar vacillation between a poetic and a prosaic mood arises for which I have no name' (ib.). In his essay *On Naive and Sentimental Poetry*, Schiller called the author of the novel the 'half-brother' of the poet. According to him, the novel offends the 'high purity of the ideal', and in terms of his norms of classicistic-idealistic aesthetics, there is too much 'chaos' in the novel (*FS* 20, 464).

In sharp contrast to the prevailing critical opinion of their time, the Schlegels unrestrainedly conceded the potentiality of true poetry in the novel. In his review of *Wilhelm Meister*, Friedrich Schlegel thematized this problem by stating that here, everything was 'poetry, high pure poetry', and by maintaining that everything in the novel was thought and uttered as though by one 'who is both a divine poet and a perfect artist' (*KFSA* 2, 132; *GM*, 64). 'Every page offers us golden fruits upon silver platters', he says, or: 'This marvellous prose is prose, and yet it is poetry' (ib.). As if he wanted to put his stamp upon the poetic character of the novel, he said in another instance: 'Goethe's purely poetical poetry is the most complete poetry of poetry' (*KFSA* 2, 206; *LF*, 197). A. W. Schlegel was of the opinion that the narrative rhythm was capable of rendering a novel poetic throughout, 'although the manner of writing must remain, of course, purely prosaic', and added that 'this seems to be really accomplished in *Wilhelm Meister*' (*AWS SW* 11, 22).

If we consider more closely the early Romantic insistence upon the poetic character of *Wilhelm Meister*, it soon becomes obvious that the arguments refer mainly to structural and linguistic features and less to questions of genre. The Schlegels were indifferent to the neoclassicistic exclusion of the novel from the list of established genres of poetry because they did not at all share this theory, which must have appeared peculiar to them. They considered the novels of Cervantes, and especially the prose in his novellas, as the highest poetry. A decisive reason for this was the striking language of Cervantes' prose, which, through its fine formulations, acquired a poetic character which distinguished it from the language of common life. Their interest in Goethe's novel thus had a specifically linguistic orientation. They wanted to know how a language obviously drawn from the 'cultivated speech of social life' (*KFSA* 2, 133; *GM*, 64) could inform a work of art which ·satisfied those rigorous demands of perfect interconnection, structure, grouping, and positioning that up to now had been exemplified by works of Sophocles and Shakespeare. In his review of *Wilhelm Meister*, Friedrich Schlegel expressly warned against reading Goethe's novel 'as it is usually taken on the social level: as a novel in which the persons and the incidents are the ultimate end and aim'. To judge this 'absolutely new and unique' book according to a conventional idea of genre was 'as if a child tried to clutch the stars and the moon in his hand and pack them into his satchel' (ib.). In his analysis of the language of *Wilhelm Meister*, Schlegel noticed that, although the 'threads of this style' are on the whole drawn from modern cultivated life, they show a 'noble and delicate development' both 'significant and pro- found'. When the poet turns to 'some aspect peculiar to this or that everyday trade or skill', or to 'spheres that according to public commonplace are utterly remote from poetry', he takes pleasure in 'rare and strange metaphors', so that even these instances come close to the most delicate of poetry. Schlegel asks: 'What is lacking in the paens of praise that Werner and Wilhelm raise to trade and to poetry but the metre, for everyone to acknowledge them as poetry?' (*KFSA* 2, 132; *GM*, 64).

Friedrich Schlegel's main argument, however, is developed through structural analysis and refers to the particular mode of connection, of 'tying', in Goethe's manner of narration. He thinks that the 'usual expectations of unity and coherence' are disappointed by this novel 'as often as they are fulfilled' (*KFSA* 2, 134; *GM*, 65). He wants to say that a new manner of shaping a poetic unity is at work here that reminds us of the one familiar in the past, but which is, nevertheless, basically different from it. Indeed, he continues that the 'reader who possesses a true instinct for system, who has a sense of totality' will discover in the novel 'the more deeply he probes, the more inner con- nections and relations and the greater intellectual coherence' (ib.). How is this to be understood? At the beginning of his review, Schlegel said that the tale proceeds like the 'quiet unfolding of an aspiring spirit' (*KFSA* 2, 126; *GM*, 59). Later he mentions the 'innate impulse of this work, so organized and organizing down to its finest detail, to form a whole' (*KFSA* 2, 131; *GM*, 63). Describing the 'organization of the whole' (*KFSA* 2, 135; *GM*, 65) more precisely, he stresses that the 'overall coherence' connecting the individual parts into a 'rounded whole' is achieved by raising expectations and interests, opening new scenes and worlds, returning the 'old figures with youth renewed', mutually mirroring the individual images, and thereby creating a peculiar kind of genetic, fluid unity which has the movement of progression. Schlegel says that 'every book opens with a new scene and a new world', or more precisely, that 'every book contains the germ of the next, and with vital energy absorbs into its own being what the previous book has yielded' (*KFSA* 2, 135; *GM*, 66). Newness is never entirely new or disruptive, and familiarity is never completely familiar or merely old.

This idea of a genetic, fluid, progressive unity can be further specified. Schlegel elucidates it with reference to the relationship of the individual parts of the work to the whole and says: 'The differing nature of the individual sections should be able to throw a great deal of light on the organization of the whole. But in progressing appropriately from the parts to the whole, observation and analysis must not get lost in overminute detail' (*KFSA* 2, 135; *GM*, 65). In order to avoid this, the reader must pause 'at those major sections whose independence is also maintained by their free treatment'. This is justified, because the poet himself has acknowledged their 'homogeneity and original unity'. One can go further and maintain that the poet's treatment consists in two apparently antagonistic inclinations by shaping rounded out, homogeneous, and unified parts of the work on the one hand, and by pulling them together and forming them into an accomplished whole on the other, always through poetic means. Schlegel says: 'The development within the individual sections ensures the overall coherence, and in pulling them together, the poet confirms their variety. And in this way each essential part of the single and indivisible novel becomes a system in itself' (ib.).

This special kind of unity can be illustrated on various levels. From a formal point of view, this progressive unfolding manifests itself in Goethe's innovative technique of narration, which operates with foreshadowings of the events, correspondences, mirroring of characters and contrasting figures, and thereby creates a type of poetic unity which is never fully present and resides in a constant progression. In this case, the unity rests on Goethe's 'manner of representation' as described in the sentence: 'It is rather the manner of the representation which endows even the most circumscribed character with the appearance of a unique, autonomous individual, while yet possessing another aspect, another variation of that general human nature which is constant in all its transformations, so that each variation is a small part of the infinite worked' (*KFSA* 2, 127; *GM*, 60). In a more specific sense, this technique becomes apparent in the first book in a 'series of varied situations and picturesque contrasts, each casting a new and brighter light on Wilhelm's character from a different, noteworthy perspective' (*KFSA* 2, 128–9; *GM*, 61). A good example of this 'manner of representation' is the figure of the Stranger in the first book – rightly called 'the Stranger', since he appears as a 'measure of the heights to which the work has yet to rise' (*KFSA* 2, 128; *GM*, 61). The *Confessions of a Beautiful Soul*, by contrast, first 'come as a surprise in their unaffected singularity, their apparent isolation from the whole, and the arbitrariness of their involvement in it'. However, just as Wilhelm, 'on closer reflection', is perhaps not without all relationship to the Aunt, these confessions prove 'some connection with the novel as a whole', at least in so far as 'these are also years of apprenticeship when nothing is learnt but how to exist' and how to live according to one's particular principles or unalterable nature (*KFSA* 2, 141; *GM*, 70). To emphasize the truly poetic character of the work in its obvious distinction from all utility and proximity to reality, Schlegel speculates that a reader who expects a particular result from these events may feel disappointed and even deceived by the end of the 'novel', for 'nothing comes of all these educational arrangements but an unassuming charm'. Such a reader discovers that 'behind all these amazing chance occurrences, prophetic hints, and mysterious appearances, there is nothing but the most lucid poetry', and he learns that the 'final threads of the entire action are guided merely by the whim of a mind cultivated to perfection' (*KFSA* 2, 144; *GM*, 72).

The most notable means for this 'manner of representation' and the 'how' of Goethe's poetic communication is, of course, 'the irony which hovers over the entire work' (*KFSA* 2, 137; *GM*, 67), which Schlegel emphasizes in many suggestive formulations. We meet irony in the third book of the second volume in the contrast between the charm of theatre and acting on the one hand, and the commonness of the real life of the actors on the other, between the nobility and the actors ('neither of whom will yield the prize for absurdity to the other'), and between 'high expectations and bad management', between 'hope and success', between 'imagination and reality'. This contrasting depiction is 'foolishness shaped into transparency', and it conveys an impression which we might call an 'ethereal merriment', which is, however, 'too fine and delicate for the mere letter of commentary for it to be reflected and reproduced' (ib.). Stylistically, this irony manifests itself in an 'illusion of dignity and importance, mocking at itself', in an 'apparent negligence' or 'seeming tautologies', in a 'highly prosaic tone in the midst of the poetic mood', or in a 'delicate breath of poetic pedantry on the most prosaic occasions' (*KFSA* 2, 137–8; *GM*, 67). Schlegel refers to this highly conscious and reflective ironic communication when he warns the reader not to let himself be 'deceived into thinking that the poet is not utterly serious about his masterpiece, even though he himself seems to take the characters and incidents so lightly and playfully, never mentioning his hero except with some irony, and seeming to smile down from the heights of his intellect upon his work'. On the contrary, we should think of this novel 'in connection with the very highest ideas, and not read it as it is usually taken, on the social level' (*KFSA* 2, 133; *GM*, 64).

A further peculiarity of *Wilhelm Meister* which produces this effect of a progressive unity is that the novel criticizes itself and is one of those books 'which carries its own judgment within it, and spares the critic his labour' (*KFSA* 2, 133–4; *GM*, 65). This is perhaps the most important point in Schlegel's review. It is closely related to the ironic character of the work and can be defined in manifold ways. The particular progressive unity of *Wilhelm Meister*, one could say, consists in the fact that it cannot be defined or identified, because it transcends critical comprehension and is, with regard to its future, engaged in an eternal development, in a never fully realized manifoldness of becoming. Someone who wished to review *Wilhelm Meister* would appear to us 'like the young man who went walking into the woods with a book under his arm' and was driven away by Philine with the cuckoo. In similar fashion, our feelings protest 'against an orthodox academic judgment of this divine organism' (ib.). Yet, the desire for a comprehensive understanding of such a work is irrefutable. Schlegel says: 'Why should we not breathe in the perfume of a flower and at the same time, entirely absorbed in the observation, contemplate in its infinite ramifications the vein-system of a single leaf?' The human being is not only interested 'in the brilliant outward covering, the bright garment of this beautiful earth', but also likes to detect 'the layering and the composition of the strata far within', and would even wish 'to delve deeper and deeper, even to the very centre, if possible, and would want to know the construction of the whole' (*KFSA* 2, 131; *GM*, 63).

Since this progressive, constantly mobile and restructuring unity does not have such a centre, however, the desire for comprehension remains, if not unsatisfied, then at least caught up in the same progression as *Wilhelm Meister* itself. As far as understanding the work in the sense of a critical review is concerned, the thought arises that perhaps 'we should judge it, and at the same time refrain from judging it; which does not seem to be at all an easy task' (*KFSA* 2, 133; *GM*, 65). This could be accomplished by means of commentaries – 'but of the sort which should on no account make everything clear for everybody' (*KFSA* 2, 135; *GM*, 66). For where there is so much to be noticed, 'there would be little point in drawing attention to something that has been there already, or recurs again and again with a few changes'. Such a commentary is excellent only 'if the reader who completely understands *Wilhelm Meister* finds it utterly familiar and if the reader who does not understand it at all finds it stupid and empty', if the reader 'who only half-understands the work' also finds the commentary 'half-comprehensible', so that 'it would enlighten him in some respects, but perhaps only confuse him all the more in others' (*KFSA* 2, 136; *GM*, 66). Another possibility of doing justice to the hermeneutic inexhaustibility of *Wilhelm Meister* would consist in 'dialogues' on the work to 'banish all one-sidedness' through a plurality of voices and views as well as through this particular form of writing. For if only one person presented his individual point of view, it would in the end 'tell us no more than that the speaker's opinions on these matters were as stated' (*KFSA* 2, 143; *GM*, 71).

In this manner, Friedrich Schlegel articulates his theory of understanding of literary works that actively resist any re- duction to a determinable meaning and instead involve the reader and critic in the infinitely progressive movement of the work of art. Only in this sense can we speak of a truly 'poetic criticism', of a genuine understanding and comprehending of the unity of *Wilhelm Meister*. Such poetic criticism does not act 'as a mere inscription, and merely say what the thing is and where it stands and should stand in the world'. For that, only one person would be required and only one insight. The poetic critic, however, intends to 'represent the representation anew', he will 'add to the work, restore it, shape it afresh'. Such criticism must do this 'because every great work, of whatever kind, knows more than it says, and aspires to more than it knows' (*KFSA* 2, 140; *GM*, 69). Goethe's novel is one of those writings that will never be fully understood and will therefore have to be 'eternally criticized and interpreted again' (*KFSA* 16, 141; 2, 149).

As far as content is concerned, the progressive unity of the novel can be seen in 'Wilhelm's infinite impulse toward higher education', in the 'sequence of grades of these apprentice years in the art of living' (*KFSA* 2, 136; *GM*, 66), indeed, in his acquiring of the 'art of all arts, the art of living' (*KFSA* 2, 143). This first refers to the progression Wilhelm makes in his knowledge of art in the usual sense, by way of a 'natural development of his own mind' and because 'others have urged him toward it', since he meets 'real experts' with whom he conducts 'conversations about art' (*KFSA* 2, 139; *GM*, 68). Viewing his development from this perspective, one could assume that it had been the 'poet's intention to set up a comprehensive theory of art, or rather to represent one in living examples and aspects' (*KFSA* 2, 131; *GM*, 63). Indeed, one could easily establish a 'system in the author's presentation of this physics of poetry', not, to be sure, by way of the 'dead framework of a didactic structure, but stage after stage of every natural history and educational theory in living progression' (*KFSA* 2, 132; *GM*, 63) – beginning with the 'puppet plays, the early childhood years of poetic instinct' (ib.) and moving from there to nature poetry, represented by Mignon and the Harpist, to the highest and most profound of all artistic poetry, Shakespeare's *Hamlet* (*KFSA* 2, 139; *GM*, 68). The fourth book, however, makes it clear that it does not deal with 'what we call theatre or poetry, but the great spectacle of humanity itself, and the art of all arts, the art of living' (*KFSA* 2, 143; *GM*, 71).

This refers to that concluding movement of the novel toward finiteness, concrete reality, and limited form, which has always been seen as its humane and humanistic message. Whereas Friedrich Schlegel had analysed the structural and narrative qualities of *Wilhelm Meister* with attention to the finest nuances, he appears most reticent and taciturn as far as this theme is concerned. He does not ignore the importance of it, but writes in his concluding sentences with astonishing brevity:

It is as if everything that had gone on before were only a witty, interesting game, and now the novel were to become serious. The fourth volume is already the work itself; the previous parts are only preparation. This is where the curtain of the holy of holies is drawn back, and we suddenly find ourselves upon a height where everything is god-like and serene and pure, and in which Mignon's exequies appear as important and significant as the necessary coming of her end. (*KFSA* 2, 146; *GM*, 73)

Critics are usually unanimous in praising Friedrich Schlegel's understanding of the finest shades of nuance in the structure of the novel, but are simultaneously disappointed at his apparently complete failure to comprehend the final goal and concretization of Wilhelm's apprenticeship.[31] Instead of giving us more information about what he saw behind the 'curtain of the holy of holies', he breaks off his review at precisely this point with a simple 'to be continued' (*KFSA* 2, 146) and leaves us uncertain as to what he had recognized as the goal, the message of the novel. It appears justified, however, to interpret his silence as deliberate, as a refusal to comment on Goethe's classical restraint and guidance on the finitude of life because it flagrantly contradicted his own Romantic objective of a movement into infinity. The phrase 'to be continued' should therefore be taken as belonging structurally to his review, as its natural end, and not as a promise of a future continuation.

This already points ahead to the critique of Goethe's *Wilhelm Meister* by the early Romantics, which is often accompanied by a recognition of the novel's high poetic qualities. This critique first manifests itself in a slight withdrawal from Goethe, as far as the articulation of the theory of the novel is concerned, and a stronger inclination toward Cervantes. The main quality of the Romantic novel is now seen as 'fantasizing the music of life' (*KFSA* 2, 283), rendering the 'chime of life', representing the 'infinite play of the world' (*KFSA* 2, 324). A poetic work like the novel is supposed to 'suspend the movement and laws of rationally thinking reason and to transplant us once again into the beautiful confusion of the imagination, into the original chaos of human nature' (*KFSA* 2, 319; *DP*, 86). Unity and inner cohesion are not thereby cancelled, but become apparent in a more complex manner than in *Wilhelm Meister*. Such a work has 'organization' and 'structure of the whole', but these phenomena manifest themselves as an 'artfully organized confusion', as a 'charming symmetry of contradictions', or as a 'wonderful perennial alternation of enthusiasm and irony' (*KFSA* 2, 319; *DP*, 86). What constitutes the novel as a coherent unity is by no means the 'dramatic thread of the story', but the 'relationship of the whole composition to a higher unity' (*KFSA* 2, 336; *DP*, 101). This is the infinite play of the world, referred to in the 'Speech on Mythology', of which poetry should create 'representations' (*KFSA* 2, 324; *DP*, 89), or the 'hieroglyph of the one eternal love and the sacred fullness of life' referred to in the 'Letter on the Novel' (*KFSA* 2, 334; *DP*, 100). Only the imagination can grasp this fullness of life and it 'strives with all its might to express it'. However, in the 'sphere of nature', in the realm of human language and experience, the imagination can 'communicate and express itself only indirectly' and therefore transforms itself into 'witty' or ironic configurations (ib.).

A. W. Schlegel was more direct in explaining how a poetic unity based on reflection, wit, and irony should be understood. Referring to *Don Quixote*, he declares:

If, however, a material cohesion is required, connecting occurrences among one another like cause and effect, means and end, so that everything is organized to accomplish something, a marriage, for instance, or other consoling things for which the great crowd of amateurs turns over the last pages of a novel – then the entire composition of *Don Quixote* is defective. (*AWS SW* 11, 410)

A. W. Schlegel is of the opinion that the novel may very well consist of facts and events, but it does not unite them in logical sequence and presents them according to the laws of the imagination, an approach which is also defined as 'witty' composition. He maintains that, for a genuine novel, the principle of progressive action is irrelevant. What matters is 'that the series of phenomena in their illusory change be harmonious, controlled by the imagination, and never interrupt the enchantment until the end' (*AWS SW* 11, 411). His brother thought that the 'great wit of Romantic poetry' could be perceived not so much in individual sections, or in 'persons, events, situations, and individual aspirations', but rather in the structure of the whole (*KFSA* 2, 334; *DP*, 100).

Early Romantic theory was at that time on its way to the notion of absolute poetry, and it established an ideal which could no longer be satisfied by any author of the eighteenth century, not even by Goethe. As Friedrich Schlegel repeatedly mentions in his notebooks, Goethe's *Wilhelm Meister* is 'modern', that is, determined by reflection, and also 'poetic', that is, produced by creative imagination, but not 'Romantic', that is, not characterized by the relationship to the infinite which distinguished the poetry of the Romantic tradition and was to be rejuvenated in the poetry of the early Romantics (*KFSA* 16, 108, 113, 133; 3, 138). He also says in these notes that the Romantic novel, like the ellipse, requires 'two centres', one of which lies in the infinite. Novalis went much further in his critique, and maintained that Goethe's *Wilhelm Meister* was unpoetic to the highest degree, a 'satire against poetry', so much so that whoever took this work truly to heart would never read another novel again (*NO* 3, 646–7). One only has to compare novels like Tieck's *Franz Sternbald's Wanderings*, Novalis' *Heinrich von Ofterdingen*, or Brentano's *Godwi* with Goethe's *Wilhelm Meister* to illustrate the differences in content and structure, although these novels were usually misunderstood as imitations of *Wilhelm Meister*. At that time, F. Schlegel wrote into his notebooks: 'We have philosophical novels (Jacobi), poetic novels (Goethe), now only a *Romantic* novel is lacking' (*KFSA* 16, 133). A little later he added: '*Don Quixote* is still the only Romantic novel throughout' (*KFSA* 16, 176). But shortly afterwards, he discovered Tieck's *Franz Sternbald* and said: 'the first novel since Cervantes that is Romantic and in that respect, far above *Meister*' (*KFSA* 24, 260). In another instance we read: '*Sternbald* [is] a Romantic novel and for that reason absolute poetry' (*KFSA* 16, 206).

The prototype of the early Romantic novel, however, was to be *Heinrich von Ofterdingen*, which originated in conscious and direct competition with Goethe's *Wilhelm Meister*.[32] That this novel remained unfinished did not really diminish its appreciation by the early Romantics, and has perhaps even contributed to increasing its reputation, since such incompleteness could be interpreted as expressing the high demand of poetry transcending every human capability. Friedrich Schlegel and Tieck edited the first part of the novel in 1802 after Novalis had died. When Schlegel presented a brief survey of the most recent German literature in his newly founded periodical *Europa* of 1803, he divided his subject into exoteric and esoteric literature. The exoteric was for him the kind 'that represented the ideal of the beautiful within the affairs of human life', thereby applying a human measurement, whereas the esoteric is that kind of poetry 'that transcends the human realm and attempts to encompass at the same time the human being and nature' (*KFSA* 3, 11). He does not give any example of the exoteric type of poetry, but we know from his notebooks and later statements that he thought of *Wilhelm Meister* in this instance (*KFSA* 3, 109–44). Esoteric poetry, however, in its 'transition from the novel to mythology', is represented for him by Novalis' uncompleted *Heinrich von Ofterdingen*. He says: 'If

Novalis had completed the cycle of novels he had projected to represent world and life from the most important different perspectives of the human mind, this would have produced a work that no other could possibly equal in forming and stimulating the imagination' (*KFSA* 3, 12). At that point, the early Romantic theory of the novel had become fully articulated, but it still remained to some extent related to Goethe, since it aimed to transcend or surpass what he had accomplished.

CHAPTER 4

Novalis and the mystical dimension
of early Romantic theory

Novalis certainly cannot be considered a mystic in the usual
sense of the word, that is, as someone who, beyond the exercise
of reason, is preoccupied with direct experience of the extra-
terrestrial, supranatural, or divine in a highly personal manner.
Yet this is precisely the meaning of the term 'mysticism' as it
was half-ironically used by Novalis and Friedrich Schlegel when
they indulged their own inclinations towards 'mysticism' and
ridiculed the common-sense or rational outlook on life as
lacking any trait of their 'mysticism'. In a certain respect, this
mysticism can be seen as the transcending, transparent quality
of the Romantic style in its attraction to the infinite. But for the
two friends, genuine mysticism leaves behind the predominantly
literary character of the Romantic style and in its broader
scope, it can better be described in philosophical terms or even
as 'religion'. In this sense, Novalis told Friedrich Schlegel in
the summer of 1798 that he had discovered the 'religion of
the visible universe', and he assured his friend: 'You will
not believe how far that reaches. I think here I will leave
Schelling far behind' (*KFSA* 24, 152). Schlegel was deeply
impressed by this project of an 'unhabitual view of habitual
life', and he readily admitted to Novalis that the latter had
the greater capacity for attaining this attitude (*KFSA* 24,
155). Earlier, in March of the same year, he had established a
certain order of rank in religious or mystical ability among the
early Romantics by according his brother the smallest and
Novalis the largest share of it, whereas he himself took a middle
position. He wrote: 'If Hardenberg [Novalis] has more religion,
then I have more philosophy of religion. And as much religion

as you have, I will always be able to bring together' (*KFSA* 24, 104).

A more precise way of delineating these differences would be to say that Novalis was a true poet among the early Romantics and that his poetry, in contrast to that of Tieck, is of a profoundly philosophical, metaphysical, indeed, mystical and religious character. He lacked almost completely the historical, critical, and philological orientation of the Schlegels, although he admired highly what they accomplished in these areas (*NO* 4, 186–7). When, in his own speculation, he had to distinguish between ancient and modern, classical and Romantic literature, he simply followed the Schlegelian schemes, but he immediately added a personal touch when he spoke about these phenomena in more concrete terms. On the interrelationship of the poetic with the Romantic and the philosophical with the prosaic, he wrote, for instance: 'Philosophy is prose. Its consonants. *Distant* philosophy sounds like *poetry* – a *poem*. *Actio in distans*. Distant mountains, distant people, distant events, etc., all this becomes Romantic, *quod idem est* – hence derives our arch-poetic nature. Poetry of night and of twilight' (*NO* 3, 302). This statement certainly was the source of the well-known fragment by Novalis: 'The art of *alienating* in an *agreeable* manner, to make an object alien and yet familiar and attractive – that is the romantic poetics' (*NO* 2, 685). As will be noticed, Novalis uses the term 'romantic' much more freely than the Schlegels and in a manner relating to himself or to poetry in general, that is, independent from and uninhibited by the great models of the Romantic tradition. In another instance, he relates poetry directly to mysticism, stating:

The sense for poetry has much in common with that for mysticism. It is the sense for the peculiar, personal, unknown, mysterious, for what is to be *revealed*, the necessary-accidental. It represents the unrepresentable. It sees the invisible, feels the unfeelable, etc. Criticism of poetry is an absurdity. Although difficult to decide, the only possible distinction is whether something is poetry or not. The poet is truly deprived in his senses – instead, everything happens within him. He represents in the most genuine manner *subject-object – mind and world*.

Hence the infinity is a good poem, the eternity. The sense for poetry has a close relationship with the sense for augury and the religious sense, with the sense for prophecy in general. The poet organizes, unites, chooses, invents – why precisely so and not otherwise, is incomprehensible even to himself. (*NO* 3, 686)

Novalis also believed that poets occurred at certain crucial times in the history of humanity, and he was certainly convinced that he was born into such a period of transition and rejuvenation. Whereas the Schlegels expressed their analogous feelings of an epochal break by means of highly reflective and intellectual metaphors like 'transcendental poetry', 'new mythology', or the 'age of rejuvenation', Novalis expressed his experience in more direct poetic language and often added a surrealistic touch to it. As already mentioned, in his essay *Christendom or Europe*, he senses 'with full certainty the traces of a new world' in the Germany of his time (*NO* 3, 519). These traces were seen in the movement towards a 'higher epoch of culture', in a 'tremendous fermentation in the sciences and the arts', and in a 'versatility without comparison'. All this represented for him 'a new history, a new humanity', and he described this new state of affairs in his characteristic manner:

The newborn will be an image of its father, a new golden age with dark, infinite eyes, a prophetic, miraculous and healing time, a consoling and life-engendering time – a great time of reconciliation, a saviour, native among humankind like a true genius, not visible but believed and adored by his believers in manifold forms, consumed as bread and wine, embraced as the beloved, breathed as air, heard as word and song, and absorbed as death with heavenly pleasure and with the most intense pain of love into the inner part of the dissolving body. (*NO* 3, 519–20)

In his relationship to philosophy, Novalis adopted a similar personal approach and lacked the broad training in the history of philosophy which the Schlegels displayed in their aesthetic writings. Instead, he studied only a few philosophers – Kant, Fichte, Schelling, and Hemsterhuis among them – not so much with a view to acquiring a general type of knowledge as to what they could teach him about the development of his own philosophical outlook. He attempted to learn from them, for instance, how to distinguish between the philosophical and the poetic outlook on life, the sense for philosophy and the sense for poetry. The study of Fichte is prominent among these exercises, because Novalis, shortly after he had completed his studies and took up his appointment as a salt-mine engineer in the summer of 1795, chose Fichte as the philosopher with whose help he hoped to acquire this sense for philosophy and train his own powers of philosophical thought. Since he had no technical philosophical terminology at his disposal, whereas Fichte had created his own terminology completely independently of tradition, this encounter has an unusual degree of immediacy and originality as far as the direct philosophical experience is concerned. Yet, because of the almost complete lack of an orientation to points of reference in traditional philosophy, these notes are also surprisingly difficult to understand. Known as Novalis' 'Fichte Studies',[1] they do not yet have the character of fragments, but rather of a continuous dialogue with another text, although some of them could clearly be seen as early Romantic fragments (in the most rigorous sense of the term). The main event to which this text bears witness is Novalis' progressive dissociation from Fichte, and his emergence as a theorist in his own right. Since Friedrich Schlegel, who conducted his own argument with Fichte, appeared on the scene at a crucial point during these studies, Novalis' quarrel with Fichte's philosophy can best be approached in a comparative fashion, taking account of Friedrich Schlegel's position in the controversy so as to demonstrate more clearly its importance to early Romantic theory.

FRIEDRICH SCHLEGEL'S AND NOVALIS' CRITIQUE OF FICHTE

Perhaps Novalis chose Fichte as the instrument of his own philosophical training mainly because the philosopher had moved to Jena University in the summer semester of 1794 and Novalis had made his personal acquaintance in the house of the philosopher Niethammer in May of the following year.[2] The question of whether one could understand the new philosophy became a test for many intellectuals in the Jena area around that time. Novalis carried out his professional duties in the little town of Tennstedt, where he lived in personal isolation, at least as far as his intellectual interests were concerned. In January 1800, he mentioned in a curriculum vitae that he had devoted his free time in 1795–6 in Tennstedt 'to old favourite ideas and an arduous investigation of Fichte's philosophy' (*NO* 4, 311). At that time, however, a more comprehensive acquaintance with Fichte was hardly possible, since Novalis wrote to his brother between 11 and 12 November 1795 that he had about three hours per day for his leisure and that these were occupied with 'introductory studies to my entire future life, the filling of essential gaps in my knowledge, and the necessary exercise of my powers of thought' (*NO* 4, 159). Only the last type of activity can be considered relevant to his Fichte studies in the proper sense. Yet, during the autumn of 1795, Novalis certainly began his study of Fichte and probably concentrated on the various introductory writings to the 'doctrine of science' that had appeared up to then, with special attention, perhaps, to the more comprehensive *Foundation of the Entire Doctrine of Science* – although such preference is hard to ascertain from his notes.

In February 1796, Novalis returned to his home in Weißenfels as an assessor in the salt-mines and probably continued his study of Fichte. A more intense preoccupation with the philosopher can be detected around the time when Friedrich Schlegel visited his friend on his way from Dresden to Jena towards the end of June and the beginning of August. In his letter of invitation to Schlegel, Novalis had written on 8 July 1796: 'My favourite study has the same name as my fiancée. Sophie is her name – philosophy is the soul of my life and the key to my innermost self. Since that acquaintance, I also have become completely amalgamated with that study' (*NO* 4, 188). Indeed, that 'study' can safely be interpreted as a reference to Fichte and becomes clear later in the letter: 'To Fichte I owe stimulation. – It is he who awakened and indirectly stifled me' (ib.). Since Schlegel had settled in Jena in August 1796, the friends continued their exchange about Fichte's philosophy in letters that were occasionally accompanied by 'written packages' (*KFSA* 23, 340), that is, Schlegel's philosophical notebooks containing his critique of Fichte (*KFSA* 18, 31–9). Novalis would have liked to answer them with a 'thick bundle of replications and additions' and wrote: 'Herewith I am returning with many thanks your philosophica. They have become most valuable to me. My head is full of them, where they have made crude breeding grounds' (*KFSA* 23, 340). In December, Schlegel visited his friend again and later remembered with pleasure the 'polemical totality' that had marked the last evening of their 'cheerful togetherness' (*KFSA* 23, 341). From 18 to 21 January 1797, he was once again in Weißenfels (ib.). During these visits the friends continued their discussion of Fichte's philosophy in hour-long talks. Schlegel remembered this activity when he wrote to Novalis on 5 May 1797: 'How nice it would be if we could sit together all by ourselves and philosophize for a few days, or as we liked to call it, Fichtecize' (*KFSA* 23, 363). If we wanted to describe the general thrust of this Fichtecizing, we would have to say that it consisted in a rising above the confines of Fichte's philosophy in an attempt to safeguard the reflective and self-critical mobility of the mind from any disciplinary (philosophy) and systematic (doctrine of science) fixation.[3]

At this time, the state of health of Novalis' fiancée, Sophia von Kühn, deteriorated, and she died on 19 March 1797 (*NO* 4, 204). After her death, Novalis wrote to Schlegel on 13 April 1797 that his main interest in the world was his theoretical concerns, but the plan to spend the summer in Jena and study Fichte's philosophy together with his friend did not now materialize. In the spring of 1797, Novalis discovered Schelling (*NO* 4, 226), and this opened a new field of study for him. By that time, Friedrich Schlegel had left the 'teacher of the doctrine of science' far behind and came to appreciate Fichte more and more as a human being, although he put the sceptical question to Novalis: 'For *you*, however, his philosophy is perhaps not liberal enough?' (*KFSA* 23, 363). Novalis answered on 14 June 1797: 'Fichte cannot move out of his doctrine of science, at least not without a transformation of himself, which appears to me to be impossible' (*NO* 4, 230). He also wrote:

As far as Fichte is concerned, you are undoubtedly right – I am moving more and more towards your point of view regarding his doctrine of science... Fichte is the most dangerous of all the thinkers I know. He encircles you with his magic. Nobody will be more misunderstood and hated than he. Yet soon the misunderstandings will die out. You are chosen to protect the aspiring original thinkers against Fichte's magic. I know from experience that such an understanding is difficult to reach. Many a hint, many a cue to orient myself in this awful labyrinth of abstraction, I owe exclusively to you and the idea I have of your free, critical mind. (*NO* 4, 230)

This also meant for Novalis the end of his interest in Fichte, as well as a broadening of his intellectual horizons. If one were to look for a precise moment for the end of these studies, it probably coincided with the death of Sophia von Kühn, which basically transformed Novalis' entire activity and personality. The well-known diary entry of 29 May 1797, 'At the border crossing [of Tennstedt] and Grüningen I had the pleasure of finding the true concept of the Fichtean Ego' (*NO* 4, 42), perhaps marks the definitive end of his interest in Fichte. Grüningen was where Sophia was buried. This entry can be linked with a corresponding note on 17 May 1797: 'My main task should be – to bring everything into a relationship to her [Sophia's] idea' (*NO* 4, 37). In August 1797, after Friedrich Schlegel had departed for Berlin, Novalis visited Fichte in Jena, but he no longer had the same medium of understanding with him. He wrote to Schlegel on 5 September 1797 about the meeting: 'At Fichte's, I got into my favourite topic. – He was not of my opinion, but, considering he regarded my opinion extravagant, what careful attention he paid it.[4] – This will remain unforgettable to me' (*NO* 4, 236).

Novalis took his leave from Fichte. For Schlegel, however, the need to separate the systematic philosopher from the artistic thinker governed his general attitude towards Fichte, and simultaneously provided an enormous inspiration for his own theory of reflective, 'transcendental' poetry. A few examples from his encounters with Fichte can illustrate the point. Shortly after his arrival in Jena at the beginning of August 1796, Schlegel visited the philosopher, whose writings had raised such enormous expectations on his part; but the first meeting, as is often the case in such situations, turned out to be disappointing. 'I do not know how it happened', he wrote to Novalis on 9 August 1796. 'I was embarrassed, and we only talked about trivial things' (*KFSA* 23, 328). But Schlegel continued to explore the philosopher in his writings, his lectures, and through personal contacts, and indeed soon became 'Fichte's friend', as he indicated to Novalis on several occasions (*KFSA* 23, 367, 369). 'I like the person Fichte more and more', he wrote, but he added that Novalis might not find his philosophy 'liberal enough' (*KFSA* 23, 363). He also mentioned his own 'polemical view of his [Fichte's] system' (*KFSA* 23, 370) and exclaimed on 26 May 1797: 'if only I could be entirely frank towards him! But I will at least never be dishonest towards him, never that' (*KFSA* 23, 369). Schlegel had begun to formulate his objections to Fichte in the fragments in his notebooks, which he, of course, could not show to the philosopher (*KFSA* 23, 367) and which he instead sent as 'written packages' to Novalis (*KFSA* 23, 340, 368, 373, 374).

In his letters to Christian Gottfried Körner in Dresden, who had followed his early writings on Greek literature, Friedrich Schlegel is rather more outspoken about his actual objections to Fichte. On 21 September 1791, he reports that he is visiting Fichte quite frequently and finds him 'occasionally better' in personal dialogue than in his writings or at the lecture podium. 'At the latter I found him admirably trivial', he said, and added: 'It is strange that he has absolutely and totally no suspicion at all that he is not' (*KFSA* 23, 333). Schlegel found him 'weak and strange in every science that has an object'. During their first conversation, Fichte earnestly told the young historian of Greek literature that he 'would rather count peas than study history' (ib.). Yet, Schlegel insisted that he defended, loved, and praised all of this not out of an 'iron obstinacy, maintaining preconceived prejudices', but out of the conviction that nothing great ever happens 'without such glaring one-sidedness, without a certain limitation' (ib.). On 30 January

1797, he told Körner that he was finished with 'Fichte's system'. He talked with him only about the external aspects and liked the person all the more since he had 'separated himself truly and decidedly from the teacher of the doctrine of science' (*KFSA* 2, 343). To this experience one should add a letter by Fichte to Friedrich Schlegel of 16 August 1800. Fichte wrote in response to Schlegel's *Dialogue on Poetry* and took issue with the idea expressed at the beginning of the *Dialogue* that there are manifold individual views of poetry and that we should try to 'grasp every other independent form of poetry' so that it may become a stimulus for our own imagination (*KFSA* 2, 284; *DP*, 53). Fichte was not only upset by the asystematic character of this view, but also by its implied historicism. The friendship between Schlegel and Fichte had deepened during these years, but their completely diverging theoretical views could not be better expressed than by Fichte's letter:

Having received the last two pieces of the *Athenaeum*, I now believe I understand completely your system of poetry that we discussed last winter in Jena. It is worthy of your mind, your love of hard work, and your historical research, although I myself consider it only provisional, only suitable for this time. Something in the material of poetry is, to be sure, individual; the main thing in it, however, its form, is thoroughly general; and in this regard, I would say contrary to you: Just as there is only one reason, there is only one true poetry.[5] Are we supposed to absorb the works of the great artists of previous times through study? – It may be that in our desiccated age we can do no better. But where then did the source for the first artist who had no predecessors originate? Could it be possible that this original source has now dried up for all time? Oh, if only we had a pure aesthetics! (*FI* 4, 282–3)

In the notebooks sent to him by Friedrich Schlegel, Novalis read of how one could 'almost always boldly contradict' what Fichte assumed as self-evident (*KFSA* 18, 31). Regarding his endless attempts at introducing his audience to the point of view of the doctrine of science, Schlegel wrote: 'I have not yet found anybody who believed in Fichte, yet many who admire him, some who know him, and the one or the other who understands him. Fichte is somehow like the drunk man who does not tire of mounting his horse from one side and, transcendingly, keeps

falling off on the other' (*KFSA* 18, 32). As to Fichte's importance
for aesthetics, Schlegel was of the opinion: 'However limited
someone might be in his sphere, at certain times he nevertheless
enjoys an outlook on aesthetics and such things' (ib.). In
general, however, Schlegel believed that Fichte's doctrine of
science was 'too narrow': 'Only Fichte's principles are deduced
in it, that is, the logical ones, and not even these completely.
And what about the practical, the moral or ethical ones? –
Society, learning, wit, art, and so on are also entitled to be deduced
here' (ib.). Fichte's theory of femininity appeared ridiculous to
Schlegel, for whom true women were not 'passive', but
'antithetical, physically as well as morally' (*KFSA* 18, 34). On
the whole, Fichte's doctrine of science appeared to him 'as
rhetorical as Fichte himself': 'With regard to individuality, it is
a *Fichtean presentation of the Fichtean spirit in Fichtean letters*' (*KFSA*
18, 33). In a more humorous vein, Schlegel considered the
doctrine of science not to be the '*formative process of pure egohood*,
but fancies and narrations of an oscillating, travelling, strolling
mystic' (*KFSA* 18, 35). Schlegel, in other words, raised the
question of Fichte's own historicity, or the historicity of what
was going on in his system, and felt that what was proclaimed
here as absolute Ego or absolute thought was nothing more than
Johann Gottlieb Fichte in Jena, including all his personal
idiosyncracies and prejudices.

In a more philosophical or theoretical formulation of his
critique, Schlegel objected to Fichte's assumption of only one
basic principle, one single axiom (*Grundsatz*), and insisted that,
to be set in motion, the transcendental process has to proceed
from two interactive principles, two reciprocal poles, or one
axiom antithetical in itself (*Wechselgrundsatz*, *KFSA* 18, 36). In its
philosophical orientation, his critique of Fichte already pre-
supposes that absolute idealism of a full-blown interaction of
subject and object, ideality and reality, ego and nature, which
Schelling and Hegel made their own after the turn of the
century.[6] Schlegel, however, never limited his view to philosophical statements alone, but sought their most productive
expression in poetry and literature. Yet, in a strictly philosophical sense, it was evident for him that idealism and realism,

subject and object, Fichte and Spinoza, were not only complementary components, but also two poles that must 'interactively make themselves possible, necessary, and real'. And he added: 'This may indeed be beyond Fichte; Schelling surmises as much' (*KFSA* 18, 66). If we take later texts by Friedrich Schlegel into consideration, this aspect of his critique of Fichte can be characterized as an objection to making only the Ego the centre of 'spirit, life, activity, movement, and change' and reducing the non-Ego or nature to a state of 'constant calm, standstill, immobility, lack of all change, movement, and life, that is, death' (*KFSA* 12, 152, 190). Nature is thereby degraded to a 'dead sensual world or a mere sediment of reflection', to a 'mere restraint and limitation of the infinitely developing spirit', even to the 'true non-being' (*KFSA* 8, 68). 'Fichtean idealism proves its incompetence by not understanding and comprehending materialism', Schlegel said in a note of 1811 (*KFSA* 17, 269). Friedrich August Hülsen, an associate of the early Romantic circle, expressed this feeling most vividly when he studied the doctrine of science in the Schwarza Valley of the Thuringian forest, formerly one of Germany's most beautiful landscapes, and, on looking up from the book, said: 'Nature approached me as if a distant friend had greeted me after a long absence.'[7]

To view Novalis' 'Fichte Studies' in a broader perspective and to give them their weight in comparison to Friedrich Schlegel's Fichte critique, one has to consider that Schlegel arrived in Jena with a fully developed concept of Fichte's philosophy. He had already organized his conception of Greek literature according to idealistic principles (*nature*: the epic, *freedom*: lyric poetry, and the *synthesis of the two*: drama), whereas Novalis was still expending much energy on working his way into this 'awful labyrinth of abstraction' (*NO* 4, 230). Schlegel's position in relation to Fichte had always been one of distance, expressing a feeling of his own superiority, whereas Novalis attempted to transpose himself into the interior of this philosophy and from there, seek to transcend it. Novalis' 'Fichte Studies' also stand at the beginning of his career as a writer and have all the features of both the importance and transitoriness of an early work. Today they are recognized as one of the most peculiar products of early Romanticism in the field of philosophy. Indeed, Novalis' 'Fichte Studies' conduct an intellectual struggle with a type of systematic thought that represents philosophy in exemplary fashion, and they come to realize, from the point of view of poetry as well as that of personal self-recognition, that philosophy is immeasurably incomplete and thereby in need of support from all sorts of other quarters.

The central subject of interest in Novalis' study of Fichte is obviously that of philosophy, which for him was certainly not the only activity of the mind, nor even the most prominent of all intellectual experiences as it was for Fichte. For Novalis, philosophy stands in a larger context where faith, love, poetry, and religion have the same right to existence. These 'Fichte Studies' can therefore be characterized in more than one respect as attempts to analyse the 'activities of the spirit' in a more comprehensive manner than Fichte had done and to create a theory of the ego with a much wider scope than the doctrine of knowledge had been able to establish. All this is carried out in the context of Fichte's philosophy, which bestows a particularistic, ephemeral character upon these notes. The real target, however, is philosophy as such. In his critique of philosophy, Novalis does not take on the whole of the history of philosophy, or an abstract, self-constructed notion of philosophy, but philosophy in its most recent expression, in its most advanced form. In his analyses, he concentrates on the theory of the ego and relates it to his own notion of personality; he sketches out a theory of the imagination in contrast to Fichte's thought process; he describes the poetic power in its distinctness from the philosophical faculty within us. In other instances, he attempts simply to clarify concepts (life – something – nothing) in order to distinguish the faculty of feeling from that of reflection, to compare 'intellectual intuition' with 'intellectual power of seeing', and he writes down everything that appears noteworthy to him and translates it into his own language and manner of thinking.

The most important theme emerging from these manifold observations – if one can single out one dominant theme at all

– is that of the relationship of philosophy to poetry, of the thinking to the poetizing power. Here Fichte maintained the absolute primacy of philosophy; for him, all questions boiled down to philosophical ones. Novalis, unlike Fichte, relativized the activity of philosophy, or rather, he gave other realms of experience autonomy, especially poetry. Many interpreters have seen the result of these studies as embodied in a fragment of a later date that seems to proclaim the absolute domination of poetry and reads: 'Poetry is the absolutely real. This is the core of my philosophy. The more poetic, the more true' (*NO* 2, 647). This statement seems to reverse the relationship between philosophy and poetry as Fichte saw it, and to introduce the reign of poetry as the core of early Romantic theory as expressed by Novalis. Yet, if one bears in mind the counter- or interactive quality of the notion of 'real' in its relationship to 'ideal', as well as other statements by Novalis, one can very well show that, like the Schlegels, he understood the relationship between poetry and philosophy in terms of an interaction (*Wechselwirkung*) and conceived of the union or fusion of philosophy and poetry not in terms of subjugating one to the other, but as a full maintenance of the mutual tension between the two poles. One of these fragments states: 'The poem of reason is philosophy – This is the highest elan that reason gives to itself – Unity of *reason* and *imagination*. Without philosophy, the human being remains discordant in his essential powers – There are two human beings – one reasonable being and one poet. Without philosophy, imperfect poet – without poetry, imperfect thinker, critic' (*NO* 3, 531). In another instance, Novalis describes the interaction of philosophy and poetry in the following way: '...the philosopher becomes a poet. *Poet* is only the highest degree of the thinker, or the perceiver, etc. (Degrees of the poet.) The separation of poet and thinker is only fictitious – and to the *disadvantage* of both – It is a sign of a sickness – and of a sickly constitution' (*NO* 3, 406). This thought continues to be formulated in the most varied contexts. Another of the entries reads: 'Poetry is the hero of philosophy. Philosophy elevates poetry to its principle. Philosophy teaches us the value of poetry. Philosophy is the *theory of poetry*.

Philosophy teaches us what poetry is, that poetry is the one and the all' (*NO* 2, 591).

If one isolated philosophy from this lively and essential interaction with poetry, as Fichte seems to propose, one would reduce philosophy to a 'mere activity of the intelligence' (*NO* 2, 269). The isolated, energy-specific activity of the intelligence, however, is its 'proper mode of thought', the seeking of grounds, the desire of an absolute grounding (*NO* 2, 269). Reduced to this tendency, philosophy becomes finite, petrified. Philosophy becomes free and an 'infinite activity', an 'infinitely free activity in us', once such a ground is no longer sought or the desire for it is satisfied only in a relative manner. This goal of a free philosophy could be called the 'absolute postulate' of philosophy, whereas all 'search for *one principle*' appears like an attempt to find the 'squaring of the circle', the 'perpetuum mobile', or 'the philosopher's stone' (*NO* 2, 270).

In general, one can say about Friedrich Schlegel's and Novalis' attitude toward Fichte's thought that, after closer acquaintance with his doctrine of knowledge, they made a decisive distinction between the project in its philosophical scope and its reflective and animating thought process, between the dogmatic ballast of Fichte's theory of consciousness and the life of the intelligence, between what they called the 'letter' and the 'spirit' of the doctrine of science. They separated, in other words, Fichte as the promulgator of a new scientific edifice or system of philosophy from Fichte as the 'inventor of an entirely new way of thinking – for which there is not yet a name in language' (*NO* 2, 524). They readily relinquished all the cognitive elements, categories of thought, and forms of self-consciousness that Fichte attempted to establish through his philosophical speculation, and focused almost exclusively on the 'art of reflection', on the lively thought and counterthought which animated this philosophy. They also felt free to transfer this informed thinking to other realms of human experience, such as poetry, art, society, politics, but especially to literary communication. When Friedrich Schlegel attempted, shortly after the dissolution of the early Romantic group, to give the readers of his Paris journal *Europa* (1803–5) some flavour of the spirit that had emanated from the new German literature and philosophy, he referred to Fichte as a most prominent figure but practically ignored all of the material part of his doctrine of science, its philosophical and systematic constructs. Instead, he focused solely on the reflective, agile character of Fichte's thought process and described his merit as having 'entirely on his own and for the first time discovered and installed the proper method in philosophy by organizing free autonomous thought as an art' (*KFSA* 3, 6). And he added that Fichte, 'by upsetting consciousness in its innermost creative depth', had provoked the 'most significant changes and revolutions in all other areas of human thought and creation' and that there was 'hardly an art or a science that had not yet been seized by the light of intellectual intuition and begun to experience the beneficial results of idealism' (ib.).

ABSOLUTE IDEALISM

Shortly after Sophia von Kühn's death, Novalis wrote to Friedrich Schlegel that his earlier plan of coming to Jena had become meaningless because projects of a much larger magnitude had arisen for his intellectual life. He wrote this letter from Tennstedt, the place close to Grüningen where he had met his fiancée and where she now was buried:

You can imagine how I feel in this neighbourhood, the old witness of my and her glory. I still feel a secret enjoyment to be so close to her grave. It attracts me ever more closely, and this now occasionally constitutes my indescribable happiness. My autumn has come, and I feel so free, usually so vigorous – something can come of me after all. This much I solemnly assure you – that it has become absolutely clear to me what a heavenly accident her death has been – the key to everything – a marvellously appropriate event. Only through it could various things be absolutely resolved and much immaturity overcome. A simple mighty force has come to reflection within me. My love has become a flame gradually consuming everything earthly. Your hope has proven right – there is much more healing power, perseverance, and resistance in my soul than I realized myself – a healing power cutting the ground from under the evil – a perseverance not to be measured by hours – a resistance against everything that could profane my sanctuary. For four years I was at universities, and one year I studied – I am twenty-five years old, and have lived only half a year. (*NO* 4, 220)

As one might expect, this personal aspect of Sophia's death has drawn much attention in Novalis research. If one subtracts from this letter, however, the momentary and acute feeling of loss and also the tone of self-consolation as well as the usual extravagance in Novalis' manner of writing, it expresses a decisive moment in the genesis of his thought. Seen in the context of his previous *Fichte Studies* and their concentration on the critique of ego-centred, subject-centred, philosophy, Novalis now steps into his own sphere as a thinker by augmenting and completing the subject by the object, the human being by nature, this world by the beyond. Only a few days after the letter just quoted had been written, Novalis reported to Friedrich Schlegel that Schelling's philosophy of nature had found 'a curious reader' in him (*NO* 4, 226). Shortly afterwards he wrote: 'I am trying to acquaint myself with Schelling, the sooner the better. In one respect he corresponds to me more than Fichte. I will soon know what significance he will have for me' (*NO* 4, 230).

Schelling's significance was certainly great, but for Novalis similar to Fichte's. While eagerly deriving the basic impulse and most productive inspiration from Schelling, the quest for a comprehensive synthesis of subject and object, he nevertheless dropped what he considered the limitation of this idea. He gave Schelling's purely philosophical formulation, including its discursive, systematic, and disciplinary characteristics, a much wider scope. When Novalis told Friedrich Schlegel about his discovery of the 'religion of the visible universe', he immediately added: 'I think that here I will leave Schelling far behind' (*NO* 4, 255) – as if a formulation like 'religion of the visible universe' did not already indicate that. On 11 May 1798, about a year after the events described in the previous section, he wrote to Schlegel that 'he had conceived of an idea, a very great, very productive idea', that would throw a 'ray of light of the highest significance upon the Fichtean system', an idea which would permit the 'realization of the most *daring* desires and premo-

nitions of all times'. But he said he could at that point only incite
the curiosity of his friend without satisfying it, and he merely
hinted at his idea by using the symbol for infinity: ∞ (*NO* 4,
254).

The most important text of this time is the collection of 114
fragments entitled *Pollen* which Novalis published in the
Athenaeum (*NO* 2, 413–63). Fragment 14 introduces his new
manner of thinking in interacting, oscillating antinomies, as
when he characterizes life as the 'beginning of death', but death
as 'both an ending and a beginning, a separation and a
tightening self-relationship' (*NO* 2, 417). The most compact of
these is Fragment 16, which reads:

Imagination posits afterlife with regard to us either in the height or in
the depth or in metempsychosis. We dream of journeys through the
universe: is not the universe within us? We do not know the depths of
our spirit. – Inward is the direction of the mysterious path. Within us
or nowhere is eternity with its past and future worlds. The external
world is the world of shadows; it casts its shadows into the realm of
light. Now it may well seem to us dark within, lonely, formless. But
how very different will it appear to us when this darkness is past and
the shadow-body has been moved away. We shall enjoy more than
ever, for our spirit has known privation. (*NO* 2, 417–19; *HN*, 66)

This expansion and reversal of perspectives leads to the most
surprising assumptions. Life appears as an incident, a play of
incidents and occurrences, which, like all play, implies surprise
and dissimulation. Many omens of ordinary people deal with
these reversed relationships: 'Bad dreams signify luck; dec-
laration of death, long life; a hare crossing one's path,
misfortune. Virtually all the superstition of ordinary people is
based on interpretations of this play.' Yet, in a similar way, the
imagination of a great poet like Goethe operates when he
occupies himself 'in a poetic manner with a mysterious play'
(*NO* 2, 425; *AF*, 64). In the last analysis, this is one of our most
important intellectual activities: 'All incidents of our life are
materials out of which we can make whatever we like. Whoever
has much intelligence will make much of his life. Every
acquaintance, every incident might, for a thoroughly intellectual person, become the first link of an infinite series, the

beginning of an unending novel' (*NO* 2, 437–9; *HN*, 68). Lastly, Novalis' broad notion of poetry as embracing mythology, religion, and philosophy is also the result of these expanding syntheses. In Fragment 71, he says:

> In the beginning, poets and priests were one; it was only in later times that they became separated. The true poet, however, has always remained a priest, just as the true priest has remained a poet. And will not the future restore this former state of affairs? (*NO* 2, 441; *AF*, 66)

The most direct way of exhibiting the contours of Novalis' new ideal realism is to compare it with Schelling's exposition of his new universal system of philosophy. There are two texts that lend themselves to such a condensed confrontation, Schelling's introduction to his *System of Transcendental Idealism* of 1800 and a section of Novalis' fragments from the collection *The General Brouillon* (*Materials for Encyclopaedistics*) of 1798–9 that articulates a thought first expressed in the *Teplitz Fragments*: 'The world is a *universal trope* of the [human] mind – a symbolic image of it' (*NO* 2, 600). Schelling's system of 1800 attempts to expand transcendental idealism to a 'system of the entirety of all knowledge' (*FWJS* 3, 330), and for him the best model for doing so lies in the genetic form of presentation, that is, in the exposition of 'all parts of philosophy in one great continuity and the entirety of philosophy as what it is, namely, a progressive history of self-consciousness' (*FWJS* 3, 331). A particular aspect of this '*gradual sequence* of perceptions through which the ego rises to consciousness in its highest exponentation' is for Schelling the 'parallelism between nature and intelligence' that had been surmised earlier, but could not be fully grasped either in transcendental philosophy or in an isolated philosophy of nature, but required the interaction of the two sciences. The same 'potencies of intuitions' operative in the ego can thereby be shown to a certain degree in nature (*FWJS* 3, 332). The ultimate basis of such harmony between subject and object would then appear as a principle of absolute identity (*FWJS* 3, 333).

The passage to be compared with Novalis' conception of idealism does not follow this long pathway of a gradual and painstaking history of consciousness, but takes the faster approach of showing that, in our knowledge and every application of it, the 'objective and the subjective are so instantly united that we cannot determine to which of the two the priority belongs': 'There is here no first, and no second; both are co-instantaneous and one' (*FWJS* 3, 339).[8] The proof of this statement is that it matters little whether I start at the one or the other pole because I will eventually be driven from the one to the other. This is the decisive point in Schelling's systematic exposition of absolute idealism of which Hegel later said in his *Lectures on the History of Philosophy*: 'Thus nature is impelled to the spirit, and spirit to nature; either may be given the first place, and both must come to pass' (*HEG* 20, 424; *HP* 3, 517). Schelling demonstrates the interaction between the two poles by calling the 'sum of all that is merely objective' *nature*, and the 'sum of all that is subjective' the *self* or *intelligence*, and then showing how the 'reciprocal concurrence of both' in 'all acts of positive knowledge' can be explained. In this interaction, the intelligence is conceived of as 'exclusively representative, nature as exclusively represented', the ego as 'conscious' and nature 'as without consciousness', as 'in itself unconscious' (*FWJS* 3, 339). The actual demonstration takes place if I take the objective as the first and then account for the 'supervention of the subjective which coalesces with it' (ib.); and subsequently take the subjective as the first and then explain 'how there supervenes on it a coincident objective' (*FWJS* 3, 341). The first task is resolved by showing that every act of our knowledge of nature tends to 'introduce theory into our views of natural phenomena' and that eventually the 'highest perfection of natural philosophy consists in the perfect spiritualization of all the laws of nature into laws of intuition and intellect' (*FWJS* 3, 340). Schelling refers to optical laws that are 'but a geometry', gravitation, the heavenly motions, and concludes from this that the complete theory of nature would resolve the whole of nature into an intelligence. Conversely, if we take the intelligence and the subject as primary, as happens in transcendental philosophy, this philosophy cannot determine itself as the point of view of the ego without absorbing the non-ego into itself and declaring it a result of the ego's activity, as Fichte did in the most radical version of that system. Transcendental philosophy thereby always relates at least indirectly to that other 'necessary basic science of philosophy' that Schelling conceived as philosophy of nature. As is already obvious from this introductory sketch to his *System of Transcendental Philosophy* of 1800, Schelling's aim is an absolutely philosophical and systematic one. He provides a 'glance into the entire system of philosophy', which, as he thought, is perfected by means of two basic sciences: 'They mutually seek and complement each other, while being opposed in their principle and tendency' (*FWJS* 3, 343).

In the relevant section of his *General Brouillon*, Novalis conceives of the realm of nature as that of the 'unknown, the mysterious', the '*result* and the *beginning* of all'. 'What cannot be comprehended is in the imperfect state of nature', he says, or: 'Nature is incomprehensible per se. Quietness and formed incomprehensibility.' What is incomprehensible, however, 'is to be made progressively comprehensible' (*NO* 3, 302). This is achieved by comprehending it, as in the case of nature, as a 'universal trope', an image of the human spirit (*NO* 2, 600). For we 'know properly only that which knows itself', that is, our own ego. Yet, Novalis adds: 'Knowledge is a means of coming again to non-knowledge' (*NO* 3, 302), implying, of course, that the firm point of our knowledge in the ego or in the subject, which is utilized for a comprehension of nature, becomes absorbed and eventually consumed by the incomprehensibility of nature. Whereas Schelling confidently saw in the interaction of his two 'basic sciences' a progressive generation of absolute knowledge, Novalis, adopting a more reflective and critical attitude, concentrates on the incomprehensibility and 'infinity' in this interrelationship. Wilhelm Dilthey made the interpretation of this section an important part of his essay on Novalis and saw its clear distinction from Schelling's point of view as its most important aspect. He characterized Novalis' perspective as the 'poetic view of nature' and said: 'Everywhere a mind of poetic formation permeates his theories.'[9] Citing formulations from the text just quoted, Dilthey characterized this view as follows:

We only know properly that which knows itself. In the light of this deep thought, the result appears to be plausible: Nature is incomprehensible per se. It is incomprehensible not because of an accidental reason, however, but because the light of consciousness meets it only from outside. But then nature appears as a universal trope of the mind, that is, as a symbolic image of it. Consequently, nature is comprehensible only through the mind. And as Hardenberg [Novalis] is now engaged in unending conjectures with regard to the innermost secret of ourselves, he also sees the corresponding innermost realm of nature in the changing illuminations of such ascending and descending conceptions. (*NO* 3, 306)

Dilthey concludes his analysis of Novalis' view with the observation:

The only thing that is wholly evident is the negative cognition that the world as we can perceive it in analogy to our ego cannot be explained solely from the point of view of reason as the basic character of our ego, but only from a fermenting depth of this ego, which, a miracle to ourselves, finds the same primary expression in the will, the soul, or the imagination. (*NO* 3, 306)

THE NATURE OF THE TRULY POETIC

On this basis, Novalis' view of poetry finds its broader context, as was indicated earlier.[10] After he had conceived of his 'very great, very productive idea', however, his absolute idealism came to coincide with his poetic view of the world, although we know that this did not mean an unrestrained poeticizing of everything, but, like Friedrich Schlegel's 'new mythology', resulted from the synthesis of philosophy and poetry. Already in his 'Fichte Studies', Novalis had employed this kind of poetic shaping, integrating the reflective, theoretical part of the ego with the object-oriented tendency of representation, as when he says:

It is coarse and dull to communicate oneself simply because of the content – content and material should not tyrannize us. We should communicate ourselves in a *suitable* manner – artfully – reflectively – our delivery should not be unworthy of ourselves – it should be appropriate to its public, to its aim. It should utilize the advantages of time and space. (*NO* 2, 281)

This now became more and more his model of poetic activity. In another passage in his 'Fichte Studies', he analysed the interaction of subject and object in poetic creation more precisely, although we have to consider that these reflections occur in the context of an exploration of Fichte's philosophy, and thereby show a natural inclination towards the side of the subject or the ego. This passage reads:

If there is an independent representative power – which simply represents in order to represent – to represent in order to represent – then it is a *free* representation. This simply indicates that not the object as such but the *ego* as base of the activity should determine the activity. The work of art thereby assumes a free, autonomous, ideal character – an imposing spirit – for it is a *visible* product of an ego. – The ego, however, posits itself distinctly in this manner because it posits itself as an infinite ego – and since it has to posit itself as an infinitely representing ego, it posits itself as free, as a distinctly representing ego. The object can only be the germ, the type, the point of investment – only the forming power develops creatively the beautiful totality at, in, and through the object. (*NO* 2, 282–3)

In his later fragments Novalis is inexhaustible in describing this particular power of the poet. One favourite example is the language used by the poet not in the sense of 'general signs', but as 'tones', or 'terms of enchantment'. He compares poets' words to the clothing of saints that enclose 'wondrous powers'. We cannot really say that, for the poet, language is too poor but only that it is 'always too general' (*NO* 2, 533; *AF*, 68–9). Another way of illustrating the particular nature of poetry is by comparing it to the other arts, especially painting and music. Like the painter who sees the visible things of this world with eyes different from those of the ordinary person, the poet sees the events of the inner and outer world in a manner different from others. No other art, however, can exemplify the nature of poetry more effectively than music. 'Nowhere', Novalis says, 'is it more conspicuous than in music that it is only the spirit that poeticizes the objects, the modifications of the material, and that the beautiful, the subject of art, is not pregiven to us and does not lie readymade in the appearances either. All sounds produced by nature are hoarse – and spiritless – only a musical soul perceives the rustling of the forest, the whistling of the wind, the song of the nightingale, the babbling of the brook as melodious and significant. The musician takes the essence of his art from himself – not even the slightest suspicion of imitation can be incurred by him' (*NO* 2, 573–4). This particular quality of perception also applies to the painter, the only difference being that he employs 'an infinitely more difficult language of signs than the musician', that he paints with the eye. In the last analysis, however, 'every human being is to a small degree already an artist'. The main difference is that the artist is able to employ this particular susceptibility as he pleases and 'without exterior solicitation', whereas the non-artist becomes susceptible only at the instigation of an external solicitation (*NO* 2, 574).

In another instance, Novalis calls this artistic susceptibility by its proper name and says: 'The imagination is that wondrous sense that can *substitute* for us all other senses – and is already to a large extent subject to our choice. While the outer senses are totally subservient to mechanical laws – the imagination is obviously not bound to the presence of and contact with outer stimulations' (*NO* 2, 650). A little later, he compares consciously artistic activity to the working of instinct and observes: 'Instinct is art *without intention* – art without knowing how and what one is doing. Instinct can be transformed into *art – by observing* the activity of art. What is done instinctively can eventually be learned to be done artistically. Art of producing the ridiculous and the romantic' (*NO* 3, 287). From this point of view poetry can be seen as the 'intentional, active, productive employment of our organs', if we understand by 'organs' our natural equipment as human beings, including the organs of perception and knowledge. Indeed, Novalis continues, 'thinking perhaps would not be much different – and thinking and poeticizing are thereby one' (*NO* 3, 563). The particular point in this fragment is, of course, that thinking is enlisted on the side of the natural, unconscious, instinctive activities of the mind, whereas poeticizing is ranked as an intentional, consicous action. Yet, the type of artistic intentionality advocated by the Schlegels is too radical for Novalis and lacks the natural component of an instinctive and unconscious creation. He comments on these relationships in a fragment on Shakespeare that reads:

When the Schlegels talk about the intentionality and artificiality of Shakespeare's works, they overlook that art belongs to nature and is, as it were, nature contemplating, imitating, and forming itself. The art of a well-developed nature is of course miles apart from the artificiality of reason and a merely reasoning spirit. Shakespeare was no calculating mind, no scholar, he was a powerful and motley soul whose inventions and works, like products of nature, bear the impression of a thinking spirit and in which even the most penetrating observer will discover new agreements with the infinite structure of the universe, correspondences to ideas not yet discovered and relationships with the higher powers and senses of humanity. His works are metaphorical and polysemous, simple and inexhaustible like these [the works of nature], and nothing more senseless could be said about them than that they were works of art in that limited and mechanical meaning of the word. (*NO* 3, 569)

Taken together, the fragments quoted so far on the poetic faculty reveal a constant oscillation, a subtle shifting of balance in their alternate predilection for the artistic or the natural, the intentional or the instinctive tendency of poetry. Some of them, especially those from or close to the *Fichte Studies*, show a clear preponderance of the subjective side, whereas others, especially the fragment on Shakespeare, are more explicitly in favour of nature. Novalis appears to adopt this oscillating manner of viewing the interrelationship in order to avoid a 'systematic' solution, a final result, as well as to keep reflection alive and open-ended for further discoveries.

Another characteristic way of describing the nature of poetry and the poetic is by analogy to the human mind (*Gemüt*). One fragment adopting this approach reads: 'Poetry is true idealism – contemplation of the world as contemplation of a *large mind* – self-consciousness of the universe' (*NO* 3, 640). That poetry is essentially a '*representation* of the *mind* – of the *inner world in its entirety*' is already indicated for Novalis by its medium, that is, its words, language, which are the revelation of this inner realm

(*NO* 3, 650). However, just as the 'representation of nature' must be 'spontaneous, peculiarly general, connecting, and creative', the 'representation of the mind' should never aim at 'how it [the mind] is, but how it could be, and ought to be' (ib.). One fragment describes the mind's particular poetic manner of 'weaving' [*verknüpfen*] more precisely:

In our mind, everything is connected in the most peculiar, pleasant, and lively manner. The strangest things come together by virtue of one space, one time, an odd similarity, an error, some accident. In this manner, curious unities and peculiar connections originate – one thing reminds us of everything, becomes the sign of many things, and is itself signified by and referred to many things. Reason and imagination are united through time and space in the most extraordinary manner, and we can say that each thought, each phenomenon of our mind is the most individual part of an altogether individual totality. (*NO* 3, 650–1)

Because of this intimate interrelationship between mind and poetry, the question of whether 'everything will in the end become poetry' coincides with the question: 'Will the world in the end become [human] *mind*?' (*NO* 3, 654). Yet the investigation into the nature of poetry remains infinite and cannot be concluded with a firm result: 'What actually constitutes the essence of poetry can definitely not be determined. It is infinitely composed and yet simple. Beautiful, romantic, harmonious are only partial expressions for the poetic' (*NO* 3, 690).

It is in this context that Novalis formulates his most avant-gardist ideas about poetry. In one of these fragments, he characterizes poetry as the 'art of exciting the mind' (*Gemütser-regungskunst*), as an 'inner *painting* and *music*' producing 'inner *moods* and pictures or visual perceptions like a "mechanical instrument" in the mind – perhaps also *spiritual* dances, etc.' (*NO* 3, 639). In such a procedure, the poet uses 'things and words like *piano keys*', and his 'entire poetry consists in an active association of ideas – of spontaneous, intentional, ideal *production of contingencies*' (*Zufallsproduktion*) (*NO* 3, 451). Unity and connection appear to be suspended in such poetry. 'A fairy-tale', Novalis says, 'is really like a dream image – without

connection – an *ensemble* of wondrous things and occurrences –
for instance a *musical fantasy* – the harmonious effects of an
aeolian harp – *nature itself*. And he adds: 'If a *story* is brought
into a fairy-tale, this is already an interference from the outside'
(*NO* 3, 454). Then the fairy-tale assumes features of 'reason', of
'connection, meaning' (*NO* 3, 455). In another instance, we
read:

Narrations without connection, yet with associations, as in *dreams*.
Poems – merely *melodious* and full of beautiful words – but also without
any meaning and connection – at the most, some stanzas comprehensible – they must appear altogether like fragments of the most
diverse things. True poetry can have at best an allegorical meaning on
the whole and, like music, exert an indirect effect: Nature is therefore
purely *poetic* – like the chamber of a magician – of a physicist – a
nursery – a storage room, a storage pantry. (*NO* 3, 572)

As some of these fragments indicate, Novalis had his own
predilections as to which literary genre was best suited to
express the truly poetic – although he never took any particular
genre in an established or traditional sense, but always added
his personal touch to it. One of his favourite genres is certainly
the novel. In his reflections on the poetic character of the novel,
he directly referred to what the Schlegels had said about the
relationship of prose and poetry, and in particular to the prose
rhythm of novelistic narration in which A. W. Schlegel had
seen the most efficient way of elevating prose to poetry. Novalis,
however, saw in melodiousness, word position, varied sentence
structure, and other such literary devices, only 'ornaments'
that could not really elevate prose to poetry, but left it on the
level of functional, goal-oriented, and thus limited speech (*NO*
4, 246). In a letter to A. W. Schlegel of 12 January 1798,
responding directly to the review of Goethe's *Hermann and
Dorothea* in which Schlegel had formulated his propositions
regarding prose rhythm, Novalis based his approach not on
prose expanding into poetry, as A. W. Schlegel had done, but
on a broad notion of poetry capable of moving into all
directions, now manifesting itself according to strict rhythmical
laws and now expanding itself into the realm of prose and the

novel. Novalis was of the opinion, however, that in the latter case, language need not be informed and embellished by rhetorical ornaments: 'The more simple, uniform, quiet the movements of the sentences are here, the more congruent their coherences on the whole, the looser the connection and the more transparent and pale the expression – the more *perfect*, in contrast to *embellished* prose, this *careless* poetry will be – a poetry apparently dependent on objects' (*NO* 4, 247). This poetry seems to relax from the rigour of strict regulations, but whoever dares to engage in this type of poetry, Novalis continues, soon becomes aware of 'how difficult it is to realize poetry perfectly in this form'. He thought that this 'expanded poetry' con- stituted the 'greatest problem' for the actual, practising poet and saw a problem here that could be resolved only by approximation, one that truly belonged to the realm of 'higher poetry', which he preferred to call the 'poetry of the infinite' (ib.).

These observations clearly point to Novalis' novel *Heinrich von Ofterdingen*, but a good many of the fragments dealing with the novel address Goethe's *Wilhelm Meister*, still regarded by Novalis in his early fragments as the *non plus ultra* of the genre. One is certainly not mistaken in attributing to the novel Novalis' technique of 'romanticizing', especially if one keeps in mind that the first two syllables of this verb contain the German word for novel (*Roman*). Novalis describes a dual, counteractive movement, similar to Friedrich Schlegel's alternation of self- creation and self-annihilation, in which romanticizing consti- tutes the expansion of the mind into the mysterious and unknown, yet eventually reverses itself into a return into the ordinary and familiar. Like Schlegel, Novalis often expressed these relationships in pseudo-mathematical terms of exponen- tiation and logarithms. The most impressive fragment on this subject reads:

The world must be romanticized. That is how we re-establish the original meaning. To romanticize is nothing but a qualitative exponentiation. The lower self becomes identified with a higher self in this operation. Just as we ourselves are such a series of qualitative exponentiation. This operation is still totally unknown. By giving the ordinary a high meaning, the habitual a mysterious appearance, the known the dignity of the unknown, the finite an infinite air – I romanticize. The reverse operation relates to the higher, unknown, mystical, infinite – it becomes logarithmized through this connection and acquires an ordinary expression. Romantic philosophy. *Lingua romana*. Alternating elevation and lowering. (*NO* 2, 545)

This device also finds manifold expression in *Heinrich von Ofterdingen* with its great variety of alternations between proximity and remoteness or the interior of the world and the infinity of the universe. This novel, although only a fragmentary work, best expresses Novalis' idea of the genre.

Closely connected with his theory of the novel, and indeed also with the structure of *Heinrich von Ofterdingen*, is Novalis' conception of the fairy-tale. Situated in the world of facts and reality, as we are, the weakness of our 'organs' and self-realization does not permit us to see ourselves in a 'fairy-world'. Here lies the importance of this genre: 'All fairy-tales are dreams of that homelike world that is everywhere and nowhere' (*NO* 2, 564). Fairy-tales are also best suited for expressing a particular 'mood of the mind' (*Gemütsstimmung*: *NO* 3, 377). Nothing, however, is more opposed to the nature of the fairy-tale than 'a moral fate – a lawful coherence'. The fairy-tale represents 'genuine natural anarchy', a world as in dreams (*NO* 3, 438). In this regard, the fairy-tale is 'canonical for poetry – everything poetic must be as in a fairy-tale', and the poet has to adore 'chance' (*NO* 3, 449).

Novalis also discusses the other forms of poetry in this manner, lyric poetry in particular, always giving his observations an original personal twist that distinguishes them from any conventional discussion of literary genres. As he had associated the prose of the novel with true poetry in his reflections, he relates the lyric genre, traditionally considered the epitome of poetry, with prose. The individual terminology for this speculation is that of a 'plus-poetry' (i.e. objective, meditative, and beautiful) and a 'minus-poetry' (i.e. subjective, reflective, and interesting). The following fragment seems like a continuation of the observations on poetry and prose in the letter to A. W. Schlegel of 12 January 1798:

It would be an appropriate question whether the lyric poem is properly a *poem*, plus-poetry, or rather prose, minus-poetry? Just as people have taken the novel for prose, they have taken the lyric poem for poetry – both unjustly. The highest, most characteristic prose is the lyric poem. (*NO* 3, 536)

To justify such an extreme claim, Novalis would probably insist on the subjective, reflective, and interesting features of lyric poetry and confront them with the objective, meditative, and beautiful elements he wished to give expression to in the novel.

Most important in these reflections on possible forms of literary expression and communication is, of course, the fragment, which not only constituted a prominent genre for Novalis, but also a manner of writing indicative of the particular era in which he lived. Yet, as with Friedrich Schlegel, Novalis' own manner of writing in fragments became the hallmark of the fragment as such. There are distinctly different nuances in the fragments of the two friends. In the case of Schlegel, writing in the form of fragments assumes what he calls a 'progressively cyclical' character. Employing a more philosophical mode of expression, Schlegel says: 'The idea of philosophy can only be accomplished through an infinite progression of systems. Its form is a circle' (*KFSA* 12, 10). This thought process is animated by contradiction and antithesis, as Schlegel notes: 'An antinomy between different parts of human development is not a real dualism but only a mutual, interactive determination' (*Wechselbestimmung*: *KFSA* 18, 301). There will always be a 'leap across into the contrary' occasioned by scepticism in this process of self-reflective thought. This scepticism, however, is not an 'absolute scepticism', not a 'scepticism as system', which could only produce 'anarchy', but a scepticism belonging essentially to thought itself and constitituing a continuous 'logical insurrection' (*KFSA* 2, 179) against the stifling bonds of a system. In this form, scepticism is as old as philosophy. Schlegel also described 'wit' as a principle of his fragmentary thought process, stating in his Cologne lectures: 'That activity, however, in which consciousness manifests itself most essentially in the fragment, is *wit*. The essence of wit consists in isolatedness and originates from the isolatedness and derivative character of consciousness itself' (*KFSA* 12, 392). Yet, this theory of wit has not become nearly as prominent as Schlegel's theory of irony. Characterized as a 'continuous alternation of self-creation and self-annihilation', irony became the best-known motivation for Schlegel's writing in the form of fragments. From the point of view of its author, irony is the expression of a mind 'that simultaneously contains within itself a plurality of minds and a whole system of persons' (*KFSA* 2, 185; *LF*, 177). From the point of view of the experience of the world, irony is the 'intellectual intuition of an eternal chaos, an infinitely abundant, ingenious, and eternally cyclical chaos' (*KFSA* 18, 228).

The rhythm of thought which animates Novalis' fragmentary writing expresses an exuberant transcendence of the self into the world of the object and a counteractive self-critical return into the self. This rhythm resembles Friedrich Schlegel's alternation of self-creation and self-annihilation, yet unlike Friedrich Schlegel's version, it assumes for Novalis more the character of a poetic experience of the inner and outer worlds in their reciprocal mirroring. His fundamental vision can best be described in terms of an interaction of these two worlds. He himself calls it the 'method of reversal' – a method which, 'while we are studying nature, refers to ourselves, to inner observations and experiences; and while we are studying our self, refers to the outer world, to outer observations and experiences' (*NO* 3, 429). These were for him the 'true bonds of a connection of subject and object' (ib.). The two movements of thought coincide in the last analysis and form a constant pulsation of the ego. Indeed, Novalis says: 'What is outside me, is really within me, is mind – and vice versa' (ib.).[11] Thus, Novalis' reflection also assumes a rotating character, yet the rhythm is of a more static nature. His thought always circles around the same phenomenon and attempts to grasp it in ever new configurations. Rahel Varnhagen had the impression, on reading Novalis' fragments, that it was 'as if only a few truths were presented and always the same was said'. Only 'variations of a few intuitions' were present in Novalis' writing, she said, without, however, considering this a flaw. On the contrary, the same observation applied for her to Fichte, Goethe, Rousseau,

Saint-Martin, and Jean Paul. 'All who say something good, say the same', she added, declaring that there is 'nothing but variations of a simple theme conceived in a moment of the highest wit'.[12]

Novalis published only a few collections of his fragments. Most of the fragments edited from his manuscripts are preliminary works, outlines and sketches. Yet even the published fragments were of only transitional importance for him. He foresaw a 'future literature', a 'beautiful period of time' when one would read 'nothing but the beautiful composition – literary works of art' (*NO* 3, 276–7). From this point of view, his fragments were only 'disjointed thoughts' or 'beginnings of interesting sequences of thought – texts for thinking'. 'Most of them are simply chips and have only a transitional value', he thought. 'Some of them, however, bear the imprint of my deepest convictions' (*NO* 2, 595). Yet, we know that these images of transitoriness and a beautiful future were only ironical metaphors which enabled the early Romantics to express all the more adequately the actual state of our knowledge and the appropriate form of our writing.[13]

EXAMPLE: NOVALIS' *HEINRICH VON OFTERDINGEN*

Mythology, symbol, and fairy-tale are the terms most spontaneously used by critics to characterize Novalis' *Heinrich von Ofterdingen*. Friedrich Schlegel saw the novel as a paradigm of his notion of 'esoteric poetry', or a 'transition from the novel into mythology' (*KFSA* 3, 12).[14] Long before its publication, he announced Novalis' work to Schleiermacher as a 'wondrous and absolutely new phenomenon', emphasizing especially the masterly skill of his friend in the shaping of the fairy-tale.[15] Solger characterized the novel as 'a mythical story, a tearing away of the veil that the finiteness of this world keeps around the infinite'.[16] On the basis of these qualities, Dilthey saw in the novel 'the most significant literary accomplishment that this first generation of Romanticism produced'.[17] According to Paul Kluckhohn, *Heinrich von Ofterdingen* was neither a realistic nor an

allegorical novel, 'but a symbolic novel, which aimed to show
the immanence of transcendence in this life, the essential nature
of the divine in the earthly realm'.[18]

The language is simple and naïve, and precisely through its
calm and composed rhythm it exposes the transparency of all
happenings. Songs and lyrical interludes accentuate respective
sections of the novel. Dialogues deal with central topics of
Novalis' theory of poetry – philosophy, history, human life,
religion, and morality. We encounter ten such dialogues in the
first part alone, but should be careful not to identify the author
with the many voices appearing in this work. There is hardly
any trace of an ironic mood in the novel, yet we find the device
of mirroring as a remarkable mirroring of the novel within the
novel. Heinrich sees a depiction of his own life in the manuscript
of the Count von Hohenzollern of which the Count relates: 'As
far as I know, it is a novel about the wondrous fortunes of a poet,
in which poesy is presented and praised in its manifold relations'
(*NO* 1, 265; *HO* 91).

Of central importance is the function of dreams, which in this
case do not relate to psychoanalysis and spiritualism, but
emphasize the relationship to the supernatural. The novel
begins with a dream, and at the beginning of the second part, a
voice named Astralis pronounces the enigmatic words: 'World
turns to dream and dream to world' (*NO* 1, 319; *HO*, 152). The
first dream is the motivating force for all subsequent events of
the novel, and Heinrich distinctly feels that this dream does not
constitute an insignificant occurrence in his life, but reaches into
his soul 'as into a giant wheel, impelling it onward with a mighty
swing' (*NO* 1, 199; *HO*, 19). His dream vision reveals the
following features:

He found himself on soft turf by the edge of a fountain, which shot up
into the air and seemed to consume itself there. Dark blue cliffs with
bright veins arose at a distance; the daylight round about him was
brighter and milder than ordinary daylight, and the sky was dark blue
and wholly clear. But what attracted him with great force was a tall,
pale flower, which stood beside the spring and touched him with its
broad glistening leaves. Around this flower were countless others of
every hue, and the most delicious fragrance filled the air. He saw

nothing but the blue flower and gazed upon it long with inexpressible tenderness. Finally, when he wanted to approach the flower, it all at once began to move and change; the leaves became more glistening and cuddled up to a growing stem; the flower leaned towards him and its petals displayed an expanded blue corolla wherein a delicate face hovered. (*NO* 1, 197; *HO*, 17)

Through its blue atmosphere the dream image emphasizes the transparent aura of the entire novel and its relationship to the transcendent world. And then all of a sudden, there appear, alongside these dreams, symbols, and suggestions of transparency, scenes of the most realistic character and a highly developed sense for historical reality. We are in the age of the Crusades, known to Novalis through Schiller's historical lectures at Jena University. The figure of the miner, a portrait of the geologist Abraham Gottlob Werner, displays the author's sharp sense of observation. The morning walk outside the gates of Augsburg can be seen as another good example of realistic depiction and representation. The most precious cultural-historical portrayal of this kind, however, is undoubtedly the description of the occupation of mining, the barrows, the miners and their customary greeting of 'Good luck', as well as their habit of communal prayers before descending into the mines (*NO* 1, 240–1; *HO*, 64–5). Penetrating the interior of the earth, however, we again move into the mysterious, into the 'hidden treasure chambers of nature' (*NO* 1, 242; *HO*, 66) and become acquainted with strange and enigmatic arts. Yet in this realm, we are also confronted with the 'king of metals', gold, which, as the basis of money, determines the mercantile dealings of the outer world. This alternation between the worlds of the miraculous and ordinary life, the inner self and the exterior world, exemplifies Novalis' literary technique of indicating the cohesion of the two spheres.

As is evident from these few observations, the novel incorporates a great variety of themes from Novalis' theoretical discussions and stands in close proximity to his philosophical outlook on life, to such an extent that it can even be seen as a poetic embodiment of the latter. From this point of view, it is almost incomprehensible that this novel has been considered by a great number of critics as an imitation or offspring of Goethe's *Wilhelm Meister*. In his notes on Goethe's novel, Novalis is quite outspoken about it. Originally, he was impressed by *Wilhelm Meister* and its manner of narration (*NO* 2, 424). He spoke of the 'grand style of representation we admire so much, and rightly so, in Goethe' (*NO* 2, 422) and even called the work a 'pure novel', that is, a 'novel par excellence' (*NO* 2, 596). In the late summer of 1798, however, Novalis applied this appreciation entirely to the practical, economical side of poetic creation and saw Goethe with respect to his works 'like the English with respect to their manufacture – pre-eminently simple, neat, convenient, and durable'. Goethe accomplished in German literature 'what Wedgewood did in the world of the English arts' (*NO* 2, 640; *AF*, 75). Later he saw *Wilhelm Meister* as an 'embarrassing and silly book' which was 'unpoetic in the highest degree', even a 'satire on poetry', a 'Candide directed against poetry', so much so that 'whoever took this work truly to heart would not read another novel' (*NO* 3, 646–7). What Novalis objected to mostly was the assimilation of the protagonist to the bourgeois world of society and practical purposes, something he labelled a 'gospel of economics' (ib.). In another comment he said more directly:

Wilhelm Meister's Apprenticeship is in a way totally *prosaic* – and modern. The romantic perishes in it – also the poetry of nature, the miraculous – it deals only with ordinary *human* things – nature and mysticism are entirely forgotten. It is a poeticized bourgeois and domestic story. The miraculous is explicitly treated as poetry and enthusiasm. Artistic atheism is the spirit of the book. A good deal of economy – the poetic effect is accomplished on the basis of a prosaic, cheap subject. (*NO* 3, 638–9)

For his own purposes, even the word 'apprenticeship' appeared too goal-oriented to Novalis, since it expressed 'a certain somewhere', and he said: 'For me this cannot mean anything but – *transitional years* from the finite to the infinite' (*NO* 4, 281).[19]

We have only the first part of his novel with the title 'Expectations' and vague sketches for the second. The first part is entirely rounded off and depicts Heinrich's growth as a poet in a series of distinct stages. At the beginning we see Heinrich at the age of barely twenty in his parental house in Eisenach, located in a modest duchy. Of special interest are the frequent comparisons between Heinrich and his father at the beginning of the novel. The father also had an important dream in his youth, very similar to the one that set a whole series of events of Heinrich's life in motion. Yet, the father did not rise to Heinrich's stature and said in a resigned way about himself: 'At that time I was still a quite different fellow too' (*NO* 1, 199; *HO*, 19). Of similar importance for Heinrich's development is the influence of the mother, which the father, in his benevolent attitude, does not resist. She realizes that Heinrich suddenly 'was far more quiet and inclined to brood than formerly' and therefore plans as a remedy for him a journey from the dreary north into the cheerful social life of the southern city of Augsburg, not without hopes that 'the charms of a girl in her native Augsburg will dispel the gloomy mood of her son and restore his former cheerful and sociable spirit' (*NO* 1, 203; *HO*, 24). The actual reason for Heinrich's introspective attitude is, of course, the dream at the beginning of the novel that had been incited by the visit of an unknown stranger and his narratives. Heinrich thought musingly: 'I wonder where the stranger really came from? None of us has ever seen a person like him' (*NO* 1, 195; *HO*, 15). In this manner, the true beginning of the novel is lost in references to ever earlier beginnings.

The journey to Augsburg begins in the company of a friendly group of merchants. We learn from them what we already know from Heinrich's previous conversation with his father, namely, that he was originally expected to become a 'competent scholar' (*NO* 1, 197; *HO*, 18). Yet, the merchants recognize, as they tell Heinrich, that he seems to have a poetic talent: 'You speak so fluently of the promptings in your heart and soul, and you have no lack of choice expressions and happy comparisons. You also incline toward the marvellous, the element of the poet' (*NO* 1, 208; *HO*, 30). Although these merchants know very little about the task of the poet and represent rather the opposite of poetic wisdom, that is, a sense for worldly profit (*NO* 1, 206–7; *HO*, 27–8), Heinrich learns quite a bit from them about his future profession. They not only convey information from their worldly perspective about the wondrous position of the poet, but also tell a revealing story in the second chapter about the unity between the poet and nature, and in the third, the myth of Atlantis which foreshadows Heinrich's own destiny and that of Mathilde.

In the fourth chapter, Heinrich meets a group of Crusaders who have in their company a 'lovely prisoner', the 'oriental girl' Zulima. The importance of this encounter seems to be that it confronts Heinrich with the opposition between the misery of war and the 'soothing fancies' of the beautiful oriental girl. He recognizes that the attraction of the 'golden distance' is not identical with the world of the warriors who want to motivate him to participate in their next Crusade, but of a more subtle nature. Then in the fifth chapter, an enormous step occurs in the development of the maturing poet when he becomes acquainted with the miner from Bohemia who introduces him to the 'auras of ancient times' (*NO* 1, 247; *HO*, 72). In the interior of the earth Heinrich senses a 'wondrous joy in things, which may have a close relation to our mysterious existence', and now 'he surveyed at a glance all his relations to the wide world around him, felt what he had become through it and what it would become to him, and grasped all the strange concepts and impulses he had often felt in contemplating it' (*NO* 1, 252; *HO*, 77). In addition, 'a thousand other recollections of his life strung themselves along a magic thread' (*NO* 1, 252; *HO*, 78). In this chapter, nature and history entwine in so far as the penetration into nature and the interior of the earth symbolizes the movement into the 'previous world' of history (*NO* 1, 253; *HO*, 78). Here Heinrich meets the hermit, whose eyes radiate an 'inexpressible serenity' and who turns out to be the Count of Hohenzollern. He familiarizes Heinrich with the historical sense, which 'develops late and more under the quiet influence of recollection than under the more violent impression of the present' (*NO* 1, 257; *HO*, 83), but is nevertheless an essential precondition for becoming a poet (*NO* 1, 259; *HO*, 85). In becoming acquainted with history, Heinrich feels 'a new unfolding of his intuitive inner life' (*NO* 1, 263; *HO*, 89).

Another stage in the development of the growing poet, usually neglected in Novalis research, consists in his education in sensuality, in the pleasures of love, wine, song, in short, the withdrawal from the simplicity of the court chaplain in the north and the turn to the pleasures of life in the south. This influence derives from the heritage of Heinrich's mother. It is manifest in her native city of Augsburg, which appears to Heinrich as the 'earthly paradise' (*NO* 1, 203; *HO*, 24). We encounter this atmosphere when Heinrich enters the 'splendid house' of grandfather Schwaning, 'lit up', animated by 'jolly music' and a 'gay party' of a 'colourful throng' (*NO* 1, 268–9; *HO*, 95–6). The grandfather, too, says of his nephew: 'It seems to me he was born to be a poet' (*NO* 1, 271; *HO*, 98), although he also remarks: 'One can tell you are from the north. We'll thaw you out here and teach you to look for pretty eyes' (*NO* 1, 270; *HO*, 97). What he means by this is obvious in the 'frivolous song' on the conflict between the hidden desires of adolescent girls and the strict prohibitions of their parents (*NO* 1, 274–5; *HO*, 99–101) which he recites during the party.

The next stage in Heinrich's formation as a poet, not yet complete however, is represented by the poet Klingsohr, whose physical appearance and expression ('He was of sturdy build, his movements were quiet and expressive, and wherever he stood, there he seemed to want to stand forever': *NO* 1, 270; *HO*, 97) are clearly reminiscent of Goethe. Up to now, Heinrich has acquired an understanding of the correspondence between mind and nature. Klingsohr reveals to him the importance of reason, craftsmanship, and the mechanical to poetry. Yet, Klingsohr's influence upon the young poet is not limited to the civilizing of a bardic notion of poetry by means of reason and technical know-how. Above all, he introduces his disciple in the eighth chapter to a dialectical comprehension of world history ruled by war and contradictions (*NO* 1, 284–5; *HO*, 113–14). Heinrich knows that history comprises 'rough and crude times of barbarism' (*NO* 1, 204; *HO*, 25), but had assumed the rhythm of history was one of a 'gradual calming of nature' creating an 'increasingly cordial harmony, a more peaceful communion, a mutual support and stimulation' (*NO* 1, 261;

HO, 87). Now he learns from Klingsohr that this 'ceaseless conflict' continues eternally and that the periods of conflict are generally those ages 'in which poets are born' (*NO* 1, 264; *HO*, 113). In such periods, 'the primal sea stirs': 'New continents are to arise, new races to come forth out of the great dissolution' (*NO* 1, 265; *HO*, 113).

Now Heinrich has matured sufficiently eventually to be initiated as a poet, a function carried out by Mathilde, Klingsohr's daughter. She appears to him as 'the spirit of her father in the loveliest disguise' (*NO* 1, 271; *HO*, 98). 'Oh!' he says on another occasion, 'she is the visible spirit of song, a worthy daughter of her father. She will dissolve me into music' (*NO* 1, 277; *HO*, 104). All the two can say after their first kiss is 'Sweet Mathilde! Dear Heinrich!' and to his mother Heinrich can only say: 'It is quite glorious' (*NO* 1, 276; *HO*, 103–4). At this point the story seems to reach its natural conclusion. Heinrich says to himself: 'Did I not feel as I did in that dream when I saw the blue flower? What strange connection is there between Mathilde and that flower? The face which inclined towards me out of the flowery calyx, that was Mathilde's heavenly face, and now I also remember having seen it in the hermit's book' (*NO* 1, 277; *HO*, 104). The decisive event, however, that makes Heinrich a poet is not this kiss, but Mathilde's death, which is anticipated in the first part in a horrible dream by Heinrich. The effect of this death, as Kluckhohn puts it, is that for Heinrich 'the barrier between this world and the beyond is removed and he feels at home in both worlds, participating in the events of the outer world, but simultaneously belonging to the inner and transcendent one, like Novalis after Sophia's death'.[20]

In the concluding ninth chapter of the first part, Klingsohr narrates a fairy-tale about the transition from the 'previous world' into the 'future world'. This fairy-tale has justly been criticized as overcharged with ideas and 'congealed in allegory'.[21] Novalis' purpose was obviously to manage, as Tieck put it, the 'transition to the second part', in which the novel 'incessantly moves from the most common into the most wondrous, and the two realms mutually interpret and complement each other'.[22] Tieck also tells us that the voice named Astralis which proclaims the prologue to the second part was supposed to return after every chapter to continue the lyrical shaping of the 'wondrous view of things' and thereby to maintain the 'eternal connection of the invisible world with the visible'.[23] Until his meeting with Klingsohr, Heinrich had traversed the natural course of his development as a poet. In his conversation with Sylvester, a new world opens up. We perceive 'summoning voices of a higher nature', and the two conversation partners conjure up a time when 'the need for all fear, all pain, all want, and evil will be removed from the universe' (*NO* 1, 330; *HO*, 164). After Heinrich's conversation with Sylvester, which moves on to such deep metaphysical themes as conscience and the existence of God, the work suddenly breaks off.

According to his own statements, Novalis had precise conceptions about the continuation of the novel. 'The plan is laid down clearly enough, and the subject is a most favourable one', he wrote to Friedrich Schlegel (*NO* 4, 330). The novel should 'progressively transform itself into fairy-tale' (ib.), he said, and remarked: 'It will become simpler and more human toward the end' (*NO* 1, 345). In another instance, he wrote: 'The ending is a transition from the real world into the concealed – death – last dream and awakening' (*NO* 1, 342). Yet these plans for continuation and Tieck's own reports of them soon assume such colossal dimensions that doubts arise whether the poet 'would have been in a position to carry them out in a reasonable manner'.[24] From the 'Cloister' and the 'Forecourt' at the beginning of the second part (*NO* 1, 317; *HO*, 151) the journey was to be continued into the worlds of previous times, the Greeks and the Orient, to the court of the Emperor Frederick II, and from there to the singers' contest at the Wartburg. Yes, Heinrich was to pass through the different realms of nature and become stone, plant, and animal, but eventually pluck the blue flower and be reunited with Mathilde and vicariously bring about the golden age, uniting time and eternity, spirit and nature. Clemens Brentano expressed his feelings at such enormous plans perhaps most cogently when he said that the perusal of the second part had left him with a most singular impression. He thought 'that in such a way, no further poetry whatsoever can originate', since it is already 'consumed with the projection of the plan – like Dido's ox's skin which, finely cut and stretched extensively around the field, can no longer serve anyone as a bed'.[25]

We have to consider, of course, that Tieck's reports are not always reliable. He even wanted to carry out the continuation himself, but fortunately Friedrich Schlegel vetoed this plan, which he found 'not only inappropriate, but also sacrilegious, abominable, godless, and impious'.[26] About the projects of a continuation as Novalis expressed them in his manuscripts, Schlegel observed, with good reason, that these were 'absolutely not valid', since his friend had told him on the last day of his life that he had altered his plan 'totally and throughout'.[27]

For a critical examination of the projected continuation of the novel, there is therefore no authentic source other than the first part itelf. Yet in an analysis of it, little material comes to light. In one instance, as mentioned earlier, the novel is mirrored within the novel by means of an ancient book in the Provençal language. When Heinrich examines the last sections of it, they appear dark and incomprehensible to him, and he has the impression that the conclusion of the book seems to be missing. The Count confirms this impression and says point-blank: 'The conclusion is missing in this manuscript, which I brought with me from Jerusalem, where I found it among the effects of a friend who had died' (*NO* 1, 265; *HO*, 91–2). In his dream about the death of Mathilde towards the end of the first part, the main events are only sketched out in a few strokes. Heinrich wanders through a foreign, distant country, he hears songs, and finds Mathilde. The reunion occurs in a strange, surrealistic atmosphere beneath a river with blue waves flowing above the two. Yet, the concluding dialogue shows where the true place of their reunion is: 'Where are we, dear Mathilde? – With our parents. – Will we remain together? – Forever, she replied as she pressed her lips to his and put her arms around him so that she could not be separated from him again' (*NO* 1, 279; *HO*, 106). At the beginning of the novel, leaving his home town of

Eisenach, Heinrich also has a premonition about where this journey is leading him. Delving into the 'blue waters of the distance', he felt as if 'after long wanderings he would return to his native land from distant regions towards which they were now travelling' and that 'it was really his native land he was approaching' (*NO* 1, 205; *HO*, 26–7).

Of all the novels of early Romanticism, *Heinrich von Ofterdingen* is certainly the most ambitious work. Yet, we cannot consider it the greatest literary production of early Romanticism as Kluckhohn and Dilthey did. We have only the first part, and this part is clearly a torso, since the centre of gravity of the novel evidently lies in its continuation. In its conception, however, *Heinrich von Ofterdingen* can indicate what enormous dimensions the early Romantic novel attempted to embrace.

CHAPTER 5

Wackenroder's and Tieck's conceptions of painting and music

Through Wackenroder and Tieck, early Romantic theory came to embrace painting and music, two forms of art that had never been strongly emphasized by the Jena group. Painting and music were almost completely absent from the early writings of the Schlegels, and although Novalis did give some consideration to these art forms in his fragments, he saw them for the most part in analogy to poetry and never really considered them in their own autonomy. In the critical writings of Wackenroder and Tieck, however, the entire concept of art is no longer envisioned according to a poetic paradigm, but follows the model or, as the two friends preferred to say, language, of painting and music. This new direction in the exploration of art is in itself almost exclusively Wackenroder's achievement. Tieck followed Wackenroder to some extent in this new orientation but was most original and successful when he dealt with these subjects through the medium of his fiction and poetry rather than theoretically. Wackenroder's influence grew incessantly and soon manifested itself in Tieck's *Franz Sternbald's Wanderings*, in August Wilhelm and Caroline Schlegel's dialogue 'The Paintings' (*AWS SW* 9, 3–101), Friedrich Schlegel's descriptions of paintings in his periodical *Europa* of 1803–5 (*KFSA* 4), and especially in the predominance of painting and music in the theories of art of later periods of Romanticism.[1]

Initially, these impulses came almost exclusively from a small and unpretentious book with the peculiar title *Outpourings of an Art-Loving Friar*. By the time it appeared in 1797, Wackenroder, the author, had already died. Out of respect for Wackenroder's father, who would have disapproved of his son's career as a writer, Tieck published the text anonymously. Wackenroder had secretly worked on the manuscript in 1794 and 1795, after he had taken up his judicial appointment in Berlin. When he visited the Dresden galleries in the summer of 1796 with Tieck, he informed him confidentially of his work, and Tieck then showed it, with Wackenroder's approval, to Johann Friedrich Reichardt, the editor of the journal *Deutschland*. In the same year Reichardt published the section of Wackenroder's text entitled 'In Pious Memory of Our Revered Forebear, Albrecht Dürer' in his journal, giving it the title 'Of an Art-Loving Friar', to which the word *Outpourings* was prefixed when the text appeared as a book. The first edition also contained a few additions by Tieck: 'To the Reader of these Pages'; 'Yearning for Italy'; 'A Letter from the Young Florentine Painter Antonio to His Friend Jacobo in Rome'; and 'Letter from a Young German Painter in Rome to His Friend in Nuremberg'.

If one concentrates on Wackenroder's contributions alone and ignores the pieces added by Tieck, the *Outpourings* show a well-structured composition. Of its fourteen individual sections, the seventh, 'In Pious Memory of Our Revered Forebear, Albrecht Dürer', forms the centre. It is surrounded by two sections which are also central to the world of art depicted here: 'A Few Words Concerning Universality, Tolerance, and Love of Humanity in Art' and 'Of Two Wonderful Languages and Their Mysterious Power' (that is, the language of nature and art). The first part consists mainly of narrations about Italian painters, beginning with Raphael as an artist on the highest level. The following ones show further possibilities in the realization of the art of painting. Following them and immediately before 'A Few Words Concerning Universality, Tolerance, and Love of Humanity in Art', Wackenroder presents two descriptions of paintings, 'The Holy Virgin with the Christ-Child and the Boy John' and 'The Adoration of the Three Wise Men from the East'. The friar seems to assume that the beauty of a painting would be prejudiced by a prose description, and he therefore uses simple verses in an attempt to copy the style of old writers of chronicles with the help of particular figures of speech. Following the central section on

Dürer, the text continues with narratives concerning Italian painters, this time highlighting Michelangelo. 'The Portraits of the Artists' compares paintings by Leonardo da Vinci, Dürer, Michelangelo, and Raphael, and turns again to poetry. 'The Painters' Chronicle' concludes the treatment of the graphic arts and also introduces the French designer and engraver Jacques Callot in addition to a great number of Italian painters. Turning to 'contemporary times', the friar then represents a new aspect of art with 'The Remarkable Musical Life of the Tone-Poet Joseph Berglinger'. Altogether, disregarding Tieck's additions, the structure of the text is as follows:

Raphael's Vision

The Remarkable Death of Francesco Francia, A Painter Renowned in His Time and the Founder of the Lombard School

Raphael and the Apprentice

The Model of an Inventive Yet Erudite Painter, As Exemplified by Leonardo da Vinci, the Renowned Founder of the Florentine School

Descriptions of Two Paintings

A Few Words Concerning Universality, Tolerance, and Love of Humanity in Art IN PIOUS MEMORY OF OUR REVERED FOREBEAR, ALBRECHT DÜRER, BY AN ART-LOVING FRIAR

Of Two Wonderful Languages and Their Mysterious Power

Concerning the Peculiarities of the Ancient Painter Piero di Cosimo of the Florentine School

How and in What Manner We Ought Properly to Contemplate the Works of the World's Great Artists and Employ Them for the Benefit of Our Souls

The Genius of Michelangelo Buonarotti Painter in Rome

The Portraits of the Artists

The Painters' Chronicle

The Remarkable Musical Life of the Tone-Poet Joseph Berglinger

One could compare this arrangement to the form of an old altarpiece. The main difference is, of course, that the sequence of saints and prophets to the left and right is represented here by artists and that the centre, usually occupied by Christ, is ceded to Dürer.

THE APPROACH TO ART IN THE *OUTPOURINGS*

While preparing these individual sections, Wackenroder paid great attention to the collection of biographies of renowned Italian artists compiled in the sixteenth century by Giorgio Vasari.[2] Vasari furnished the material for the seven sections dealing with particular events in the lives of Raphael, Francesco Francia, Piero di Cosimo, Michelangelo, and some of the lesser-known painters who appear in the section 'The Painters' Chronicle'. The manner in which Wackenroder utilizes Vasari's collection is most revealing. Among the usually quite comprehensive materials on individual artists, he focuses only on one particular point and ignores the rest. He also eschews historical preambles such as 'There is the report...', to avoid having to account for the derivation of such stories, and thus gives his own text a sharper profile. Wackenroder also avoids biographical presentation and only rarely considers individual works of art that are given such attention by Vasari. In the sections of his work devoted to the old German school of painting and to Albrecht Dürer, he follows the biography of Dürer by Joachim von Sandrart.[3] As far as composition is concerned, the *Outpourings* are a most carefully constructed work of literature. Rudolf Köpke, Tieck's biographer, says of the appearance of the text:

Reichardt invented the title under which these images were to be released to the public. They were animated by the spirit of a happy belief in art, deriving from a past period in which enthusiasm still balanced the dissolving tendency of reason. Such consideration of the work of art was hardly any longer possible in a time of loud and self-conscious activities. It was attributed to a simple monk who had devoted his youth to art and decided to end his life in monastic silence. The world and his youth are behind him, but the enthusiasm for art inspires him as before and has become part of his faith. He formulates this faith in artless, yet captivating words and in a tranquillity that has found a firm anchoring that can never be torn away again. This pious simplicity is reminiscent of the friar in Lessing's *Nathan*. Reichardt therefore proposed the fitting title *Outpourings of an Art Loving Friar*. Tieck added the preface and a few essays. Then the book appeared in 1797 with the Berlin publishing house Unger.[4]

The text originated in complete independence of the theories of the Jena group. After his move to Berlin in the late summer of 1797, Friedrich Schlegel became acquainted with Wackenroder and spontaneously appreciated him as the most interesting representative of the entire Berlin school of art. This happened, however, only shortly before Wackenroder became mentally ill and eventually died on 17 February 1798. The *Outpourings* appeared shortly afterwards, and were the subject of a substantial review by A. W. Schlegel in the *ALZ*. When the elder Schlegel republished his review in 1801, he added the notes:

This notice I wrote without knowing anything personal about the author who perhaps would subsequently have become a friend had his early and harsh death not thwarted all such hopes. His bosom friend Tieck edited his posthumous writings in the *Fantasies on Art* together with some of his own related studies. Tieck also honoured his memory with some touching poems. (*AWS SW* 10, 371)

The most remarkable among these poems appears towards the end of the first part of the *Fantasies on Art for Friends of Art* of 1799, in which Tieck represents his relationship with Wackenroder in allegorical manner, describing the two on a communal walk through life and asking his departed friend to stay with him, at least in spirit, while he traverses the vast land of art (*TI PhK*, 98–104). Indeed, Tieck's and Wackenroder's writings became closely interwoven, first through the edition of the *Fantasies on Art for the Friends of Art*, which contained more of Tieck's own writings than the few additions he contributed to the *Outpourings*, but also through Tieck's own Romantic novel *Franz Sternbald's Wanderings*. This novel begins in the milieu of Albrecht Dürer's Nuremberg and leads the protagonist, Franz Sternbald, a young apprentice in the art of painting, through various stages in his accomplishments to Rome, where not only his art, but also his attitude towards life come to maturity, and the relationship between art and life assumes a less rigorous and more conciliatory stance.[5] The irreconcilability of art and life is a dominant theme in the *Outpourings*, especially in the last section on the musician Berglinger. By continuing the treatment of this theme in his novel *Franz Sternbald* and including the decisive 'Letter from a Young German Painter in Rome to his Friend in Nuremberg' in the first edition of the *Outpourings*, Tieck seems to imply that Wackenroder's presentation of this theme was not the final word and that only with *Franz Sternbald's Wanderings* do we have a full view of the problems as the two friends envisioned them. Indeed, according to Rudolf Haym's account, Tieck and Wackenroder projected this plan together.[6]

This projection leads to the central figure, the art-loving friar, who presents the images of art and of artists in a seemingly simple manner, and who has been too easily identified, in the criticism of the nineteenth and twentieth centuries, with Wackenroder and his attitude towards art. Overall, critical literature likes to refer to Wackenroder's 'faithful idealism', his 'pure enthusiasm', his 'enthusiastic feelings for the divine and the beautiful', his 'pure and chaste adoration of art'.[7] One easily forgets that we are not talking about Wackenroder, but about his creation, the friar. The *Outpourings*, in other words, are not taken as the communication of an author, a writer, but as a 'confession of faith', a 'gospel', since Wackenroder had supposedly nothing in common with 'sceptical moods', with the 'reasoning of systematic theoreticians', and expressed his thoughts on art in 'devotions on art', in 'piety about art', in true words and images. The friar is not seen as a mask or persona for Wackenroder, but as his direct and immediate embodiment. Tieck's contributions are seen as foreign bodies in this pure and immediate sequence of direct communication. Tieck's first piece, the introductory section, 'To the Reader of these Pages', shows a level of reflection that does not occur in the other sections and almost gives the impression of a stylistic rupture. The next, 'Yearning for Italy', is so different from the rest in its transition into lyric poetry that Tieck noticed this himself and designated these 'jottings' as having been written in the friar's 'early youth' (*WA*, 10; *OF*, 10). Finally, the 'Letter from a Young German Painter in Rome to his Friend in Nuremberg' already belongs to the context of *Franz Sternbald's*

Wanderings. The entire Catholic atmosphere, the mass, and the depiction of the elevation of the Host, are all considered as especially intrusive. These obsevations certainly carry weight. Yet, it would be a similar distortion to consider the *Outpourings* as lacking any ironic distancing by the author, as Wackenroder's final word on art. Once one has granted the text the aspect of a perspective and the friar the function of a mask, the further development in *Franz Sternbald* seems less disconcerting and perhaps the most natural consequence of the *Outpourings* and their unresolved problem of life and art.

A. W. Schlegel, of course, appreciated the *Outpourings* not as the direct expression of Wackenroder's true feelings, but as 'pleasant writing' opposed to the manner of thinking of its time and therefore rightfully avoiding the 'language of fashion'. The unknown author 'chose a foreign costume in order to express most vividly his intimate feeling about the sacredness and dignity of art and did not even step out of it in the preface' (*AWS SW* 10, 364). To communicate his opinion to 'future artists and amateurs' in the most effective manner, 'he everywhere resists a certain complacent air of the connoisseur'. A. W. Schlegel sees 'the character of a spiritual hermit' as, from this point of view, perhaps 'the most appropriate that could be found to lay the basis for such a mood, to expound such doctrines impressively'. Even the 'tinge of enthusiasm' appeared justified for this purpose: 'Who will blame the simple, but cordial religious hermit when he extols the divine that is only to be found in the human being and when he compares the incomprehensibility of artistic enthusiasm with other higher and immediate inspirations and also confuses them with the former' (*AWS SW* 10, 364-5). We, as readers, need not become confused and 'can easily translate his language into our manner of speaking'. His language, because it is antiquated, furthermore assumes the 'attraction of novelty'. As far as the relationship between art and religion is concerned, A. W. Schlegel is of the opinion that 'however distinct the free play of the imagination, as constituting the enjoyment of art, may be from that devotion that requires a contrite self-abnegation and, as it were, an immediate suspension of earthly existence, it is nevertheless undeniable that modern art at its renaissance and during its greatest period was in a close alliance with religion' (*AWS SW* 10, 365). He thought there was no reason not to have a positive attitude towards Christian fables and habits 'otherwise alien to our manner of thinking', since in our relationship to works of art, we are also tolerant towards 'mythological dreams of antiquity' (*AWS SW* 10, 36). This attitude contrasted sharply with Goethe's opinion of Wackenroder's *Outpourings*, which, precisely because of these features, was hostile from the beginning and later led Goethe to alter the review of this text by his friend Heinrich Meyer ('art Meyer') in the *ALZ* of 1805. With great indignation, Goethe referred to the 'klosterbruderisierende, sternbaldisierende Unwesen' (the excessive mischief in the style of the art-loving friar and Franz Sternbald) and saw here a greater danger for art than from 'all the Calibans who clamour for greater realism'. At that time, Wackenroder's *Outpourings* had found strong support in Friedrich Schlegel's depictions of paintings in the periodical *Europa*, and this aspect of early Romantic art theory was soon to be enthusiastically received by the young generation of painters in Germany, especially by the group of the Nazarenes who were then living in Rome.

A. W. Schlegel gives particular attention to Wackenroder's use of Giorgio Vasari's biographical collections *Lives of the Most Excellent Painters, Sculptors, and Architects* and considers Wackenroder's utilization of the work excellent. What A. W. Schlegel has in mind becomes obvious if one looks at the Italian original, especially the lives of Francesco Francia, Leonardo da Vinci, and Piero di Cosimo, and realizes 'how favourably the author, through arrangement, omission, depictions, and inserted meditations, has transformed his subject' (*AWS SW* 10, 367). A. W. Schlegel refers to the 'life of Leonardo' as a particularly illustrative example showing, in Wackenroder's own words, 'that the genius of art associates willingly enough with the stern Minerva,[8] and that a great and generous soul, even when concentrated upon one main activity, reflects the entire and varied picture of human science in perfect harmony and beauty' (*WA* 28; *OF*, 28). He claims that Wackenroder's image of

Albrecht Dürer is 'so well modelled after the honourable character and the straight manners of that time that it deceptively transposes the reader into it' (ib.). Wackenroder's style makes it obvious for him 'that he chose as his model the greatest master in representational prose of our language', that is, Goethe. Schlegel also discusses the many poems in Wackenroder's text that reveal a 'true and hearty feeling' and considers the device of introducing the respective persons in his depictions of paintings by way of dialogue (*WA*, 41-4; *OF*, 40-4) as 'original' and in some cases 'very appropriate'. Of the story about the 'unfortunate musician' Berglinger, he says: 'This story impresses the mind of the reader in a melancholy manner because of the fact that independence of character is an indispensable prerequisite of the artist, so that he can resolutely overcome adverse reality and maintain, while dependent in many ways, the freedom of his mind and does not waver between fantastic exaggeration and sickly ennervation' (*AWS SW* 10, 370).

Of particular significance for Wackenroder's treatment of art with the help of anecdotes about artists is the section 'Raphael's Vision', which depicts the vision of a Madonna that the early Raphael is reported to have had on the wall of his bedroom. The friar got hold of this story when he was searching through the rich store of old manuscripts in the monastery and, 'among many a worthless dusty parchment', chanced upon 'some pages of the hand of Bramante,[9] whose presence here I am at a loss to explain' (*WA*, 7; *OF*, 7). On one of these sheets Bramante relates the story of how he pressed Raphael to reveal to him 'whom on earth he had used as a model for the incomparable beauty, the touching countenance, and the unsurpassed expressiveness of his Holy Virgins'. One day Raphael told him that, since his earliest years, he had felt a special devotion to the Virgin Mary, and when he turned to painting, he had thought himself unequal to the task of painting her in perfection. The form he beheld of her always slipped from his mind, and he never caught more than a fleeting glimpse of her features. Once when he was again working on a painting of the Holy Virgin, however, he awakened in the middle of the night, and his eye was drawn to the wall where his unfinished painting 'was now completed and had come to life in a warm radiance':

The divine presence in this picture had so overwhelmed him that he had burst out in a flood of tears. The eyes had gazed at him with an expression infinitely touching, and it had seemed as if the figure might move at any moment; indeed, he had the impression that it did in fact move. The greatest miracle of all was that it seemed that this was the picture which he had always wanted to paint, though he had never had more than a vague and confused notion of it. He had no recollection of how he fell asleep again. Next morning he had awakened as if newborn. The vision was imprinted forever on his soul and his senses, and from then on he was able to portray the Mother of God as he had always envisioned her, and he had always felt a certain reverence for his own pictures. (*WA*, 8–9; *OF*, 8–9)

This story has some biographical background, in so far as it relates to a quotation from a letter which Raphael once wrote to Count Castiglione.[10] The letter, and in particular the quotation, found attention in Germany when Johann Joachim Winckelmann referred to it in his *Thoughts on the Imitation of Greek Works* of 1756. In the quotation, Raphael says: 'Since one encounters so few beautiful female figures, I cling to a certain image which dwells within me' (*WA*, 7; *OF*, 7). Raphael, in other words, cited as the model of his artistic creation not the Aristotelian theory of representation, but the Platonic one of inspiration. The quotation, however, does not relate, as A. W. Schlegel immediately recognized, to a Madonna, but to a goddess of the sea, to Galatea as Raphael had painted her in the Farnesina, a prominent villa in Rome, traversing the foaming ocean in a carriage of shells drawn by dolphins. Such a painting, Raphael said in his letter to Count Castiglione, had to be created after a model. Since he so rarely encountered beautiful women in this world, however, he made use of a 'certain idea' in his mind. When Winckelmann referred to this incident in his writing on the imitations of the Greeks, he wanted to illustrate Raphael's creation of the true taste of antiquity and the notion that we could find in Raphael the calm and quietness of the ancient artists. For Winckelmann, Raphael was the master who had found again in the modern age the true character of the

ancients. Winckelmann recognized, for instance, in the countenance of the Sistine Madonna the happy divine peace of
classical physiognomies.[11] These advantages now assumed
through Wackenroder a Christian character. A. W. Schlegel,
who so far had been quite tolerant of Wackenroder's Christian
inclinations and interpreted his attitude as a clever means of
communication in a time alienated from art, now insisted that
there was no reason for the mysterious meaning which Wackenroder attributed to Raphael's words (*AWS SW* 10, 369) and
maintained that Wackenroder's interpretation was in this sense
more or less a falsification.

THE CONCEPTION OF PAINTING

If one looks in these texts for a theory of painting, very little
comes to light. Most of Wackenroder's contemplations attempt
to describe the origin of art in this world and deal with painting
chiefly as the preferred medium for such deliberations. The
periods under consideration are the Italian Renaissance of the
fifteenth and sixteenth centuries and the so-called Old German
School of Painting as represented by Albrecht Dürer during the
same time period. Wackenroder describes these centuries,
however, as if they were part of the Middle Ages, that is, a time
of unquestioned faith in and an unbroken relationship to the
divine. His depictions of the origin of art in the great painters of
this period thereby assume a strong religious colouring, as was
already obvious in his handling of Raphael's letter to Count
Castiglione on the true model of his Galatea. What is described
in the theories of the Jena group as the shaping power of creative
imagination appears in the friar's description as an influence of
divine grace and revelation. We could interpret this tendency as
a preference for unconscious creation à la Schelling and oppose
it to the Schlegelian notion of an artistic, intentional creation.
Yet, it soon turns out that the conception of art in this text
cannot so easily be ascertained and in reality also has the
opposite inclination towards craftsmanship, learning, theory,
and reflection. Whereas Raphael seems to incorporate the
spontaneous creative aspect of art, Michelangelo and even more

so Leonardo da Vinci represent the learned artist. Dürer seems to combine both aspects. A great number of other artists display different nuances. The best way of illustrating Wackenroder's theoretical position is by turning to some of the portraits themselves.

'Raphael's Vision', Wackenroder's first section, is of prime importance for this investigation. This artist is 'the brightest star in the heaven of art' and incorporates what the friar calls 'the divinity of art' (*WA*, 7; *OF*, 6–7), that is, an art without reflection, without effort, and also without self-criticism. Yet, he also refutes the modern talk of a merely artistic type of creation and enthusiasm. After revealing to his readers the true meaning of Raphael's words about the image in his mind, the friar asks himself:

Will they, enlightened by this manifest revelation of heavenly omnipotence, now grasp the profound and noble significance of those simple words spoken from the depths of this innocent soul? Will they now finally come to see that all this profane gossip about artistic inspiration is downright blasphemous – and acknowledge that it is to be attributed to nothing short of the direct intermediation of God? (*WA*, 10; *OF*, 9)

A number of other painters serve to underline this point by confirmation and contrast.[12] Francesco Francia is the example of a painter who had advanced through industriousness and effort and, after much public praise, gained the impression that he was a great artist. However, when confronted with an altar panel by Raphael towards the end of his life, he realized the difference between his art and the creations of this master and 'achieved undisputed greatness through the awareness of his own insignificance in comparison to the heavenly Raphael' (*WA*, 18; *OF*, 17–18). The following incident is related to the same theme. A young apprentice in the art of painting, Antonio, does not really get on with his training and asks Raphael in a letter to reveal to him the secret of his art. Raphael, however, confesses that he does not know it and recommends that Antonio 'continue to practise art with love' (*WA* 23; *OF*, 23). The 'Letter from the Young Florentine Painter' contains another version of this topic. Antonio has all of a sudden had an insight into 'what human beings have called nature and the beauty of this earth' (*WA* 24; *OF*, 24) and now is able to paint almost without consciousness. His friend in Rome responds that this fortune had not been granted to himself, but also warns him not to let all his sentiments 'wander off uncontrolled in one direction only' or sacrifice his 'many-sided talent to one single feeling' (*WA*, 27; *OF*, 27).

Leonardo da Vinci, however, represents a different possibility of a life devoted to art. In contrast to the divine blessing of Raphael, his attitude can be characterized as 'the model of a truly learned and profoundly scholarly artist and the epitome of a tireless and yet imaginative worker' (*WA*, 28; *OF*, 28). Leonardo demonstrates 'that the genius of art associates willingly enough with the stern Minvera' (ib.). Through his work, he taught 'that a painter should make himself universal and portray all things with respect for their special peculiarities' (*WA*, 31; *OF*, 31). The 'questioning spirit of the earnest scientist' and the 'creative spirit of the artist' were both his genius (*WA*, 35; *OF*, 34–5). Wackenroder refers to the fresco the 'Last Supper in the refectory of the Dominicans in Milan' (*WA*, 37; *OF*, 36) and the 'portrait of Lisa del Giocondo' and is more specific in this section than in any other (*WA*, 37; *OF*, 37). Towards the end, he lets his friar ask himself self-critically whether he wishes to set up Leonardo da Vinci 'as the foremost and most superlative of all painters' (*WA*, 38; *OF*, 39). The answer, of course, is 'that one can admire two spirits of a very dissimilar nature, as long as both possess great qualities'. Yet, the answer is by no means that easy, because 'when the magic word beauty rings out', our mind acts involuntarily and intuitively. Similarly, when Leonardo and Raphael, usually called 'the divine', are compared, spontaneous preferences of the mind are set in motion. This section concludes: 'Such like fancies, when they come to our minds, often cast a wondrous light on objects, illuminating them more brightly than the logical processes of reason. Besides the so-called higher powers of perception there is, perhaps, a magic mirror in our souls which may sometimes show us things in their most vivid form' (*WA*, 40; *OF*, 39–40).

The section entitled 'Universality, Tolerance, and Love of Humanity in Art' confirms this result from a completely different perspective. The creator of this world is capable of embracing at one glance the infinitely varied appearances of his creation. He hears the human beings 'talk different languages in different time zones at different times and hears them quarrel and fail to reach understanding', whereas for him 'everything resolves into harmony'. Art, too, appears in 'ever-changing forms', and to the heavenly creator the Greek temple is as pleasing as the war song of savages (*WA* 46; *OF*, 45–6). In the human world, however, people are 'embroiled in disputes and misunderstandings' and are 'incapable of surveying the whole':

Stupid men cannot understand how there are antipodes on our earth and how they themselves are antipodes. They always imagine that where they are standing is the centre of everything – and their spirit lacks the wings with which they might fly round the globe and embrace with one gaze the whole earth, which is founded in itself.

Likewise they regard their own feelings as the measure of all beauty in art and pronounce decisive judgments on everything as if from a judge's seat, without considering that no one appointed them to be judges or that those whom they condemn might just as easily set themselves up as judges.

Why do you not condemn the Indians for speaking Indian and not our language?

And yet you would condemn the Middle Ages for not building the same kind of temples as the Greeks built? (*WA*, 47; *OF*, 46)

If we do not succeed in feeling our way 'into all other beings and sense their works through a sympathy with their souls', then we should 'at least try to reach this understanding indirectly through the logic of reason' (*WA*, 47; *OF*, 47). At this point, however, a conflict between reason and feeling arises similar to the one described in the previous section on Leonardo and Raphael. Reason attempts to establish 'a strict system by means of the art of reasoning' and would force all human beings to feel in accordance with the rules and regulations of reasoning. The friar has harsh words for such an attitude: 'Whoever believes in a system has banished universal love from his heart! Intolerance of feeling is preferable to intolerance of reason;

superstititon is better than belief in systems' (*WA*, 49; *OF*, 48). The resolution of this conflict is 'to let every mortal creature and every people under the sun have their own beliefs and their own kind of happiness'. The age in which the friar and his contemporaries live is a privileged one, and it makes them feel as if they were 'standing on the summit of a lofty mountain and beholding clearly with our own eyes many lands and ages laid around us at our feet'. The task is to 'strive to sense what is *human*' in all these various appearances. Yet, every human being is bound to its own self and 'sees ideal beauty only it itself': 'Just as each mortal eye receives its own impression of the rainbow, a different impression of beauty is reflected into every eye from the world around it' (*WA*, 49–50; *OF*, 49).

The following text is devoted to Albrecht Dürer and forms the centre of the entire *Outpourings*. The preceding contrast between Raphael and Leonardo and the reflections on tolerance have helped prepare this decisive step in these thoughts on art. The reflection now focuses on a German artist surrounded, left and right, by groups of Italian painters. One could, of course, also explain this extraordinary position of Dürer by the fact that he is the only German artist whom Wackenroder could discover. At any rate, the contemplation leads us into the 'winding streets' of Nuremberg, when the city was 'the vigorous centre of German art', and when within its walls 'there lived and thrived an artistic spirit' (*WA* 50; *OF*, 49). Considering the exorbitant praise of Italian art on the previous pages, a new conflict seems to arise which the friar attempts to assuage with the words:

Are Rome and Germany not on *one* earth? Has our heavenly Father not built roads from north to south, and from east to west to encompass the whole earth? Is one human life too short for all this? Can the Alps not be crossed? – If not, then more than *one* kind of love must dwell in the human breast. (*WA*, 51; *OF*, 50)

Inspired by such feelings, the friar begins his contemplations on the graveyard outside the walls of Nuremberg where the bones of Dürer lie amid countless gravestones, among which flourish tall sunflowers. He feels glad to be a German (*WA*, 51; *OF*, 51). A saying of Luther comes to his mind according to which 'music is foremost among all the arts and sciences' (*WA*, 53; *OF*, 52). Art is thereby considered with 'profound veneration'. If the creative arts have such an important position, he argues, it is an undignified attitude to turn away from Dürer's human figures simply because they are not painted in that resplendent beauty that has become almost the sole criterion of art or because they are not yet presented in depth, but only side by side without being artfully formed into an organized group. He decides to concentrate on his 'unadorned simplicity', the 'soul and deeper significance' of Dürer's figures (*WA*, 54; *OF*, 53) and leave it to others that 'Dürer did not have Titian or Correggio as his teachers, or that people in those days wore quaint, old-fashioned clothes' (*WA* 55; *OF*, 54). He feels no regret at Dürer's not having lived 'in Rome for a time and learnt from Raphael what real beauty is and what "the Ideal" means in art', but thanks God for having given 'to Germany a genuine national painter' (*WA*, 57; *OF*, 55–6).

What distinguished Dürer from the 'idealism or the noble simplicity of a Raphael' was his ability to show us human beings 'as they really lived around him'. This equal value of the two artists is illustrated toward the end of this section by a dream in which fiction and reality mingle. The friar refers to the time in his youth when he first saw paintings by Raphael in the same picture gallery as paintings by Dürer, saying that, of all the artists represented in this room, these two had a particularly close affinity to his heart. He was so occupied with these impressions that they recurred in his dream in which he returned to the castle[13] and found his way with a torch to the picture gallery:

When I came to the door I heard an indistinct murmur within; I opened – and gave a sudden start, for every corner of the vast hall was illuminated by an eerie light, and before several paintings there stood in person the imposing figures of their creators, wearing the old costumes in which I had seen them in pictures. One whom I recognized told me that they often came down from heaven to earth, to linger in the still of night in this or that gallery and inspect the still-loved works of their hands. I recognized many Italian painters, but very few Netherlanders were to be seen. Reverently I passed among them –

and then, o wonder! there before my very eyes, standing hand in hand apart from all the others, were Raphael and Albrecht Dürer, looking calmly and in amiable silence at their paintings hanging together. I did not have the courage to address the divine Raphael; awe and a secret dread sealed my lips. I was just about to greet Albrecht, however, and pour forth my love for him – when there was a crash, everything faded, and I awoke in violent agitation. (*WA*, 58; *OF*, 56–7)

The friar also refers to the 'writings of old Vasari' where he could read of Raphael and Dürer 'how during their lifetimes these two sublime painters, though they never met, had become friends through their works, and how Raphael had admired the honest, truthful works of the old German and had not thought them unworthy of his love' (ib.).

The essay 'Of Two Wonderful Languages' moves away from this centre and deals with the distinction between the 'languages of words' and the language of art and nature. By means of the former 'we have dominion over all of nature' and acquire with ease 'all the treasures of the earth'; only the 'invisible spirit which reigns above us' is inaccessible to this language. The latter is spoken only by a few chosen human beings (*WA*, 60–1; *OF*, 59). Basically, we do not know 'what a tree is, or what a meadow is, or what a rock is', since we cannot talk to them and are 'capable of communicating only among ourselves'. And yet we have a 'marvellous sympathy for these things without ever having the appropriate and precise words for them' (*WA*, 62; *OF*, 60).

The language of art is of a different kind, and together with the language of nature, it forms the two kinds of language which the friar designates in the title as 'wonderful'. The language of art has a 'marvellous power over the human heart' and speaks through 'pictorial representations', employs a 'hieroglyphic language whose signs we recognize and understand on sight'. Contrary to the language of words and of reason, it merges the spiritual and the sensuous in its figures 'in such an effective and admirable fashion that the whole of our selves and every fibre of our being is doubly moved and shaken utterly'. At this point, in order to illustrate the power of this language, the friar refers to a painting representing the torture of Saint Sebastian 'standing naked and bound to a tree while an angel draws the arrows from his breast and another angel descends from heaven with a garland of flowers for his head'. He tells his readers: 'To this painting I owe the most profound and lasting Christian sentiments, and even yet I can scarcely recall its details without tears coming to my eyes' (*WA*, 63; *OF*, 61). In a more theoretical manner, he derives the extraordinary power of this language from the fact that it is able to 'touch our senses as well as our minds', or rather to merge our being 'into one single part of perception, which in this twofold way grasps and comprehends heavenly mysteries' (*WA*, 63; *OF*, 62).

The story of the 'Ancient Painter Piero di Cosimo' continues the sequence of old painters' chronicles found in Vasari and other 'histories of the ancient painters' (*WA*, 65; *OF*, 64) which serve in the *Outpourings* to illustrate the manifold options in the world of art. Piero di Cosimo loved most of all to depict 'wild Baccanals and orgies, dreadful monsters, and other terrifying images'. But the friar doubts that he 'truly possessed the genuine artistic temperament' (*WA*, 70–1; *OF*, 69–70), because 'the artistic temperament should be no more than a functional aid for perceiving nature in its totality and infusing it with the human spirit so that it may be born again in beautifully transfigured form' (*WA*, 71; *OF*, 69). The text 'How and in What Manner We Ought Properly to Contemplate the Works of the World's Great Artists' compares 'picture galleries', which ought to be 'temples', with 'county fairs', and the true reception of works of art to 'prayer' (*WA*, 72–3; *OF*, 70–1). The works of the artists are not there so that our eye may see and our mind decipher them, 'but so that we may enter them sympathetically, and live and breathe in them' (*WA*, 74; *OF*, 72).

The essay 'The Genius of Michelangelo Buonarotti' brings to the fore a painter who continues the sequence of great paradigms of art drawn so far from Raphael, Leonardo da Vinci, and Dürer. With him, God sent an artist into the world who was 'to teach mankind the meaning of perfection in the arts of drawing, craftsmanship, and chiaroscuro (by means of which paintings capture the fullness of life)'. As an architect, he showed 'how buildings should be invested with stability, comfort, beauty of proportion, charm, and wealth of architectural embellishment' (*WA*, 77; *OF*, 75). In this section, Wackenroder formulates his aesthetic principles more distinctly and with a rare precision. It is not sufficient to say of a work of art that it is 'excellent and beautiful', because these qualities can be applied to the most diverse productions. We must 'give ourselves over entirely to every great artist', 'comprehend natural objects through his eyes', and be able to say: 'This work is in its own fashion accurate and well-founded' (*WA*, 78; *OF*, 76). Painting is described as a 'kind of poetry employing images of human beings'. As in poetry, works of painting are animated by different feelings which the artist 'has breathed into them'. This feature can illustrate the difference between Raphael and Michelangelo. We could call Raphael 'the painter of the New Testament' and Michelangelo 'the painter of the Old Testament'. The first embodies 'the divine and tranquil spirit of Christ', while on the second 'there reposes the spirit of the inspired prophets, of Moses, and the other prophets of the Orient'. Michelangelo had a tendency to depict 'prodigious and monstrous forces and expressed a superhuman tension and energy through his figures' (*WA*, 79; *OF*, 76–7). His was the time of 'truly original painters': 'Who painted like Correggio before Correggio, or like Raphael before Raphael?' At the same time one comes to think 'that nature, in her prodigality, had squandered all her wealth of artistic genius during this period'. Masters of later times down to the present day do little more 'than to imitate one or another (or even several together) of those early original standard-setting-painters' (*WA*, 81; *OF*, 78). In 'The Portraits of the Artists', a muse enters a picture gallery in the company of a young artist and comments with him in lyric verses on the accomplishments of Leonardo, Dürer, Michelangelo, and Raphael. The section 'The Painters' Chronicle' ends the portrayals of painters with a great variety of representatives and also serves the function of paying tribute to Vasari, who had furnished the material for so many parts of the *Outpourings*. This is done by interlacing the story with parts of Wackenroder's own biography, referring to the time when, as a student at Erlangen University, he used to visit the picture gallery at Château Weißstein near Pommersfelden in Upper Franconia. On one of his early visits, an old Italian priest watched the uninformed enthusiasm noticeable in his eager scrutiny of these paintings, especially those by Raphael, and advised him how much more pleasure he would derive from them if he had some knowledge of the artists who created them. The book he most strongly recommended to him in this regard was the history of the lives of the painters by Giorgio Vasari (*WA*, 95; *OF*, 93). It was this unknown person who had motivated the study of the history of the artists expounded in the *Outpourings* (*WA*, 104; *OF*, 102).

In its deliberately naïve tone of narration and skilful use of Christian imagery, Wackenroder's early writing breaks with the belief in the stable system of rationalism and the Enlightenment as well as in absolute norms that are accessible to the human mind. In his Berlin milieu, the author is still unaware of the new articulation of reason and systematic philosophy accomplished by transcendental idealism. Yet, in his own way, he shows that the language of reason is only one means of facilitating our contact with reality, and as powerful as it may prove in subjugating the world to our purposes, it is quite impotent in understanding the deeper meaning of life. Art is the human capability of relating to this divine language. To be sure, the text says very little about art except for these general phrases and hardly anything about painting beyond biographical, mostly legendary information taken over from old Italian sources. If one compares the various portraits of these painters drawn by the friar, one comes to realize that art has a source other than reason, is in fact incapable of being reduced to reason, and manifests itself in a variety of different perspectives that no logical system will ever be able to encompass.

THE CONCEPTION OF MUSIC

The last section of the *Outpourings* has the title 'The Remarkable Musical Life of the Tone-Poet Joseph Berglinger' and transposes us to the 'present time', that is, to the period of the 'early youth' of the friar and his close friendship with an artist who devoted his life to music. We are in a little town in southern Germany, and the name of the friend is Joseph Berglinger. Because of the unhappy ending of the story and Wackenroder's own early death, the two events have, of course, been brought together in the sentimental literary histories of the nineteenth and twentieth centuries. Beyond that, the notion that art has a life-endangering character, that a basic antagonism exists between life and art, has been drawn from this story and can be traced in the tales of E. T. A. Hoffmann, the literature on art as vital decadence in the nineteenth century, and the literary production of Thomas Mann. From the beginning, these features of the Romantic theory of music portrayed it as an art form of the greatest refinement, but also of the greatest danger. Rudolf Köpke, Tieck's biographer, himself postulated a close relationship between Berglinger and Wackenroder and thus gave the myth of the life-consuming character of art an early biographical confirmation:

In Joseph Berglinger's musical life and his *Outpourings*, Wackenroder had represented the painful state of mind [of his own life, torn between an undesired juridical profession and devotion to art.] He was that young man who, with his desire and enthusiasm for music, stood before an active and rationalistic father who intended to employ him usefully just as he himself had been. It was he who read every page of his textbooks ten times without comprehending them, while his soul sang inner fantasies. He recollected dreams from the time of his studies when he let the suffering protagonist flee from his paternal house to devote himself to art. He might have had secret doubts whether he was capable of the highest creative profession when he lets Berglinger confess with a feeling of bitter disappointment that yearning and fantasy promise more than talent and life gratify, that the enthusiasm to overcome the resistance of life has to be of a stronger nature, and that his vocation was perhaps more to enjoy than to practise art. His [Wackenroder's] enthusiasm was a quiet passion permeating everything he thought and said, but also consummating his youth and life.[14]

This story puts music into the centre of aesthetic interest. Berglinger becomes totally convinced 'that God had set him on the earth to become a musical genius, and at times he imagined that heaven would raise him to even greater heights of glory on account of the depressing restrictions and privations which he had to suffer in his youth' (*WA*, 113; *OF*, 111). In some of the poems he composes at that time, he directs himself to St Cecilia, the patroness of music, and asks:

> Let my soul dissolve in anthems
> Which so sweetly charm my heart.
>
> (*WA*, 114; *OF*, 111)

Through his father, who opposes this inclination to music with a rigorous sense of duty, music and art assume the attraction of a forbidden fruit for Berglinger. One day, he leaves his father's house and returns to the episcopal seat where he becomes a conductor and lives in great splendour. Yet now he feels trapped in a new cage. He has to perform in the concert hall and cannot express his feelings as freely as he wishes (*WA*, 119; *OF*, 117). Considering his audience, he says disdainfully: 'And it is for souls like these that I exhaust my inspiration! For these I spare no effort so that their feelings might be stirred! This is the noble destiny for which I believed I was born!' (ib.). As an artist he is involved at court in all sorts of 'disgusting jealousies', 'malicious intrigues', and 'subordination of art to the will of the court'. It is not sufficient for the execution of the art of music to express a simple feeling; one needs 'many hands before one work may come into being'. Whereas in his youth he thought that, through music, he could escape 'all earthly woe', he now finds himself 'more firmly bogged down in the mire' (*WA*, 120; *OF*, 118). Of his father's wishes that he become a doctor so that he might alleviate the sufferings of others, Berglinger thinks: 'Perhaps it would have been better that way' (*WA*, 123; *OF*, 121). When his father is on his death-bed, Berglinger is reconciled with him, and this gives him the stimulation to compose a Passion which, according to the friar, 'with its insinuating melodies expressing all the agonies of suffering, will forever remain a masterpiece' (*WA*, 124; *OF*, 122).

Shortly thereafter Berglinger dies in the flower of his youth. The friar attempts to draw a lesson from his life by asking the question: 'Why it was the will of heaven that the conflict between his ethereal enthusiasm and the baseness and wretchedness of earthly existence should so embitter his whole life and should in the end sever forever body from spirit in his divided self?' The answer is that Raphael, Reni, Dürer, in spite of all the adversities of life, produced magnificent works, but Berglinger, 'whose harmonious works possess such mysterious beauty, was different from all of these!' His 'sublime fantasy' consumed him, and perhaps he was 'born to enjoy art rather than to practise it'. The 'unfathomable power to create' is perhaps something quite different, 'something still more wonderful and more divine than the power of the imagination'. The artistic power will forever remain a mystery to human beings. After he has articulated these recollections and his reflections on them, the friar hopes that they 'may serve to awaken good thoughts in some unknown reader' (*WA*, 125–6; *OF*, 123–4).

When Tieck published the *Fantasies on Art for Friends of Art* in 1799, he included a much larger part of his own contributions than he did in the edition of the *Outpourings* of 1797. The first part of the *Fantasies*, mainly devoted to painting and painters, is a continuation in the biographical, legendary style created by Wackenroder and is mostly, except for two pieces, by Tieck.[15] The second part deals with music, has Wackenroder as its main author,[16] and the name of Joseph Berglinger is conspicuous. Since Wackenroder did not reveal his work on these subjects to Tieck until the summer of 1796, fell ill in December 1796,[17] and died in February 1797, work on these pieces must have taken place in the few months between these events and been interrupted by fits of Wackenroder's mental sickness. At this time, the two friends must also have drawn up their plan for the novel *Franz Sternbald's Wanderings*, which Tieck carried out by himself following Wackenroder's death, not without linking the plan, however, to the publication of the *Outpourings* by inserting the 'Letter from a Young German Painter in Rome to His Friend in Nuremberg' (*WA*, 113–18; *OF*, 79–86).

The mask of the friar is dropped in the *Fantasies*, and Wackenroder's introductory remarks to his 'fantasies on the art of music' do not continue the mournful mood of the section on Berglinger in the *Outpourings*. Instead, we read: 'His convictions about art agreed with mine in an amazing manner, and through frequent outpourings of our hearts, our feelings became more and more united' (*TI PhK*, 50). The first of these essays bears the strange title 'A Wondrous Oriental Fairy-Tale about a naked Saint'. This naked saint was a hermit in the deserts of the Near East, a madman who did not live in a human way and cut himself off from all contact with society. Most people, however, considered him a 'higher genius from the realm of the firmament who had gone astray and assumed a human figure' (*TI PhK*, 51). He lived in a cave near a river and was possessed by the feeling that the 'wheel of time' rotated through his entire being with an enormous roaring and imbued him with an unimaginable pressure and a feeling of being hurried. He could not rest nor execute any activity, and as soon as anything seemed to come to a halt, he became agitated and undertook the most desperate efforts to prevent time from standing still. When people came to watch him, he became enraged because of their standing there. When someone collected herbs or pieces of wood around his cave, he became furious and laughed wildly at such idle activities while the wheel of time was incessantly moving on. He jumped out of his cave and killed the blasphemer with one stroke. He could not do anything like other human beings – stretch out a hand, set one foot before the other – because a 'vibrating anxiety' pervaded his entire being. Only during beautiful nights when the moon stood before his cave did he sink to the ground and whine and cry in despair because the wheel of time did not give him any rest. He obviously was in search of something distinct, yet unknown to him (*TI PhK*, 53). One night, however, two lovers came in their boat up the river. The moon had inspired their feelings, and soft music from the boat developed into a magic and floating world of sounds. The unknown desire on the part of the naked saint was all of a sudden satisfied. His figure disappeared, and travelling cara-vans saw instead an angelic form move into the heavens which they interpreted as the 'genius of love and music' (*TI PhK*, 55).

To explain the 'Magic of the Art of Sounds', as the next section is entitled, Wackenroder employs a great number of similes, but the most convincing consists for him in the questions of the composer who asks: 'Is not the whole of life a beautiful dream? a lovely soap-bubble? Well, my piece of music is the same' (*TI PhK*, 55). Another way of explaining this magic is to ask how human beings acquired this art. They obviously wanted to preserve their agreeable feelings, and for this purpose, all beautiful arts originated. Music, however, was the most wonderful among these inventions 'because it depicted human feeling in a superhuman manner'. All movements of our mind are represented in an incorporeal manner. Music speaks a language 'which we do not know in ordinary life, which we have learnt but do not know where and how' (*TI PhK*, 58). One particular impression conveyed by music is that, while listening to one special piece, we spontaneously consider it to be the most exquisite and forget about all others. Wackenroder sees in this feeling the criterion for a true enjoyment of art as well as for the excellence of a particular work of art, namely, 'that we forget about all other works of art and do not have any inclination to compare it with others' (*TI PhK*, 61). It would, of course, be odd to remain with this particular work or to stay with one single art form and not expand our experience into the entire world of art. The most interesting relationships thereby come into play. In this section, 'Of the Different Genres in Each Art, and Especially of the Different Kinds of Church Music', Wackenroder envisions a comparative study of art and focuses on spiritual art forms as they exist in poetry, painting, and music for the sake of worship of the divine. He sees these three arts as competing to come as close as possible to God's throne, but considers music as the most daring in the praise of God 'because it dares to speak of the heavenly things in a strange, untranslatable language, with a bold resonance, a vigorous movement and a harmonious union of a whole group of living beings' (*TI PhK*, 62).

The following reflection is presented as a 'Fragment of a Letter by Joseph Berglinger' and takes its starting-point from a pleasant summer evening when outside the walls of the city a brass band is playing and various classes of citizens spend their leisure time relaxing to its music. A little later, everything is covered by night, and Berglinger grieves over the 'incessant, monotonous change of thousands of days and nights'. The only consolation he finds is art, which reaches out its hand to us from heaven 'so that we hover above the desolate abyss in a bold position, between heaven and earth' (*TI PhK*, 67). The section, 'The Particular Inner Essence of the Art of Sounds and the Psychology of Today's Instrumental Music' is Wackenroder's most concrete attempt to investigate the nature and special attraction of music. He analyses the physics, mathematics, and sensuous power of sounds, and explains on the basis of its medium why music in its present state of development is the youngest of all the arts (*TI PhK*, 68). Yet, the most significant feature of this art, in contrast to all others, is for him that music is the most direct expression of human feeling. He says:

In the mirror of sounds, the human heart learns to know itself; through these sounds we learn to *feel feeling*; they give a living consciousness to many dreamy thoughts living in hidden corners of the mind and thereby enrich our inner self through entirely new and magic forms of feeling. (*TI PhK*, 71)

Another letter by Berglinger concludes Wackenroder's contributions to the *Fantasies*.[18] This letter is again written in a gloomy, desperate mood and expresses the feeling of forlornness on the part of the artist, who, in order to carry out his profession, has separated himself by a vast intermediate space from the rest of humanity (*TI PhK*, 75). This includes a certain lack of sociability, indeed, even a degree of selfishness and narcissism that is needed to live the life of an artist: 'Art is a seductive, forbidden fruit; whoever has tasted its inner, sweet juice, is irretrievably lost for the active, living world. He will move in an ever more constricting way into his own selfish enjoyment of himself, and his hand will lose the strength to reach out actively to a fellow human being' (*TI PhL*, 76). Berglinger feels with bitterness that he is incapable of leading a 'beneficient, god-pleasing life'. He speaks of the 'deadly poison which is inwardly hidden in the apparently harmless germ of artistic enjoyment'. Even irony does not help in this situation because all self-mockery is shown in the last analysis to be 'miserable play-fulness' (*TIPhK*, 78). The greatest misery is that a human being totally absorbed by art deeply despises reason and philosophy, which for the normal human being constitute firm points of reference: 'The philosopher contemplates his soul as a systematic book and finds beginning and end, truth and untruth spelled out in distinct words. The artist contemplates it as a painting or a piece of music and knows of no firm conviction and considers everything beautiful which stands in its appropriate place.' Berglinger resigns himself to the thought: 'Thus my soul will for its entire life resemble the hanging Aeolian harp, and its strings will be breathed through by a strange, unknown air, producing at pleasure changing melodies' (*TI PhK*, 79). We know that this is a depiction of Berglinger's opinion and that Wackenroder, together with Tieck, projected a more diversified and pluralistic answer to the nagging antagonism of life and art. Yet, Wackenroder had already died when Tieck carried out this project, which he did not complete either.

EXAMPLE: TIECK'S NOVEL
FRANZ STERNBALD'S WANDERINGS

Ludwig Tieck's *Franz Sternbald's Wanderings* is the first important manifestation of the novel during the period of early Romanticism, or rather its recreation if we relate this novel back to its older Romantic prototypes such as Cervantes.[19] Since its appearance at the Easter book fair in 1798, however, the novel has been measured against ideals and judged according to norms it does not obey and according to Tieck's intentions did not pursue at all. The fact that the novel remained unfinished gave the two first parts a merely provisional character and made one expect that the main portion was still forthcoming. Tieck's notice in the postscript to the first part about Wackenroder's share in the planning of the work[20] gave critics like Rudolf Haym the idea that the blueprint of the novel was a 'variation of the motifs of the *Art-Loving Friar*'. Wackenroder's death, however, dissipated the 'chaste view of the friar' which was then replaced by a 'frivolous artist morality', by 'lascivious, coarsely sensuous bath adventures'.[21] Most frequently *Franz Sternbald* was understood as a novel à la *Wilhelm Meister*, and critics usually explained the obvious difference to Goethe's novel by Tieck's exaggerated imagination or the supposed inability of the author to follow his great model in an appropriate manner. Caroline Schlegel fell asleep while reading the novel on 14 October 1798, and shared Goethe's opinion that there was not really any action in the novel and that the work was peculiarly devoid of content. She wrote: 'A fantasy which constantly flaps its wings and flutters, but never really takes off the ground' (*CA* 1, 460). In his attempt to understand the novel as an artist novel, Goethe found 'too little art' and 'too much morning sun' in it as well as too many 'nice sunrises'. He thought that everything was in it 'except for the painter' (*GOE* 12, 268). Critics of our time have found a confusing indecisiveness in the novel insofar as it does not become clear whether art is defended against life (first part) or life against art (second part). With this criticism, we are not far from more substantial criticisms of the novel's thematic rupture and consequent failure.[22] In an exercise in 'ideological criticism', the wanderings depicted here have even been interpreted as the 'attempted escapes of city-dwellers incorporated in money society' – attempted escapes, however, which, because of a lack of real alternatives, become an end in themselves and manifest themselves as 'autonomous escapes'. In this manner, the author departs before having finished the third part, 'just as Sternbald and Roderigo disappear before the accomplished union'.[23]

In order to do justice to this frequently maligned novel, we have to ask what exactly constitutes the poetic unity of the work. The answer is that *Franz Sternbald* represents the abundance and variety of life in the medium of the imagination. *Franz Sternbald* represents that particular variation of the early Romantic novel that can be called its fantastic type, and which, because of its proximity to the 'marvellous', 'fanciful', 'improbable', 'exotic', and so forth, comes closest to the old 'romance'. The theme of travelling, highlighted in the title, underscores this feature, and the numerous poems and songs, especially in the second part, in their constant alternation of prose and poetry, represent the switch from real life to the life of fancy. This fantastic principle of unity is operative, however, through what is almost exclusively the pleasant and benevolent type of imagination and not, as in other works of Tieck, its sinister, demonic form. We also notice that this fantastic unity is never broken or interrupted by irony and that, except for the abrupt ending, the author does not appear personally in his work. Only rarely, and virtually indiscernibly, is the thread of narration interrupted, as for instance when the author intertwines elegiac reflections on the 'life of youth' with the body of the story. We search in vain for a 'smiling down' of the author upon his work, as Goethe had done in his *Wilhelm Meister*, or for a deliberate destruction of poetic illusion such as we might expect from the author of the drama *Puss in Boots*. Yet, we do not encounter a merely naïve form of narration. Whoever has an ear for it will notice that the voice of the narrator changes considerably from the first to the second part, that is, during the transition from the old German past into a timeless landscape. Altogether, although they are scarcely detectable, a great number of narrative perspectives, specifically called 'masks' (*TI FS*, 190), appear in this novel and manifest the author's ironical distance, his mastery of his work.

The principle of fantastic and romance-like unity explains the other characteristics of the novel without great difficulty, especially its alleged lack of content. At first glance, we definitely gain the impression that nothing is actually occurring in the work. The 'action' encompasses a period of about one-and-a-half years (*TI FS*, 398). With its change of seasons, cities, and landscapes, this time span corresponds to Franz Sternbald's inner development, revealing itself in a seemingly erratic roaming that Tieck called 'wanderings'. Friedrich Schlegel, who had a distinct sense for such unsensational happenings, went so far as to characterize the novel as a fantasizing on the imagination when he said: 'The romantic spirit seems to fantasize pleasantly about itself' (*KFSA* 2, 245; *LF*, 231). The movement of this novel is not circular, however, because the arabesque direction of these travellings assumes the character of a search – for parents, brothers and sisters, the unknown beloved, but also for the self and its realization.

It corresponds to the particular focus of interest in early German Romanticism that this search, development, and finding are the acts of an artist. The novel presents us with a young apprentice in the art of painting who, in various stages, finally achieves mastery in his art.[24] The development of the painter is simultaneously a training in the art of living, in Franz's personality, in his health, vitality, his point of view, and this process finally culminates in the finding of his beloved. The maturation of the artist and that of the human being are inseparably interwoven. In retrospect, one could easily show how each moment, each conversation and acquaintance has furthered Franz on his wanderings, even if some of these events threatened to lead him astray. At the beginning of the novel we meet him as a young person full of restlessness and apprehension as to whether he will in time become a great artist (*TI FS*, 34–5). Dürer, who understands his disciple, knows through his own great wisdom that the latter belongs to those emergent artists who do not thrive best in seclusion, but who do better when they enjoy the 'sight of manifoldness' (*TI FS*, 122).

This 'sight of manifoldness', this movement out of oneself, pursued through all these wanderings (and especially those in Italy), becomes incorporated toward the end of the first part in a figure that almost dominates the second. This is the Italian Florestan, who appears to Franz as the incarnation of that enjoyment of life which expresses itself only in an immediate fashion. After he has entertained the party on the boat to Rotterdam with his joyful songs, Florestan explains: 'The main idea in them is a cheerful view of the world' (*TI FS*, 142). The sweet desire for travelling which sees everything present as too narrow and limited finds an even better representative during the course of the novel in Roderigo, and perhaps its strongest expression in Ludoviko. Indeed, a spontaneous inclination towards adventure and instability unites these three fellow-travellers. We notice, however, that Franz, in spite of his great admiration for Rudolf Florestan, would not like to be identical to him, but stubbornly pursues his own peculiar way, knowing very well how to distinguish between his own pensive meditation and melancholy and Florestan's immediate enjoyment of life (*TI FS*, 161–2, 204, 220). Finally, on his own impulse, he separates himself from the enjoyable romantic company in the most beautiful romantic garden and continues his wanderings with a pitiful pilgrim. He has realized that with these companions he would 'almost totally forget his goal' (*TI FS*, 322) and the year might end before he would arrive in Italy (*TI FS*, 332).

The 'view of manifoldness' opened to Franz by Rudolf Florestan also brings the young man a decisive initiation into the pleasures of love. This experience is closely connected with Franz's development as a painter and the general formation of his personality, and it gives his entire orientation in life a new note. A comparative glance at the timid youth leaving Nuremberg at the beginning of the novel and the vivacious young man appearing at the side of the voluptuous Lenore in Rome makes this obvious. This emergence from himself in the experience of sensuousness, however, almost leads Franz to lose himself and depart from his way. Indeed, Tieck has followed this danger of complete self-surrender to its extreme in his novel. Yet, Franz is able to terminate the 'previous rashness in his life conduct' on his own, even feel sorry for it and find himself again on a new level of life (*TI FS*, 397) that leads almost of its own accord to the reunion with his beloved.[25]

This change also leads to an awakening of a 'new love for art' (*TI FS*, 397). In Italy Franz has come to experience the 'sight of the manifold' in art. He was simply overwhelmed by the beauty he had seen there and 'experienced so much that he did not have time to order his impressions' (*TI FS*, 392). The conversations on art in the Castellani Salon were dominated by a historical scepticism and relativism according to which no work of art, no painter, and no epoch could possibly attain an absolute value. Franz's enthusiasm, his 'impetuousness' in the veneration of Dürer and Raphael, were smiled at with the knowledge that his was the attitude of a young man still quite inexperienced (*TI FS*, 392). These impressions now gradually replace Dürer and Nuremberg in his concerns (*TI FS*, 397), just as the image of the beloved is dissipated. Franz's reappropriation of himself in the realm of art that occurs in parallel to his regaining of his personality on the ethical-moral level is occasioned by a contemplation of Michelangelo's fresco *The*

Last Judgment in the Sistine Chapel.[26] What Franz Sternbald had written in the spring from Alsace to Sebastian in Nuremberg has now been fulfilled. At that time, he had dreamed that his artistic mind would develop like a tree, without any pressure or force. He was also convinced that the angelic image in his mind would become real. At that time this image had stood only as an 'uncertain, passing phenomenon' before his soul, and he wrote that he 'ardently stretched his senses and memory to perceive it really and truly and to make it his property' (*TI FS*, 200).

Tieck's novel is not only an artist novel depicting the developing and maturing of a young artist, however, but also a novel on art itself, making art its central theme and presenting a particular notion of art. Because this concept or theory of art is acquired progressively by the protagonist and eventually constitutes his intellectual distinction, it is not unrelated to the events of the novel, but is rather most intimately integrated with them. In this sense, Eichendorff called Tieck's novel an 'apotheosis of art'.[27] Most of the active figures in the novel are involved in art, and 'art conversations' occupy a considerable space in *Franz Sternbald*. At the beginning, Franz participates somewhat silently when Dürer and Lukas von Leiden debate the themes of artistic invention and the imitation of nature, following their arguments without 'distinctly grasping the thought' (*TI FS*, 116). When Dürer presents art as a revelation of the 'wondrous human spirit', however, he suddenly becomes fully involved (*TI FS*, 116–20).

The development of a certain theory of art not only results in the work of great masters such as Dürer and Lukas von Leiden, but also takes shape in many seemingly sporadic conversations with people who have nothing directly to do with art, who are not artists of life like Ludoviko or singers and poets like Florestan. On numerous occasions, Florestan attempts to divert his friend from his ascetic 'old German' notion of art and to open his eyes to the sensuous beauties of the world. In a remarkable conversation, Ludoviko unveils to the amazed Franz a type of painting that has completely departed from traditional techniques and accomplishes 'something totally unheard of', provoking 'surprise and horror'. 'Strange figures from the world of insects, worms, and plants', yet full of 'wondrous similarity to human characters' appear here in a 'confused, almost incomprehensible union' (*TI FS*, 314–15). The sculptor Bolz who, as an absolutist, is of the opinion that in comparison to Michelangelo all other artists are only preparations, happens to be together with Franz at an iron-works one evening where in the midst of black rocks, flying sparks, glowing masses of ore and hammering, the workers present a strange view. 'If one could only paint this', exclaims Franz, who now begins to think of paintings as completely devoid of action and composition, and presenting instead nothing but glitter, confused figures, moods, and an artificial, almost trifling play of colours. Such creations would lead beyond the periphery of objects and, in a way, let us look into them (*TI FS*, 341–2). Considering Bolz, who thinks according to degrees of perfection, Franz is convinced that art, like nature, has more than one kind of beauty (*TI FS*, 342).

Of special importance for these convictions are Franz Sternbald's visits to the eccentric hermit who lives as a painter high up in the solitude of the mountains. This hermit sees himself as a 'failed artist' who, because of his way of life, has not accomplished real mastery in his field. In his conversations with Franz, however, he reveals deep insights into art, which are intensified in their meaning because Franz accidentally discovers a portrait of his unknown beloved in the hut of the old man. Their conversation culminates in the notion of allegorical art which first occurred to Franz while contemplating Strasburg Cathedral, which appeared to him at that time 'as though it were an image of infinity' (*TI FS*, 217–18). In his discussion with the old hermit, Franz specifies allegorical art as an attempt to express the infinite abundance of life while not rendering the objects of the world in an isolated fashion, but in their inner relationships with one another and 'by ascribing to the singular a general meaning' (*TI FS*, 258). Allegorical art is furthermore that type of creation that does not copy its objects in any objective manner but rather represents their mirroring in the mind, in the interaction of subject and object (ib.). Later Franz speaks with a high degree of self-assurance to Rudolf Florestan about allegorical art. It is not through figures, landscapes, or events that the painter reveals his imagination or his 'sense for the magic of art'. These are only incidents that transform 'that play of ideas, that music' into 'miraculous miracles' (*TI FS*, 282–3). As a particularly accomplished example of such a work of art reflecting the totality of life, Rudolf Florestan mentions *The Triumph of Death* on the Campo Santo in Pisa, a work that spontaneously conjures up for him the 'image of grand human life'. Here, 'nobody knows of the other and all move around blind and deaf' (*TI FS*, 284).

Tieck's novel not only fantasizes about art and discusses aesthetics, but also attempts to portray the interconnection of art with life in general. The conviction that life and art form an antagonism and cannot be reconciled seems to find expression in Wackenroder's *Outpourings of an Art-Loving Friar*, especially in the narrative 'The Remarkable Musical Life of the Tone-Poet Joseph Berglinger'. Tieck varies the idea of the irreconcilability of personal happiness in life and an artistic vocation in numerous forms in his novel. Already outside the gates of Nuremberg, Franz Sternbald experiences a conflict between the enjoyment of unrestrained travelling and the happiness of a simple domestic life. In his conversations with Messy, a black-smith, a contrast appears between the usefulness of a handicraft and the social irresponsibility of art (*TI FS*, 22–5). In the second part, Ludoviko emphasizes the discrepancy between art and life. 'One who devotes himself to art', he explains to Franz, 'has to sacrifice what he is and can be as a human being' (*TI FS*, 313). These and other instances have induced readers to assume that Tieck intended to depict in *Franz Sternbald* the irreconcilability of life and art or the mutual 'strangeness' and 'estrangement' of these two realms. The scene just quoted from his wanderings, however, shows Franz at a stage in his life when he can calmly refer Ludoviko to great artistic figures 'who remained untouched by such foolishness' (*TI FS*, 313), and Ludoviko responds immediately by saying that his words now appear to him 'as a slander of human dignity' (*TI FS*, 314). Shortly before this scene, Franz had met with the hermit in the mountains, someone who demonstrated to him, through his despair, the end to which the separation of art and life leads (*TI FS*, 261–3). Towards the end of the novel, it is Sebastian who finds it foolish to continue to work and forget all about life around him and who, reviewing his work, poses the gloomy question to Franz: 'For what?' (*TI FS*, 335). Franz, however, is no longer able to follow his friend. He drops his letter and exclaims: 'Yes, I am happy, I feel how happy I am! My life spins off like a golden thread' (*TI FS*, 335). To Sebastian he responds: '...do not lose your courage in life...The world and art are much richer than I was able to believe before' (*TI FS*, 368).

On the basis of these various observations, we can claim that the novel aims to integrate all of its elements into a harmonious union. This goes far beyond the artistic perfection and personal maturity of Franz Sternbald, and comprises the human being and the world, art and life, north and south, past and future, ideality and reality. Richard Alewyn had this reconciling tendency in mind when he described the novel in terms of 'converging lines': 'the union of the lovers, the reunification of the relatives, the disentanglement of all complications, and the solution of all riddles'. Alewyn refers to a fragment from the continuation of the novel describing the 'union of the lovers, the fusion of past and present, memory and desire, world and ego as the return into the lost paradise of childhood'.[28]

This thrust of the novel is most evident in its structure. The first two parts are so fundamentally disparate in their narrative prose, content, and entire atmosphere that many critics have been unable to see any relationship between them at all. To visualize a relationship, however, one has to start from the premise that the transition from the old German past into the beautiful manifoldness of the Italian Renaissance, which almost looks like a complete reversal, is necessary for Franz Sternbald's artistic and personal development. This confrontation leads him to that task of self-discovery and integration in which the two worlds will fuse. This is a path from unity to plurality, from self-concentration to manifoldness, from 'self-constitution of the ego' to an 'emergence of the ego from itself'. This self-realization of the ego, in the sense of an identity of the self and the world, can also be seen in the religious tendencies of the two parts. With its praise of Martin Luther and the Reformation, the first represents Protestantism, whereas the second takes a pronounced turn to Catholicism. The solution of this conflict is obviously to be found in a higher synthesis of these confessions. From the point of view of nationalism, the predilection for Germany in the first part changes into an admiration of Italy in the second, a disparity which apparently was to be resolved in a synthesis of northern seriousness and southern light-heartedness.

The way in which the first part of the novel necessitates its second and then requires the third is already obvious in the 'Letter from a Young German Painter in Rome to His Friend in Nuremberg' which Tieck inserted into Wackenroder's *Outpourings*. If we accept Tieck's words about a planned division of labour on the part of the two friends as far as their communal writing of the novel was concerned (*TI FS*, 191–2), we are perhaps not mistaken if we attribute to Wackenroder the sections on Nuremberg and Dürer, and to Tieck the ones on Italy and the Renaissance artists. This seems to be confirmed by the *Letter*, the author of which is easily recognized as Franz Sternbald. He confesses to Sebastian that he has converted to Catholicism and is about to marry his beloved. He is inexpressibly happy and in this emotional state thinks of Nuremberg, Sebastian, and Dürer:

In my thoughts I can see the artful Master Albrecht sitting on his stool, carving an intricate little piece of wood with childish, almost touching diligence, reflecting ponderously on his subject and its effectuation, and looking again and again at the work of art which he has begun. I can see his spacious panelled room with its round-panel windows, and you copying one of his works with boundless industry and fidelity. I can see, too, the younger apprentices walking to and fro, and old Master Dürer interjecting many a wise and many a merry word. Then I see Mistress Dürer come in, or the eloquent Willibald Pirckheimer, who inspects the paintings and drawings and begins a lively dispute with Albrecht. And when I imagine all this in detail I really cannot understand how I have come to this place and how everything is so different here. (*WA*, 82–3; *OF*, 80)

He also exemplifies the enormous difference between these two worlds by imagining how he himself would have felt in Nuremberg if he had suddenly been confronted with these experiences:

Yet heaven alone knows what I would have said or felt then if Raphael's transfigured faces had been revealed to my childish eyes. Ah! my dear Sebastian, if I had understood them I would surely have sunk to my knees, and in the fullness of my young heart would have dissolved in devotion, tears, and adoration. Despite everything, you see, one can still perceive the earthly element in our great Dürer. One can understand how an artful and skilful man might light upon these faces or arrive at these inventions, and if we look very closely at his pictures, we can almost dismiss their painted figures and uncover the empty, unadorned panel beneath. With Raphael, on the other hand, my dear Sebastian, everything is contrived so wonderfully that you quite forget that there is any such thing as paint or painting, and inwardly you can feel only humility and the warmest love for his heavenly and yet so profoundly human figures and devote your heart and soul to them. Do not imagine that I am exaggerating out of youthful ardour, for you cannot imagine or grasp these things unless you come and see them with your own eyes. (*WA*, 83–4; *OF*, 81–2)

Critics have often speculated how the third part of the novel would have been executed. Tieck himself gave important indications of his intentions in the postscript to his last edition of *Franz Sternbald* of 1843, in a fragment on the continuation,[29] and in the 'Letter from a Young German Painter in Rome to his Friend in Nuremberg'. According to these drafts, Franz Sternbald, who had converted to Catholicism, was about to marry Marie. Franz was to become more and more consicous of his happiness. Especially his childhood with all its scenes and personalities was to return in his thoughts. In the mountains near Florence he would even become reunited with his father. The story was supposed to end in Nuremberg at Dürer's grave and in Sebastian's company. Tieck pursued this plan for a long time and, as he said, tried again and again 'to raise his pen and continue and conclude the book'. Yet, he added that he did not find himself in the mood necessary for a continuation and that the narrative thus remained unfinished.[30] When he made the novel a part of his *Collected Writings*, he merely changed the structure of the finished parts to some extent and rounded off some scenes and episodes by making occasional additions.

Critics have naturally considered this hesitancy as more than a mere inability to regain a past poetic mood, and have maintained that the discrepancy between the two parts became too wide to be bridged in a concluding third section. It remains uncertain whether Tieck would have been able to synthesize Nuremberg and Rome, Protestantism and Catholicism, the Ego and the world, ideality and reality, time and eternity. Yet, the novel is definitely intended to comprise these grand unifications. Towards the end of the second part, when Franz Sternbald meets Marie, we are led to the threshold of these events. Both Franz and Marie are overwhelmed by the significance of this moment in which the goal of the entire action becomes visible and the ideal enters reality. 'Oh, that I see you again', Marie exclaims stammeringly. 'Your image has followed me every-where.' – 'I will never comprehend it', she says a little later: 'You are like a friend known from long ago, you are not strange to me.' Franz answers: 'From this moment on my life begins, oh, it is wondrous and still true. Why should we comprehend it?' The fragment of the continuation of the novel depicts this moment in an exclamation by Marie: 'Oh happy presence! Now past and future have disappeared and eternity has penetrated into time.' Yet all these formulations indicate sufficiently that *Franz Sternbald's Wanderings* had found its natural conclusion toward the end of the second part and that it is not Tieck's inability, but the inner structure of the novel itself that explains why the third part was never written.

CHAPTER 6

Theory of language, hermeneutics, and encyclopaedistics

Originally, the Jena group was not at all aware of the new approaches to art pursued by Wackenroder and Tieck, especially to painting and music. Through A. W. Schlegel's reviews in the *ALZ* and Friedrich Schlegel's move to Berlin in the summer of 1797, the Jena Romantics became the first intellectuals in Germany, however, to take cognizance of these new trends and connect them with their own endeavours. With Friedrich Schlegel's departure from Jena, the centre of gravity of early Romanticism occasionally shifted to Berlin. It was here that the *Athenaeum*, the journal that soon became the target of widespread polemics in Germany, was published, and that A. W. Schlegel delivered his grand lecture courses on Romantic critical theory.[1] Another publication closely linked with Berlin and also subject to violent attacks was Friedrich Schlegel's novel *Lucinde* of 1799. In the wake of these events, one can no longer speak of a Jena Romanticism in the same tone as during the time prior to Friedrich Schlegel's move, although as far as Romanticism is concerned, the great days for Jena were still to come. They occurred in the autumn of 1799, when Friedrich Schlegel moved back to Jena, followed by Dorothea, and when Ludwig and Amalie Tieck also settled there. For a short time, a union of the early Romantic school took place in A. W. Schlegel's and Caroline's house on the Löbdergraben. Novalis, living close by in Weißenfels, was a frequent participant in this circle, as was Schelling, a philosophy professor at the university.

Schleiermacher never came to Jena, but his impact on the theory of early Romanticism is noticeable through Friedrich Schlegel, with whom he entertained a close friendship until about 1802. Their common interest can be characterized as a philosophy or theory of morality in the broadest sense of the term, focusing on notions such as individuality, independence, friendship, and love. They conceived of morality as an enormously wide field encompassing the social position of women, the relationship of the sexes, even problems of economy, politics, society, and themes relating to manners, courtesy, and good behaviour.[2] Closely related to these topics were problems of understanding and interpretation which, in turn, raised the question of the range and capacity of human language as a means of communication.

Schleiermacher also gave the early Romantic notion of religion a new impulse when he published his first major work, *On Religion. Speeches to its Cultured Despisers*, in 1799 and presented religion as an independent, autonomous realm of human experience. Far beyond any dogmatic or orthodox conception, the young theologian and priest defined religion as a feeling for the infinite, and developed a notion of God that was hard to reconcile with that of the Christian tradition, depicting him as dwelling in nature and in human beings.[3] We have seen earlier in the writings of Novalis and Friedrich Schlegel how the new ideal realism of an interaction between nature and human beings assumed the character of mysticism and, indeed, of a new religion.[4] Schleiermacher's *On Religion* is a much more resolute expression of this tendency and considers religion in the light of these new experiences. Religion is for him a particular and irreducible state of mind, an immediate feeling for the infinite and the eternal. Here, religion is sharply distinguished from philosophy (metaphysics), morality, and art. Schleiermacher wants especially to separate religion from philosophy and morality, as when he says:

In order to take possession of its own domain, religion herewith renounces all claims to whatever belongs to those others and gives back everything that has been forced upon it. It does not wish to determine and explain the universe according to its nature, as does metaphysics; it does not desire to continue the universe's development and perfect it by the power of being, as morals do. Religion's essence is neither thinking nor acting, but intuition and feeling. It wishes to intuit the universe, wishes devoutly to overcome the universe's own manifestations and actions, longs to be grasped and filled by the universe's immediate influences in childlike passivity. Thus, religion is opposed to these two in everything that makes up its essence and in everything that characterizes its effects. (*FDES ÜR*, 28–9; *OR*, 101–2)

As these few remarks indicate, Schleiermacher's treatment of religion is based on the conviction that there are several independent tendencies of the human mind which form autonomous spheres of human culture, also described as 'elements of humanity'. These are philosophy, morality, art, and religion. Friedrich Schlegel shared this opinion, and his notebooks from the time of his contact with Schleiermacher reflect the individual attitudes and intellectual styles of these various expressions of humanity. 'The four elements of humanity are poetry, philosophy, morality, and religion', he wrote (*KFSA* 18, 309); and he said in the *Athenaeum*: 'Religion is the all-animating world-soul of culture, the fourth invisible element besides philosophy, morality, and poetry' (*KFSA* 2, 256; *LF*, 241). Yet these distinctions, forming the basis for a truly manifold encyclopaedia of human education and culture, also contained the seed for Friedrich Schlegel's eventual break with Schleiermacher. He obviously had the impression that, in his friend's cultural encyclopaedia, religion came to dominate the other spheres and sucked out their life blood, a critique already noticeable in his review of Schleiermacher's *On Religion* which he published in the *Athenaeum* shortly after that work's appearance. Schlegel emphasized the author's view 'that religion is originally and eternally an autonomous part of human culture', noting that Schleiermacher had '*constituted* religion as a co-citizen in the realm of human culture' and the 'focal point' for the rays of everything beautiful in the other spheres (*KFSA* 2, 276). Schleiermacher in fact occasionally seemed to treat 'the other innate peculiarities of the human being, that is, poetry, philosophy, and morality, rather badly and not with sufficient religiosity'. He offered 'not at all a harmony of the whole', but only something equal, perhaps, to morality (*KFSA* 2, 278).

With the publication of the *Athenaeum*, however, the more

powerful organ of the Romantic school in German intellectual and literary life, these ideas became a public issue, and provoked debate and counterdebate. In this context of greater public attention and reaction, the linguistic and communicative ability of human beings, the capacity to understand and interpret, as well as the notion of totality in the sense of an encyclopaedic unity, become prominent in the formation of early Romantic theory.

THEORY OF LANGUAGE

The early Romantic theory of language is still virtually unknown, since it has never been methodically investigated, or made the focus of concerted research. The copious material which the Romantics provided for comparative linguistics, the study of families of languages, language relationships, and the search for an underlying original language (*Ursprache*),[5] have all been recognized as specific contributions to a comparative science of language, as a genetic discipline.[6] This type of Romantic linguistics, which attempted to comprehend language in terms of its origins, has become almost a cliché, and has obscured the profounder reflections on language in the writings and fragments of the early Romantics, particularly with regard to the importance of language for poetry, the process of understanding in human communication, and the interaction of human beings with the world. Some of these observations have already been noted in the context of the previous chapters, and they indicate the prominence of language in early Romantic theory. In analogy to Kant's Copernican revolution in philosophy, we find here what one may call the 'linguistic revolution' in thought and poetry, the recognition of language as the most basic component for our functioning as human beings.

To introduce this radical insight into the importance of language for our self-recognition and contact with the world, we can begin with Fichte's essay 'On the Ability to Speak and the Origin of Language' of 1795. Friedrich Schlegel recommended this essay to his brother, who was working in Amsterdam on his

'Letters on Poetry, Metre, and Language' for Schiller's *Horae* in 1795, and he wrote to him: 'I wish you would read for your investigations into language, etc., a treatise on this by Fichte. You should not fear Schillerian scholasticism because when he has to, this thinker can leave Kant and Spinoza behind, and as soon as he wishes to speak, can also surpass Rousseau' (*KFSA* 23, 263).[7] However, when Fichte's essay appeared in Niethammer's *Philosophical Journal*, Schlegel reversed his opinion and wrote disappointedly to his brother:

Listen: where it is appropriate, I love and honour with body and soul, but not in a stupid manner. This origin of language is not by the immortal founding father Fichte, but by the 'revealer' who became famous by a ridiculous mistake.[8] This is a miserable thing. The first thought, however, is still good. Whoever does not know how language *ought* to originate, can stay at home. Everybody can dream about how it might originate. (*KFSA* 23, 281)

Fichte had, indeed, thought it his task in his essay to demonstrate how human language as we know it was invented and not to set up a hypothesis on how language might have originated under the influence of various occurrences. Such possibilities were so numerous that no research could possibly exhaust them (*FI* 3, 97). Fichte did not want to set up another genetic theory of the origin of language, but aimed at an a priori deduction of language 'from the most essential dispositions of human nature'. He wanted to show that language, as a use of 'arbitrary signs', is part of the basic endowment of human nature, of our anthropological equipment. Fichte thereby turned against numerous writings of that time which dealt with the 'origin' or the 'development' of language on the basis of a determinable historical knowledge. Towards the end of the eighteenth century in Europe, there were three main hypotheses: the theory of a progressive transition from animalistic cries to a human means of communication (Rousseau); the theory of an agreement on the use of signs in human society (Condillac); and the theory of a divine inspiration (Süßmilch) which offered an explanation for something that cannot be deduced from natural causes. There is an amazingly rich literature on all of these models in late eighteenth-century Europe, including the contest of the Prussian Academy of Sciences on the origin of language in 1770. As the genetic model gained prominence, Fichte set about transforming it into a transcendental mode of explanation. Friedrich Schlegel believed that Fichte had fallen prey to the transcendental philosopher's prejudice of taking pure thought as a zone prior to language and that he saw language merely as a translation, a transposition of thought into a sensuous, perceptible medium of communication. Indeed, Fichte often says that language is 'an expression of our thoughts through arbitrary signs' (*FI*, 97) and asks: 'How has the human being come to express his thoughts through arbitrary signs?' (*FI*, 98). But the idea that thought is already a manifestation of language did not occur to him, which is why Friedrich Schlegel dismissed his text as a 'miserable thing'.

The genetic explanation of language found a remarkable reformulation in Herder's essay 'On the Origin of Languages' of 1770. This essay was obviously the most important impulse for the early Romantic theory of language, especially in the case of A. W. Schlegel. In this text, Herder rejects the supranatural theory of an origin of language as a divine gift, an instantaneous communication from God, but also the natural explanation of language as a long process of development by habit and repetition from animal cries to human articulations. The first theory can be considered the dominant German model and was closely connected with the Prussian Academy, especially with Johann Peter Süßmilch, its most outstanding exponent at that time.[9] The second is the French model, and Condillac and Rousseau were its main spokesmen. Yet, Herder knew Rousseau's theory only on the basis of his reading of the *Essay on the Origin and the Reason of Inequality among Men*, which has but a brief section on language, rather than Rousseau's comprehensive 'Essay on the Origin of Languages', which was later edited from Rousseau's manuscripts.[10] He also disregards a number of other important theories of language, such as those of Leibniz and Vico, in order to concentrate on the opposition between a supranatural and a naturalistic derivation of language, its origin from either God or animal. Herder takes his own position midway between the two extremes and explains language as a human phenomenon, its origin as a human process.

The chief result of Herder's analysis was to equate language with humanity, to consider the human being and language as coexistent (*HE* 5, 27; *OL*, 108). One of his many arguments in the essay begins with the 'entire disposition of man's forces', the 'total economy of his sensuous and cognitive, of his cognitive and volitional nature' (*HE* 5, 28–9; *OL*, 109–10), that is, wit, perspicacity, fantasy, reason, and will. These are not isolated forces to be found in anthropological textbooks or metaphysical abstractions, but are separated from the rest merely 'because our feeble minds cannot consider them at once': 'They appear in chapters, not because they work in nature chapter by chapter, but because an apprentice finds it easiest to develop them for himself in that fashion' (ib.). Herder says:

If we have grouped certain activities of the soul under certain major designations, such as wit, perspicacity, fantasy, and reason, this does not mean that a single act of the mind is ever possible in which only wit or only reason is at work; it means no more than that we discern in that act a prevailing share of the abstraction which we call wit or reason, as for instance the comparison or the elucidation of ideas; yet in everything the total undivided soul is at work. (*HE* 5, 30; *OL*, 111)

Herder includes this whole economy of the human soul in the notion of 'reflection' (*Besonnenheit*: *HE* 5, 31; *OL*, 112), which does not occur in the human being only now and then, but always and already 'in the first state in which he is a human being'. The human being 'in the state of reflection which is peculiar to him' is already in possession of language, or 'did invent language'. Reflection and language are coexistent, and the 'invention of language is therefore as natural to the human being as it is to him that he is a human being' (*HE* 5, 37; *OL*, 115). Reflection is basically of a dialogical nature for Herder, although the dialogue in question is an inner one, just as his entire model of an origin of language is an image of solitude, of the human being existing solely with himself. Yet, with this model, there is no thought in the human mind that is not reflective, not dialogical, not language. Herder says: 'I cannot think the first human thought, I cannot align the first reflective argument without dialoguing in my soul or without striving to dialogue' (*HE* 5, 47; *OL*, 128).[11]

Another argument relates to the 'ear' as the 'first teacher of language' and shows that as 'a listening, a noting creature', the human being is 'naturally formed for language', that the 'entire, multisonant divine nature' is a 'teacher of language' for human beings (*HE* 5, 48–50; *OL*, 129–30). The first vocabulary was collected from the 'sounds of the world', 'sounding verbs' constituting the first elements and nouns the first to 'move towards abstraction' (*HE* 5, 49–53; *OL*, 132–3). From this point of view, poetry is older than prose because the first language was nothing but 'a collection of elements of poetry'. Herder refers to a tradition in classical antiquity which claimed that song was 'the first language of the human race'. Interpreting this in the sense of a 'sounding language', he believes that 'this song – eventually sublimated and refined – gave rise to the oldest poetry and music' (*HE* 5, 56–9; *OL*, 136–7). What is of special importance in this argument is that reflection, the same 'single focus' which for Herder forms the origin of language, is also the origin of poetry (ib.).

A further demonstration of the origin of language from the entire nature of the human being refers to the world of sensuous perception and questions how those words that relate to soundless things originated and how the human being is capable of 'changing into sound what is not sound' (*HE* 5, 60; *OL*, 138). The answer is that as human beings we are a *sensorium commune*, that among all sense perceptions there is an intimate, strong, and ineffable bond which leads to the most different 'interconnections of the most different senses', and that for 'sensuous beings who perceive through many diverse senses at once, such an assembly of ideas is inevitable' (*HE* 5, 61–2; *OL*, 139–40). The distinctions between sensations defined by Buffon, Condillac, and Bonnet are mere 'abstractions'. In reality, they all belong to 'one single tissue' (*HE* 5, 62; *OL*, 140) and are 'nothing but forms of feeling of one soul' (*HE* 5, 64; *OL*, 142). The older and more original languages are, the more they will show what Herder calls the 'analogy of the senses' (*HE* 5, 70;

OL, 148), which is simultaneously for him the reason for the metaphorical character of language, its 'spirit of metaphors' (*HE* 5, 71; *OL*, 149). Herder speaks of the invention at the beginning of the formation of language as of 'bold verbal metaphors' which survive for a long time and are even 'extended and increased in sheer imitation or for the love of things past' (*HE* 5, 73; *OL*, 171). Such 'bold verbal labours', such 'transpositions of feelings', were originally 'ruleless and lineless meshings of ideas'. Herder looks with amusement at these 'verbal trials' of a nascent language when they are taken as basic concepts for a dogma or system and enlarged to 'word idols', unknown to the original inventor (*HE* 5, 75; *OL*, 152).

As far as the concrete process of language formation is concerned, Herder envisions the following stages of development. The oldest language was an inexhaustible 'dictionary of nature' for poetry, and the first grammar an attempt to structure this original 'poetry' more regularly. The most recent form of language, however, is best suited for axioms and demonstrations (*HE* 5, 84; *OL*, 165). Whereas the first part of Herder's essay deals with the human capacity to invent language, the second attempts to show the way in which human beings must have invented language and aims at a philosophical demonstration of necessary laws. From here, Herder does not really move to a systematic consideration of language, but simply reapplies his genetic approach in various formulations. The origin of language is for him an inner urge, like the push of the foetus towards birth at the moment of maturity (*HE* 5, 96). All states of reflection are seen as states of language (*HE* 5, 99).

Fichte, however, pursued this systematic, transcendental aspect, but relates his story of the formation of language exclusively to a priori reason. Language has the function of expressing thoughts of reason and serves to communicate ideas. In his desire to subjugate 'raw and animalistic nature', to form nature according to his purpose, and to 'conquer hostile nature', one human being finds an ally in the other, who agrees with him, and with whom he wants to enter into 'interaction' (*FI* 3, 100–802). For this purpose, an exchange of thought, which enlarges the role of language, is necessary, but this language is entirely rational. The first language, the 'first signs of things', was simply an imitation of nature, perceived through seeing or hearing, expressed in the sand or through sounds. Progressively, language became established in sounds that became fixed through the invention of letters. From this point, the formative process of language moved further, always motivated by the impulse to communicate, to express abstract concepts such as that of the thing, of being in general, of anything at all, of the world, or of God (*FI* 3, 111). In contrast to Herder, Fichte emphasizes the communicative drive in the formation of language, and reduces the rich potentialities of language to a mere instrument of reason. Of his attempt to maintain a language-free zone for reason, he says: 'Language according to my conviction has been taken much too seriously, since people have believed that no use of reason could possibly take place without it' (*FI* 3, 103).

In the same year, i.e. 1795, A. W. Schlegel published his 'Letters on Poetry, Metre, and Language', a text which gives a good impression of the early Romantic theory of language in its first formulation. Here, A. W. Schlegel considers language the 'most miraculous creation of the human poetic power', the 'great, never accomplished poem in which human nature represents itself' (*AWS SW* 7, 104). He seems to assume a kind of original poetry of humanity, an original creativity of the human mind which underlies all specific, developed languages in which the basic ability to understand resides. Language is, therefore, not the product of reason alone, but of a deeper, more comprehensive power of which reason is merely a part and in which the imagination also participates. Informed by reason, the developed languages grow and gain in usefulness and precision, while losing their original power. The language of science conveys hardly any impression of this original language, and appears to be a collection of signs established through agreement. And yet, even in this language, the infinite language of humanity lies hidden, as is proven by the continuous recurrence of poetry in the most abstract stages of language, as well as our ability to understand poetry immediately. The poet rediscovers this language and knows how to convey it to others.

A. W. Schlegel says: 'The degree of clarity in which this is possible determines the poetic force of a language' (*AWS SW* 7, 105).

Brushing aside the question of the origin of language, Schlegel relegates it to the same order as asking about the original state of human beings (*AWS SW* 7, 111). When theoreticians make use of such models of thought, they do it to communicate circumstances without specifying them according to space and time. The gap between our oldest documents and these original states is so wide 'that one can bridge it only by a fatal leap'. Many have taken such a leap and met with failure. In these attempts, he says, people have used certain philosophical etymologies which are understood by neither the linguist nor the philosopher. Attempting to derive all languages from one single root, such theorists have pretended that this actually constitutes a philosophical theory of the origin of language. In discussing the origin of language, A. W. Schlegel distinguishes between three possible theories. 'Language has originated either only from sounds of feeling, or only from imitations of objects, or together from both' (*AWS SW* 7, 112). The first theory is Herder's, the second that of Condillac, and the third his own, whereby imagination and reason are both involved in the formation of language.

We observe daily that human beings have signs of communication for both feelings and thoughts, and that these consist in the 'lively delivery of speech' as well as in gestures, which are the language of feeling and equal in value to words. Schlegel refers to the countenance of a sad person and, in accordance with an old dictum, compares the entire human body to the strings of a lyre, which, when touched by the soul, express different sounds (*AWS SW* 7, 114). An 'intimate bond of common feeling' unites humanity for him, and this is of greater importance to our capacity for communicating than any rational relationships can provide: 'Otherwise we would be lonely in the midst of society, deserted in suffering by all compassion, and even in happiness damned to the dead enjoyments of egoism' (*AWS SW* 7, 114–15). This general communicability reaches so far that it includes every child, every 'savage', human beings from the most distant zones, and even, if we could call them back into life, from the farthest centuries. This is for Schlegel 'the true, eternal, generally valid language of the human race' and the 'primordial' basis of all particular languages (*AWS SW* 7, 116). For an interpretation of language, however, both of the opposed systems are useful, and they are wrong only 'when they maintain their basic law concerning the origin of language as the only one, to the exclusion of the other' (*AWS SW* 7, 118).

A. W. Schlegel developed his theory in Amsterdam and chose Frans Hemsterhuis as his guide.[12] Many philosophers before him had taken a similar middle course by recognizing two sources in the formation of language. Most of them, however, accorded too little importance to the sensual and imaginative realm by relegating it to an early stage of sensuality and passion which would be eliminated progressively through the refinement of the human mind. For Schlegel, however, this share of feeling, emotion, and imagination continues and accompanies all stages of linguistic development (*AWS SW* 7, 120).[13] He illustrates this cooperation of the two formative forces of the human mind through a brief discussion of the 'origin of poetry', about which we know historically, of course, 'just as little as about the origin of language'. If the oldest language really was the result of 'those two communally active dispositions of human nature', it was 'totally image and metaphor, totally the effect of the passions'. This is certainly what was meant when, according to an ancient tradition, the oldest language was described as poetry and music. This is not to be understood as a poetry and music formed according to technical requirements, but more in the sense of a primordial imagery and sound. It is precisely this realm to which we return at various stages of the formed languages when the sense of poetry awakens (*AWS SW* 7, 121–2).[14]

We could say that, by focusing on language as a medium of communication and understanding, A. W. Schlegel reflected on what language is capable of or entitles us to. His argument is less concerned with Friedrich Schlegel's and Novalis' emphasis on the limits of communication and understanding in view of the fact that we are bound to language. To give an example of this critical kind of reflection on language, we can refer to Novalis' remarkable 'Monologue', which outlines in a few genial strokes the mischievous character of language which prevents us from doing precisely what we are trying to accomplish with its help, that is, to achieve an orderly and complete presentation of an idea. People assume 'that their talk is about things', Novalis argues, but they overlook the fact that language is concerned only with itself 'and that discourse turns out to be nothing but wordplay'. If someone wants to speak about something specific, 'the capricious nature of language will cause him to say the most ridiculous and mistaken things', but if someone 'speaks just in order to speak' and without any purpose in mind, 'he pronounces the most magnificent and original truths'. Certain people hate language because of these intricacies, but they should be made aware 'that it is with language as with mathematical formulas – they constitute a world by themselves, they play only among themselves, express nothing but their own marvellous nature, and for that reason they are so expressive and mirror the singular interplay of things' (*NO* 2, 672; *AF*, 82).

Up to this point, the fragment reads as an exercise in linguistic scepticism, although the reader will certainly not overlook the strong ironic mood in this brief text. While outlining the limits of our linguistic capability, however, Novalis all of a sudden turns his argument into a discovery of the tremendous abilities of our language, for it is precisely this unintentional speaking that explains 'the nature and function of poetry as clearly as possible'. 'So it is with language', and:

whoever is sensitive to its touch, its tempo, its musical spirit, whoever hearkens to the gentle workings of its inner nature and moves his tongue and hand accordingly, will be a prophet; however, whoever knows it well enough but possesses neither ear nor understanding for it will write truths like these but be taken in by language and mocked by men, like Cassandra by the Trojans.

Novalis is ironical enough, however, to give yet another twist to his own speaking and writing by assuming that what he is producing here could itself, 'without my knowledge and conviction, be poetry and elucidate a mystery of language'. For a writer is, after all, 'but one who is inspired by language' (ib.).

THEORY OF UNDERSTANDING AND INTERPRETATION

Friedrich Schlegel entertained thoughts about language very similar to those of Novalis. We should be careful, however, not to confuse their ideas, which can be characterized as reflections upon the limits or barriers of language, with pejorative descriptions of language as a prison. Their attitude is rather a joyful acceptance of the limited character of our language as appropriate to the human condition, but it also reflects the true character of the human being as residing in a constant attempt to transcend these limits through poetry, play, and irony. Friedrich Schlegel and Novalis did not mourn the loss of full communication in an irretrievable past, or project it into a utopian future, but would have instead considered a fully accomplished system of knowledge and understanding as the real prison of the human race: 'Verily, you would take fright if, as you demand, the whole world were ever to become totally and really comprehensible' (*KFSA* 2, 370; *LF*, 268).

One essential means for attaining a full comprehension of the world and perfecting our understanding, Friedrich Schlegel argues sarcastically, would be a 'real language' which permitted us to 'stop rummaging about for words and pay attention to the power and source of all activity' (*KFSA* 2, 364; *LF*, 260). Such a language would appear as the appropriate endowment of an age that proudly congratulates itself on being the 'critical age', and that raises the expectation 'that soon everything is going to be criticized, except the age itself, and everything is going to become more and more critical', and that 'artists can already begin to cherish the just hope that humanity will at last rise up in a mass and learn to read' (*KFSA* 2, 364–5; *LF*, 261). Christoph Girtanner of Göttingen[15] had already put forward this idea of a 'real language', holding out the glorious prospect that 'in the nineteenth century man will be able to make gold'. With Girtanner's prediction and Schlegel's comments, we are at the close of the eighteenth century, when all sorts of expectations were held for the future. He had always admired 'the objectivity of gold', Schlegel assures us, and 'even worshipped it'. In every part of the world, 'where there is even a little enlightenment and education, silver and gold are comprehensible, and through them, everything else'. Once artists possess these materials in sufficient quantity, we can expect them to write their works 'in bas-relief, with gold letters on silver tablets'. 'Who would want to reject such a beautifully printed book with the vulgar remark that it is incomprehensible?' Schlegel asks. Yet, all of these expectations are now 'merely chimeras or ideals' because Girtanner is dead, and with great artistry we might extract 'only so much iron out of him as might be necessary to immortalize his memory by way of a little medallion'. Furthermore, the complaints about incomprehensibility have not yet subsided, but have recently shown a new vigour by directing themselves at the *Athenaeum* (*KFSA* 2, 365; *LF*, 262).

Philosophical reflection and meditation also lead, for Schlegel, to the theme of incomprehensibility. Certain subjects 'stimulate us to ever deeper thought', he argues, and we 'lose ourselves in these subjects' while contemplating them. These subjects become more and more integrated, until they eventually converge to comprise everything else, including 'the nature of things' or 'the destiny of man'. Other subjects, however, lead to the 'opposite pathway' by 'multiplying themselves and becoming more complicated upon more minute reflection'. They also do not lend themselves to consideration in isolation and 'holy seclusion', but require us to communicate with other people. Wondering 'what could be more fascinating than the question of whether such communication is actually possible', Schlegel speculates that one could not find 'a better opportunity for carrying out a variety of experiments to test this possibility or impossibility than by writing a journal like the *Athenaeum* or taking part in it as a reader' (*KFSA* 2, 363; *LF*, 259). Usually, one would conclude 'that the basis of the incomprehensible is to be found in incomprehension', and he certainly detests 'incomprehension, not only the incomprehension of the uncomprehending but even more the incomprehension of the comprehending'. But above all, he is convinced 'that all comprehension is relative' and that 'words often understand themselves better than do those who use them'. From this point of view, we are not far from the assumption 'that the purest and most genuine incomprehension emanates precisely from science and the arts – which by their very nature aim at comprehension and at making themselves comprehensible' (*KFSA* 2, 364; *LF*, 260).

With these reflections, Friedrich Schlegel addresses the theme of incomprehensibility directly and wonders whether incomprehensibility really is 'something so unmitigatedly contemptible and evil'. One could rather argue that 'the salvation of families and nations rests upon it', and also that of 'states and systems', as well as the 'most artificial productions of man'. 'Even man's most precious possession, his own inner happiness, ultimately depends on some point of strength that must be left in the dark, but nonetheless supports the whole burden, although it would crumble the moment one subjected it to rational analysis' (*KFSA* 2, 370; *LF*, 268). In an inverse type of reflection, Schlegel maintains that all the 'greatest truths of every sort are completely trivial', and 'nothing is more important than to express them in ever new ways and wherever possible, ever more paradoxically, so that we will not forget that they still exist and that they can never be expressed in their entirety' (*KFSA* 2, 366; *LF*, 263).

The most direct approach from this point to the themes of understanding and interpretation in their literary and critical relevance is to ask how one can understand an author better than he understood himself. This is an old and humorous dictum of philological, editorial practice, relating to the emendation of texts, but it is also present in our daily communication with others when we automatically and tacitly correct another's slip of the tongue. During the early Romantic period, this dictum gained new prominence, as can easily be shown with reference to the three great philosophers of the time: Kant, Fichte, and Schelling. When, in the *Critique of Pure Reason*, Kant came to Plato's doctrine of ideas, he thought it necessary to modify Plato's argumentation slightly, justifying his procedure by saying 'that it is by no means unusual, upon comparing the thoughts which an author has expressed in regard to his subject, whether in ordinary conversation or in writing, to find that we understand him better than he has understood himself. As he has not sufficiently determined his concept, he has sometimes spoken, or even thought, in opposition to his own intention' (*KA* 3, 246; *CPR*, 310). Here, better understanding relates to the greatest philosopher of the West, Plato, and aims at establishing the author's real intention. Fichte pursued a similar goal when, in his lectures on the vocation of the scholar, he came across certain contradictions in Rousseau and assured his audience: 'We wish to discover this point and will resolve the contradiction. We will thus come to understand Rousseau better than he understood himself and will then find him to be in complete agreement with himself and with us' (*FI* 3, 61; *EPW*, 178).

When Fichte interpreted Kant's philosophy as entirely congruent with his own, however, and Kant protested at this interpretation, Fichte threatened to interpret Kant 'according to the spirit' of his philosophy if interpretation according to the letter did not get on well enough. Such an interpretation leaves the letter of the text as well as its authorial intention far behind and discovers new meanings from a historically or intellectually advanced position. The third model of better understanding relates to Schelling's philosophy of identity and is founded on the theory of unconscious creation. The link between author and work, intention and text, which was dissolved in Fichte's model, is reestablished here, though in an unconscious rather than a conscious manner. In this sense, Schelling says in his *System of Transcendental Idealism*: 'The basic character of a work of art is thus an *unconscious infinity*. The artist seems instinctively to have presented in his work, apart from what he has put into it with obvious intent, an infinity which no finite understanding can fully unfold' (*FWJS* 3, 619; *PI*, 209).

If one tried to classify the early Romantic theory of understanding, especially that of Friedrich Schlegel and Novalis, according to these three models, one would choose the Fichtean type of better understanding, although the broad scope of early Romantic theory and its artistic character differ from Fichte's philosophical focus and unartistic attitude. Friedrich Schlegel also loosened the bond between author and work, granting the text its own autonomy and saying in this regard: 'The question of what the author intends can be settled; not, however, the question of what the work is' (*KFSA* 18, 318). This did not result from a layer of meaning placed unconsciously in the work by its author, but from the artistic character of the work itself, which, as Schlegel put it, 'knows more than it says, and aspires to more than it knows' (*KFSA* 2, 140; *GM*, 69). Schleiermacher, however, associated his notion of understanding with Schelling's theory of unconscious creation. This is obvious in his own lectures on hermeneutics,[16] in Boeckh's almost literal repetition of the respective sections,[17] and in the writings by Dilthey, who declared the better understanding of an author as the necessary result of the doctrine of unconscious creation.[18] In this tradition, Schleiermacher's position was interpreted as the prototype of Romantic hermeneutics and the 'Romantic revolution' in hermeneutics. The more recent literature on this subject contends that the formation of a hermeneutic philosophy or theory took place according to a scheme of several successive phases, in which Romantic hermeneutics was assigned its firmly determined position. These phases consist in the sequence of Schleiermacher (Romantic hermeneutics), Dilthey (foundation of the human sciences), Heidegger (ontological turn), and Gadamer (universal hermeneutics).[19]

It is obvious that, in this tradition of hermeneutics, there is no room for Friedrich Schlegel, who is indeed placed as a footnote to Schleiermacher. This is particularly evident in Dilthey, who, of all the modern representatives and historiographers of hermeneutics, had the best knowledge of early Romanticism. In his analysis of the conditions for Schleiermacher's 'grand design of a universal hermeneutics', Dilthey also discusses Friedrich Schlegel and characterizes him as 'Schleiermacher's guide to philosophy as an art'. The writings by Schlegel to which Dilthey refers are his 'brilliant essays on Greek poetry, Goethe, and Boccacio'. Dilthey describes the guiding concepts of these essays as those 'of the inner form of the work, the genesis of the author and the work, and the structured totality of literature'. However, he devalues all these accomplishments as merely auxiliary to Schleiermacher's work and says that, 'behind such individual accomplishments of a recreating philological art was the project of a science of criticism, an *ars critica*, to be based on a theory of the productive literary power. How close this project was to Schleiermacher's project of hermeneutics and criticism!'[20] One could also say that Dilthey relates Friedrich Schlegel to an alleged ideal of hermeneutics and criticism that Schlegel certainly did not wish to pursue. Only recently and sporadically have critics looked at Schlegel's hermeneutic thought in its own right.[21]

How soon early Romantic theory of interpretation was forgotten and replaced by an organic model of understanding can best be exemplified by Schleiermacher himself. In his lecture to the Prussian Academy of August 1829 entitled 'On the Concept of Hermeneutics', Schleiermacher summarized the central idea that gave him his pioneering position in the history of hermeneutics. This is the transcendence of the usual scope of hermeneutics as represented by F. A. Wolf and Friedrich Ast, who confined it to the interpretation of literary, juridical, and theological works. Schleiermacher expanded this scope to include every written or spoken subject-matter and refused to limit hermeneutics to written texts, insisting that 'I quite often catch myself in hermeneutic operations right in the middle of private conversations'. An even more characteristic feature of Schleiermacher's hermeneutics comes to light in this lecture when he defines understanding as the 'divination of an author's individual manner of combination'.[22] Although such divination cannot be proven in a demonstrative fashion, it can still attain a particular type of certainty. At this point, Schleiermacher refers to a 'paradoxical dictum' pronounced by a 'first-rate mind' who had recently died. This dictum declares that to *state* something is far more valuable than to *prove* it. It is evident that this 'first-rate mind' can only be Schleiermacher's former friend Friedrich Schlegel, who had died in January of the same year. More specifically, Schleiermacher is referring to Fragment 82 of the *Athenaeum*, which says: 'If both were to be done equally well, it is indisputably far more difficult to state something than to prove it' (*KFSA* 2, 177; *LF*, 171). Yet, Schleiermacher is surely also alluding to his years of friendship with Schlegel and their common work on hermeneutics.

Another dictum characterizing their early work on hermeneutics relates to the better understanding of an author by his interpreter. This dictum refers to a common device in the field of philological practice, but the two friends also gave it an ironical twist in trying to bring it closer to their own notions concerning the infinity and impossibility of true understanding. With this attention in mind, Friedrich Schlegel had said in Fragment 401 of the *Athenaeum*: 'In order to understand someone who only partially understands himself, you first have to understand him completely and better than he himself does, but then only partially and precisely as much as he does himself' (*KFSA* 2, 241; *LF*, 227–8). In this version, the better understanding is evidently the first action, which succeeds immediately, while the second, the true understanding, is ironically described as partial understanding. These relationships are more obvious in an earlier, handwritten version of this fragment, which defines the hierarchy of understanding in three steps and puts better understanding at the beginning as the lowest form. The text reads:

In order to understand someone, you first have to be more intelligent than he is, but then also just as intelligent and then just as stupid. It is not sufficient to understand the real meaning of a confused work better than the author understood it himself. You must also comprehend the confusion, including its principles, and be able to characterize and even reconstruct it. (*KFSA* 18, 63)

The special point of this fragment is that better understanding is the first step, and the correction of the confusion the second, but the comprehension of the principles of confusion follows as the last and most complex act. We could also designate the comprehension of the principles of confusion of an author as an ironic formulation for the true understanding of someone's individuality, which is, of course, an infinite and never fully accomplishable task and thereby infinitely deferred. To ill-

ustrate the basic difference between Schlegel and Schleiermacher by means of a simple formula, we could ask what
occurs more easily and faster according to their theory,
understanding or better understanding. We immediately realize
that, for Friedrich Schlegel, better understanding comes first,
whereas for Schleiermacher, understanding is the first action,
and better understanding follows as the second and more
difficult task. In this academy lecture on hermeneutics and
criticism, Schleiermacher indeed describes the process in such a
way that we first 'understand the speech just as well and then
better than its author' by bringing much to consciousness 'that
can remain unconscious for the author'.[23] For Schlegel, the
relationship is precisely the reverse. For him, better understanding occurs by itself and is the spontaneous, immediate,
easier action, while true understanding is a more complicated
task which will never be fully accomplished. To understand
someone better than he understands himself is a daily occurrence. The subject of this understanding has to be distrustful.
In this manner Julius, the protagonist in Schlegel's novel
Lucinde, exclaims to his beloved: 'Many would understand me
better than I understand myself, but only one completely, and
that is you' (*KFSA* 5, 24; *LF*, 62). In this way, Schlegel
immediately understood Goethe's *Wilhelm Meister* better than
Goethe himself, who was most satisfied with that inasmuch as he
repeated in conversations with Caroline many of Schlegel's
formulations, 'and especially the ironical ones' (*KFSA* 24,
176–7).

For Friedrich Schlegel the aim of criticism was simply 'to
understand an author better than he understood himself', that
is, it was 'nothing but a comparison between the spirit and the
letter of a piece of writing' (*KFSA* 16, 168). The truth of the
great works, to be sure, will never be revealed by this approach.
Schlegel says: 'A classical text must never be entirely comprehensible. But those who are cultivated and who cultivate
themselves must always want to learn more from it' (*KFSA* 2,
149; *LF*, 144–5). In his unpublished fragments, he distinguishes
between 'a merely negative and a positive not understanding'
(*KFSA* 18, 129) for one 'has to have much understanding in

order not to understand certain things' (*KFSA* 18, 114). Considering the incomprehensible character of existence, Schlegel comments urbanely: 'It shows a high and perhaps the ultimate stage of education if one posits the sphere of incomprehensibility and confusion in oneself' (*KFSA* 18, 277). Here it becomes obvious that his theory of understanding relates to themes like Erasmus' *laus stultitiae*, Nicolaus Cusanus' *docta ignorantia*, and Socratic ignorance. We could also say that, according to Schlegel, we always get stuck at better understanding and therefore never arrive at true understanding. We constantly interpret according to our own measurements and never see the real relationships. We continuously arrange things according to our own points of view, to what we desire.

By associating himself with Schelling's theory of unconscious creation, Schleiermacher did not really represent the early Romantic theory of understanding and interpretation, but a position of idealistic philosophy. When he later took up Friedrich Schlegel's thoughts on understanding and better understanding, he no longer understood it and reversed the order of steps by determining the hermeneutic task as first 'to understand a speech just as well and then better than its author'. He also explained this better understanding by means of the theory of unconscious creation, observing that 'we attempt to bring to consciousness much of what can remain unconscious for the author'.[24] The further reception of this postulate eventually led to a gross distortion of Friedrich Schlegel's ironic meaning. August Boeckh continued Schleiermacher's reversal by maintaining that the interpreter had to make conscious what the author had produced unconsciously.[25] Wilhelm Dilthey finally considered the device of understanding an author better than he understood himself as the quintessence of modern hermeneutics and interpreted this step as the necessary result of the doctrine of unconscious creation.[26] Heinrich Nüsse, a contemporary critic, comments on this process: 'Instead of Friedrich Schlegel's subtle postulate, which has vanished in history, a mere formula was transmitted without being understood.'[27]

By declaring a full understanding impossible, Friedrich

Schlegel also provided new impulses to literary criticism as an interpretation of individual works. He did not conceive of interpretation as establishing a final meaning that would close the book and relegate it to the past, but as an involvement in the infinite task of deciphering that relates the text to the future of the world and keeps it alive. In this process, notions like meaning, wholeness, and the unity of literary works gain a new significance, as is obvious in his review of *Wilhelm Meister*, and impose themselves upon the critic with a new rigour. 'Thorough understanding' of the most subtle peculiarities in all their ramifications together with the genesis of the work and its author are the most important requirements (*KFSA* 3, 60). The goal is the enunciation of this understanding in distinct words, and this results in a judgment which deals with its object not in scientific, moral, or social terms, but in aesthetic ones (*KFSA* 1, 191). Such judgments require intense familiarity with the organization and treatment of their objects. They need that type of study, reading, and re-reading which is referred to in one of Schlegel's fragments as 'ruminating' or 'chewing the cud' (*KFSA* 2, 149). Otherwise, 'I shall be damned' would be the best judgment of the worthiest work of art. 'There are critiques', Schlegel adds, 'which say nothing more, but only take much longer to say it' (*KFSA* 2, 154; *LF*, 150). Yet, what matters most in these judgments is that they render a 'representation of the impression' that the work of art has made upon the critic. This should not be achieved in the style of mere impressionistic criticism. It should not result in a 'poem about the poem' demonstrating the critic's brilliance, nor should the critic merely convey the 'impression the work has made yesterday or makes today on this or that reader, but the impression it should make on any civilized person at any time' (*KFSA* 1, 499).[28]

THE EARLY ROMANTIC NOTION OF ENCYCLOPAEDIA

'Encyclopaedia', 'encyclopaedic', or 'encyclopaedistic' are frequent terms in early Romantic discourse. They obviously relate to a form of comprehension and totality that is not marked by systematic structure and by the metaphysical implications of that type of unity, but nevertheless maintain a certain coherence among all branches of human knowledge and experience. Similar ambitions were encountered in the early Romantic notion of the fragment and the idea of a 'system in fragments'.[29] An analogous attempt is at work in the conception of basic human 'elements' of education, of constituent cultural spheres in the process of an education of the human race (philosophy and poetry, morality and religion).[30] In the light of this ambivalent tendency to reject the metaphysical-ontological implications of any type of absolute systematization on the one hand, but without altogether denying notions of totality and coherence on the other, 'encyclopaedia' – in the sense of the totality of all human knowledge and experience – appears to be the most suitable concept for the early Romantic project as a whole, and it indeed occurs regularly at certain points within early Romantic thought. The importance of this notion is also recognized by some critics and historians.[31]

The most famous encyclopaedia available at the time of early Romanticism was undoubtedly the *Encyclopédie ou Dictionnaire raisonné des sciences, des arts et des métiers*, which Diderot and d'Alembert published from 1751 to 1772 in 35 volumes. All previous attempts at encyclopaedic knowledge in classical antiquity (ἐγκύκλιος παιδεία, *encyclios disciplina*), the Middle Ages (Vincent de Beauvais, *Speculum historiale, naturale, doctrinale, et morale*, 1260), the Renaissance (*disciplina orbicularis quam Encyclopaediam Graeci vocant*), or the modern age (Francis Bacon, *De dignitate et augmentis scientiarum*, 1623, and Leibniz, *Characteristica universalis*), and in the encyclopaedias of the early eighteenth century (Chambers) were outdone by this work, which combined a systematic thrust with the most ramified knowledge of details. The systematic character of this encyclopaedia is often overlooked because of its mechanical arrangement of facts in alphabetical order. It is sustained, however, through the 'enchainment of knowledge', through references in the articles to Bacon's division of the human mind into memory, imagination, and reason (*E* I, LXXIX–LXXXVIII), and through d'Alembert's introductory essay which establishes the genealogy and filiation of all our knowledge (*E* I, V–LXXIV).

At first glance, we notice numerous features which link Diderot's and d'Alembert's encyclopaedia with the early Romantic project.[32] We encounter the idea of a mutual interpenetration of all sciences and arts and an awareness of the most refined ramifications of human knowledge and ability. The future-oriented aspirations of the encyclopaedists and their idea of the infinite perfectibility of the human race are a common bond with the early Romantics. Above all, the idea of a non-institutionalized association of 'gens de lettres' seems to correspond to what was perceived by contemporaries as a 'Romantic school' or the 'new school'. People of diverse backgrounds and orientations came together to accomplish communal works (*KFSA* 2, 185; *LF*, 177–8). Yet, the early Romantics did not associate themselves with this most prominent encyclopaedic project of the age.[33] If asked why they resisted this apparently most advanced expression of encyclopaedic knowledge, we must presumably conclude that the encyclopaedists' sensualistic, empiricist conception of the human mind was the main obstacle, and this was reinforced by a progressively negative reaction to the French Revolution, for which the *Encyclopédie* was usually considered to have been one of the main preparatory forces. In a fragment of 1799, Friedrich Schlegel said: 'The encyclopaedia of the French is totally a wrong tendency – whereas this project is native to Germany' (*KFSA* 18, 348). This seems to imply that the encyclopaedia could better be realized on the basis of transcendental idealistic thought than on the basis of empiricism and sensualism. In his Berlin lectures on the *Encyclopaedia* of 1803, A. W. Schlegel designated the *Encyclopédie* as an 'aggregation' of materials totally dominated by 'empiricism' and confronted it with Bacon, who 'had undertaken a most laudable encyclopaedic attempt'. He overlooked, however, that the French encyclopaedia was built on Bacon's 'System of Human Knowledge' (*E* I, LXXIX).

Indeed, the impetus for encyclopaedic thinking in Germany did not come from France, but from transcendental philosophy, especially that of Kant.[34] Kant saw the task of an encyclopaedia as 'designating a science's position in the horizon of all knowledge' (*KA* 9, 42–3), without, however, carrying out this task or ever visualizing it beyond the horizon of philosophy and the sciences. When he says in the *Critique of Judgment* that each science 'has to have its place in the encyclopaedia of all sciences', Kant visualizes a universal encyclopaedia, which does not, however, comprise all the arts, as in the French or early Romantic concept of an encyclopaedia. Another important stimulus for encyclopaedic thinking came from classical philology, especially from F. A. Wolf. At Halle University, Wolf had delivered lectures on the *Encyclopaedia of the Classical Disciplines*.[35] Although these lectures were published only much later, Friedrich Schlegel was familiar with Wolf's encyclopaedic conception (*KFSA* 16, 33–81). Wolf emphasized the humanistic angle of an encyclopaedia by stressing the importance of classical studies for the formation of the human mind. But his notion of an encyclopaedia could not be reduced to the assumption that a particular discipline, classical studies, could represent or be a substitute for the entire cosmos of human knowledge. When Wolf delivered lectures or published texts on the encyclopaedia of classical studies, he intended to present everything worth knowing in his particular field. It is in this sense of a disciplinary comprehensiveness that the term 'encyclopaedia' was used in Germany as applied to encyclopaedias of juridical studies, of religious studies, and so forth. The universal notion of an encyclopaedia thus tended to form a paradoxical link with specific disciplinary attitudes.

There is one discipline, however, that claims to be fundamental and contain the principles of all other disciplines within itself. This is philosophy, which is nowhere more succinctly defined than in Hegel's statement: 'What is true in any one science is so through and by virtue of philosophy, whose encyclopaedia thus comprises all true sciences' (*HEG*, see *EPO*, 53). The other, ordinary encyclopaedia is distinguished from this philosophical one in that it is only an assemblage, an aggregation of knowledge that has arisen empirically in a more or less accidental fashion. Here, one also finds disciplines that 'bear the names of sciences but are otherwise only collections of bits of information' (*HEG*, see *EPO*, 53). As well as disciplines

of a merely 'aggregational' character, such as classical philology, Hegel's encyclopaedia excludes those which have 'arbitrariness' as their basis, as, for instance, heraldry. Other
disciplines, such as jurisprudence, are considered only in so far
as their 'rational basis and origin' links them with philosophy.
As far as their 'empirical distinctiveness and reality' are
concerned, they are irrelevant to the encyclopaedic project. The
same applies to sciences such as natural history, geography, and
medicine, which spread out into specialities governed by
'external chance and play, not by reason'. Hegel even counts
history among these disciplines, since it resides in 'contingencies
and in the field of arbitrariness'. Those expressions of philosophy which are founded on 'anthropology, facts of consciousness, inner intuition, or external experience' do not belong
to the sphere of a philosophized encyclopaedia either (*HEG* 8,
61–2).

It is against this manifold background that the early
Romantic project of an encyclopaedia of all of the arts and
sciences has to be viewed. There is one particular aspect worth
mentioning, if only as a way of contrasting the early Romantic
concept of an encyclopaedia with its extreme opposite. In 1812,
long after the early Romantic school of Jena had dispersed,
Hegel was asked by the Bavarian Ministry of Education to
present a statement on how to teach philosophy as a pro-
paedeutic discipline, and he wrote:

> The encyclopaedia, as it is meant to be philosophical, precludes the
> literary encyclopaedia, which is in any case insubstantial and worthless
> for youth. The encyclopaedia can contain nothing but the general
> content of philosophy, that is, the basic concepts and principles of its
> particular branches, of which I count three main ones:
>   1. logic; 2. philosophy of nature; 3. philosophy of spirit.
> All other sciences, considered as non-philosophical, belong origin-
> ally to these and should be considered in the encyclopaedia because
> it is philosophical only in relation to these origins.[36]

As is obvious from these remarks, Hegel's encyclopaedia was
closely related to general education, and Hegel believed that
philosophy, not literature, provided the best model for this
purpose. The one who most strongly promoted the literary type

of general education and maintained that the principles of knowledge could best be gained through the encyclopaedia of literature was Friedrich Schlegel, who here again constituted the direct opposite to Hegel.

Within the contours of early Romantic thought, Novalis, A. W. Schlegel, and Friedrich Schlegel created characteristic conceptions of what constitutes an encyclopaedia. Novalis' sketches, stemming mostly from 1798–9, are included in that section of his manuscripts entitled *The General Brouillon* (*NO* 3, 242–478) and are explicitly designated 'Materials for Encyclopaedistics'. His main idea is that there is a general analogy between the different individual sciences, which constantly create new affinities and coordinates. No branch of knowledge – 'physics, mineralogy, astronomy, physiology, sociology, history, linguistics, music, poetics, but also the doctrines of mining, financing, cooking, and furnishing' (*NO* 3, 238) – is foreign to the others, but all are related through intimate relationships. This part of Novalis' work is still uninvestigated. Tieck said in the preface to the first edition of Novalis' writings (Berlin, 1802) that Novalis had 'outlined the plan for an encyclopaedic œuvre in which experiences and ideas from the most different sciences were mutually to explain, support, and confirm each other'. Novalis did not plan this work in the form of fragments, and what we have in his manuscripts from that period is merely a preliminary collection of materials (*NO* 3, 238).

A. W. Schlegel left behind the most complete Romantic encyclopaedia. In May 1803, he began a course of lectures in Berlin on the *Encyclopaedia of Sciences*, of which we have almost a thousand pages in manuscript. A. W. Schlegel's project has likewise never been investigated in its entirety and was published only recently (*AWS VO* 3).[37] The lectures present the theme of the encyclopaedia in its entirety by including all the sciences and arts. Their special character, however, is that human language and communication are taken as the most universal bond among all of these various disciplines.

Friedrich Schlegel's notion of the encyclopaedia is closely related to Wolf's project of an encyclopaedia of classical disciplines, but opens it up to literature in its entirety, classical and modern, antique and Romantic. Schlegel does not use the term 'world literature', although this concept, with its strongly comparative focus, certainly lies behind his project. This notion of the encyclopaedia is also intimately related to Schlegel's project of hermeneutics and to that understanding of Western literary works in their entirety to which both Schlegels devoted most of their lives. In his book *On the Language and Wisdom of the Hindus* of 1808, Friedrich Schlegel said:

Just as in the history of mankind the Asians and Europeans form one great family, and Asia and Europe one inseparable unity, so one should strive to regard the literature of all educated peoples as a continuous progression and a single intimately connected structure, as one great totality; then many one-sided and prejudiced views would disappear by themselves, much would be clarified when placed in this context, and everything would appear new in this light. (*KFSA* 8, 315)

The most concrete expression of Friedrich Schlegel's project of an encyclopaedia can be found at the beginning of his Paris lectures of 1803–4 on ancient and modern literature. He begins these lectures with the humanist thought that literature and an acquaintance with 'the most prominent works of poetry, philosophy, and history' necessarily belong to a higher education that aims at a 'development of the higher faculties of reason, imagination, and will'.[38] Schlegel refers not only to classical literature, but also emphasizes the importance of literary creations among the modern nations of Europe and sees European literature 'as a coherent whole in which all branches are most intimately interwoven, one founds itself upon the other and finds explanation and complementation in this context'. The importance of the study of literature is obvious, and is highlighted by numerous arguments relating to ancient and modern literature. The essence of Schlegel's argumentation is that the study of literature enables us to develop the 'powers and abilities of the human being to a whole'.

By singling out one fundamental and broad discipline – i.e. literature – as essential to the entire process of education, Schlegel comes close to Hegel, who established philosophy, especially the study of its principles, as the core of an

encyclopaedic education. This notion of a literary encyclopaedia was mentioned earlier as a characteristic concept of the
Romantic area. It occurred in Goethe's novel *Wilhelm Meister's
Apprenticeship*, where it is argued that Shakespeare, in whom
nature and art are one, seems to have a special connection to the
creative world spirit. Consequently, the modern human being
can find no better path to an encyclopaedic education than
through this poet, who, having special access to the structure of
the world, functions as its interpreter. Yet, Friedrich Schlegel's
early Romantic notion of an encyclopaedia could not possibly
find realization in one particular field of the arts and sciences,
not even in a branch of human experience as comprehensive
and universal as literature. Any concentration on one particular
field calls forth an opposite tendency of the mind. Thus, to
consider literature the best medium for an encyclopaedia calls
forth the opposite intellectual tendency, which looked to the
counterbalancing option of philosophy. Here again, we are at
the nexus, the interaction, and mutual interdependence of
philosophy and poetry, creation and reflection, which is perhaps
the most enduring legacy of early Romanticism in Germany.

EXAMPLE: FRIEDRICH SCHLEGEL'S *LUCINDE*

Friedrich Schlegel's novel *Lucinde* of 1799 can be seen as an
attempt to create allegorical art in the form of a novel, and its
best description among the many varieties of early Romantic
narrative would indeed be that of an allegorical novel. *Lucinde* is
itself distinct from a novel like *Franz Sternbald* in that the
fantastic principle of unity has been replaced by allegory, and
that reason, reflection, and theory play a much larger part in its
construction. The transition from action to song and poetry is
lacking, and instead of lyrical digressions, we have reflections,
fantasies, and allegories. Julius, the protagonist, says to his
beloved Lucinde: 'I want at least to suggest to you in divine
symbols what I can't tell you in words' (*KFSA* 5, 58; *LF*, 104).
Yet, *Lucinde* is not merely an attempt to provide allegorical
representations of otherwise ineffable states of mind and feeling;
in its union of theory and practice, it also contains within it the

theory of the allegorical novel. One can refer here to Friedrich Schlegel's 'Letter on the Novel' where he says of his proposed narrative theory: 'Such a theory of the novel would have to be itself a novel, which would reflect imaginatively every eternal tone of the imagination' (*KFSA* 2, 337; *DP*, 102–3). Yet, for an understanding of the allegorical novel, it would not suffice to concentrate on the many instances in *Lucinde* where the author reflects on this subject, since Schlegel applied the notion of theory in its original Greek meaning of intellectual intuition, *theoria*. Only in its totality can *Lucinde* provide an impression, an intellectual intuition of the theory it represents.

Perhaps no more than two or three contemporary readers (certainly Fichte and Schleiermacher) and only a few interpreters in our century have approached the novel in such a complex manner. Most other commentators have either ridiculed or rejected the novel with moral indignation. These numerous opinions about *Lucinde* can be reduced to two phrases pronounced by Wilhelm Dilthey: 'shameless sensuality' and 'aesthetically considered, a little monster'.[39] Rudolf Haym varied these judgments slightly by calling the novel an 'aesthetic outrage' and 'at the same time a moral outrage'.[40] In more recent times, a new dimension has been added to these arguments against *Lucinde* with the claim that the 'revolutionizing of love' professed in the novel could not replace the revolutionizing of work, and that the 'elitist disdain of reality' represented by this 'Romantic anticapitalism' failed to provide guidelines for 'meaningful action'.[41]

Such judgments mostly reveal, as Wolfgang Paulsen has noted, that their authors have not succeeded 'in approaching the truly artistic' aspect of this novel, or that they have forgotten 'the artistic in favour of some type of content'.[42] Most frequently, the novel has been seen as representing persons of the Romantic circle under fictitious names or the love affair between the young Friedrich Schlegel and the divorced Dorothea Veit. One could also gain the impression, as Dilthey put it, that the author had little talent for 'broad, comfortable narration'. To understand the novel, however, we should begin with the artistic character of the work, which immediately reveals that *Lucinde* is not an offspring of *Wilhelm Meister*, in the tradition of the German educational novel (*Bildungsroman*), and that its artistic structure derives from a clearly developed conception of novelistic composition.

In terms of form, H. A. Korff thought it inconceivable that 'Friedrich Schlegel, or another or even a greater poet, could have expressed what he had in mind other than in the form of reflections',[43] and Wolfgang Paulsen had the impression that the novel was extremely well composed.[44] Building on these observations, Hans Eichner and Karl Konrad Polheim have developed a new understanding of the artistic character of this often misrepresented work of literature. To emphasize the rigorous will to form which is manifest in this novel, one should consider that Schlegel's goal was to create a 'shaped, artistic chaos' and that the whole was meant to be 'chaotic and yet systematic'. How these paradoxical formulations are to be understood is best illustrated by the novel itself, for one has only to open the first pages to see how it is executed. Julius begins a letter to Lucinde that is meant to communicate to her his present state of happiness and how this bliss has occurred, but he then interrupts the logical thread of his narration for the sake of destroying 'at the very outset all of that part we call "order", so as to remove it, and explicitly claim and actually affirm the right to charming confusion' (*KFSA* 5, 9; *LF*, 45). Why does he do this? The answer is that the material which life and love offer to the writer is 'so incessantly progressive and so unbendingly systematic' that it would make the written text 'insufferably unified and monotonous' and prevent the author from creating what he intends: 'the re-creation and integration of the most beautiful chaos of sublime harmonies and fascinating pleasures' (ib.). Julius therefore claims an 'undeniable right to confusion', making use of it by taking one page here and another there from the many dispersed pages he has written and putting them into this or that part of the novel. That he is guided by a very intentional idea of composition, however, becomes obvious when we consider the novel in its entirety.

Disregarding its title and prologue, *Lucinde* consists of thirteen parts with a strictly symmetrical structural form. The centre-piece, 'Apprenticeship for Manhood', is surrounded on each side by six sections that balance one another with regard to their length and formal structure, but also show correspondences in content. The sections are entitled:

Julius to Lucinde
A Dithyrambic Fantasy on the Loveliest Situation in the World
A Character Sketch of Little Wilhelmine
Allegory of Impudence
An Idyll of Idleness
Fidelity and Playfulness
APPRENTICESHIP FOR MANHOOD
Metamorphoses
Two Letters
A Reflection
Julius to Antonio
Yearning and Peace
Dalliance of the Imagination

In his 'Letter on the Novel', Schlegel had referred to 'arabesques and confessions' as the basic products of the Romantic mind (*KFSA* 2, 337; *DP*, 103). We can say that the six pieces at the beginning and end of *Lucinde* are arabesque in character and reflective in nature, while the narrative centre-piece represents a progressive story, the development of the protagonist from uncertain, yearning youthfulness to personal maturity and artistic knowledge. The clear difference between the arabesque sections of the frame and the confessional centre-piece is also obvious in the narrative voice, which is represented in the frame sections by Julius or Julius in dialogue with Lucinde, while in the 'Apprenticeship of Manhood' an anonymous voice objectively reports the story of Julius. From a chronological point of view, the first six frame sections describe the state of feeling realized by Julius through his union with Lucinde, the happy present occasionally accentuated by glances back into the melancholy past. The narrative middle section represents the yearning past of the protagonist up to his union with his beloved, and it shows how Julius attains harmony in his life through the influence of love. The concluding six frame sections relate to the future and deal with Julius' entrance into the social world. The first six parts, corresponding to the emotional and mental state of the protagonist at the end of the 'Apprenticeship of Manhood', treat the happiness of love in a most varied manner and link it with themes such as naturalness, leisure, proper conduct, and fidelity. The concluding six parts turn to new metamorphoses of the loving mind, but also to such complicated topics as property, division of classes, sickness, decadence, death, and decay. References to centre-piece and frame sections should not give the impression, however, that the emphasis lies in the centre. As Karl Konrad Polheim has correctly observed, confessions were for Friedrich Schlegel 'on a much lower level than arabesques'.[45]

According to Hans Eichner, Schlegel solved the problem of how to end this 'novel', which has hardly any action at all, in a most skilful manner by concluding with the 'Dalliance of the Imagination'. In this last section, the novel resorts to increasingly 'fragile and transparent prose and eventually dissolves into nothingness'.[46] The only aggravating blemish in the novel is the inclusion of 'First Part' in the title, for Schlegel made desperate efforts to continue his work. The fragments of the continuation that have survived, including some sixty poems composed for that purpose, actually prove what a careful reading reveals, namely that there is nothing to be added to the novel and that its poetic as well as thematic potentiality is exhausted with the text as we now have it. One might, however, have continued the novel by completely reversing the perspectives and having the same events and moods narrated by Lucinde, a female voice, whereby Julius and Lucinde would reflect each other like focal points in an ellipse.

The themes of *Lucinde* occur on different levels or, in Friedrich Schlegel's language, in different 'potencies'. The first and most obvious is love, for it is a love story. In this respect, the jubilant exclamation of Julius which, according to Hans Eichner, forms the core of the entire novel moves into the centre and begins with the words: 'Yet, I would have thought it a fairy-tale that there could be such happiness and such love as I feel now – and such a woman, at once the most delicate lover, the most wonderful companion, and the most perfect friend' (*KFSA* 5, 10; *LF*, 471). To comprehend this state of happiness fully, one should compare it to the consuming longing, taciturnity, and hopeless loneliness which characterize Julius at the beginning of his apprenticeship, or to Friedrich Schlegel in his early letters to his brother. In the arms of Lucinde, this lonely and desperate man gains new confidence, and all his 'suppressed faith and sympathy broke out in streams of words that were interrupted only by embraces' (*KFSA* 5, 54; *LF*, 99). What surprised Julius most in his relationship with Lucinde was her difference from what 'habit or stubbornness calls feminine', that is, her capacity for a total relationship in love. In sharp contrast to the Christian-Platonic, Cartesian, or modern bourgeois dualism of body and soul, this total relationship manifests itself by engaging all parts of the personality 'from the most passionate sensuality to the most spiritual spirituality' (*KFSA* 5, 11; *LF*, 47). As portrayed in the novel itself, this type of love unites everything: 'friendship, pleasant society, sensuality, and passion, too; and all these must be present in love, and the one must soften and strengthen the other, animate and ennoble it' (*KFSA* 5, 35; *LF*, 76). To render this union of mind and body in language, Schlegel uses numerous oxymora such as 'spiritual voluptuousness' and 'sensuous beatitude'.

This total relationship also manifests itself in the attempt to relate to the entire personality of the beloved, without overlooking any part of him or her. Julius says to Lucinde that she takes everything of him 'so solemnly and so negligently', but also so completely that she does not 'relinquish any part of me to the state, to posterity, or to my friends' (*KFSA* 5, 11; *LF*, 47). This love is not only, as Diotima had revealed to Socrates, 'the quiet longing for eternity: it is also the holy enjoyment of a lovely presence'. It is not merely a mixture, 'a transition from mortal to immortal; rather it is the total union of both' (*KFSA* 5, 60; *LF*, 106).

What becomes constituted and integrated through these manifold relationships is marriage, but marriage in the state of nature, without any sanctioning by the state or by the Church, and for that very reason the most intimate union of the two persons. In the last of the first six frame sections, the two lovers appear before us for the first time and, while caressing each other, conduct a dialogue leading up to their sexual union. Schlegel modelled this part on a Greek bucolic poet, Bion, who composed an amorous dialogue in hexameters that, verse by verse, proceeded to the physical union of the two lovers. While in this classical model, however, a young virgin is seduced by a shepherd and the dialogue is mostly conducted by the male partner (*KFSA* 1, 388–9), the dialogue in the section 'Fidelity and Playfulness' is between two mature partners in a witty, playful discussion of fidelity and jealousy. The play of words and thoughts kindles an eroticism which renders thoughts sensuous and sensuality spiritual.

In terms of gender criticism, it is obvious that the novel is written entirely from the male perspective and that the only conceivable second part of *Lucinde* would be an exchange of the male for the female voice. Yet it is equally obvious, and this leads to the last 'potency' of the work, that this revolutionary view of love rests on the absolute equality of the loving partners and thereby produces a new view of woman. This 'emancipatory' tendency has often been noticed, but never fully discussed. Such reluctance to acknowledge Schlegel's radicalism may simply be a result of the flowery language in which it is clothed. The equal status of the loving partners does not mean that man and woman, Julius and Lucinde, were identical for Schlegel, but that their relationship is rather elliptic, like that of an 'I' and a 'Thou'. 'Only in the answer of its "you" can every "I" wholly feel its boundless unity', Julius writes to Lucinde (*KFSA* 5, 61; *LF*, 106); or we read of their union: 'They were completely devoted and joined to each other, and yet each was wholly himself, more than he had ever been before' (*KFSA* 5, 55; *LF*, 99). For this type of relationship, the Fichtean terms of 'reciprocal effect' and 'mutual determination' appear entirely appropriate. This does not mean that it is man's or woman's fate to be always and eternally on this or that side of the ellipse. Emancipation should have a reciprocal effect, and we know from the 'Dithyrambic Fantasy on the Loveliest Situation in the

World' that man and woman should 'exchange roles and in childish high spirits compete to see who can mimic the other more convincingly' (*KFSA* 5, 12; *LF*, 49). As we know from Schlegel's theoretical writings, he found 'overloaded femininity' and 'exaggerated masculinity' equally ugly and repelling, and desired 'autonomous femininity' and 'gentle masculinity' (*KFSA* 1, 93), or, as he said in *Lucinde*, 'the development of man and woman to full and complete humanity' (*KFSA* 5, 13; *LF*, 49).

'When one loves as we do, then human nature returns to its original state of divinity' (*KFSA*, 67; *LF*, 113), Julius assures Lucinde. This is perhaps the most important aspect of the novel, namely the beneficial results which naturally emanate from the revolutionizing of love, the equal position of woman, and the natural relationship of the sexes. We find ourselves in the Romantic utopia of a new earth and a new humanity of which Julius dreamt when he said: 'The happy dreams come true, and the pure outlines of a new world arise from Lethe's waves, beautiful as Anadyomene, and unfold their shapes in place of the vanished darkness' (*KFSA* 5, 60; *LF*, 106). This new state is manifest in a regained innocence, in the freedom from prejudices and false modesty represented by little Wilhelmine. Or it shows itself in the 'divine art of laziness', the *dolce far niente* of a 'pure vegetating' (*KFSA* 5, 27; *LF*, 66). This is an attitude towards life which stems from a good conscience, but has its counterpart in a highly reflective mentality that prompts Julius to say: 'I did not simply enjoy but felt and enjoyed the enjoyment itself' (*KFSA* 5, 8; *LF*, 44). Schlegel sharply contrasted leisure and idleness to the figure of Prometheus, 'tied down by a long chain and working with great haste and strain' (*KFSA* 5, 26; *LF*, 66), and to the 'empty, restless activity' of the modern world, this 'unremitting aspiration and progress without rest and purpose' which is 'nothing but a Nordic barbarity', an 'antipathy toward the world', and which impels the protagonist to exclaim: 'industry and utility are the angels of death who, with fiery swords, prevent man's return to Paradise' (ib.). In addition, this type of love in an effortless and natural form of behaviour results in fidelity (*KFSA* 7, 32; *LF*, 74).

In this manner, *Lucinde* leads from the present world of greed, objects, utility, property, and acquisitiveness to the happy state of nature and new health (*KFSA* 5, 64; *LF*, 110). In the last analysis, it is love that causes this substantial change and makes us, as Julius writes to Lucinde, 'true and complete human beings and is the essence of life' (*KFSA* 5, 64; *LF*, 110). Julius senses 'a great change' in his being and describes it as a 'general softness and sweet warmth' in his soul and mind (*KFSA* 5, 65; *LF*, 111). In this state, the two love everything they had loved before, only more so, and Julius says: 'It is only now that a feeling for the world has really dawned on us' (*KFSA* 5, 67; *LF*, 113). He is now ready to earn together with Lucinde their place 'in this lovely world', and with her, he wants to enter 'into the dance of humanity', to 'sow and reap for the future and the present' (*KFSA* 5, 62; *LF*, 106).

Schlegel does not refrain from depicting this great change in a most realistic manner. Lucinde is pregnant, and in the six concluding arabesque frame sections, Julius shows a new sense for utility, breaking out in 'rapturous praises about how good it is to have one's own home and how honourable domesticity is' (*KFSA* 5, 62; *LF*, 108). We also see him as a concerned husband plagued during Lucinde's illness by visions of her death and a desire for his own death. He goes so far as to say retrospectively: 'What existed between us before was only love and passion' (*KFSA* 5, 61; *LF*, 107), and he designates their earlier state of feeling as also suspended 'in the vacuum of a universal enthusiasm' (*KFSA* 5, 62; *LF*, 108).

The conception of paradise has changed considerably from the first six frame sections to the concluding ones, and an unmistakable narrowing into the sphere of the bourgeois and respectable world becomes noticeable.[47] At this point, we should remember that *Lucinde* was conceived as an allegorical novel and that the fate of Julius and Lucinde represents the new earth and the new humanity of the Romantic utopia. These are by no means limited to parenthood and domesticity, but marriage also relates to the community of classes and social groups and to the 'universal brotherhood' among them (*KFSA* 5, 63; *LF*, 109). Julius' and Lucinde's domesticity is directly linked to that state of the earth in which 'lovely houses and charming cottages' will adorn the world and replace the decayed and sick condition in the present cities (ib.). The hymnic love-dialogue 'Yearning and Peace' shortly before the end of the novel connects love, night, and death in a symbolic manner and far exceeds any utopian ideas of the early Romantic revolution. We read:

Oh eternal yearning! Still at last the fruitless yearning and vain brilliance of the day shall vanish and expire, and a great night of love make itself felt in eternal peace (*KFSA* 5, 80; *LF*, 127).

Conclusion: early German Romanticism and literary modernity

Early German Romantic literary theory, as it developed during the last five or six years of the eighteenth century, certainly relates to the formation of the Romantic movement in Germany and Europe during the first decades of the nineteenth century and thereby participates in the great epochal change from the Enlightenment and the classicist doctrine to Romanticism. Yet, we can easily recognize features of this theory that make it an event of far greater significance than merely incepting Romanticism and relate it directly to the origin of our own modernity. Obviously the term 'early Romanticism' is a subsequent and retrospective designation unknown at the time when this theory arose. The original name for the phenomenon was 'Romantic school', but this label proved to be misleading because of its close association with the later Romantic movement in Germany. 'Early Romanticism', however, did not originate as a period designation until the beginning of our century and became an established category only during the latter half of it.[1] The idea underlying this term is obviously to ascertain at the very beginning of the Romantic period a distinct body of thought and literature that is hard to bring into line with any other intellectual trend of the time. For want of a better name, but also because of the favoured use of the term 'Romantic' among its representatives, this brief phenomenon of decisive change gained the title 'early Romanticism'.

The trouble with all period designations modified by a *prae* or a *post* is, of course, that they suggest that the main event is either anticipated or already past and that the respective time period relates to this event only by way of expectation or succession.

Names like 'late antiquity' or the 'early Middle Ages' have this connotation and almost automatically evoke the idea of a high or accomplished form still to emerge or already gone. Such an idea, however, is not at all intended by the term 'early Romanticism'. The modifier 'early' denotes a mentality still untouched by the often reactionary attitude of later Romanticism in Germany. This is particularly manifest in the early Romantics' affirmative attitude towards the French Revolution, in the republican conviction, or in their cosmopolitan attitude toward their intellectual tradition. All this differs sharply from what the name 'Romanticism' came to stand for in Germany, not to speak of the early Romantics' predilection for the fragment, for infinite reflection, and indirect communication. An early Romantic is, furthermore, someone who looks at literary texts with a good dose of irony, who in his relationships with other people displays an infinite amount of wit, and who in philosophy exercises constantly higher exponential series of thought. To be an early Romantic can also mean to push things a little too far – a tendency, however, easily redeemed by the quality of youth also implied in the term. The early Romantic ignores what this one calls his philosophy and that one his poetry and instead develops a form of communication uniting not only philosophy and poetry, but also morality and religion. Like postmodernism, early Romanticism describes an attitude apart from the habitual sequence of epochs – early Romanticism anticipating and displaying many features of our literary modernity, and postmodernism playing off our modern inheritance in a parody of its styles. Both early Romanticism and postmodernism, however, seem to assume a twisted posture toward modernism marked by a radical reflection on its conditions or, as Friedrich Schlegel would put it, on the 'impossibility and necessity' of its full realization.[2]

One decisive step undertaken by the early Romantics toward a consciously developed sense of literary modernity concerns the nature of the literary work and art in general. Adam Müller, a contemporary of the Schlegels, characterizes the essence of the 'literary revolution' brought about by these brothers as having made the 'meaning, the tendency of a work of art' the most important aspect in our dealing with aesthetic phenomena. Whereas during previous ages, art objects appeared to be condemned to having a 'closed, immutable authority', to being the subject for 'repeated and desperate imitations', they now assumed the function of an 'everlasting growth and life, of an infinite mobility and active effect upon art history'.[3] We could also characterize this basic shift in the appreciation of art and literature as a move away from the model of representation to that of creation, from mimetic imitation to creative production. The representational model is that of the classical and classicist period basically deriving from Plato and Aristotle. This model was reformulated during the course of the centuries in a variety of ways but dominated Western thought about literature until the end of the eighteenth century. The main idea was that the task of the arts and literature consists in representing and imitating a pregiven reality – nature as it surrounds us, the great events of history, the figures and fables of mythology, eventually the revelations and historical events of Christianity, or the great literary works of art. According to this theory, literature is seen as representation, as mimesis, as imitation.

Perhaps no classical or classicist author has ever so directly and one-sidedly declared literature to be nothing but that. Not even Plato could be reduced to this doctrine. He, of course, reproached the poet for being an imitator, and a poor one at that, but was mostly concerned about the poet's ability to arouse the emotions of his audience, and this has little to do with imitation.[4] He also thought that the poet produced his works not in a state of sobriety and equanimity, but in ecstasy, even in madness, a theory more of inspiration than imitation.[5] Aristotle defended literature against Plato as a completely natural or legitimate form of imitation.[6] Describing the activity of the poet more closely, however, he compares him to the historiographer, who depicts real happenings and executes a real imitation, whereas the poet works in the realm of the possible, the imaginative.[7] When Aristotle says that a work of literature should have a beginning, a middle, and an end,[8] he suggests that the artist, in his imitation, has to make choices in the conscious structuring of his work, something again distancing literature from a merely mimetic procedure. Longinus saw the essence of poetry in the creation of the sublime style, of what moves the soul and inspires the mind through its vehemence[9] – something far from mimesis. Dante and Boccaccio distinguished between the literal and allegorical dimensions of the literary text and assumed a plurality of meaning, a polysemy in poetic works.[10] Even a dramatist like Corneille who wanted to abide by the rules of imitation had to violate them occasionally in order to create greater beauties for his audience.[11] Dryden saw the distinctive quality of Shakespeare not in his mimetic talent, but in the fact that he possessed 'the largest and most comprehensive soul', and in his 'wit', too, the innovative and combinatory power of the mind.[12]

In spite of these and many other deviations, we still feel entitled to characterize the classical and classicist views of literature as a theory of imitation, of mimesis, because of the belief in a pregiven reality for poetry, the assumption that literature relates to something outside, to an already existing reference point in the real world. The early German Romantics brought about an entirely new understanding of the literary work and no longer conceived of it as relating to a pregiven reality but rather emerging from a creative principle in the human mind, creative imagination, that power of genius capable of producing entire works of its own. Of course, poetry takes its materials from the outer world as it surrounds us, but creates a unique world differing from the real world and meaningful in its own way. This world has its own order of time and place, of communication and truth, and is created by the poet in a highly conscious manner. In this kind of creation, the poet shapes an individual unity, fusing together a multiplicity of discordant and even oppositional elements until they form a structured and coherent whole. According to the early Romantic model, the poetic work is the result of conscious artistry, and the poet is in absolute control of his creation. We should add at this point, however, that perhaps no early Romantic ever espoused the theory of poetic creativity as pronouncedly as it is depicted here. We always notice a characteristic antagonism between conscious and unconscious creation, a fine line between deliberate and natural creativity. Yet, we feel entitled to speak about the early Romantic literary theory in terms of creativity because whatever the reference of poetry to the outer world and to nature may be, these phenomena are never seen in terms of imitating, representing, miming a pregiven reality, but essentially in relationship to the poet's mind that makes the poetic experience of the world possible and constitutes its 'condition of possibility'.

This new view of the literary work goes hand-in-hand with a fully developed historical consciousness. Modernism and historicism, latent in the battle between the ancients and the moderns, came to a juncture in early Romanticism, and from then on the view of literature and history remained inseparable. The notion of an infinite perfectibility, of a constant striving toward an absolute goal, of a 'universally progressive poetry', best expresses the early Romantic conception of history. Perfectibility in its early Romantic understanding, however, does not mean a naïve belief in progress and optimism, but includes a reflection on the losses that are unavoidable through movement, time, and history. Perfectibility instills the double feeling of confidence and melancholy. Here we realize the radical theoretical shift from a normative theory of literature in the classicist style to a historical investigation into the nature of literature. What literature is can only be told by history, or even more directly: the theory of literature is its own history. In the last analysis, however, no theory can possibly exhaust the notion of poetry because 'that, in fact, is its real essence: that it should forever be becoming and never be perfected' (*KFSA* 2, 183).

Looked at from the standpoint of the quarrel between the ancients and the moderns, this status of perfectibility certainly indicates a victory of the moderns over the ancients, in that no classical standard any longer determines the course of modern poetry in its future-oriented direction. The price to be paid for this independence, however, is the relegation of pure beauty and perfection to a past age of classical harmony and the ascription of alienation, imperfection, and deficiency to the status of modernity. Modernism now appears as a post-classical age in which the classical structures of self-possession and identity are lost. In this view, classicism and modernism enter into a close relationship of interactive rapport lacking in previous treatments of the quarrel between the ancients and the moderns. In a paradoxical formulation we could say that the most advanced type of modernity is the one that stands in the liveliest interaction with the classical age.

Yet, to experience the full tension in this interaction of classicism and modernism, we have to realize that the classical world of an assumed perfect literature and 'pure beauty' is also one of perfectibility and represents art only at a certain time and under certain conditions. This world by no means embodies a beauty above which nothing more beautiful can be thought, but only a 'relative maximum', which like the modern maximum is bound to time, place, and, above all, to the medium of poetry, language. The construction of an absolute classicism is just as self-destructive as that of an absolute modernism. Just as modernism is driven into the search for an absolute classicism, at least an 'infinitely growing' one, classicism results in an infinitely growing modernism.

If we wanted to determine the particularly modern character of the new poetic and critical discourse brought about by the early German Romantics, we would have to abandon the dominance of one single principle (creative imagination, reason, fragment, structure, progress, perfectibility, classicism, modernism, and so forth) and stress the counteractive movement of several tendencies (affirmation and scepticism, enthusiasm and melancholy) as the characteristic mark of their modernity. We would have to add that this attitude implies a critique of any straightforward type of modernism lacking an autocritical assessment of its own position and an awareness of its own limitations. We should perhaps also add that the attitude of self-criticism permeating the early Romantic expression of literary modernity does not have a nostalgic character and is not to be understood as a melancholic reflection on a loss or limitation of the human being. Critical self-reflection in the early Romantic style rather implies a joyful affirmation and acceptance of the human condition, the limits of which can very well be extended by means of language games, irony, and indirect communication.

Notes

INTRODUCTION

1 See René Wellek, 'Immanuel Kant's Aesthetics and Criticism', *Discriminations. Further Concepts of Criticism* (New Haven: Yale University Press, 1970), 122–42.

2 The first presentation of early Romanticism from this point of view is that of Hermann Hettner, *Die romantische Schule in ihrem inneren Zusammenhange mit Goethe und Schiller* (Brunswick: Vieweg, 1850).

3 Fritz Strich, *Deutsche Klassik und Romantik oder Vollendung und Unendlichkeit.* 4th edn (Bern: Francke, 1949).

4 Eliza M. Butler, *The Tyranny of Greece over Germany. A Study of the Influence Exercised by Greek Art and Poetry over the Great German Writers of the Eighteenth, Nineteenth, and Twentieth Centuries* (Cambridge University Press, 1935).

5 Johann Wolfgang Goethe, 'Literarischer Sanskulottismus', *Gedenkausgabe*, ed. Ernst Beutler (Zurich: Artemis, 1948–53), Vol. 14, 180.

6 Adam Müller, *Kritische, ästhetische und philosophische Schriften*, ed. Walter Schroeder and Werner Siebert (Neuwied: Luchterhand, 1967), Vols. 1, 23, 38, 39, 41.

7 See Ernst Behler, *Unendliche Perfektibilität. Europäische Romantik und Französische Revolution.*

8 E.g., Hans-Georg Gadamer, *Truth and Method*, trans. Joel Weinsheimer and Donald G. Marshall. 2nd, rev. edn (New York: Crossroad, 1990).

9 See Josef Körner, *Die Botschaft der deutschen Romantik an Europa* (Augsburg: Filser, 1929).

10 E.g., Rudolf Haym, *Die romantische Schule. Ein Beitrag zur Geschichte des deutschen Geistes.*

11 Especially in the third book of the novel.

12 G. W. F. Hegel, *Nürnberger Schriften*, ed. Johannes Hoffmeister (Leipzig: 1938), 439. See also G. W. F. Hegel, *Encyclopaedia of the*

Philosophical Sciences in Outline and Critical Writings, ed. Ernst Behler (Continuum: New York, 1990) and my introduction, pp. xxii–xxvi.

13 *L'Absolu littéraire. Théorie de la littérature du romantisme allemand*, ed. Philippe Lacoue-Labarthe and Jean-Luc Nancy (Paris: Editions du Seuil, 1978). See, especially, *Die Aktualität der Frühromantik*, ed. Ernst Behler and Jochen Hörisch.

14 Jürgen Habermas, *The Philosophical Discourse of Modernity*, trans. Frederick Lawrence (Cambridge, Mass.: MIT Press, 1987).

1 FORMATION AND MAIN REPRESENTATIVES OF EARLY ROMANTICISM IN GERMANY

1 Jochen Hörisch, '"Sein ist gut." Ein Jenaer Geistergespräch vom Mai 1795 im Hause Niethammer mit Fichte, Hölderlin und Hardenberg', *Athenaeum: Jahrbuch für Romantik*, ed. Ernst Behler, Alexander von Bormann, Jochen Hörisch, and Günter Oesterle (1991), Vol. 1, 279–82.

2 Schiller expresses these views in a long introduction to the periodical.

3 *Crabb Robinson in Germany. 1800–1805. Extracts from his Correspondence*, ed. Edith J. Morley (Oxford University Press, 1929), 116–18.

4 See especially '*Romantic' and its Cognates. The European History of a Word*, ed. Hans Eichner, which also lists all previous investigations on this subject. Especially useful to the present discussion is René Wellek, 'The Concept of Romanticism in Literary History', *Concepts of Criticism* (New Haven: Yale University Press, 1963), 128–98.

5 Raymond Immerwahr, '"Romantic" and its Cognates in England, Germany, and France before 1790' in *Romantic and its Cognates*, ed. Hans Eichner, 18.

6 Hans Eichner, 'Germany: Romantisch–Romantik–Romantiker' in '*Romantic' and its Cognates*, 100.

7 Raymond Immerwahr, '"Romantic" and its Cognates' in '*Romantic' and its Cognates*, 19.

8 Nicolas Boileau-Despreaux, *Oeuvres complètes* (Paris: Bibliothèque de la Pléiade, 1966), 170, 158, 171.

9 Quoted from the edition of Geneva (Pellet), 1777, Vol. 29, 376.

10 Hans Eichner, 'Germany: Romantisch–Romantik–Romantiker' in '*Romantic' and its Cognates*, 102.

11 See René Wellek, 'The Concept of Romanticism in Literary History', *Concepts of Criticism*, 128–98.

12 Hermann Hettner, *Die romantische Schule in ihrem inneren Zusammenhange mit Goethe und Schiller* (Brunswick: Vieweg, 1850).

13 Rudolf Haym, *Die romantische Schule. Ein Beitrag zur Geschichte des deutschen Geistes.*

14 Heinrich Heine, *Die romantische Schule*, Sämtliche Werke, ed. Klaus Briegleb. Vol. 3 (Munich: Hanser, 1971), 361.

15 Rudolf Haym, *Die romantische Schule.*

16 Wilhelm Dilthey, *Leben Schleiermachers* (Berlin: Reimer, 1870), 215.

17 Ludwig Geiger, *Dichter und Frauen – Abhandlungen und Mitteilungen* (Berlin, 1899), 95.

18 Ib.

19 Henriette Herz, *Ihr Leben und ihre Erinnerungen*, ed. J. Fürst (Berlin: Herz, 1858).

20 Adam Müller, *Kritische, ästhetische und philosophische Schriften*, ed. Walter Schröder and Werner Siebert (Neuwied: Luchterhand, 1967), Vol. 1, 23, 38, 39.

21 Diana Behler, 'Henry Crabb Robinson as a Mediator of Early Romanticism to England', *Arcadia* 12 (1977), 119.

22 See the 'Example' to Ch. 3.

23 See Carl Schmitt, *Politische Romantik* (Munich: Duncker und Humblot, 1924).

24 *Lessings Werke*, ed. Georg Witkowski (Leipzig and Vienna: Bibliographisches Institut), Vol. 7, 448.

25 Henriette Herz, *Ihr Leben und ihre Erinnerungen*, ed. J. Fürst (Berlin: Herz, 1858), 268–9.

26 Jean Paul, *Werke*, ed. N. Miller (Munich: Hanser, 1966), Vol. 6, 344.

27 *Deutsche Literatur und Französische Revolution*, ed. Richard Brinkmann (Göttingen: Vandenhoeck und Ruprecht, 1974), 175.

28 Georg Lukács, *Kurze Skizze einer Geschichte der neueren deutschen Literatur* (Neuwied: Luchterhand, 1975), 79; Hans Mayer, *Von Lessing zu Thomas Mann. Wandlungen der bürgerlichen Literatur in Deutschland* (Pfullingen: Neske, 1959), 25.

29 See Wilfried Malsch, '*Europa*'. *Poetische Rede des Novalis. Deutung der Französischen Revolution und Reflexion auf die Poesie in der Geschichte.*

30 See on the following Ernst Behler, *Unendliche Perfektibilität: Europäische Romantik und Französische Revolution.*

31 See Ch. 2, 'Ancient and modern, classical and Romantic poetry', pp. 95–109, below.

2 POETRY IN THE EARLY ROMANTIC THEORY OF THE SCHLEGEL BROTHERS

1 See A. W. Schlegel's Berlin lectures on aesthetics of 1801: 'Poetry, in a general sense, is that which is common to all arts and modifies itself according to specific spheres' (*AWS V* 1, 186). On the encyclopaedic projects of the Schlegels, see A. W. Schlegel's Berlin lectures 'Über Enzyklopädie' (*AWS V* 3) and F. Schlegel's Paris lectures entitled 'Geschichte der europäischen Literatur', *KFSA* 11, 3–18, as well as Ch. 6 below.

2 See my essay '"The Theory of Art is its own History": Herder and the Schlegel Brothers', *Herder Today. Contributions from the International Herder Conference*, ed. Kurt Mueller-Vollmer (Berlin: de Gruyter, 1990), 246–67.

3 The Kantian distinction between *Verstand* and *Vernunft* is rendered as 'understanding' (*Verstand*) and 'reason' (*Vernunft*).

4 Friedrich Schlegel reverses the Kantian relationship between understanding and reason by calling 'reason' what Kant named 'understanding'. This brings a slightly confusing note into the following section. A. W. Schlegel, however, follows the Kantian usage.

5 See *Mythos und Moderne. Begriff und Bild einer Rekonstruktion*, ed. Karl-Heinz Bohrer (Frankfurt: Suhrkamp, 1985).

6 See especially Schlegel's late studies on Jacobi: *KFSA* 8, 585–616.

7 See Ch. 3, pp. 154–64, below.

8 Since these arguments were formulated at a much later period than that of the appearance of Kant's work (1790, 1793), namely at the height of the early Romantic theory (1801–2), they easily convey an impression of unfairness. Schlegel argued from a position based on completely different philosophical principles. The aim of these lectures was, however, to summarize the early Romantic theory, and in this context Schlegel had to deal with Kant because much of the early throught had been developed as a counter-position to Kant.

9 See on this Peter C. Simpson, 'The Critique of Wordplay during Early German Romanticism: Critical Construction of a Literary Style'. Diss. Cornell University, 1985.

10 This is the main text by Karl Philipp Moritz in the field of aesthetics the general thrust of which can be described as a theory of creative imitation. Next to the passive human 'sensitive power' (*Empfindungskraft*) is the human creative 'formative power' (*Bildungskraft*) which is able to concentrate the entirety of nature on a reduced scale as a structured whole.

11 Goethe, for instance, used them in an early essay called 'Einfache Nachahmung der Natur, Manier, Stil' of 1788 (*GOE* 13, 66–71).

12 Friedrich Schlegel is referring to Quintilian, *Inst.* II, 8.

13 See Thomas G. Sauer, *A. W. Schlegel's Shakespearean Criticism in England.*

14 See on the following Ernst Behler, *Unendliche Perfektibilität: Europäische Romantik und Französische Revolution.*

15 *Encyclopédie ou Dictionnaire raisonné des sciences, des arts et des métiers, par une société de gens de lettres* (Geneva: Pellet, 1777), Vol. 2, 608–11.

16 Denis Diderot, *Oeuvres complètes*, ed. J. Assézat and M. Tourneux (Paris: Garnier, 1875–9), Vol. 3, 323.

17 Voltaire, *Le Siècle de Louis XIV*, in: Voltaire, *Oeuvres complètes* (Kehl: Imprimerie de la Société Typographique, 1785), Vol. 20, 189–91.

18 He completed the text and submitted it to the publisher toward the end of 1795, but the essay did not appear until January, 1797.

19 Rudolf Haym, *Die romantische Schule*, p. 190.

20 On Schlegel's double-edged usage of the terms 'classical' and 'modern' see Raymond Immerwahr, 'Classicist Values in the Thought of Friedrich Schlegel', *Journal of English and Germanic Philology* 79 (1980), 376–89.

21 See the 'Example' to Ch. 1: 'Early German Romanticism and the French Revolution', pp. 54–71, above.

22 See Ch. 1, section on the words 'romantic' and 'romanticism', pp. 24–33, above.

23 See the special issue *The Nineteenth-Century Rediscovery of Euripides*, ed. William M. Calder III, in: *Greek Roman and Byzantine Studies* 27 (1986), 4.

24 M. S. Silk and J. P. Stern, *Nietzsche on Tragedy* (Cambridge, 1981), 311.

25 See the 'Example' to Ch. 6: Friedrich Schlegel's *Lucinde.*

26 Theodore Distel, 'Wielands Tadel an Böttiger', *Goethe-Jahrbuch* 33 (1912), 216–18; cf. Uwe Petersen, *Goethe und Euripides. Untersuchungen zur Euripides-Rezeption in der Goethezeit* (Heidelberg, 1974), esp. 106–16 ('Schlegel's *Jon*') and 151–60 ('Goethe and A. W. Schlegel').

27 Albert R. Schmitt, 'Wielands Urteil über die Brüder Schlegel. Mit ungedruckten Briefen des Dichters an Karl August Böttiger', *Journal of English and German Philology* 65 (1966), 637–61.

28 Schlegel, for example, sent copies of his lecture notes to Schelling, who was at the time lecturing on aesthetics at the University of Jena: E. Behler, 'Schellings Aesthetik in der Überlieferung von Henry Crabb Robinson', *Philosophisches Jahrbuch* 83 (1976), 137–9

and Ernst Behler, *Studien zur Romantik und zur idealistischen Philosophie*, 171–95 (reprint of the essay).

29 *August Wilhelm Schlegels Vorlesungen über schöne Literatur und Kunst*, ed. Jakob Minor, 3 vols. (Heilbronn: 1884).

30 A. W. Schlegel, *A Course of Lectures on Dramatic Art and Literature*, tr. John Black (London 1815). A second edition appeared in 1840, and a 'Revised Edition According to the Last German Edition' was published by A. J. W. Morrison (London 1846) and became part of Bohn's Standard Library. Black's translation was reprinted in Philadelphia in 1833.

31 *Poet.* 1453a10.

32 Plato, *Republic* III.

33 *Comparaison entre la 'Phèdre' de Racine et celle d'Euripide* (Paris 1807 (= *AWS SW* 14, 333–405)).

34 *Briefe von und an August Wilhelm Schlegel*, ed. Josef Körner (Vienna 1930), Vol. 2, 200.

35 In, for example, the *Journal de l'Empire* of 16 and 24 February and 4 March 1808, as well as in the *Mercure de France*. See Josef Körner, *Die Botschaft der deutschen Romantik an Europa* (Augsburg: Filser, 1929), 12.

36 See his letters to Eichstädt of 23 September and 18 November 1807, and to Frau von Stein on 19 November 1807.

37 A. W. Schlegel, *Observations sur la langue et la littérature provençales*, *AWS SW* 14, 149–250.

38 *Spanisches Theater*, 2 volumes, ed. Eduard Böcking (Leipzig 1845). See E. Behler, 'The Reception of Calderón among the German Romantics', *Studies in Romanticism* 20 (1981), 437–60.

39 A. W. Schlegel, 'Über das spanische Theater', *Europa*, ed. Friedrich Schlegel (Frankfurt 1803), Vol. 1, 72–87.

40 On the continuation of this story, see the publication quoted in n. 23, above, especially William M. Calder, 'Ulrich von Wilamowitz-Moellendorff: Sospitator Euripides'.

3 THE THEORY OF ROMANTIC POETRY

1 Ernst Behler, *Die Zeitschriften der Brüder Schlegel* (Darmstadt: Wissenschaftliche Buchgesellschaft, 1983), 50–2.

2 Dionysius of Halicarnassus, *Opera omnia*, 6 vols. (Leipzig: Teubner, 1889–1905).

3 Karl Jaspers, *Vernunft und Existenz* (Munich: Piper, 1960), 20.

4 Raymond Immerwahr, 'Die symbolische Form des Briefes über den Roman', *Zeitschrift für deutsche Philologie*. Special issue: *Friedrich Schlegel* 88 (1970), 41–610.

5 *KFSA* 2, 397–419; 3, 46–102.

6 Parts of the following discussion can also be found in Ernst Behler, *Irony and the Discourse of Modernity* (Seattle: University of Washington Press, 1990), 73–110.

7 Beda Allemann, *Ironie und Dichtung* (Pfullingen: Neske, 1956).

8 Adam Müller, *Kritische, ästhetische und philosophische Schriften*, ed. Karl Schroeder and Werner Siebert. 2 vols. (Neuwied: Luchterhand, 1967), Vol. 1, 234.

9 Norman Knox, *The Word Irony and its Context* (Durham: Duke University Press, 1961), 184.

10 Aristotle, *Rhet.* 3.18.1419b7. Aristoteles is quoted from *Aristotelis Opera*, edn of Academia Borussia (reprint, Darmstadt: Wissenschaftliche Buchgesellschaft, 1960). References are given by title, book, chapter, and page number of this edition.

11 Aristotle, *Eth. Nic.* 2.7.1108a19–23; 1127a20–26.

12 Cicero, *Acad. Pr.* 2.5.15.

13 Cicero, *De or.* 2.67.270.

14 Quintilian, *Inst.* 9.2.44.

15 Quintilian, *Inst.* 9.2.46.

16 Aristophanes, *Nubes* 443.

17 Plato, Republic 337a. Plato is quoted from the edition Platon, *Oeuvres complètes*, ed. Guillaume Budé (reprint, Paris: Les Belles Lettres, 1953). References to this edition are given with the counting according to Henri Stephanus (1528–98), a counting used in most editions of Plato.

18 Aristotle, *Eth. Nic.* 4.13.1127b22–6.

19 Aristotle, *Phys.* 3.808a27.

20 Aristotle, *Hist. Animal.* 1.491b17.

21 Plato, *Symposium* 216d.

22 Hans Krämer, 'Fichte, Schlegel und der Infinitismus in der Platon-Deutung', *Deutsche Vierteljahresschrift* 62 (1988), 583–621.

23 This relates directly to the manuscript of his 'Critical Fragments': *KFSA* 2, 147–63; *LF*, 143–59.

24 *KFSA* 3, 46–102. These are only Friedrich Schlegel's own critical parts of the anthology. The texts selected from Lessing's writings will appear in *KFSA* 34.

25 See Ernst Behler, 'Das Fragment', *Prosakunst ohne Erzählen*, ed. Klaus Weissenberger (Tübingen: Niemeyer, 1985), 125–43.

26 A. W. Schlegel, *Spanisches Theater*, 2 vols. (Berlin: Reimer, 1803–9) and A. W. Schlegel 'Über das spanische Theater', *Europa*, ed. Friedrich Schlegel (Frankfurt: Wilmans, 1803–5), Vol. 1, 2, 72–87. These texts appeared together in the second edition of A. W. Schlegels *Spanisches Theater*, 2 vols. ed. Eduard Böcking (Leipzig:

Wiedmann, 1845). See also A. W. Schlegel, *Blumensträuße italie-nischer, spanischer und portugiesischer Poesie* (Berlin: Reimer, 1804).

27 See Ch, 1, section 'The words "romantic" and "romanticism"'', pp. 24–32, above.

28 E.g., '*Three dominant genres*: 1. *Tragedy* with the Greeks; 2. *Satire* with the Romans; novel with the moderns' (*KFSA* 16, 88). – 'Just as the novel colours all of modern poetry, so satire...colours the whole of Romantic poetry' (*KFSA* 2, 188; *LF*, 180). – 'Just as our literature began with the novel, so the Greek began with the epic and eventually dissolved in it' (*KFSA* 2, 335; *DP*, 101). See Hans Eichner, *Friedrich Schlegel*, 53–4: '...it was because of his conviction of the dominant role played in the literature of the last thousand years by the *Roman* – i.e., by the rhymed epic in a modern vernacular, the romance, the novel, and even certain types of drama, all considered as variants of one and the same literary form – that Schlegel termed the essence of this literature "romantic"'.

29 See Ch. 4, section 2 'Novalis' absolute idealism', pp. 184–95, below.

30 See Melitta Gerhard, 'Goethes "geprägte Form" im romantischen Spiegel', in Melitta Gerhard, *Leben und Gesetz: Fünf Goethe-Aufsätze* (Bern and Munich: Francke 1966), 64–78; Raymond Immerwahr, 'Friedrich Schlegel's Essay "On Goethe's *Meister*"', *Monatshefte* 49 (1957), 1–21; Clemens Heselhaus, 'Die *Wilhelm Meister*-Kritik der Romantiker und die romantische Romantheorie', *Nachahmung und Illusion. Kolloquium Gießen 1963*, ed. H. R. Jauß (Munich: Eidos 1964), 113–209; Jacob Steiner, 'Äther der Fröhlichkeit, Zur Frage nach einer dichterischen Ironie', *Orbis Litterarum* 13 (1958), 64–80; Henry Hatfield, '*Wilhelm Meisters Lehrjahre* und "Progressive Universalpoesie"', *The Germanic Review* 36 (1961), 221–29; Hans Eichner, 'Über Goethes *Meister*', in *Kritische Friedrich Schlegel Ausgabe*, (Paderborn and Munich, 1967), Vol. 2, LXXI–LXXIX; Hans-Joachim Mähl, 'Goethes Urteil über Novalis', *Jahrbuch des Freien Deutschen Hochstifts* (1967), 130–207; Karl Robert Mandel-kow, 'Der Roman der Klassik und Romantik', *Neues Handbuch der Literaturwissenschaft*, Vol. 14: *Europäische Romantik*, ed. Karl Robert Mandelkow (Wiesbaden: Athenaion, 1982), 393–428.

31 See, especially, Melitta Gerhard, 'Goethes "geprägte Form" im romantischen Spiegel', 64–78.

32 See Ch. 4 'Example': 'Novalis' *Heinrich von Ofterdingen*'.

4 NOVALIS AND THE MYSTICAL DIMENSION OF EARLY ROMANTIC THEORY

1 The text consists of manuscripts of approximately 500 pages which were preserved in the Hardenberg family archives. They contain notes on philosophers of that time, especially Kant, Fichte, and Hemsterhuis. The sections on Fichte were first published in the critical Novalis edition by Paul Kluckholm in 1928, but then again in a completely reorganized manner, following the order of the manuscripts, by Joachim Mähl: *NO* 2, 102–296.

2 See Ch. 1, section 3, 'The members of the ealy Romantic school', pp. 33–54, above.

3 In June 1797, Friedrich Schlegel wished that he and his friend could practise their 'Fichtecizing' once again 'as heartily, as agreeably, as cosily as it had happened a few times last winter' (*KFSA* 23, 371). At that time, however, their dissociation from Fichte's philosophical project was obvious.

4 Certainly the opinion according to which everything was to be brought into a relationship to the idea of Sophia: see the following section of this chapter, pp. 195–201, below.

5 Friedrich Schlegel had said at the beginning of his *Dialogue on Poetry*: 'There is only one reason, and for everyone it remains the same; but just as every human being has his own nature and his own love, so does he bear within him his own poetry which must and should remain his own as surely as he is himself, as surely as there is anything original in him' (*KFSA* 2, 284; *DP*, 53).

6 Reinhard Lauth, 'Fichtes Verhältnis zu Jacobi unter besonderer Berücksichtigung der Rolle Friedrich Schlegels in dieser Sache', *Friedrich Heinrich Jacobi. Philosoph und Literat der Goethezeit*, ed. Klaus Hammacher (Frankfurt: Klostermann, 1971), 191. Josef Körner, 'Friedrich Schlegels philosophische Lehrjahre', in his edition of Friedrich Schlegel, *Neue philosophische Schriften* (Frankfurt: Schulte-Bulmke, 1935), 3–114, especially 19–20.

7 Reported by Hendrik Steffens, *Was ich erlebte*, 10 vols. (Breslau: Max, 1840–4), Vol. 4, 64. On another occasion Hülsen said about Fichte: 'I felt odd with regard to his manner when I figured out for myself his way of perception; he must never have vividly perceived any tree, any animal, and especially not any rich landscape' (Vol. 4, 165).

8 Coleridge, in Ch. 12 of his *Biographia Literaria*, took over these passages from the introduction of Schelling's *System of Transcendental Idealism* and translated them without indicating their origin: Samuel Taylor Coleridge, *Biographia Literaria*, ed. J. Showcross, 2 vols. (Oxford University Press, 1907), Vol. 1, 173–7.

His purpose was to introduce the 'Occasion of the *Lyrical Ballads*' and how they were originally proposed, namely, as a 'poetry of nature' (Wordsworth) and a poetry of the 'supernatural' (Coleridge). Similar to Schelling's scheme, it was Wordsworth's task 'to give the charm of novelty to things of every day, and to excite a feeling analogous to the supernatural'. Coleridge's 'endeavours should be directed to persons and characters supernatural', yet with the intention of letting them appear as natural: *Biographia Literaria*, Vol. 2, 5–6. I have used Coleridge's translations as a help for my own rendering of these passages in English.

9 Wilhelm Dilthey, 'Novalis', in *Das Erlebnis und die Dichtung*, 3rd edn (Leipzig: Teubner, 1910), 304. References to this essay are given in parenthesis in the text.

10 See above, p. 195.

11 See also *NO* 3, 376, 302, 374.

12 *Rahel. Ein Buch des Andenkens für ihre Freunde* (Berlin: Reimer, 1834), Vol. 3, 139–40.

13 See above, p. 71.

14 See above, p. 179.

15 *Aus Schleiermachers Leben. In Briefen*, ed. Ludwig Jonas and Wilhelm Dilthey (Berlin: Reimer, 1861), Vol. 3, 178–9.

16 K. W. F. Solger, *Nachgelassene Schriften und Briefwechsel* (Leipzig: Brockhaus, 1826), Vol. 1, 95.

17 Wilhelm Dilthey, *Das Erlebnis und die Dichtung*, 3rd edn (Leipzig: Teubner, 1910), 337.

18 Paul Kluckhohn, *Friedrich von Hardenbergs Entwicklung und Dichtung*, in *NO* 1, 56.

19 Novalis writes 'from the infinite to the finite'.

20 Paul Kluckhohn in *NO* 1, 57.

21 Paul Kluckhohn in *NO* 1, 43.

22 *NO* 1, 360. Referring to Tieck's 'Account of the Continuation'.

23 This also refers to Tieck's 'Account of the Continuation'.

24 Richard Samuel, '*Heinrich von Ofterdingen*', *Der deutsche Roman. Vom Barock bis zur späten Romantik*, ed. Benno von Wiese (Düsseldorf: Bagel, 1965), 296.

25 Reinhold Steig, *Achim von Arnim und Clemens Brentano* (Stuttgart: Cotta, 1894), vol. 1, 136.

26 *Friedrich Schlegels Briefe an seinen Bruder August Wilhelm*, ed. Oskar Walzel (Berlin: Speyer und Peters, 1890), 477.

27 Ib.

5 WACKENRODER'S AND TIECK'S CONCEPTIONS OF PAINTING AND MUSIC

1 The dominance of music in Schopenhauer's aesthetics is the most conspicuous example for this trend.

2 Giorgio Vasari, *Vite de' più eccelenti pittori, scultori ed architetti* (Florence: Giunti, 1550). Wackenroder probably used the second edition which is considerably enlarged. Both editions were available to him during his studies at Göttingen University.

3 Joachim von Sandrart, *Deutsche Akademie der edlen Bau-, Bild- und Malerkünste*, 2 vols. (Nuremberg: Sandrart, 1675–9).

4 *Ludwig Tieck. Erinnnerungen aus dem Leben des Dichters nach dessen mündlichen und schriftlichen Mitteilungen*, ed. Rudolf Köpke, 2 vols. (Leipzig: Brockhaus, 1855), Vol. 1, 221–2.

5 See the 'Example' to this chapter, pp. 248–59, below.

6 Rudolf Haym, *Die romantische Schule*, 129.

7 See on this and the following especially Rudolf Haym, *Die romantische Schule*, 124.

8 The goddess of manufacturing artisanship.

9 Bramante, properly Donato d'Angelo (1444–1514), was a famous Italian architect who was originally a painter.

10 Baldaserre Count Castiglione (1478–1529) was a famous Italian statesman and author of that period.

11 Johann Joachim Winckelmann, *Gedanken über die Nachahmung der griechischen Werke in der Malerei und Bildhauerkunst*, in the series Deutsche Literaturdenkmale, (Heilbronn: Henninger, 1885), vol. 20, 14.

12 Wackenroder for this purpose also utilized the biographies of painters in Giovanni Pietro Bellori, *Le vite de' pittori, scultori ed architetti moderni* (Rom: Mascardi, 1672).

13 Wackenroder is referring to Château Weißstein near Pommersfelden in Upper Franconia where he visited the art gallery as a student at Bamberg University.

14 Ludwig Tieck, *Erinnerungen des Dichters nach dessen mündlichen und schriftlichen Mitteilungen*, ed. Rudolf Köpke (Leipzig: Brockhaus, 1855), Vol. 1, 223–4.

15 The first section, 'Description How the Old German Artists Have Lived', and the fifth, 'St Peter's Cathedral', are by Wackenroder. I could not locate an English translation of this text.

16 Tieck contributed the last four sections: 'Unmusical Tolerance', 'The Sounds', 'Symphonies', 'The Dream. An Allegory'.

17 See above, p. 54.

18 Tieck reports in the preface that he did not include an unfinished

essay on Rubens and a cantata which had not satisfied Wackenroder himself (*TI PhK*, 4).

19 See above, p. 167.

20 Tieck stated that after the completion of the *Outpourings* the two
friends had planned to write the 'story of an artist', and that this
was the origin of the present novel; 'In a certain sense, part of this
work belongs to my friend, although his sickness prevented him to
actually working out the sections which he had taken on. The
reader certainly loses a lot because I had to finish the work without
his help' (*TI FS*, 191–2). Tieck also mentioned that the novel was
supposed to appear under the name of the art-loving friar, and
that this explains the tone in certain sections of it (*TI FS*, 191).

21 Rudolf Haym, *Die romantische Schule*, 129.

22 J. L. Sammons, 'Tieck's *Franz Sternbald*: The Loss of Thematic
Control', *Studies in Romanticism* 5 (1965), 30–43; A. Anger,
'Nachwort', in L. Tieck, *Franz Sternbalnds Wanderungen*, ed. Alfred
Anger (Stuttgart: Reclam, 1966), 543–83; E. Mornin, 'Art and
Alienation in Tieck's *Franz Sternbalds Wanderungen*', *Modern Lan-
guage Notes* 94 (1979), 510–23.

23 H. Hillmann, 'Ludwig Tieck', *Deutsche Dichter der Romantik*, ed.
Benno von Wiese (Berlin: Schmidt, 1983), 114–38.

24 Most strongly emphasized in William J. Lillyman, *Reality's Dark
Dream. The Narrative Fiction of Ludwig Tieck* (Berlin: de Gruyter,
1979), 61–76.

25 See Richard Alewyn, 'Ein Fragment der Fortsetzung von Tiecks
Sternbald', *Jahrbuch des Freien Deutschen Hochstifts* (1962), 58–68; H.
Geulen, 'Zeit und Allegorie im Erzählvorgang von Tiecks Roman
Franz Sternbalds Wanderungen', *Germanisch-Romanische Monatsschrift*
18 (1968), 281–98; and William J. Lillyman, *Reality's Dark Dream.
The Narrative Fiction of Ludwig Tieck*.

26 See William J. Lillyman, *Reality's Dark Dream*, 68.

27 Eichendorff, *Der deutsche Roman des achtzehnten Jahrhunderts in seinem
Verhältnis zum Christentum* (Leipzig, 1851).

28 Richard Alewyn, 'Ein Fragment', 68.

29 Ib.

30 Ludwig Tieck, *Schriften* (Berlin: Reimer, 1828), Vol. 16, 415.

6 THEORY OF LANGUAGE, HERMENEUTICS, AND ENCYCLOPAEDISTICS

1 A lecture course of three sections, 'Literature and Fine Arts'
(1801–2), 'Classical Literature' (1802–3), 'Romantic Literature'
(1803–4), are in *AWS V*.

2 In his notes and fragments Schleiermacher often took issue with Adolf Franz Friedrich Knigge, author of the well-known book, *On the Behavior toward Others* (*Über den Umgang mit Menschen*), which was reprinted until far into our century and explained interpersonal relationships in a merely formal and sometimes egoistical manner.

3 This attitude dominates the first edition and obliged Schleiermacher to recast his notions of religion and God in the second (1806) and third (1821) editions and to make them conform more with his Christian beliefs.

4 See above, p. 181.

5 The most important text for this investigation is Friedrich Schlegel's *On the Language and Wisdom of the Hindus* of 1808 which deals in its first part with language and investigates the plurality of languages from these points of view: *KFSA* 8, 105–440.

6 See Ferdinand de Saussure, *Course in General Linguistics*, trans. Wade Baskin (New York: McGraw-Hill, 1966), 1–3.

7 Rousseau is mentioned here because of his prominence for a theory of language. Rousseau's comprehensive 'Essay on the Origin of Language' ('Essai sur l'origine des langues'), in *Oeuvres complètes de Jean-Jacques Rousseau* (Paris: Henri Feret, 1827), 469–564, was not too well known at that time. References to Rousseau as a theoretician of language mostly relate to the much more succinct sections in his *Discourse on the Origin and Foundation of Inequality among Mankind*, ed. Lester G. Crocker (New York: Washington Square Press, 1967), 214–18. The early Romantics, however, especially the Schlegels, seem to have been familiar with the later and more comprehensive work.

8 The mistake of taking Fichte's anonymous writing on revelation as a Kantian text: see above, p. 17.

9 Johann Peter Süßmilch, *Attempt at a Demonstration that the First Language Took its Origin not from the Human Being, but solely from the Creator* (Berlin: Academy of Sciences, 1766).

10 See note 5, above.

11 In this instance Herder considers language as a means of communication with others. This is presented by him, however, as an afterthought, as an application of what has occurred in the soul: 'The first human thought is hence in its very essence a preparation for the possibility of dialoguing with others. The first characteristic mark which I conceive is a characteristic word for me and a word of communication for others' (ib.).

12 A. W. Schlegel refers especially to Hemsterhuis' 'Letter on the Human Being and his Relationships', in *Oeuvres philosophiques de M. F. Hemsterhuys*, Vol. 182–90.

13 See *AWS SW* 7, 104, where A. W. Schlegel discusses the way children learn how to speak.

14 See *AWS V* 1, 524, 527, where A. W. Schlegel discusses this return in terms of sleep and dream.

15 Christoph Girtanner (1760–1800) was a physician and a popular writer who published widely on medicine, chemistry, political history, and political observations of his own time.

16 F. D. Schleiermacher, *Hermeneutik*, ed. Heinz Kimmerle (Heidelberg: Akademie der Wissenschaften, 1959), 87–8.

17 August Boeckh, *Enzyklopädie und Methodologie der philologischen Wissenschaften* (Leipzig: Teubner, 1877), 87.

18 Wilhelm Dilthey, *Gesammelte Schriften* (Stuttgart: Teubner, 1957), Vol. 5, 335.

19 *Seminar: Philosophische Hermeneutik*, ed. Hans-Georg Gadamer and Gottfried Boehm (Frankfurt: Suhrkamp, 1976; *Klassiker der Hermeneutik*, ed. Ulrich Nassen (Paderborn: Schöningh, 1982); *Hermeneutische Positionen: Schleiermacher, Dilthey, Heidegger, Gadamer*, ed. Hendrik Birus (Göttingen: Vandenhoeck und Ruprecht, 1982); *The Hermeneutics Reader. Texts of the German Tradition from the Enlightenment to the Present*, ed. Kurt Müller-Vollmer (New York: Continuum, 1985).

20 Wilhelm Dilthey, 'Die Entstehung der Hermeneutik', *Gesammelte Schriften*, Vol. 5, 317–38, especially 328.

21 Heinrich Nüsse, *Die Sprachtheorie Friedrich Schlegels*; Hermann Patsch, 'Friedrich Schlegels "Philosophie der Philologie" und Schleiermachers frühe Entwürfe', *Zeitschrift für Theologie und Kirche* 63 (1966); Kenichi Sagara, '"Wissenschaft der Literatur." Gedanken aus Friedrich Schlegels Nachlaßschriften', *Doitsu Bungaku* 47 (1971); Vittorio Santoli, *Philologie und Kritik* (Bern: Franke, 1971); Hinrich C. Seeba, 'Wirkungsgeschichte der Wirkungsgeschichte. Zu den romantischen Quellen (F. Schlegel) einer neuen Disziplin', *Jahrbuch für internationale Germanistik* 3 (1971) 145–67; Klaus Weimar, *Historische Einleitung zur literaturwissenschaftlichen Hermeneutik* (Tübingen: Siebeck, 1975); Willy Michel, 'Die Aktualität des Interpretierens', *Klassiker der Literaturtheorie*, ed. Horst Türk (Heidelberg: Winter, 1978); Norbert Bolz, 'Der Geist und die Buchstaben. Friedrich Schlegels hermeneutische Postulate', *Texthermeneutik, Aktualität, Geschichte, Kritik*, ed. Ulrich Nassen (Paderborn: Schöningh, 1979); Hans Dierkes, *Literaturgeschichte als Kritik* (Tübingen: Siebeck, 1980); Hendrik Birus, 'Hermeneutische Wende? Anmerkungen zur Schleiermacher-Interpretation', *Euphorion* 74 (1980) 213–22; Willy Michel, *Ästhetische Hermeneutik und frühromantische Kritik* (Göttingen: Vandenhoeck und Ruprecht

1982); Ernst Behler, 'Friedrich Schlegels Theorie des Verstehens: Hermeneutik oder Dekonstruktion?' *Die Aktualität der Frühromantik*, ed. Ernst Behler and Jochen Hörisch, 141–60.

22 *Friedrich Schleiermachers Sämtliche Werke*, Section 3, (Berlin: Reimer, 1835), 344–86. Reprinted in *Schleiermacher, Hermeneutik und Kritik*, ed. Manfred Frank (Frankfurt: Suhrkamp, 1977), 309–46.

23 Friedrich E. D. Schleiermacher, 'Hermeneutik und Kritik mit besonderer Beziehung auf das NT', *Sämtliche Werke*, Vol. 17, 32.

24 Ib.

25 See note 15, above.

26 See note 16, above.

27 Heinrich Nüsse, *Die Sprachtheorie Friedrich Schlegels*, 95.

28 This critical side of Friedrich Schlegel's early theory has found a much better reception than his hermeneutic theory and has been explored after the Second World War in critical studies by Heinrich Henel, Victor Lange, René Wellek, and Hans Eichner – in a reception which took place almost exclusively on the North American continent: Heinrich Henel, 'Friedrich Schlegel und die Grundlagen der modernen literarischen Kritik', *The Germanic Review* 20 (1945), 81–93; Victor Lange, 'Friedrich Schlegel's Literary Criticism', *Comparative Literature* 7 (1955), 289–305; René Wellek, 'Friedrich Schlegel', *A History of Modern Criticism*, (New Haven: Yale University Press, 1955), Vol. 2, 5–35; Hans Eichner, 'Friedrich Schlegels Theorie der Literaturkritik', *Zeitschrift für deutsche Philologie* 88 (1970), 2–19; Ernst Behler, 'Friedrich Schlegels Begriff der Philologie', *Beiträge zur deutschen Literatur* (Sophia-Universität Tokyo, 1981), 1–22.

29 See above, p. 153.

30 See above, p. 262.

31 Rudolf Haym, *Die romantische Schule*, 864; Ernst Behler, 'Friedrich Schlegels *Enzyklopädie der literarischen Wissenschaften* im Unterschied zu Hegels *Enzyklopädie der philosophischen Wissenschaften*', *Studien zur Romantik und zur idealistischen Philosophie* (Paderborn: Schöningh, 1988), 236–263.

32 See Ulrich Dierse, *Enzyklopädie. Zur Geschichte eines philosophischen und wissenschaftstheoretischen Begriffs* (Bonn: Bouvier, 1977).

33 Fritz Schalk, 'Die Wirkung der Diderotschen Enzyklopädie in Deutschland', *Studien zur französischen Aufklärung* (Munich: M. Hueber, 1964), 139–47.

34 See the text referred to in note 32 above.

35 Friedrich August Wolf, *Vorlesungen über die Altertumswissenschaft*, ed. J. D. Gürtler (Leipzig: Lehnhold, 1832–5), Vol. 1: *Vorlesung über die Enzyklopädie der Altertumswissenschaft*.

36 G. W. F. Hegel, *Nürnberger Schriften*, ed. Johannes Hoffmeister (Leipzig: Meiner, 1938), 439.

37 Josef Körner published some of the sections on language: Josef Körner, 'August Wilhelm Schlegel. Die griechische und lateinische Sprache', *Romantikforschungen* (Halle, 1929), 53–62. Other mentions of the text in critical literature are insignificant.

38 See on the following *KFSA* 11, 3–8.

39 Wilhelm Dilthey, *Leben Schleiermachers* (Berlin: Reimer, 1870), 492.

40 Rudolf Haym, *Die romantische Schule*, 501.

41 G. Mattenklott, 'Der Sehnsucht eine Form. Zum Ursprung des modernen Romans bei F. Schlegel', *Zur Modernität der Romantik* (Stuttgart: Metzler, 1977), 143–66.

42 Wolfgang Paulsen, 'F. Schlegels' *Lucinde* als Roman', *The Germanic Review* 21 (1946), 173–90.

43 H. A. Korff, *Geist der Goethezeit* (Leipzig: Koehler, 1954), Vol. 3, 89.

44 W. Paulsen, 'F. Schlegels *Lucinde*', 178.

45 Karl Konrad Polheim, 'F. Schlegel's *Lucinde*', *Zeitschrift für deutsche Philologie* 88 (1970), 61–89.

46 Hans Eichner, '*Lucinde*', *Kritische Friedrich Schlegel Ausgabe* (Paderborn: Schöningh, 1962), Vol. 5, xvii–lxx.

47 Wolfgang Paulsen, 'F. Schlegels *Lucinde*', 185.

7 CONCLUSION: EARLY GERMAN ROMANTICISM AND LITERARY MODERNITY

1 The first reference I could find occurs in *Caroline. Briefe aus der Frühromantik*, ed. Erich Schmidt (Leipzig: Insel, 1913), but this is certainly not the earliest instance.

2 See Ernst Behler, *Irony and the Discourse of Modernity* (Seattle: University of Washington Press, 1990), 37–72.

3 Adam Müller, *Kritische, ästhetische und philosophische Schriften*, ed. Walter Schroeder and Werner Siebert, 2 vols. (Neuwied: Luchterhand, 1967), Vol. 1, 38.

4 Mainly in the *Republic* III and X.

5 The early dialogue *Ion* is the best known example for this opinion.

6 Aristotle, *The Poetics*; Longinus, *On the Sublime*; Demetrius, *On Style*, The Loeb Classical Library, Vol. XXIII (Cambridge, Mass., 1973), 30.

7 Aristotle, *Poetics*, p. 35 of the Loeb edition quoted in note 6, above.

8 Ib., p. 31.

9 Longinus, *On the Sublime* (edition quoted in note 6, above).

10 Dante, especially in his 'Letter to Can Grande della Scala', of

1319, in *Epistolae*, ed. with trans. Paget Toynbec (Oxford: Clarendon Press, 1920); and Boccaccio in his *Vita di Dante*. See James Robinson Smith, *The Earliest 'Lives' of Dante* (New Haven: Yale University Press, 1901).

11 Especially in his *Discourses* on dramatic poetry of 1660.

12 John Dryden, 'An Essay of Dramatic Poesy', *Essays of John Dryden*, ed. W. P. Ker (New York: Russell and Russell, 1961) Vol. 1, 64–126.

Select bibliography

Abrams, M. H., *Natural Supernaturalism. Tradition and Revolution in Romantic Literature* (New York: Norton, 1971)

Bänsch, Dieter, ed., *Zur Modernität der Romantik* (Stuttgart: Metzler, 1977)

Behler, Ernst, *Friedrich Schlegel* (Reinbek: Rowohlt, 1966)

Studien zur Romantik und zur idealistischen Philosophie (Paderborn: Schöningh, 1988)

Unendliche Perfektibilität. Europäische Romantik und Französische Revolution (Paderborn: Schöningh, 1989)

Behler, Ernst, et al., eds., *Die europäische Romantik* (Frankfurt: Athenäum, 1972)

Behler, Ernst, and Jochen Hörisch, eds., *Die Aktualität der Frühromantik* (Paderborn: Schöningh, 1987)

Bohrer, Karl Heinz, *Der romantische Brief. Die Entstehung ästhetischer Subjektivität* (München: Hanser 1987)

Die Kritik der Romantik (Frankfurt: Suhrkamp, 1989)

Bollacher, Martin, *Wackenroder und die Kunstauffassung der frühen Romantik* (Darmstadt: Wissenschaftliche Buchgesellschaft, 1983)

Borries, Kurt, *Die Romantik und die Geschichte* (Berlin: Deutsche Verlagsgesellschaft, 1925)

Brinkmann, Richard, ed., *Romantik in Deutschland. Ein interdisziplinäres Symposium* (Stuttgart: Metzler, 1978)

Brown, Marshall, *The Shape of German Romanticism* (Ithaca: Cornell University Press, 1979)

Dick, Manfred, *Die Entwicklung des Gedankens der Poesie in den Fragmenten des Novalis* (Bonn: Bouvier, 1967)

Dierkes, Hans, *Literaturgeschichte als Kritik. Untersuchungen zu Theorie und Praxis von Friedrich Schlegels frühromantischer Literaturgeschichtsschreibung* (Tübingen: Niemeyer, 1980)

Eichner, Hans, *Friedrich Schlegel* (New York: Twayne, 1970)

Eichner, Hans, ed., *'Romantic' and its Cognates. The European History of a Word* (University of Toronto Press, 1972)

Ewton, R. W., *The Literary Theories of A. W. Schlegel* (Den Haag: Mouton, 1971)
Frank, Manfred, *Das individuelle Allgemeine. Textstrukturierung und - interpretation nach Schleiermacher* (Frankfurt: Suhrkamp, 1977)
Der kommende Gott. Vorlesungen über die neue Mythologie (Frankfurt: Suhrkamp, 1982)
Einführung in die frühromantische Ästhetik (Frankfurt: Suhrkamp, 1989)
Das Problem 'Zeit' in der deutschen Romantik. Second edition (Paderborn: Schöningh, 1990)
Garber, Frederick, ed., *Romantic Irony*, (Budapest: Akadémiai Kiadó, 1988)
Günzel, Klaus, ed., *König der Romantik. Das Leben des Dichters Ludwig Tieck in Briefen, Selbstzeugnissen und Berichten* (Tübingen: Wunderlich, 1981)
Haym, Rudolf, *Die romantische Schule. Ein Beitrag zur Geschichte des deutschen Geistes.* Second edition (Berlin: Weidmann, 1906)
Hennemann Barale, Ingrid, *Poetisierte Welt.* Studi sul primo romanticismo tedesco (Pisa: ETS Editrice, 1990)
Hoffmeister, Gerhart, *Deutsche und europäische Romantik.* Second edition (Stuttgart: Metzler, 1990)
Hoffmeister, Gerhart, ed., *European Romanticism. Literary Cross-Currents, Modes, and Models* (Detroit: Wayne State University Press, 1990)
Hörisch, Jochen, *Die fröhliche Wissenschaft der Poesie. Der Universalitätsanspruch von Dichtung in der frühromantischen Poetologie* (Frankfurt: Suhrkamp, 1976)
Immerwahr, Raymond, *Romantisch. Genese und Tradition einer Denkform* (Frankfurt: Athenäum, 1972)
Janz, Rolf Peter, *Autonomie und soziale Funktion der Kunst. Studien zur Ästhetik von Schiller und Novalis* (Stuttgart: Metzler, 1973)
Kautzenbach, Friedrich Wilhelm, *Schleiermacher* (Reinbek: Rowohlt, 1967)
Kluckhohn, Paul, *Das Ideengut der deutschen Romantik* (Tübingen: Niemeyer, 1961)
Lacoue-Labarthe, Philippe and Jean-Luc Nancy, eds., *The Literary Absolute: The Theory of Literature in German Romanticism* (Albany: State University of New York Press, 1988)
Lillyman, William J., *Reality's Dark Dream. The Narrative Fiction of Ludwig Tieck* (Berlin: de Gruyter, 1979)
Lützeler, Paul Michael, ed., *Romane und Erzählungen der deutschen Romantik* (Stuttgart: Reclam, 1981)
Mähl, Hans-Joachim, *Die Idee des goldenen Zeitalters im Werk des Novalis. Studien zur Wesensbestimmung der frühromantischen Utopie und zu ihren ideengeschichtlichen Voraussetzungen* (Heidelberg: Winter, 1965)

Malsch, Wilfried, '*Europa*'. *Poetische Rede des Novalis. Deutung der Französischen Revolution und Reflexion auf die Poesie in der Geschichte* (Stuttgart: Metzler, 1965)

Michel, Willy, *Ästhetische Hermeneutik und frühromantische Kritik. Friedrich Schlegels fragmentarische Entwürfe, Rezensionen, Charakteristiken und Kritiken* (Göttingen: Vandenhoeck und Ruprecht, 1982)

Nüsse, Heinrich, *Die Sprachtheorie Friedrich Schlegels* (Heidelberg: Winter, 1962)

Paulin, Roger, *Ludwig Tieck* (Stuttgart: Metzler, 1987)

Polheim, Karl Konrad, *Die Arabeske. Ansichten und Ideen aus Friedrich Schlegels Poetik* (Paderborn: Schöningh, 1966)

Sauer, Thomas G., *A. W. Schlegel's Shakespearean Criticism in England* (Bonn: Bouvier, 1982)

Schanze, Helmut, *Romantik und Aufklärung. Untersuchungen zu Friedrich Schlegel und Novalis* (Nürnberg: Carl, 1966)

Schanze, Helmut, ed., *Friedrich Schlegel und die Kunsttheorie seiner Zeit* (Darmstadt: Wissenschaftliche Buchgesellschaft, 1985)

Scholtz, Gunter, *Die Philosophie Schleiermachers* (Darmstadt: Wissenschaftliche Buchgesellschaft, 1984)

Schulz, Gerhard, *Novalis* (Reinbeck: Rowohlt, 1969)

Schulz, Gerhard, ed., *Novalis. Beiträge zu Werk und Persönlichkeit Friedrich von Hardenbergs*. Second edition (Darmstadt: Wissenschaftliche Buchgesellschaft, 1986)

Segebrecht, Wulf, ed., *Ludwig Tieck* (Darmstadt: Wissenschaftliche Buchgesellschaft, 1976)

Seyhan, Azade, *Representation and its Discontents. The Critical Legacy of German Romanticism* (Berkeley: University of California Press, 1992)

Strack, Friedrich, *Im Schatten der Neugier. Christliche Tradition und kritische Philosophie im Werk Friedrichs von Hardenberg* (Tübingen: Niemeyer, 1982)

Timm, Hermann, *Die heilige Revolution. Schleiermacher – Novalis – Friedrich Schlegel* (Frankfurt: Syndikat, 1978)

Walzel, Oskar F., *German Romanticism*, trans. Alma E. Lussky (New York: Putnam, 1932)

Wiese, Benno von, ed., *Deutsche Dichter der Romantik*. Second edition (Berlin: Schmidt, 1983)

Index of works cited and primary sources

Index of subjects and names

Abrams, M. H., 323
absolute idealism, 199, 201
absolute poetry, 2, 7, 9, 157, 178, 179
action, 91, 112, 119
Adorno, Th. W., 8
Aeschylus, 91, 110, 115, 116, 118, 121,
    124, 127
aesthetics, 1, 23, 36, 72, 133
aesthetic horizon, 157
aesthetic modernism, 8
affirmation, 304
Agamemnon, 115
age, 65, 97, 273
Alcestis, 121
Alcibiades, 145, 146
Alembert, Jean le Rond d', xii, 283, 284
Alewyn, Richard, 256, 317
Alexander the Great, 97
alienation, 182
allegory, 2, 161, 206, 212, 218, 254–5,
    297, 302
Allemann, Beda, 312
Amsterdam, 34, 41
anarchy, 69
Anaxagoras, 120
ancient and modern poetry, 74, 95–110,
    132
ancient and modern taste, 26, 27
ancient and modern tragedy, 123
ancients, 99, 303
ancients and moderns the, 10, 26,
    95–109, 122, 303
Anger, Alfred, xvi, 317
animality, 81
Anstett, Jean-Jacques, xiv
antisystematic, 140, 152, 189
antithesis, 70, 94
antithetical, 190

Aphrodite, 127
Appia, P. J., 19
arabesque, 292, 293
architecture, 239–40
Ariosto, 166
Aristophanes, 81, 87, 88, 89, 110, 114,
    118, 129, 144, 150, 312
Aristotle, 73, 74, 85, 96, 111, 120, 123,
    142, 143, 145, 167, 301, 312, 321
Arnim, Achim von, 30
ars poetica, 3, 74, 111, 136
art, 38, 131, 139, 175–6, 194, 225–32,
    237, 247, 251, 252, 253, 261, 262,
    284, 286
art, antagonism with life, 53, 226–7,
    242–6, 249, 255–6
art of living, 175–6, 251
art versus nature, 78
Artemis, 127, 128
artificiality, 204
artist, 203
artistic judgment, 135
Ast, Friedrich, 278
atheism, 20, 21
Augustus, Caesar, 97

Bacon, Francis, 65, 283, 284
Bamberg, 53
Bänsch, Dieter, 323
Barraclough, June, xi
Barth, Karl, 48
Baskin, Wade, 318
Baudissin, Dorothea von (née Tieck), 52
Baudissin, Wolf Graf von, 52
Batteux, Charles, 3
Baudelaire, Charles, ix
beautiful, the, 1, 38, 76, 77, 80, 85, 106,
    137, 240

334